Nissan Stanza Automotive Repair Manual

by Peter G Strasman and John H Haynes
Member of the Guild of Motoring Writers

Models covered

Nissan/Datsun Stanza Deluxe and XE Sedan and Hatchback versions with 2.0 liter (120 cu in)) engine.

Covers 4- & 5-speed manual and 3-speed automatic transmission

ISBN 1 85010 676 2

© **Haynes North America, Inc.** **1984, 1986, 1988, 1989, 1990**
With permission from J.H. Haynes & Co. Ltd.

ABCDE
FGH

2

Printed in the USA   *(12W7 - 981)*

X

Haynes Publishing Group
Sparkford Nr Yeovil
Somerset BA22 7JJ England

Haynes North America, Inc.
861 Lawrence Drive
Newbury Park
California 91320 USA

Acknowledgements

Thanks are due to the Nissan Motor Company Limited of Japan for the provision of technical information and certain illustrations. Duckhams Oils provided lubrication data. The Champion Sparking Plug Company supplied the illustrations showing the various spark plug conditions. Sykes-Pickavant provided some of the workshop tools. Thanks to Mead & Taylor (Yeovil) Ltd. for their assistance. Thanks are also due to all those people at Sparkford who helped in the production of this manual.

About this manual

Its aim

The aim of this manual is to help you get the best value from your vehicle. It can do so in several ways. It can help you decide what work must be done (even should you choose to get it done by a garage), provide information on routine maintenance and servicing, and give a logical course of action and diagnosis when random faults occur. However, it is hoped that you will use the manual by tackling the work yourself. On simpler jobs it may even be quicker than booking the car into a garage and going there twice, to leave and collect it. Perhaps most important, a lot of money can be saved by avoiding the costs a garage must charge to cover its labour and overheads.

The manual has drawings and descriptions to show the function of the various components so that their layout can be understood. Then the tasks are described and photographed in a step-by-step sequence so that even a novice can do the work.

Its arrangement

The manual is divided into thirteen Chapters, each covering a logical sub-division of the vehicle. The Chapters are each divided into Sections, numbered with single figures, eg 5; and the Sections into paragraphs (or sub-sections), with decimal numbers following on from the Section they are in, eg 5.1, 5.2, 5.3 etc.

It is freely illustrated, especially in those parts where there is a detailed sequence of operations to be carried out. There are two forms of illustration: figures and photographs. The figures are numbered in sequence with decimal numbers, according to their position in the Chapter – eg Fig. 6.4 is the fourth drawing/illustration in Chapter 6. Photographs carry the same number (either individually or in related groups) as the Section or sub-section to which they relate.

There is an alphabetical index at the back of the manual as well as a contents list at the front. Each Chapter is also preceded by its own individual contents list.

References to the 'left' or 'right' of the vehicle are in the sense of a person in the driver's seat facing forwards.

Unless otherwise stated, nuts and bolts are removed by turning anti-clockwise, and tightened by turning clockwise.

Vehicle manufacturers continually make changes to specifications and recommendations, and these, when notified, are incorporated into our manuals at the earliest opportunity.

Whilst every care is taken to ensure that the information in this manual is correct, no liability can be accepted by the authors or publishers for loss, damage or injury caused by any errors in, or omissions from, the information given.

Introduction to the Nissan/Datsun Stanza

The Nissan/Datsun Stanza was first introduced early in 1982. It is powered by a completely new transversely-mounted engine, through a new gearbox to provide front wheel drive.

The combination of well chosen gear ratios and a lightweight body provides excellent fuel consumption and satisfying performance.

The fully independent strut suspension with a dual shock absorber system gives the Stanza good handling and a comfortable ride.

The level of standard equipment is high, but a range of optional extras is available.

Working on the Stanza is well within the scope of the DIY home mechanic. The mechanical design is not too complicated and does not incorporate some of the complexities found in early transversely-mounted engines.

Contents

Nissan/Datsun Stanza 1.6 SGL 5-door

Nissan/Datsun Stanza 1.6 GL 4-door

General dimensions, weights and capacities

Dimensions

Except North America

Overall length:	
All except 3-door Hatchback	4280 mm (168.6 in)
3-door Hatchback	4225 mm (166.5 in)
Overall width	1665 mm (65.6 in)
Overall height:	
All except 3-door Hatchback	1390 mm (54.8 in)
3-door Hatchback	1370 mm (53.9 in)
Wheelbase	2470 mm (97.3 in)
Track (front)	1430 mm (56.3 in)
Track (rear)	1410 mm (55.6 in)
Road clearance (unloaded)	165 mm (6.5 in)

North America

Overall length:	
3-door Hatchback	4340 mm (170.9 in)
5-door Hatchback	4405 mm (173.4 in)
Overall width	1665 mm (65.6 in)
Overall height:	
3-door Hatchback	1370 mm (53.9 in)
5-door Hatchback	1390 mm (54.7 in)
Road clearance	165 mm (6.5 in)
Wheelbase	2470 mm (97.2 in)
Track (front)	1430 mm (56.3 in)
Track (rear)	1410 mm (55.5 in)

Weights

Except North America

Kerb weight:	
4-door Saloon	930 kg (2050 lb)
3-door Hatchback	945 kg (2083 lb)
5-door Hatchback (1.6)	950 kg (2095 lb)
5-door Hatchback (1.8)	975 kg (2149 lb)
Trailer load (with brakes)	1100 kg (2425 lb)
Trailer load (without brakes)	600 kg (1323 lb)

North America

Kerb weight:	
3-door Hatchback deluxe	964 kg (2152 lb)
3-door Hatchback XE	980 kg (2160 lb)
5-door deluxe	1004 kg (2211 lb)
5-door XE	1008 kg (2220 lb)

Capacities

Fuel tank	54.0 litre, 11.9 Imp gal, 14.3 US gal
Engine oil (without filter change)	3.5 litre, 6.2 Imp pt, 3.7 US qt
Engine oil (with filter change)	3.9 litre, 6.9 Imp pt, 4.8 US qt
Manual transmission:	
4-speed	2.6 litre, 4.6 Imp pt, 5.4 US pt
5-speed	2.7 litre, 4.75 Imp pt, 5.75 US pt
Automatic transmission	6.0 litre, 5.25 Imp qt, 6.3 US qt
Cooling system	7.3 litre, 12.8 Imp pt, 7.7 US qt
Power steering system	1.0 litre, 1.7 Imp pt, 1.06 US qt

Use of English

As this book has been written in England, it uses the appropriate English component names, phrases, and spelling. Some of these differ from those used in America. Normally, these cause no difficulty, but to make sure, a glossary is printed below. In ordering spare parts remember the parts list may use some of these words:

English	American	English	American
Accelerator	Gas pedal	Locks	Latches
Aerial	Antenna	Methylated spirit	Denatured alcohol
Anti-roll bar	Stabiliser or sway bar	Motorway	Freeway, turnpike etc
Big-end bearing	Rod bearing	Number plate	License plate
Bonnet (engine cover)	Hood	Paraffin	Kerosene
Boot (luggage compartment)	Trunk	Petrol	Gasoline (gas)
Bulkhead	Firewall	Petrol tank	Gas tank
Bush	Bushing	'Pinking'	'Pinging'
Cam follower or tappet	Valve lifter or tappet	Prise (force apart)	Pry
Carburettor	Carburetor	Propeller shaft	Driveshaft
Catch	Latch	Quarterlight	Quarter window
Choke/venturi	Barrel	Retread	Recap
Circlip	Snap-ring	Reverse	Back-up
Clearance	Lash	Rocker cover	Valve cover
Crownwheel	Ring gear (of differential)	Saloon	Sedan
Damper	Shock absorber, shock	Seized	Frozen
Disc (brake)	Rotor/disk	Sidelight	Parking light
Distance piece	Spacer	Silencer	Muffler
Drop arm	Pitman arm	Sill panel (beneath doors)	Rocker panel
Drop head coupe	Convertible	Small end, little end	Piston pin or wrist pin
Dynamo	Generator (DC)	Spanner	Wrench
Earth (electrical)	Ground	Split cotter (for valve spring cap)	Lock (for valve spring retainer)
Engineer's blue	Prussian blue	Split pin	Cotter pin
Estate car	Station wagon	Steering arm	Spindle arm
Exhaust manifold	Header	Sump	Oil pan
Fault finding/diagnosis	Troubleshooting	Swarf	Metal chips or debris
Float chamber	Float bowl	Tab washer	Tang or lock
Free-play	Lash	Tappet	Valve lifter
Freewheel	Coast	Thrust bearing	Throw-out bearing
Gearbox	Transmission	Top gear	High
Gearchange	Shift	Torch	Flashlight
Grub screw	Setscrew, Allen screw	Trackrod (of steering)	Tie-rod (or connecting rod)
Gudgeon pin	Piston pin or wrist pin	Trailing shoe (of brake)	Secondary shoe
Halfshaft	Axleshaft	Transmission	Whole drive line
Handbrake	Parking brake	Tyre	Tire
Hood	Soft top	Van	Panel wagon/van
Hot spot	Heat riser	Vice	Vise
Indicator	Turn signal	Wheel nut	Lug nut
Interior light	Dome lamp	Windscreen	Windshield
Layshaft (of gearbox)	Countershaft	Wing/mudguard	Fender
Leading shoe (of brake)	Primary shoe		

Buying spare parts and vehicle identification numbers

Buying spare parts

Replacement parts are available from many sources, which generally fall into one of two categories – authorized dealer parts departments and independent retail auto parts stores. Our advice concerning these parts is as follows:

Retail auto parts stores: Good auto parts stores will stock frequently needed components which wear out relatively fast, such as clutch components, exhaust systems, brake parts, tune-up parts, etc. These stores often supply new or reconditioned parts on an exchange basis, which can save a considerable amount of money. Discount auto parts stores are often very good places to buy materials and parts needed for general vehicle maintenance such as oil, grease, filters, spark plugs, belts, touch-up paint, bulbs, etc. They also usually sell tools and general accessories, have convenient hours, charge lower prices and can often be found not far from home.

Authorized dealer parts department: This is the best source for parts which are unique to the vehicle and not generally available elsewhere (such as major engine parts, transmission parts, trim pieces, etc.).

Warranty information: If the vehicle is still covered under warranty, be sure that any replacement parts purchased – regardless of the source – do not invalidate the warranty!

To be sure of obtaining the correct parts, have engine and chassis numbers available and, if possible, take the old parts along for positive identification.

Vehicle identification numbers

The *Vehicle Identification Number* is located inside the engine compartment on the rear bulkhead. On North American models, the number is repeated on the top of the facia just inside the windscreen (photo).

The *engine number* is stamped onto the right-hand side of the cylinder block.

The *FMVSS label* is located on the edge of the door on North American vehicles.

The *tyre pressure label* is located on the body centre (B) pillar (photo).

The *emission control label* is located on the underside of the bonnet lid on North American models.

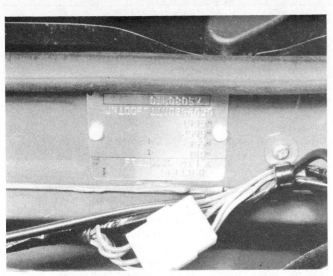

Vehicle identification plate

Tyre pressure label

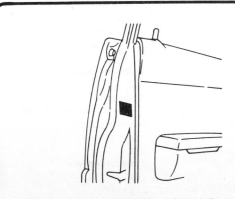

Location of FMVSS label (North America)

Location of Emission Control label (North America)

Tools and working facilities

Introduction

A selection of good tools is a fundamental requirement for anyone contemplating the maintenance and repair of a motor vehicle. For the owner who does not possess any, their purchase will prove a considerable expense, offsetting some of the savings made by doing-it-yourself. However, provided that the tools purchased are of good quality, they will last for many years and prove an extremely worthwhile investment.

To help the average owner to decide which tools are needed to carry out the various tasks detailed in this manual, we have compiled three lists of tools under the following headings: *Maintenance and minor repair, Repair and overhaul,* and *Special.* The newcomer to practical mechanics should start off with the *Maintenance and minor repair* tool kit and confine himself to the simpler jobs around the vehicle. Then, as his confidence and experience grow, he can undertake more difficult tasks, buying extra tools as, and when, they are needed. In this way, a *Maintenance and minor repair* tool kit can be built-up into a *Repair and overhaul* tool kit over a considerable period of time without any major cash outlays. The experienced do-it-yourselfer will have a tool kit good enough for most repair and overhaul procedures and will add tools from the *Special* category when he feels the expense is justified by the amount of use to which these tools will be put.

It is obviously not possible to cover the subject of tools fully here. For those who wish to learn more about tools and their use there is a book entitled *How to Choose and Use Car Tools* available from the publishers of this manual.

Maintenance and minor repair tool kit

The tools given in this list should be considered as a minimum requirement if routine maintenance, servicing and minor repair operations are to be undertaken. We recommend the purchase of combination spanners (ring one end, open-ended the other); although more expensive than open-ended ones, they do give the advantages of both types of spanner.

> Combination spanners - 10, 11, 12, 13, 14 & 17 mm
> Adjustable spanner - 9 inch
> Spark plug spanner (with rubber insert)
> Spark plug gap adjustment tool
> Set of feeler gauges
> Brake bleed nipple spanner
> Screwdriver - 4 in long x $\frac{1}{4}$ in dia (flat blade)
> Screwdriver - 4 in long x $\frac{1}{4}$ in dia (cross blade)
> Combination pliers - 6 inch
> Hacksaw (junior)
> Tyre pump
> Tyre pressure gauge
> Oil can
> Fine emery cloth (1 sheet)
> Wire brush (small)
> Funnel (medium size)

Repair and overhaul tool kit

These tools are virtually essential for anyone undertaking any major repairs to a motor vehicle, and are additional to those given in the *Maintenance and minor repair* list. Included in this list is a comprehensive set of sockets. Although these are expensive they will be found invaluable as they are so versatile - particularly if various drives are included in the set. We recommend the $\frac{1}{2}$ in square-drive type, as this can be used with most proprietary torque wrenches. If you cannot afford a socket set, even bought piecemeal, then inexpensive tubular box spanners are a useful alternative.

The tools in this list will occasionally need to be supplemented by tools from the *Special* list.

> Sockets (or box spanners) to cover range in previous list
> Reversible ratchet drive (for use with sockets)
> Extension piece, 10 inch (for use with sockets)
> Universal joint (for use with sockets)
> Torque wrench (for use with sockets)
> 'Mole' wrench - 8 inch
> Ball pein hammer
> Soft-faced hammer, plastic or rubber
> Screwdriver - 6 in long x $\frac{5}{16}$ in dia (flat blade)
> Screwdriver - 2 in long x $\frac{5}{16}$ in square (flat blade)
> Screwdriver - 1$\frac{1}{2}$ in long x $\frac{1}{4}$ in dia (cross blade)
> Screwdriver - 3 in long x $\frac{1}{8}$ in dia (electricians)
> Pliers - electricians side cutters
> Pliers - needle nosed
> Pliers - circlip (internal and external)
> Cold chisel - $\frac{1}{2}$ inch
> Scriber
> Scraper
> Centre punch
> Pin punch
> Hacksaw
> Valve grinding tool
> Steel rule/straight-edge
> Allen keys
> Selection of files
> Wire brush (large)
> Axle-stands
> Jack (strong scissor or hydraulic type)

Special tools

The tools in this list are those which are not used regularly, are expensive to buy, or which need to be used in accordance with their manufacturers' instructions. Unless relatively difficult mechanical jobs are undertaken frequently, it will not be economic to buy many of these tools. Where this is the case, you could consider clubbing together with friends (or joining a motorists' club) to make a joint purchase, or borrowing the tools against a deposit from a local garage or tool hire specialist.

The following list contains only those tools and instruments freely available to the public, and not those special tools produced by the vehicle manufacturer specifically for its dealer network. You will find occasional references to these manufacturers' special tools in the text of this manual. Generally, an alternative method of doing the job without the vehicle manufacturers' special tool is given. However, sometimes, there is no alternative to using them. Where this is the case and the relevant tool cannot be bought or borrowed, you will have to entrust the work to a franchised garage.

> Valve spring compressor
> Piston ring compressor
> Balljoint separator
> Universal hub/bearing puller
> Impact screwdriver
> Micrometer and/or vernier gauge
> Dial gauge
> Stroboscopic timing light

Dwell angle meter/tachometer
Universal electrical multi-meter
Cylinder compression gauge
Lifting tackle (photo)
Trolley jack
Light with extension lead

Buying tools

For practically all tools, a tool factor is the best source since he will have a very comprehensive range compared with the average garage or accessory shop. Having said that, accessory shops often offer excellent quality tools at discount prices, so it pays to shop around.

Remember, you don't have to buy the most expensive items on the shelf, but it is always advisable to steer clear of the very cheap tools. There are plenty of good tools around at reasonable prices, so ask the proprietor or manager of the shop for advice before making a purchase.

Care and maintenance of tools

Having purchased a reasonable tool kit, it is necessary to keep the tools in a clean serviceable condition. After use, always wipe off any dirt, grease and metal particles using a clean, dry cloth, before putting the tools away. Never leave them lying around after they have been used. A simple tool rack on the garage or workshop wall, for items such as screwdrivers and pliers is a good idea. Store all normal wrenches and sockets in a metal box. Any measuring instruments, gauges, meters, etc, must be carefully stored where they cannot be damaged or become rusty.

Take a little care when tools are used. Hammer heads inevitably become marked and screwdrivers lose the keen edge on their blades from time to time. A little timely attention with emery cloth or a file will soon restore items like this to a good serviceable finish.

Working facilities

Not to be forgotten when discussing tools, is the workshop itself. If anything more than routine maintenance is to be carried out, some form of suitable working area becomes essential.

It is appreciated that many an owner mechanic is forced by circumstances to remove an engine or similar item, without the benefit of a garage or workshop. Having done this, any repairs should always be done under the cover of a roof.

Wherever possible, any dismantling should be done on a clean, flat workbench or table at a suitable working height.

Any workbench needs a vice: one with a jaw opening of 4 in (100 mm) is suitable for most jobs. As mentioned previously, some clean dry storage space is also required for tools, as well as for lubricants, cleaning fluids, touch-up paints and so on, which become necessary.

Another item which may be required, and which has a much more general usage, is an electric drill with a chuck capacity of at least $\frac{5}{16}$ in (8 mm). This, together with a good range of twist drills, is virtually essential for fitting accessories such as mirrors and reversing lights.

Last, but not least, always keep a supply of old newspapers and clean, lint-free rags available, and try to keep any working area as clean as possible.

Spanner jaw gap comparison table

Jaw gap (in)	Spanner size
0.250	$\frac{1}{4}$ in AF
0.276	7 mm
0.313	$\frac{5}{16}$ in AF
0.315	8 mm
0.344	$\frac{11}{32}$ in AF; $\frac{1}{8}$ in Whitworth
0.354	9 mm
0.375	$\frac{3}{8}$ in AF
0.394	10 mm
0.433	11 mm
0.438	$\frac{7}{16}$ in AF
0.445	$\frac{3}{16}$ in Whitworth; $\frac{1}{4}$ in BSF
0.472	12 mm
0.500	$\frac{1}{2}$ in AF
0.512	13 mm
0.525	$\frac{1}{4}$ in Whitworth; $\frac{5}{16}$ in BSF
0.551	14 mm
0.563	$\frac{9}{16}$ in AF
0.591	15 mm
0.600	$\frac{5}{16}$ in Whitworth; $\frac{3}{8}$ in BSF
0.625	$\frac{5}{8}$ in AF
0.630	16 mm
0.669	17 mm
0.686	$\frac{11}{16}$ in AF
0.709	18 mm
0.710	$\frac{3}{8}$ in Whitworth; $\frac{7}{16}$ in BSF
0.748	19 mm
0.750	$\frac{3}{4}$ in AF
0.813	$\frac{13}{16}$ in AF
0.820	$\frac{7}{16}$ in Whitworth; $\frac{1}{2}$ in BSF
0.866	22 mm
0.875	$\frac{7}{8}$ in AF
0.920	$\frac{1}{2}$ in Whitworth; $\frac{9}{16}$ in BSF
0.938	$\frac{15}{16}$ in AF
0.945	24 mm
1.000	1 in AF
1.010	$\frac{9}{16}$ in Whitworth; $\frac{5}{8}$ in BSF
1.024	26 mm
1.063	$1\frac{1}{16}$ in AF; 27 mm
1.100	$\frac{5}{8}$ in Whitworth; $\frac{11}{16}$ in BSF
1.125	$1\frac{1}{8}$ in AF
1.181	30 mm
1.200	$\frac{11}{16}$ in Whitworth; $\frac{3}{4}$ in BSF
1.250	$1\frac{1}{4}$ in AF
1.260	32 mm
1.300	$\frac{3}{4}$ in Whitworth; $\frac{7}{8}$ in BSF
1.313	$1\frac{5}{16}$ in AF
1.390	$\frac{13}{16}$ in Whitworth; $\frac{15}{16}$ in BSF
1.417	36 mm
1.438	$1\frac{7}{16}$ in AF
1.480	$\frac{7}{8}$ in Whitworth; 1 in BSF
1.500	$1\frac{1}{2}$ in AF
1.575	40 mm; $\frac{15}{16}$ in Whitworth
1.614	41 mm
1.625	$1\frac{5}{8}$ in AF
1.670	1 in Whitworth; $1\frac{1}{8}$ in BSF
1.688	$1\frac{11}{16}$ in AF
1.811	46 mm
1.813	$1\frac{13}{16}$ in AF
1.860	$1\frac{1}{8}$ in Whitworth; $1\frac{1}{4}$ in BSF
1.875	$1\frac{7}{8}$ in AF
1.969	50 mm
2.000	2 in AF
2.050	$1\frac{1}{4}$ in Whitworth; $1\frac{3}{8}$ in BSF
2.165	55 mm
2.362	60 mm

A Haltrac hoist and gantry in use during a typical engine removal sequence

General repair procedures

Whenever servicing, repair or overhaul work is carried out on the car or its components, it is necessary to observe the following procedures and instructions. This will assist in carrying out the operation efficiently and to a professional standard of workmanship.

Joint mating faces and gaskets

Where a gasket is used between the mating faces of two components, ensure that it is renewed on reassembly, and fit it dry unless otherwise stated in the repair procedure. Make sure that the mating faces are clean and dry with all traces of old gasket removed. When cleaning a joint face, use a tool which is not likely to score or damage the face, and remove any burrs or nicks with an oilstone or fine file.

Make sure that tapped holes are cleaned with a pipe cleaner, and keep them free of jointing compound if this is being used unless specifically instructed otherwise.

Ensure that all orifices, channels or pipes are clear and blow through them, preferably using compressed air.

Oil seals

Whenever an oil seal is removed from its working location, either individually or as part of an assembly, it should be renewed.

The very fine sealing lip of the seal is easily damaged and will not seal if the surface it contacts is not completely clean and free from scratches, nicks or grooves. If the original sealing surface of the component cannot be restored, the component should be renewed.

Protect the lips of the seal from any surface which may damage them in the course of fitting. Use tape or a conical sleeve where possible. Lubricate the seal lips with oil before fitting and, on dual lipped seals, fill the space between the lips with grease.

Unless otherwise stated, oil seals must be fitted with their sealing lips toward the lubricant to be sealed.

Use a tubular drift or block of wood of the appropriate size to install the seal and, if the seal housing is shouldered, drive the seal down to the shoulder. If the seal housing is unshouldered, the seal should be fitted with its face flush with the housing top face.

Screw threads and fastenings

Always ensure that a blind tapped hole is completely free from oil, grease, water or other fluid before installing the bolt or stud. Failure to do this could cause the housing to crack due to the hydraulic action of the bolt or stud as it is screwed in.

When tightening a castellated nut to accept a split pin, tighten the nut to the specified torque, where applicable, and then tighten further to the next split pin hole. Never slacken the nut to align a split pin hole unless stated in the repair procedure.

When checking or retightening a nut or bolt to a specified torque setting, slacken the nut or bolt by a quarter of a turn, and then retighten to the specified setting.

Locknuts, locktabs and washers

Any fastening which will rotate against a component or housing in the course of tightening should always have a washer between it and the relevant component or housing.

Spring or split washers should always be renewed when they are used to lock a critical component such as a big-end bearing retaining nut or bolt.

Locktabs which are folded over to retain a nut or bolt should always be renewed.

Self-locking nuts can be reused in non-critical areas, providing resistance can be felt when the locking portion passes over the bolt or stud thread.

Split pins must always be replaced with new ones of the correct size for the hole.

Special tools

Some repair procedures in this manual entail the use of special tools such as a press, two or three-legged pullers, spring compressors etc. Wherever possible, suitable readily available alternatives to the manufacturer's special tools are described, and are shown in use. In some instances, where no alternative is possible, it has been necessary to resort to the use of a manufacturer's tool and this has been done for reasons of safety as well as the efficient completion of the repair operation. Unless you are highly skilled and have a thorough understanding of the procedure described, never attempt to bypass the use of any special tool when the procedure described specifies its use. Not only is there a very great risk of personal injury, but expensive damage could be caused to the components involved.

Jacking, towing and wheel changing

Jacking

Use the jack supplied with the vehicle only for wheel changing during roadside emergencies (photos). Chock the wheel diagonally opposite the one being removed.

When raising the vehicle for repair or maintenance, preferably use a trolley jack with a wooden block as an insulator to prevent damage to the underbody (photo).

Locate the jack only under the points indicated and once the vehicle is raised, place safety stands under the side members as shown.

To avoid repetition, the procedure for raising the vehicle in order to carry out work under it is not included before each relevant operation described in this manual.

It is to be preferred and certainly recommended that the vehicle is positioned over an inspection pit or raised on a lift. Where such equipment is not available, use ramps or jack up the vehicle as previously described, but always supplement the lifting device with axle stands.

Towing

Towing hooks are welded to the front and the rear of the vehicle and should only be used in an emergency, as their designed function is as lash-down hooks, for use during transportation (photos).

When towing vehicles equipped with automatic transmission, restrict the distance towed to 20 miles (30 km) and the towing speed to 20 mph (30 kmh). If these conditions are likely to be exceeded, then the front wheels will have to be raised off the road.

When being towed, remember to insert the ignition key and turn it to Position I. Expect to apply greater pressure to the footbrake, as servo assistance will not be available after the first few brake applications.

Wheel changing

To change a roadwheel, first remove the plastic caps from the wheel bolts.

If the car is fairly new, the roadwheels and tyres will have been balanced on the vehicle during production. In order to maintain this balance then the position of the roadwheel in relation to the mounting hub must be marked before removing the wheel.

Release but do not remove each roadwheel bolt, and then raise the vehicle with the jack. Remove the bolts and take off the wheel.

Fit the wheel and screw in the bolts. Finally tighten the bolts after the vehicle has been lowered to the ground.

Sill jacking point

Front tow hook

Rear tow hook

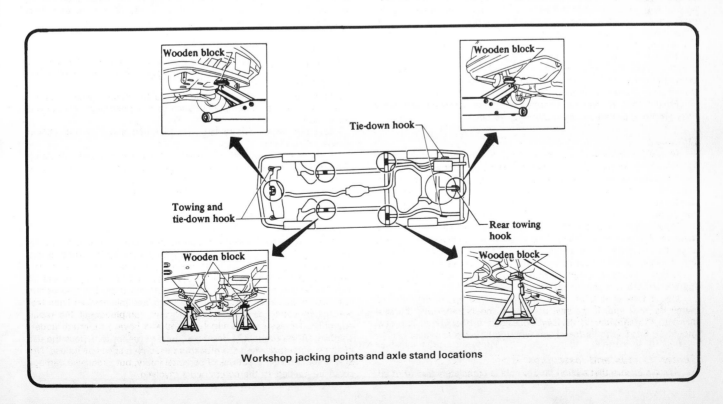
Workshop jacking points and axle stand locations

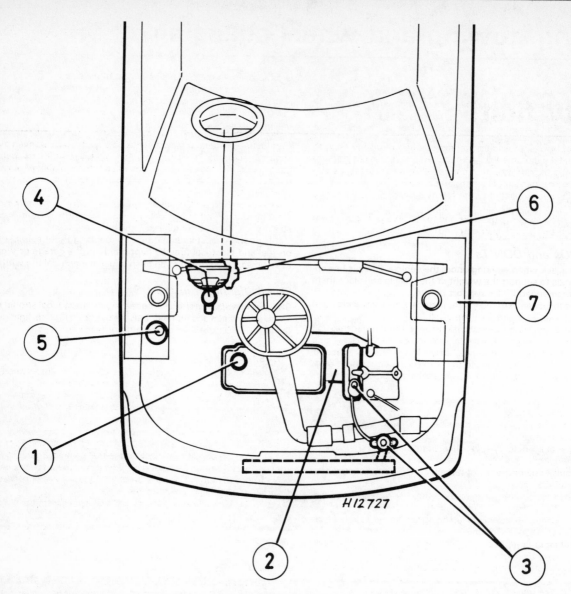

H12727

Recommended lubricants and fluids

Component or system	Lubricant type/specification	Duckhams recommendation
1 Engine	Multigrade engine oil, viscosity range SAE 10W/30 to 20W/50, to API SE	Duckhams QXR, Hypergrade, or 10W/40 Motor oil
2 Transmission		
Manual	Hypoid gear oil, viscosity SAE 80W/90, to API GL4	Duckhams Hypoid 80
Automatic	Dexron type ATF	Duckhams D-Matic
3 Cooling system	Antifreeze to BS 3151, 3152 or 6580	Duckhams Universal Antifreeze and Summer Coolant
4 Braking system	Hydraulic fluid to FMVSS 116 DOT 3	Duckhams Universal Brake and Clutch Fluid
5 Power-assisted steering	Dexron type ATF	Duckhams D-Matic
6 Steering rack	Multi-purpose lithium-based grease, to NLGI No 2	Duckhams LB 10
7 Hub bearings	Multi-purpose lithium-based grease, to NLGI No 2	Duckhams LB 10

Safety first!

Regardless of how enthusiastic you may be about getting on with the job at hand, take the time to ensure that your safety is not jeopardized. A moment's lack of attention can result in an accident, as can failure to observe certain simple safety precautions. The possibility of an accident will always exist, and the following points should not be considered a comprehensive list of all dangers. Rather, they are intended to make you aware of the risks and to encourage a safety conscious approach to all work you carry out on your vehicle.

Essential DOs and DON'Ts

DON'T rely on a jack when working under the vehicle. Always use approved jackstands to support the weight of the vehicle and place them under the recommended lift or support points.

DON'T attempt to loosen extremely tight fasteners (i.e. wheel lug nuts) while the vehicle is on a jack — it may fall.

DON'T start the engine without first making sure that the transmission is in Neutral (or Park where applicable) and the parking brake is set.

DON'T remove the radiator cap from a hot cooling system — let it cool or cover it with a cloth and release the pressure gradually.

DON'T attempt to drain the engine oil until you are sure it has cooled to the point that it will not burn you.

DON'T touch any part of the engine or exhaust system until it has cooled sufficiently to avoid burns.

DON'T siphon toxic liquids such as gasoline, antifreeze and brake fluid by mouth, or allow them to remain on your skin.

DON'T inhale brake lining dust — it is potentially hazardous (see Asbestos below)

DON'T allow spilled oil or grease to remain on the floor — wipe it up before someone slips on it.

DON'T use loose fitting wrenches or other tools which may slip and cause injury.

DON'T push on wrenches when loosening or tightening nuts or bolts. Always try to pull the wrench toward you. If the situation calls for pushing the wrench away, push with an open hand to avoid scraped knuckles if the wrench should slip.

DON'T attempt to lift a heavy component alone — get someone to help you.

DON'T rush or take unsafe shortcuts to finish a job.

DON'T allow children or animals in or around the vehicle while you are working on it.

DO wear eye protection when using power tools such as a drill, sander, bench grinder, etc. and when working under a vehicle.

DO keep loose clothing and long hair well out of the way of moving parts.

DO make sure that any hoist used has a safe working load rating adequate for the job.

DO get someone to check on you periodically when working alone on a vehicle.

DO carry out work in a logical sequence and make sure that everything is correctly assembled and tightened.

DO keep chemicals and fluids tightly capped and out of the reach of children and pets.

DO remember that your vehicle's safety affects that of yourself and others. If in doubt on any point, get professional advice.

Asbestos

Certain friction, insulating, sealing, and other products — such as brake linings, brake bands, clutch linings, torque converters, gaskets, etc. — contain asbestos. *Extreme care must be taken to avoid inhalation of dust from such products since it is hazardous to health.* If in doubt, assume that they *do* contain asbestos.

Fire

Remember at all times that gasoline is highly flammable. Never smoke or have any kind of open flame around when working on a vehicle. But the risk does not end there. A spark caused by an electrical short circuit, by two metal surfaces contacting each other, or even by static electricity built up in your body under certain conditions, can ignite gasoline vapors, which in a confined space are highly explosive. Do not, under any circumstances, use gasoline for cleaning parts. Use an approved safety solvent.

Always disconnect the battery ground (−) cable *at the battery* before working on any part of the fuel system or electrical system. Never risk spilling fuel on a hot engine or exhaust component.

It is strongly recommended that a fire extinguisher suitable for use on fuel and electrical fires be kept handy in the garage or workshop at all times. Never try to extinguish a fuel or electrical fire with water.

Torch (flashlight in the US)

Any reference to a "torch" appearing in this manual should always be taken to mean a hand-held, battery-operated electric light or flashlight. It DOES NOT mean a welding or propane torch or blowtorch.

Fumes

Certain fumes are highly toxic and can quickly cause unconsciousness and even death if inhaled to any extent. Gasoline vapor falls into this category, as do the vapors from some cleaning solvents. Any draining or pouring of such volatile fluids should be done in a well ventilated area.

When using cleaning fluids and solvents, read the instructions on the container carefully. Never use materials from unmarked containers.

Never run the engine in an enclosed space, such as a garage. Exhaust fumes contain carbon monoxide, which is extremely poisonous. If you need to run the engine, always do so in the open air, or at least have the rear of the vehicle outside the work area.

If you are fortunate enough to have the use of an inspection pit, never drain or pour gasoline and never run the engine while the vehicle is over the pit. The fumes, being heavier than air, will concentrate in the pit with possibly lethal results.

The battery

Never create a spark or allow a bare light bulb near a battery. They normally give off a certain amount of hydrogen gas, which is highly explosive.

Always disconnect the battery ground (−) cable *at the battery* before working on the fuel or electrical systems.

If possible, loosen the filler caps or cover when charging the battery from an external source (this does not apply to sealed or maintenance-free batteries). Do not charge at an excessive rate or the battery may burst.

Take care when adding water to a non maintenance-free battery and when carrying a battery. The electrolyte, even when diluted, is very corrosive and should not be allowed to contact clothing or skin.

Always wear eye protection when cleaning the battery to prevent the caustic deposits from entering your eyes.

Mains electricity (household current in the US)

When using an electric power tool, inspection light, etc., which operates on household current, always make sure that the tool is correctly connected to its plug and that, where necessary, it is properly grounded. Do not use such items in damp conditions and, again, do not create a spark or apply excessive heat in the vicinity of fuel or fuel vapor.

Secondary ignition system voltage

A severe electric shock can result from touching certain parts of the ignition system (such as the spark plug wires) when the engine is running or being cranked, particularly if components are damp or the insulation is defective. In the case of an electronic ignition system, the secondary system voltage is much higher and could prove fatal.

Routine maintenance

The Routine Maintenance instructions listed are basically those recommended by the vehicle manufacturer. They are sometimes supplemented by additional maintenance tasks proven to be necessary.

The maintenance intervals recommended are those specified by the manufacturer. They are necessarily something of a compromise, since no two vehicles operate under identical conditions. The DIY mechanic, who does not have labour costs to consider, may wish to shorten the service intervals. Experience will show whether this is necessary.

Where the vehicle is under severe operating conditions (extremes of heat or cold, dusty conditions, or mainly stop-start driving), more frequent oil changes may be desirable. If in doubt consult your dealer.

Weekly or before a long journey

Check the engine oil level and top up if necessary (photo)
Check battery electrolyte level (except maintenance free type)
Check coolant level in expansion tank (photo)
Check and top up washer fluid reservoirs (photo)
Check tyre pressures, including the spare
Check operation of all lamps, flashers and wipers

At the first 1600 km (1000 miles) service (new vehicles)

Check torque wrench setting of cylinder head bolts
Check and adjust valve clearances
Check and adjust idle speed and mixture
Adjust tension of drivebelts
Check rear hub bearing adjustment
Check ignition timing
Check tightness of exhaust manifold and downpipe flange nuts
Although not specified by the manufacturer, it is recommended that the engine oil is changed
Check the brake hydraulic fluid level in the reservoir (photo)

Every 10 000 km (6000 miles)

Renew engine oil and filter
Adjust idle speed and mixture
Check condition of distributor points and adjust dwell angle (mechanical breaker distributors only)
Clean and re-gap spark plugs
Check and top up (if necessary) brake master cylinder reservoir
Check and top up power steering fluid reservoir (if fitted)
Check and top up fluid level in manual transmission or automatic transmission
Check brake disc pads for wear
Lubricate all hinges, locks and controls
Check clutch pedal adjustment

Topping up engine oil

Every 20 000 km (12 000 miles)

Check and adjust valve clearances
Check drivebelts for condition and tension
Check cooling system hoses for condition
Renew contact points (mechanical breaker distributor)
Renew spark plugs
Check crankcase (PCV) system hoses for cleanliness, condition and security
Check all suspension and steering components for wear and condition
Move position of roadwheels to even out tyre wear. Rebalance if necessary
Check brake drum linings for wear
Check front wheel alignment

Every 50 000 km (30 000 miles)

Renew fuel filter
Renew air cleaner element
Renew air induction valve filter (North America emission control) and clean EGR system

Every two years

Renew coolant
Renew brake hydraulic fluid
Check performance of hydraulic struts on front and rear suspension
Although not specified by the vehicle manufacturers, it is recommended that the transmission oil or fluid (automatic) is renewed

Topping up coolant

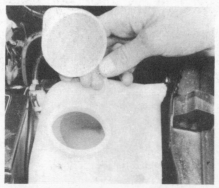

Washer fluid reservoir cap

Topping up brake fluid

Engine compartment from above (air cleaner removed for photographic purposes)

1 Windscreen wiper motor
2 Brake vacuum servo
3 Brake master cylinder
4 Carburettor

5 Heater blower cover
6 Front suspension strut upper mounting
7 Fuel pump

8 Cooling system expansion tank
9 Battery
10 Washer fluid reservoir
11 Ignition coil

12 Distributor
13 Air intake trunking
14 Headlamp

15 Bonnet lock
16 Radiator pressure cap
17 Oil filler cap

Front end from below

1	Exhaust expansion box	4	Exhaust flexible connection	6	Track control arm
2	Gearchange stabiliser rod	5	Track control arm support	7	Undershield
3	Gearchange control rod		plate	8	Driveshaft

9	Engine sump pan drain plug
10	Transmission oil drain plug

Rear end from below

1 Radius rod
2 Handbrake cable
3 Exhaust silencer
4 Fuel tank
5 Handbrake equaliser

Fault diagnosis

Introduction

The vehicle owner who does his or her own maintenance according to the recommended schedules should not have to use this section of the manual very often. Modern component reliability is such that, provided those items subject to wear or deterioration are inspected or renewed at the specified intervals, sudden failure is comparatively rare. Faults do not usually just happen as a result of sudden failure, but develop over a period of time. Major mechanical failures in particular are usually preceded by characteristic symptoms over hundreds or even thousands of miles. Those components which do occasionally fail without warning are often small and easily carried in the vehicle.

With any fault finding, the first step is to decide where to begin investigations. Sometimes this is obvious, but on other occasions a little detective work will be necessary. The owner who makes half a dozen haphazard adjustments or replacements may be successful in curing a fault (or its symptoms), but he will be none the wiser if the fault recurs and he may well have spent more time and money than was necessary. A calm and logical approach will be found to be more satisfactory in the long run. Always take into account any warning signs or abnormalities that may have been noticed in the period preceding the fault – power loss, high or low gauge readings, unusual noises or smells, etc – and remember that failure of components such as fuses or spark plugs may only be pointers to some underlying fault.

The pages which follow here are intended to help in cases of failure to start or breakdown on the road. There is also a Fault Diagnosis Section at the end of each Chapter which should be consulted if the preliminary checks prove unfruitful. Whatever the fault, certain basic principles apply. These are as follows:

Verify the fault. This is simply a matter of being sure that you know what the symptoms are before starting work. This is particularly important if you are investigating a fault for someone else who may not have described it very accurately.

Don't overlook the obvious. For example, if the vehicle won't start, is there petrol in the tank? (Don't take anyone else's word on this particular point, and don't trust the fuel gauge either!) If an electrical fault is indicated, look for loose or broken wires before digging out the test gear.

Cure the disease, not the symptom. Substituting a flat battery with a fully charged one will get you off the hard shoulder, but if the underlying cause is not attended to, the new battery will go the same way. Similarly, changing oil-fouled spark plugs for a new set will get you moving again, but remember that the reason for the fouling (if it wasn't simply an incorrect grade of plug) will have to be established and corrected.

Don't take anything for granted. Particularly, don't forget that a 'new' component may itself be defective (especially if it's been rattling round in the boot for months), and don't leave components out of a fault diagnosis sequence just because they are new or recently fitted. When you do finally diagnose a difficult fault, you'll probably realise that all the evidence was there from the start.

Electrical faults

Electrical faults can be more puzzling than straightforward mechanical failures, but they are no less susceptible to logical analysis if the basic principles of operation are understood. Vehicle electrical wiring exists in extremely unfavourable conditions – heat, vibration and chemical attack – and the first things to look for are loose or corroded connections and broken or chafed wires, especially where the wires pass through holes in the bodywork or are subject to vibration.

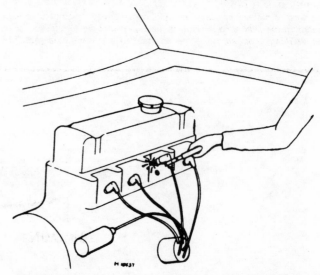

Crank engine and check for spark. Note use of insulated tool!

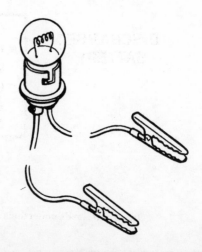

A simple test lamp is useful for tracing electrical faults

All metal-bodied vehicles in current production have one pole of the battery 'earthed', ie connected to the vehicle bodywork, and in nearly all modern vehicles it is the negative (–) terminal. The various electrical components – motors, bulb holders etc – are also connected to earth, either by means of a lead or directly by their mountings. Electric current flows through the component and then back to the battery via the bodywork. If the component mounting is loose or corroded, or if a good path back to the battery is not available, the circuit will be incomplete and malfunction will result. The engine and/or gearbox are also earthed by means of flexible metal straps to the body or subframe; if these straps are loose or missing, starter motor, generator and ignition trouble may result.

Assuming the earth return to be satisfactory, electrical faults will be due either to component malfunction or to defects in the current supply. Individual components are dealt with in Chapter 10. If supply wires are broken or cracked internally this results in an open-circuit, and the easiest way to check for this is to bypass the suspect wire temporarily with a length of wire having a crocodile clip or suitable connector at each end. Alternatively, a 12V test lamp can be used to verify the presence of supply voltage at various points along the wire and the break can be thus isolated.

If a bare portion of a live wire touches the bodywork or other earthed metal part, the electricity will take the low-resistance path thus formed back to the battery: this is known as a short-circuit. Hopefully a short-circuit will blow a fuse, but otherwise it may cause burning of the insulation (and possibly further short-circuits) or even a fire. This is why it is inadvisable to bypass persistently blowing fuses with silver foil or wire.

Spares and tool kit

Most vehicles are supplied only with sufficient tools for wheel changing; the *Maintenance and minor repair* tool kit detailed in *Tools and working facilities,* with the addition of a hammer, is probably sufficient for those repairs that most motorists would consider attempting at the roadside. In addition a few items which can be fitted without too much trouble in the event of a breakdown should be carried. Experience and available space will modify the list below, but the following may save having to call on professional assistance:

Spark plugs, clean and correctly gapped
HT lead and plug cap – long enough to reach the plug furthest from the distributor
Distributor rotor, condenser and contact breaker points
Drivebelt(s) – emergency type may suffice
Spare fuses
Set of principal light bulbs
Tin of radiator sealer and hose bandage
Exhaust bandage
Roll of insulating tape
Length of soft iron wire
Length of electrical flex
Torch or inspection lamp (can double as test lamp)
Battery jump leads
Tow-rope
Ignition waterproofing aerosol
Litre of engine oil
Sealed can of hydraulic fluid
Emergency windscreen
Worm drive hose clips
Tube of filler paste

If spare fuel is carried, a can designed for the purpose should be used to minimise risks of leakage and collision damage. A first aid kit and a warning triangle, whilst not at present compulsory in the UK, are obviously sensible items to carry in addition to the above.

When touring abroad it may be advisable to carry additional spares which, even if you cannot fit them yourself, could save having

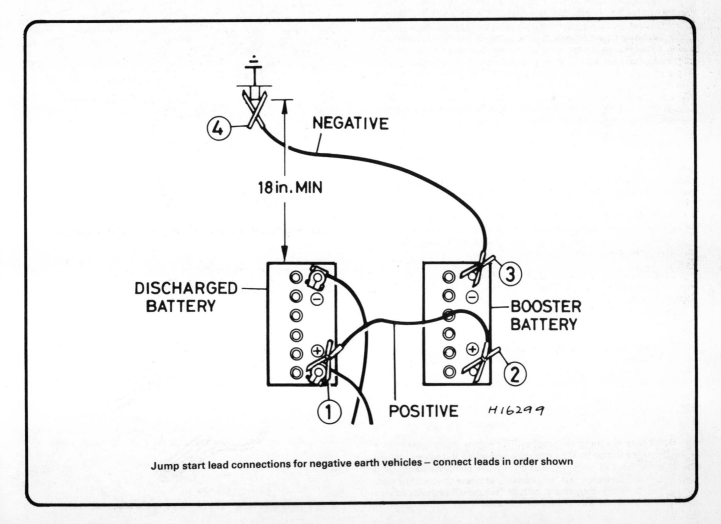

Jump start lead connections for negative earth vehicles – connect leads in order shown

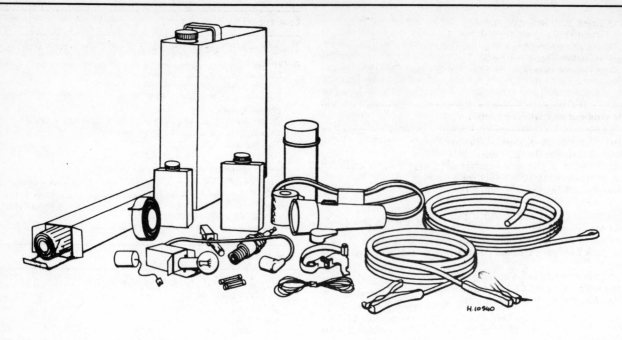

Carrying a few spares can save a long walk!

to wait while parts are obtained. The items below may be worth considering:

Clutch and throttle cables
Cylinder head gasket
Alternator brushes
Fuel pump repair kit
Tyre valve core

One of the motoring organisations will be able to advise on availability of fuel etc in foreign countries.

Engine will not start

Engine fails to turn when starter operated
Flat battery (recharge, use jump leads, or push start)
Battery terminals loose or corroded
Battery earth to body defective
Engine earth strap loose or broken
Starter motor (or solenoid) wiring loose or broken
Automatic transmission selector in wrong position, or inhibitor switch faulty
Ignition/starter switch faulty
Major mechanical failure (seizure)
Starter or solenoid internal fault (see Chapter 10)

Starter motor turns engine slowly
Partially discharged battery (recharge, use jump leads, or push start)
Battery terminals loose or corroded
Battery earth to body defective
Engine earth strap loose
Starter motor (or solenoid) wiring loose
Starter motor internal fault (see Chapter 10)

Starter motor spins without turning engine
Flat battery
Starter motor pinion sticking on sleeve
Flywheel gear teeth damaged or worn
Starter motor mounting bolts loose

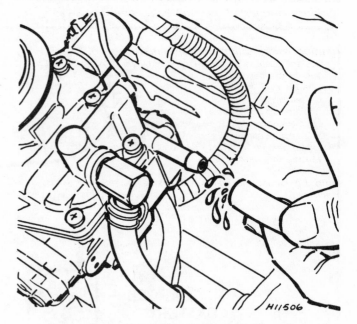

Check for fuel delivery at carburettor

Engine turns normally but fails to start
Damp or dirty HT leads and distributor cap (crank engine and check for spark)
Dirty or incorrectly gapped distributor points (if applicable)
No fuel in tank (check for delivery at carburettor)
Excessive choke (hot engine) or insufficient choke (cold engine)
Fouled or incorrectly gapped spark plugs (remove, clean and regap)
Other ignition system fault (see Chapter 4)
Other fuel system fault (see Chapter 3)
Poor compression (see Chapter 1)
Major mechanical failure (eg camshaft drive)

Engine fires but will not run
Insufficient choke (cold engine)
Air leaks at carburettor or inlet manifold
Fuel starvation (see Chapter 3)
Ballast resistor defective, or other ignition fault (see Chapter 4)

Engine cuts out and will not restart

Engine cuts out suddenly – ignition fault
Loose or disconnected LT wires
Wet HT leads or distributor cap (after traversing water splash)
Coil or condenser failure (check for spark)
Other ignition fault (see Chapter 4)

Engine misfires before cutting out – fuel fault
Fuel tank empty
Fuel pump defective or filter blocked (check for delivery)
Fuel tank filler vent blocked (suction will be evident on releasing cap)
Carburettor needle valve sticking
Carburettor jets blocked (fuel contaminated)
Other fuel system fault (see Chapter 3)

Engine cuts out – other causes
Serious overheating
Major mechanical failure (eg camshaft drive)

Engine overheats

Ignition (no-charge) warning light illuminated
Slack or broken drivebelt – retension or renew (Chapter 2)

Ignition warning light not illuminated
Coolant loss due to internal or external leakage (see Chapter 2)
Thermostat defective
Low oil level
Brakes binding
Radiator clogged externally or internally
Electric cooling fan not operating correctly
Engine waterways clogged
Ignition timing incorrect or automatic advance malfunctioning
Mixture too weak

Note: *Do not add cold water to an overheated engine or damage may result*

Low engine oil pressure

Gauge reads low or warning light illuminated with engine running
Oil level low or incorrect grade
Defective gauge or sender unit
Wire to sender unit earthed
Engine overheating
Oil filter clogged or bypass valve defective
Oil pressure relief valve defective
Oil pick-up strainer clogged
Oil pump worn or mountings loose
Worn main or big-end bearings

Note: *Low oil pressure in a high-mileage engine at tickover is not necessarily a cause for concern. Sudden pressure loss at speed is far more significant. In any event, check the gauge or warning light sender before condemning the engine.*

Engine noises

Pre-ignition (pinking) on acceleration
Incorrect grade of fuel
Ignition timing incorrect
Distributor faulty or worn
Worn or maladjusted carburettor
Excessive carbon build-up in engine

Whistling or wheezing noises
Leaking vacuum hose
Leaking carburettor or manifold gasket
Blowing head gasket

Tapping or rattling
Incorrect valve clearances
Worn valve gear
Worn timing chain or belt
Broken piston ring (ticking noise)

Knocking or thumping
Unintentional mechanical contact (eg fan blades)
Worn drivebelt
Peripheral component fault (generator, water pump etc)
Worn big-end bearings (regular heavy knocking, perhaps less under load)
Worn main bearings (rumbling and knocking, perhaps worsening under load)
Piston slap (most noticeable when cold)

Chapter 1 Engine

Refer to Chapter 13 for specifications and information applicable to 1984 and later models

Contents

Specifications

Engine type .... Four cylinder in-line overhead camshaft transversely mounted

General

Designation and displacement:

C16 .... 1598 cc (97.51 cu in)
C18 .... 1809 cc (110.39 cu in)
C20 .... 1974 cc (120.45 cu in)

Bore:

C16 .... 78.0 mm (3.071 in)
C18 .... 83.0 mm (3.268 in)
C20 .... 84.5 mm (3.327 in)

Stroke:

C16 and C18 .... 83.6 mm (3.291 in)
C20 .... 88.0 mm (3.46 in)

Compression ratio:

C16 .... 9.0:1
C18 .... 8.8:1
C20 .... 8.5:1

Cylinder compression pressures .... 11.9 bar (173 lbf/in^2) at 350 rev/min
Minimum cylinder compression pressures .... 9.0 bar (131 lbf/in^2) at 350 rev/min

Output:

C16 .... 59 kW (81 bhp) at 5200 rev/min (DIN)
C18 .... 65 kW (88 bhp) at 5200 rev/min (DIN)
C20 .... 65 kW (88 bhp) at 5200 rev/min (SAE)

Torque:

C16 .... 130 Nm (96 lbf ft) at 3200 rev/min (DIN)
C18 .... 142 Nm (105 lbf ft) at 3200 rev/min (DIN)
C20 .... 152 Nm (112 lbf ft) at 2800 rev/min (SAE)

Firing order (No. 1 at timing end) .... 1 - 3 - 4 - 2

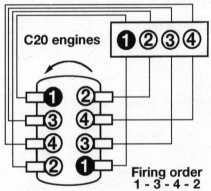

Firing order
1 - 3 - 4 - 2

Front

C16 and C18 engines

981-1-specs Haynes

Cylinder location and distributor rotation

Cylinder block (crankcase)

Material .... Cast-iron

Bore diameter:

C16 .... 77.950 to 78.00 mm (3.0689 to 3.0709 in)
C18 .... 83.000 to 83.050 mm (3.2677 to 3.2697 in)

Permitted taper .... Less than 0.02 mm (0.0008 in)
Permitted out of round .... Less than 0.02 mm (0.0008 in)

Crankshaft

Number of main bearings .... Five
Journal diameter .... 52.951 to 52.964 mm (2.0847 to 2.0852 in)
Crankpin diameter .... 44.961 to 44.974 mm (1.7701 to 1.7706 in)

Permitted taper of journal and crankpin .... 0.03 mm (0.0012 in) maximum
Permitted out of round of journal and crankpin .... 0.03 mm (0.0012 in) maximum
Crankshaft endfloat .... 0.05 to 0.18 mm (0.0020 to 0.0071 in)
Main bearing running clearance .... 0.04 to 0.06 mm (0.0016 to 0.0024 in)
Wear limit .... 0.1 mm (0.004 in)
Main bearing undersizes .... 0.25 mm (0.0098 in), 0.50 mm (0.0197 in)

Connecting rods
Rod side clearance .... 0.2 to 0.3 mm (0.008 to 0.012 in)
Wear limit .... 0.1 mm (0.004 in)
Connecting rod big-end bearing running clearance .... 0.02 to 0.06 mm (0.0008 to 0.0024 in)
Big-end bearing undersizes .... 0.08 mm (0.0031 in), 0.12 mm (0.0047 in), 0.25 mm (0.0098 in), 0.50 mm (0.020 in)

Camshaft
Number of bearings .... Five (non-renewable)
Diameter of camshaft journal .... 45.935 to 45.955 mm (1.8085 to 1.8092 in)
Camshaft endfloat (wear limit) .... 0.2 mm (0.008 in)
Cam height (inlet and exhaust):
    C16 .... 38.240 to 38.290 mm (1.5055 to 1.5075 in)
    C18 .... 38.834 to 38.884 mm (1.5289 to 1.5309 in)
    C20 .... 38.842 to 38.884 mm (1.5292 to 1.5309 in)
Wear limit .... 0.2 mm (0.008 in)

Pistons and rings
Material .... Light alloy
Diameter:
    C16 .... 77.915 to 77.965 mm (3.0675 to 3.0695 in)
    C18 .... 82.965 to 83.015 mm (3.2663 to 3.2683 in)
    C20 .... 84.465 to 84.515 mm (3.3254 to 3.3274 in)
Oversizes .... 0.50 mm (0.0197 in), 1.00 mm (0.0394 in)
Piston to cylinder bore clearance .... 0.025 to 0.045 mm (0.0010 to 0.0018 in)
Gudgeon pin outside diameter .... 19.995 to 20.000 mm (0.7872 to 0.7874 in)
Gudgeon pin to piston clearance .... 0.008 to 0.012 mm (0.0003 to 0.0005 in)
Interference fit of gudgeon pin in connecting rod .... 0.017 to 0.038 mm (0.0007 to 0.0015 in)

Cylinder head
Material .... Light alloy
Maximum permissible distortion of sealing face .... 0.1 mm (0.004 in)
Valve clearance (hot):
    Inlet and exhaust .... 0.30 mm (0.012 in)
Stem to guide clearance:
    Inlet .... 0.020 to 0.053 mm (0.0008 to 0.0021 in)
    Exhaust .... 0.040 to 0.073 mm (0.0016 to 0.0029 in)
Wear limit .... 0.1 mm (0.004 in)
Valve face angle .... 45° 15' to 45° 45'
Valve length:
    Inlet .... 105.15 to 105.66 mm (4.14 to 4.16 in)
    Exhaust .... 106.42 to 106.68 mm (4.19 to 4.20 in)
Valve stem diameter:
    Inlet .... 6.965 to 6.980 mm (0.2742 to 0.2748 in)
    Exhaust .... 6.945 to 6.960 mm (0.2734 to 0.2740 in)
Valve guide outside diameter .... 11.023 to 11.034 mm (0.4340 to 0.4344 in)
Interference fit of valve guide in cylinder head .... 0.027 to 0.059 mm (0.0011 to 0.0023 in)
Valve guide inside diameter (reamed) .... 7.000 to 7.018 mm (0.2756 to 0.2763 in)

Valve springs
Type .... Dual
Free height:
    Inner .... 44.10 mm (1.7362 in)
    Outer .... 49.98 mm (1.9677 in)

Flywheel
Permitted out of true .... Less than 0.15 mm (0.0059 in)

Lubricant
Type/specification .... Multigrade engine oil, viscosity range SAE 10W/30 to 20W/50, to API SE (Duckhams QXR, Hypergrade, or 10W/40 Motor Oil)

Oil pump
Clearances:
    Inner gear to crescent .... 0.12 to 0.23 mm (0.0047 to 0.0091 in)
    Outer gear to crescent .... 0.21 to 0.32 mm (0.0083 to 0.0126 in)
    Outer gear to body .... 0.11 to 0.20 mm (0.0043 to 0.0079 in)
    Gear endfloat .... 0.05 to 0.11 mm (0.0020 to 0.0043 in)

Torque wrench settings

	Nm	lbf ft
Timing belt tensioner bolts	20	15
Coolant pump bolt	18	13
Alternator adjuster link	20	15
Crankshaft pulley bolt (engines without damper)	130	96
Crankshaft damper bolt (engines with damper)	130	96
Crankshaft damper-to-pulley bolts (engines with damper)	9	7
Inlet manifold bolts and nuts	20	15
Alternator bracket	55	41
Fuel pump mounting nut	12	9
Carburettor mounting nut	18	13
Exhaust manifold nut	24	18
Cylinder head bolts:		
Stage 1	25	18
Stage 2	50	37
Stage 3	75	55
Rocker shaft bolt	20	15
Camshaft sprocket bolt	55	41
Fuel pump cam bolt	85	63
Spark plug	20	15
Rocker arm screw locknut	20	15
Main bearing cap bolt	50	37
Connecting rod big-end nut	35	26
Oil pan bolt	7	5
Oil pump bolts	15	11
Flywheel or driveplate bolts	100	74
Clutch cover bolts	20	15
Starter motor bolts	38	28
Flywheel (or torque converter) housing to engine bolts	55	41
Rear oil seal retainer bolts	6	4
Camshaft cover plate bolts	10	7
Air conditioner compressor bracket bolt	75	55
Idler bracket bolt	58	43
Exhaust air induction system union nut	44	32
Engine mounting pivot bolts	50	37
Engine mounting bracket bolts	50	37
Right-hand engine mounting torsion rod link bolt	75	55
Exhaust downpipe flange nuts	30	22
Roadwheel nut	95	70
Suspension lower balljoint nuts	60	44
Suspension strut upper mounting nuts	23	17

1 General description

The engine is of four cylinder overhead cam type mounted transversely at the front end of the vehicle.

The cylinder head is of light alloy construction and the cylinder block/crankcase is of cast iron.

The crankshaft is of five main bearing type whilst the belt-driven camshaft runs in a similar number of non-renewable bearings in the cylinder head.

The oil pump is mounted at the timing belt end of the crankshaft and supplies pressurised oil to all moving parts after the oil has first passed through an externally mounted full-flow cartridge type filter.

The engine is available in three capacities, the larger engine displacements being obtained by increasing the bore on C16 and C18 versions, and bore and stroke on the C20.

All engines have some form of emission control system, but on models destined for operation in North America, a modified engine type NAPS-X (Nissan anti-pollution system) is fitted. This engine incorporates two spark plugs per cylinder, mixture sensor and 'fast-burn' design of cylinder head, all in the interest of reducing the level of unburned hydrocarbons.

2 Engine oil and filter

1 The engine oil level may be checked either with the engine hot or cold. If the engine has been running then leave it for a few minutes after switching off then allow the oil to drain back into the sump pan.
2 Withdraw the dipstick, wipe it clean, re-insert it and withdraw it for the second time and read off the oil level. The level should be between the L and H marks. If it is not, top up with the correct grade of oil (photo).
3 At the intervals specified in Routine Maintenance, the engine oil and filter should be changed. Drain the oil when it is hot by unscrewing

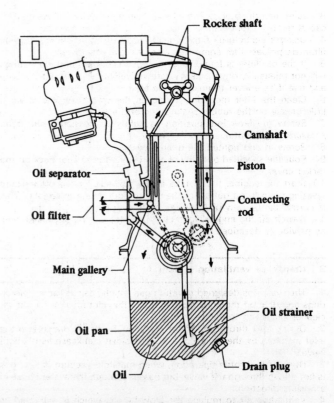

Fig. 1.1 Engine lubrication circuit (Sec 1)

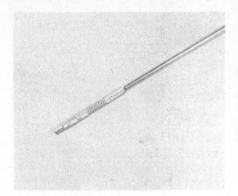

2.2 Engine oil dipstick

2.3 Engine sump drain plug

2.7 Screwing on oil filter

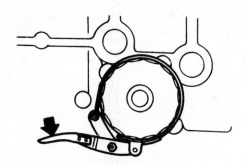

Fig. 1.2 Removing oil filter (Sec 2)

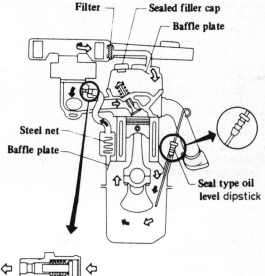

Filter — Sealed filler cap

Baffle plate

Steel net

Baffle plate

Seal type oil level dipstick

P.C.V. valve

Fig. 1.3 Typical crankcase ventilation system (Sec 3)

Fig. 1.4 Testing PCV valve (Sec 3)

1

the sump pan drain plug. The oil will drain more quickly if the oil filler cap is removed (photos).

4   Using a suitable oil filter wrench, unscrew the cartridge type oil filter. Be prepared for some loss of oil as it is unscrewed.

5   If the old filter is found to be exceptionally tight and the wrench will not release it, drive a heavy screwdriver through the filter casing and use it as a lever to unscrew the filter.

6   Clean the filter mounting flange on the crankcase and smear a little grease on the rubber sealing ring of the oil filter.

7   Screw the filter into position as tightly as possible *using hand pressure only* (photo).

8   Screw in and tighten the drain plug.

9   Pour the specified quantity of engine oil into the filler neck on the rocker cover.

10 Start the engine. It will take a few seconds for the oil pressure warning lamp to go out or for the oil pressure gauge to register. This is normal as the new oil filter has to fill with oil.

11 Switch off the engine, then check and top up the engine oil level as previously described.

---

3   Crankcase ventilation system

1   The system is designed to return gas which has passed the piston rings and entered the crankcase, to either the inlet manifold or the air cleaner according to engine load.

2   During part throttle operation the blow-by gas is drawn into the inlet manifold by the action of a PCV (positive crankcase ventilation) valve.

3   During full throttle operation, when manifold vacuum is low, gas is not drawn through the valve, but passes through the system hose in a reverse direction.

4   Ventilating air to replace the blow-by gas which is extracted, is drawn into the rocker cover from the clean side of the air cleaner.

5   On a worn engine having a large volume of blow-by gas to be extracted, some gas will pass into the air cleaner at all times.

6   At the intervals specified in Routine Maintenance clean the connecting hoses of the system free from oil and sludge.

7   Check the operation of the valve by having the engine idling and

3.8 Crankcase breather oil separator and hoses

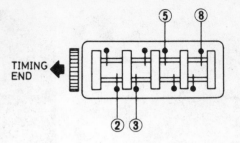

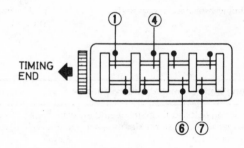

then pull the hose from the valve. A hissing noise should be heard and strong suction felt if a finger is placed over the hole in the valve.

8   The oil separator is a press fit in its hole in the crankcase. It may be levered out to clean (photo).

Fig. 1.5 Valve identification (Sec 5)

4   Major operations possible without removing engine from vehicle

The following work can be carried out without having to remove the engine:

Valve clearances – adjustment
Timing belt – removal and refitting
Cylinder head – removal and refitting
Sump pan – removal and refitting
Oil pump – removal and refitting
Piston rings and big-end bearings – renewal
Engine mountings – renewal

Warning – *vehicles equipped with air conditioning.*

Whenever overhaul of a major nature is being undertaken to the engine and components of the air conditioning system obstruct the work, and such items of the system cannot be unbolted and moved aside sufficiently far within the limits of their flexible connecting pipes to avoid such obstruction, then the system should be discharged by your dealer or a competent refrigeration engineer.

As the system must be completely evacuated before recharging, the necessary vacuum equipment to do this is only likely to be available at your dealer.

The refrigerant fluid is Freon 12 and although harmless under normal conditions, contact with the eyes or skin must be avoided. If Freon comes into contact with a naked flame, then a poisonous gas will be created which is injurious to health.

5   Valve clearances – adjustment

1   As a routine service operation, the valve clearances should be checked and adjusted while the engine is hot. After overhaul of the engine, the valve clearances will obviously have to be set cold initially and then re-set when the engine has been run to normal operating temperature.

2   Remove the air cleaner (Chapter 3).

3   Unclip and disconnect the spark plug leads.

4   Remove the rocker cover.

5   Turn the crankshaft until No. 1 camshaft lobe is pointing directly downwards. No. 1 camshaft lobe is the one nearest the timing belt end

5.6 Checking a valve clearance

of the engine. The crankshaft can be turned by using a spanner on the crankshaft pulley bolt or by using the starter motor.

6   Adjust the clearances on valves number 1 – 4 – 6 – 7. To do this, insert a feeler blade between the end of the valve stem and the rocker arm. The blade should be a stiff sliding fit. If the clearance is incorrect, release the rocker arm adjuster screw locknut and turn the adjuster screw. Once the clearance is correct, tighten the locknut without altering the position of the screw (photo).

7   Having adjusted the clearances of the first four valves, turn the crankshaft until No. 1 camshaft lobe points directly upwards. Adjust valves 2 – 3 – 5 – 8 as previously described. The valve clearances for inlet and exhaust valves are the same.

8   Fit the rocker cover using a new gasket if there is any doubt about the condition of the original one.

6.12A Timing belt mark at camshaft sprocket

6.12B Timing belt mark at crankshaft sprocket

6.14 Timing belt cover screw

6 Timing belt – removal and refitting

1   The timing belt should be inspected for wear, cuts or fraying at the intervals specified in Routine Maintenance. Unless the belt is in perfect condition, renew it.
2   Disconnect the HT leads from the spark plugs, unclip the distributor cap and move it aside.
3   Remove the drivebelts (Chapter 2) and then unbolt and take off the coolant pump pulley.
4   Extract the screws and remove the timing belt upper cover.
5   Support the engine on a jack placed under the sump pan using a wooden block as an insulator.
6   Unbolt the right-hand front mounting from both the crankcase and the body.
7   Extract the screws from the timing belt lower cover and remove it.
8   Turn the crankshaft by means of its pulley bolt until the marks on the timing belt are in alignment with the marks on the camshaft and crankshaft sprockets. It will not be possible to see the mark on the crankshaft sprocket until the crankshaft pulley/damper has been removed, do this now.
9   In order to unscrew the crankshaft pulley bolt, the crankshaft must be held against rotation. On manual transmission models, select a gear and have an assistant apply the footbrake hard. On automatic transmission models, the torque converter housing lower cover plate or the starter motor will have to be removed and the teeth of the driveplate ring gear jammed with a suitable blade.
10   Release the belt tensioner bolts, prise the tensioner pulley away from the belt.
11   Note the running direction of the timing belt and then remove it.
12   Fit the belt so that its running direction is correct and the marks on the belt are in alignment with the timing marks on the sprockets (photos).
13   Check that the belt tensioner spring is hooked onto the bolt and the bracket of the tensioner and then tighten the tensioner lower bolt B followed by the upper bolt A. The timing belt is now automatically tensioned.
14   Fit the belt cover with sealing strips (photo).
15   Fit the crankshaft pulley/damper, tighten the bolt to the specified torque while holding the crankshaft against rotation as described in paragraph 6.
16   Fit and tension the drivebelts as described in Chapter 2.

7 Cylinder head – removal and refitting

1   Disconnect the battery, drain the cooling system.
2   Remove the air cleaner.
3   Unbolt and remove the hot air collector from the exhaust manifold together with flexible duct. Disconnect the exhaust downpipe from the manifold.
4   Disconnect the ignition leads from the spark plugs and the coil. Also disconnect the distributor vacuum hose and unbolt and remove the distributor.

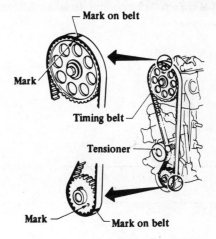

Fig. 1.6 Timing marks (Sec 6)

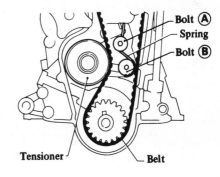

Fig. 1.7 Timing belt tensioner bolts (Sec 6)

5   Disconnect the hoses from the fuel pump and plug them. Unbolt and remove the pump.
6   Disconnect the fuel hose from the carburettor. Also disconnect the throttle control cable and electrical leads which connect to the automatic choke and fuel cut-off valve.
7   Disconnect the brake vacuum servo hose, crankcase ventilation hose and coolant hose. Then unbolt and remove the inlet manifold complete with carburettor. On North American vehicles, disconnect the emission control components including the EGR valve and anti-backfire valve (refer to Chapter 3).
8   Unbolt and remove the rocker cover and spark plugs.
9   Remove the drivebelts and then unbolt and withdraw the timing belt cover.

10 Turn the crankshaft until the marks on the bolt are aligned with the marks on the sprockets. It will only be possible to observe the marks on the camshaft sprocket with the crankshaft pulley/damper in position.

11 Remove the camshaft sprocket bolt and pull the sprocket from the camshaft. Mark its position on the shaft flange as it can be refitted in two positions.

12 Slip the belt from the camshaft sprocket and tie it up or clip the two runs of the belt together to prevent it from becoming disengaged from the teeth of the crankshaft sprocket.

13 Loosen the cylinder head bolts in the sequence shown, one half of a turn at a time.

14 Remove the cylinder head. If it is stuck tight, do not attempt to release it by inserting a tool in the gasket joint, but tap the sides of the head carefully with a plastic-faced hammer or if using an ordinary hammer, use a block of hardwood as an insulator.

15 If the cylinder head is to be dismantled and decarbonised, refer to Section 18.

16 Before refitting the cylinder head, the mating surfaces of both head and block must be perfectly clean and free from old pieces of gasket. Take care when cleaning the cylinder head not to dig or score its surface. Clean the bolt holes in the cylinder block free from dirt and oil.

17 Locate a new cylinder head gasket on the cylinder block (photo).

18 Check that No. 1 piston is still at TDC and slacken all the rocker arm adjuster screws right off.

19 Lower the cylinder head into position and screw in the lightly oiled bolts, but only finger tight. Final tightening should be carried out after the timing belt and its cover have been fitted. The longer bolt is located at the distributor mounting position (photo).

20 Engage the timing belt with the camshaft sprocket so that the belt and sprocket marks are in alignment then bolt the sprocket onto the camshaft, again aligning the marks.

21 Fit the belt cover.

22 Tighten the cylinder head bolts to the specified torque in the sequence shown.

23 Using new gaskets on clean mating faces, bolt on the inlet and exhaust manifolds (photo).

24 Bolt the hot air collector to the exhaust manifold (photo).

25 Fit the distributor as described in Chapter 4.

26 Reconnect the ignition leads to the spark plugs and coil.

27 Reconnect the vacuum and coolant hoses to the inlet manifold.

28 Reconnect the control cable and electrical leads to the carburettor.

29 Refit the fuel pump and connect the hoses.

30 On North American models, refit and reconnect the emission control components.

7.17 Cylinder head gasket

7.19 Fitting cylinder head

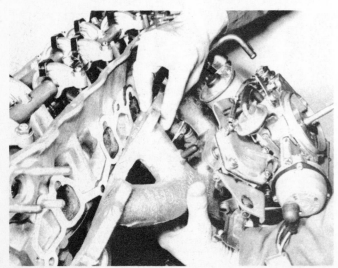

7.23 Fitting intake manifold and carburettor

7.24 Exhaust manifold hot air collector

7.33 Fitting rocker cover

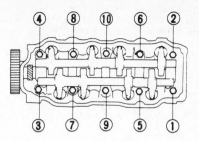

Fig. 1.8 Cylinder head bolt loosening sequence (Sec 7)

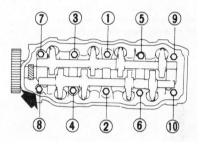

Fig. 1.9 Cylinder head bolt tightening sequence (Sec 7)

Location of longer bolt arrowed

31 Refit and tension the drivebelts (Chapter 2).

32 Set the valve clearances (Section 4).

33 Fit the rocker cover with gasket, screw in the spark plugs (photo).

34 Fit the timing belt upper cover with sealing strips. Connect the battery, fill the cooling system.

35 After the engine has been run to normal operating temperature, allow it to cool and then check the torque of the cylinder head bolts. Do this by unscrewing the first bolt through a quarter of a turn and then tightening it to the specified torque. Repeat the operations (one bolt at a time) in the correct sequence (Fig. 1-9).

36 Start the engine and again bring it to normal working temperature then check and adjust the valve clearances.

8 Sump pan – removal and refitting

1 Remove the engine undershield (if fitted).

2 Disconnect the battery.

3 Unbolt the exhaust downpipe from the manifold.

4 Release the exhaust system forward mounting, and then pull the front of the system down as far as the flexible connection will allow.

5 Drain the engine oil.

6 Unscrew the sump pan bolts and the corner reinforcement tube bolts. Pull the pan downwards and remove it.

7 Clean away the old joint gasket.

8 Stick a new gasket and sealing strips in position on the crankcase using a smear of jointing compound and then put a blob of compound over the joints where the sealing strips overlap the side gaskets. Later models have a one piece rubber gasket (photo).

9 Offer up the sump pan, screw in the bolts evenly in diagonal sequence (photo).

10 Reconnect the exhaust pipe and mounting.

11 Fit the engine undershield.

12 Fill the sump with oil.

1

8.8 Sump pan sealing strip

8.9 Lowering sump pan into position

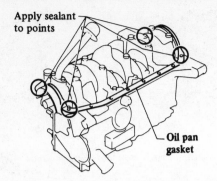

Fig. 1.10 Sump pan gaskets (Sec 8)

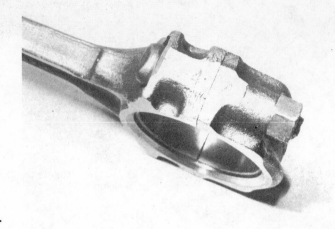

10.4 Connecting rod numbers

9 Oil pump – removal and refitting

1   Drain the engine oil.
2   Remove the sump pan as described in the preceding Section.
3   Unbolt and remove the oil pick-up pipe and strainer.
4   Remove the drivebelts.
5   Unbolt and remove the crankshaft pulley and damper as described in Section 6, paragraph 9.
6   Remove the timing belt also as described in Section 6.
7   Unbolt the timing belt tensioner and remove it.
8   Pull off the crankshaft sprocket. Remove the Woodruff key.
9   Unbolt and remove the oil pump from the front face of the crankcase. Discard the joint gasket.
10 The oil pump can be examined as described in Section 19 and renewed if worn.
11 Before refitting the oil pump, always renew the oil seal and grease the seal lips. Use a new joint gasket.
12 As the oil pump is offered into position, align the inner gear with the flats on the crankshaft. Tape the shoulder on the crankshaft to prevent damage to the oil seal lips during fitting of the pump. Remove the tape when the pump is in position.
13 Fit the crankshaft Woodruff key and sprocket so that its timing mark is visible.
14 Fit the timing belt and tensioner as described in Section 6.
15 Fit the crankshaft pulley/damper.
16 Fit the oil pick-up pipe and strainer.
17 Fit the sump pan as described previously.
18 Refill with engine oil.

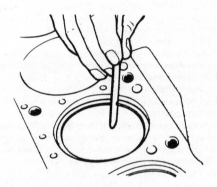

Fig. 1.11 Checking piston ring gap (Sec 10)

10 Piston rings and big-end bearings – renewal

1   Remove the cylinder head (Section 7).
2   Remove the engine sump pan (Section 8)
3   Unbolt and remove the oil pick-up pipe and strainer.
4   Note that the connecting rod big-end cap and rod are numbered at adjacent points. Number 1 is at the timing belt end of the engine (photo).
5   Feel the top of the cylinder bore for a wear ridge. If a thick one is felt then it should be removed using a ridge reamer or by careful scraping, in order to enable the piston rings to pass out of the bore during removal.
6   Unscrew the big-end cap bolts and take off the cap with shell bearing.
7   Push the piston/rod assembly out of the top of the block.
8   If the bearing shells are to be used again, tape them to their original cap or rod.
9   Repeat the operations on the three remaining assemblies.
10 If the reason for removal of the piston/rod assemblies was to fit new piston rings to reduce oil consumption, then either standard or special proprietary rings may be fitted.
11 To remove a piston ring, slide three feeler blades behind the top ring and space them at equidistant points.
12 Remove the ring by pulling it off the top of the piston using a twisting motion.

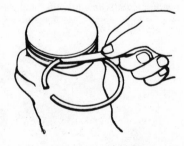

Fig. 1.12 Checking piston ring groove clearance (Sec 10)

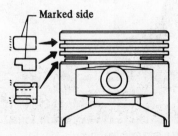

Fig. 1.13 Piston ring arrangement (Sec 10)

10.20 Piston/connecting rod component parts

10.23A Fitting piston/rod with piston ring clamp

10.23B Piston front mark

13 Repeat on the remaining rings, always removing them from the crown of the piston.
14 Clean the piston ring grooves of carbon. A piece of broken piston ring is useful for this.
15 Make sure that the oil return holes at the base of the ring grooves are clear.
16 Push the piston rings down their cylinder bore one at a time and check the ring end gap using a feeler blade. If not as specified, carefully grind the end of the ring.
17 Check each ring in its groove for side clearance again using a feeler blade. If the clearance is too small then the piston grooves can be widened by your engine reconditioner or the ring width reduced by rubbing it on abrasive sheeting located on a very flat surface.
18 Fit the rings by reversing the removal operations. Stagger the ring gaps at equidistant points.
19 If new rings have been fitted, then to assist them to bed in rapidly, the hard glaze in the cylinder bores should be removed. Do this using a rotary type flap wheel in an electric drill or with fine glasspaper rubbed up and down at an angle to give a cross-hatch effect.
20 If new bearing shells are fitted, make sure that shells of the same size as the originals are used. The shells will be marked on their backs either standard or undersize (photo).
21 Fit the shells to caps and rods.
22 Oil the piston rings liberally and fit a piston ring compressor.
23 Lower the rod of No. 1 piston into its cylinder bore so that the compressor sits squarely on the surface of the block. Make sure that the mark on the piston crown is towards the timing belt end of the engine (photos).

24 Place the wooden handle of a hammer against the middle of the piston crown and then strike the head of the hammer with the hand to drive the piston with rings into the cylinder. The compressor will be released (photo).
25 Pull the rod down onto the crankshaft and fit the big-end cap (with shell) so that the matching numbers are adjacent.
26 Screw on the cap nuts and tighten to the specified torque wrench setting (photo).
27 Repeat the operations on the remaining pistons.
28 Fit the oil pick-up pipe and strainer, the sump pan and the cylinder head all as described earlier in this Chapter.
29 Fill the engine with oil.

11 Engine/transmission mountings – renewal

1 The mountings can be renewed provided the weight of the engine and transmission is taken on a hoist or jack.
2 The component which incorporates the flexible insulator should be renewed if the rubber has become sticky or has perished or becomes deformed as the result of the weight of the power train.

12 Engine – method of removal

1 The engine should be removed complete with transmission by lifting it out upwards from the engine compartment.

10.24 Driving piston into cylinder bore

10.26 Tightening connecting rod cap nut

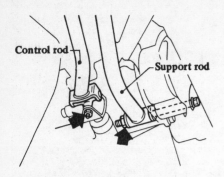

Fig. 1.14 Gearchange rod and support
rod attachment at transmission end
(Sec 13)

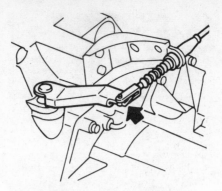

Fig. 1.15 Clutch cable connection at
release lever (Sec 13)

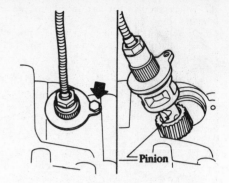

Fig. 1.16 Speedometer cable at
transmission (Sec 13)

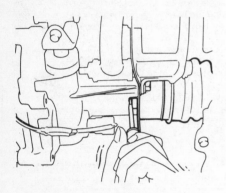

Fig. 1.17 Releasing right-hand driveshaft
(Sec 13)

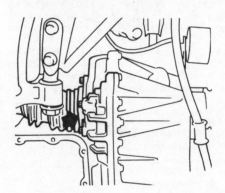

Fig. 1.18 Releasing left-hand driveshaft
(Sec 13)

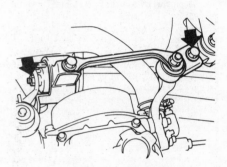

Fig. 1.19 Right-hand engine mounting
and torsion rod (Sec 13)

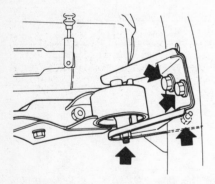

Fig. 1.20 Left-hand engine mounting
(Sec 13)

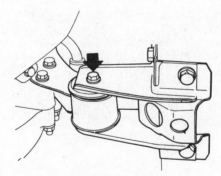

Fig. 1.21 Front engine mounting
(Sec 13)

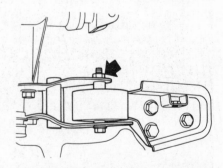

Fig. 1.22 Rear engine mounting (Sec 13)

13 Engine/manual transmission – removal and separation

1   Open the bonnet and then with the help of an assistant remove it
as described in Chapter 12.
2   Remove the battery, the cooling system expansion tank and the
battery support tray.
3   Remove the air cleaner.
4   Working under the vehicle remove the undershield (photo).
5   Drain the cooling system, disconnect the hoses (photo).
6   Remove the radiator/cooling fan as described in Chapter 2.
7   Where power-assisted steering is fitted, remove the power
steering pump (Chapter 11).

8   If air conditioning is fitted, unbolt the compressor and tie it
securely to one side of the engine compartment (refer to Section 4
warning note).
9   Disconnect the exhaust downpipe from the manifold (photo).
10 Release the exhaust system front mounting.
11 Disconnect the gearchange control rod and its support rod from
the transmission.
12 Disconnect the clutch operating cable from the release lever at the
transmission.
13 Unscrew the lockbolt and pull the speedometer pinion driven gear
from the transmission.
14 Disconnect the throttle control cable from the carburettor.
15 Disconnect the electrical leads from the carburettor, noting the

clip which secures the multi-pin plug and locks the throttle cable (photo).

16 Disconnect the ignition leads from the coil.

17 Disconnect the electrical leads from the starter motor and the alternator (photo).

18 Disconnect the leads from the reversing lamp switch, oil pressure switch and temperature sender (photo).

19 Disconnect the engine stabiliser bar from the timing belt end of the engine and the top of the engine mounting (photo).

20 Disconnect the brake servo vacuum hose from the inlet manifold (photo).

21 Disconnect the heater hoses (photos).

22 Disconnect the fuel supply hose from the pump and plug the hose.

23 On North American vehicles, disconnect emission control system leads and hoses as appropriate (see Chapter 3).

24 Drain the engine oil.

25 Disconnect the driveshafts. Do this by raising the front of the vehicle and supporting it securely. Remove the roadwheels. Disconnect the front suspension lower balljoints by removing the three bolts which hold it to the track control arm. Unscrew, but do not remove the three nuts on the suspension strut top mounting to provide greater flexibility.

26 Using a lever inserted between the inboard joint of the driveshaft and the transmission casing, prise the shaft against the resistance of the circlip until it is released from the transmission.

27 Insert a dummy bar or a U-shaped piece of wire into the hole in the transmission left by removal of the driveshaft to prevent the differential side gears being displaced.

28 Disconnect the driveshaft on the opposite side on a similar way.

29 Connect lifting eyes and a hoist to the engine. Attachment to front and rear of the cylinder head will provide a good balance for the unit during removal.

13.4 Engine undershield

13.5 Cooling system hose clip

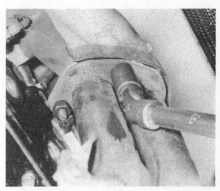
13.9 Unscrewing exhaust downpipe flange nut

13.15 Wiring plug at throttle cable bracket

13.17 Alternator wiring harness and manifold heater hose

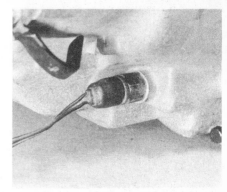
13.18 Reversing lamp switch

1

13.19 Engine stabiliser bar

13.20 Brake servo hose

13.21A Heater hose at metal coolant pipe

13.21B Heater hose and coolant hose connection

13.21C Heater hose connection at engine mounting

13.30A Engine mounting at timing end

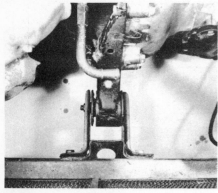

13.30B Engine front mounting

13.30C Engine rear mounting viewed from below

13.30D Engine/transmission left-hand mounting

13.30E Left-hand mounting (body) bracket

13.30F Engine rear mounting bracket under steering rack

13.30G Engine front mounting (body) bracket

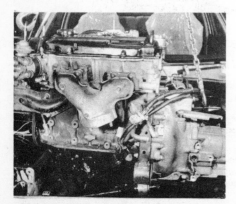

13.31 Removing engine/transmission

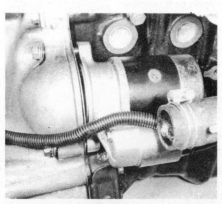

13.33 Removing starter motor

13.35 Transmission separated from engine

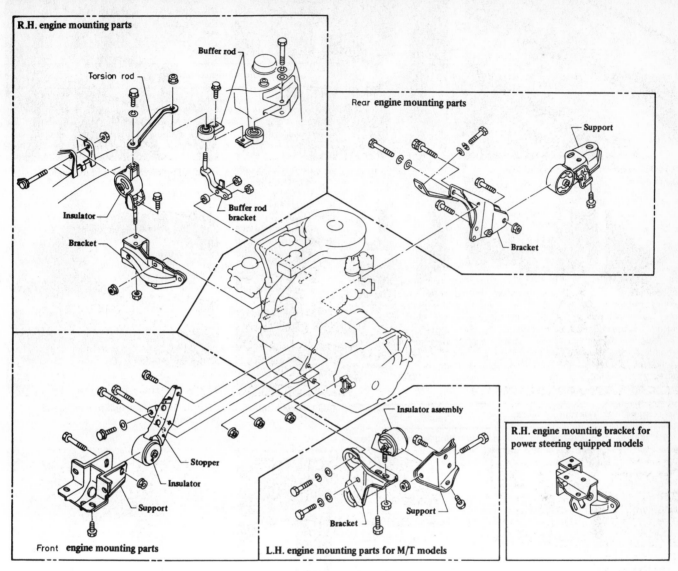

Fig. 1.23 Engine/transmission mounting
components (Sec 13)

30 Just take the weight of the engine on the hoist and then
disconnect the four engine/transmission mountings. Do this by unscrewing the pivot bolts on all mountings except the front left-hand
one. On this one, remove the three bolts holding the mounting bracket
to the transmission case (photos).
31 Hoist the engine carefully up and out of the engine compartment
(photo).
32 Clean away external oil and dirt using paraffin and a stiff brush or
a water-soluble solvent. Unbolt the metal coolant pipe and mounting
bracket.
33 Unbolt and remove the starter motor (photo).
34 Unbolt and remove the cover plate from the lower face of the
flywheel housing.
35 Unscrew and remove the bolts which connect the flywheel
housing to the engine, support the weight of the transmission and
withdraw it from the engine (photo).

14 Engine/automatic transmission – removal and separation

1   The operations are very similar to those described in the preceding
Section for manual transmission, but note the following differences.
2   Ignore all reference to the clutch cable.
3   Disconnect the speed selector control control linkage from the
transmission.

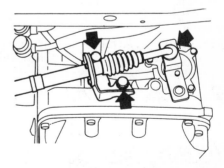

Fig. 1.24 Automatic transmission speed
selector linkage (Sec 14)

4   Observe the difference in design of the left-hand engine mounting.
5   Disconnect and plug the transmission fluid cooler hoses.
6   With the engine/transmission removed, separate the assemblies in
the following way.
7   Remove the metal coolant pipe and the mounting bracket. Unbolt
and remove the cover plate from the base of the torque converter
housing.

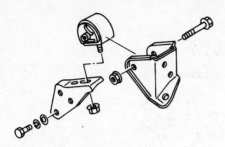

Fig. 1.25 Left-hand engine/transmission mounting (automatic transmission) (Sec 14)

8   Mark the relationship of the torque converter to the driveplate with quick-drying paint and then unscrew the converter to driveplate connecting bolts. The crankshaft will have to be turned by means of the crankshaft pulley bolt to bring the connecting bolts into view within the aperture left by removal of the cover plate.
9   Support the weight of the transmission and withdraw it from the engine. As the transmission comes away, make sure that the torque converter is pressed fully towards the transmission to prevent it coming out of engagement with the fluid pump.

15 Engine – dismantling general

1   It is best to mount the engine on a dismantling stand, but if this is not available, stand the engine on a strong bench at a comfortable working height. Failing this, it will have to be stripped down on the floor, but at least place a sheet of hardboard down first.
2   Clean each component in paraffin as it is removed.
3   Never immerse parts with oilways in paraffin (eg crankshaft and camshaft). To clean these parts, wipe down carefully with a paraffin dampened rag. Oilways can be cleaned out with wire. If an air line is available, all parts can be blown dry and the oilways blown through as an added precaution.
4   Re-use of old gaskets is false economy. To avoid the possibility of trouble after the engine has been reassembled **always** use new gaskets throughout.
5   Do not throw away the old gaskets, for sometimes it happens that an immediate replacement cannot be found and the old gasket is then very useful as a template. Hang up the gaskets as they are removed.
6   To strip the engine, it is best to work from the top down. When the stage is reached where the crankshaft must be removed, the engine can be turned on its side and all other work carried out with it in this position.
7   Wherever possible, refit nuts, bolts and washers finger tight from wherever they were removed. This helps to avoid loss and muddle. If they cannot be fitted then arrange them in a sequence that ensures correct reassembly.
8   Make sure that you have a valve grinding tool, a valve spring compressor and a torque wrench.

16 Engine ancillary components – removal

1 Before engine dismantling commences, remove the following ancillary components:

   Alternator (Chapter 10)
   Inlet manifold with carburettor (Chapter 3)
   Distributor (Chapter 4) with cap and leads
   Coolant pump (Chapter 2)
   Exhaust manifold (Chapter 3)

2   It is also recommended that the engine mounting brackets are removed. This will make the engine easier to handle.

3   Where appropriate, remove the emission control components, the air conditioner compressor, the power steering pump mountings and idler.

17 Engine – complete dismantling

1   Remove the alternator adjuster link.
2   Unscrew the bolt and take off the crankshaft pulley/damper. To prevent the crankshaft turning during this operation, either jam the teeth of the starter ring with a suitable tool or have an assistant hold the flywheel by passing a lever between the heads of two flywheel bolts.
3   Remove the timing belt outer guide disc.
4   Remove the inlet manifold support.
5   Unscrew and discard the oil filter.
6   Unscrew the oil pressure switch and remove it as this is easily damaged.
7   Remove the timing belt and tensioner (Section 6).
8   Remove the rocker cover.
9   Remove the cylinder head (Section 7).
10 Turn the engine on its side and unbolt the sump pan.
11 Remove the oil pick-up pipe with strainer.
12 Remove the crankshaft sprocket and the timing belt inner guide disc.
13 Unbolt and remove the oil pump from the front face of the crankcase.
14 Remove the piston/connecting rods as described in Section 10.
15 Unbolt and remove the flywheel bolts and remove the flywheel having first marked its position in relation to the mounting flange.
16 Take off the engine rear plate.
17 Unscrew the crankshaft rear oil seal retainer bolts and remove the retainer.
18 Remove the main bearing cap bolts.

17.19 Main bearing cap number

19 Note the caps are numbered 1 to 5 from the timing end of the engine and the numbers are read from the same end (photo).
20 Remove the caps, tapping them off if necessary with a copper-faced hammer.
21 If the bearing shells are to be used again keep them with their respective caps.
22 Lift the crankshaft from the crankcase.
23 Remove the remaining half shells from their crankcase seats and again keep them in their original sequence if they are to be refitted.
24 Unbolt and remove the baffle plate from inside the crankcase.

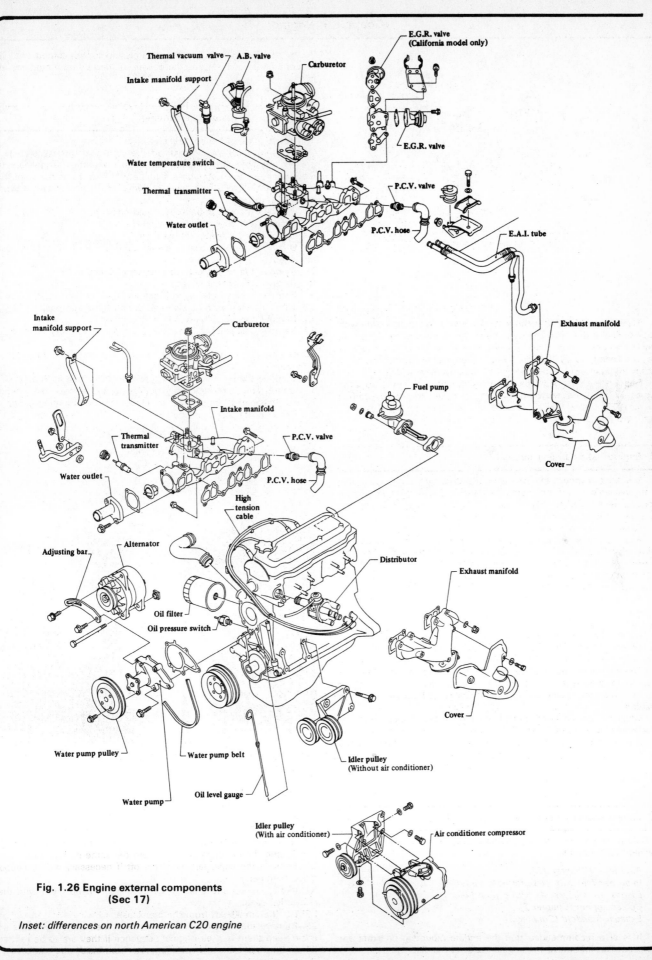

Fig. 1.26 Engine external components (Sec 17)

Inset: differences on north American C20 engine

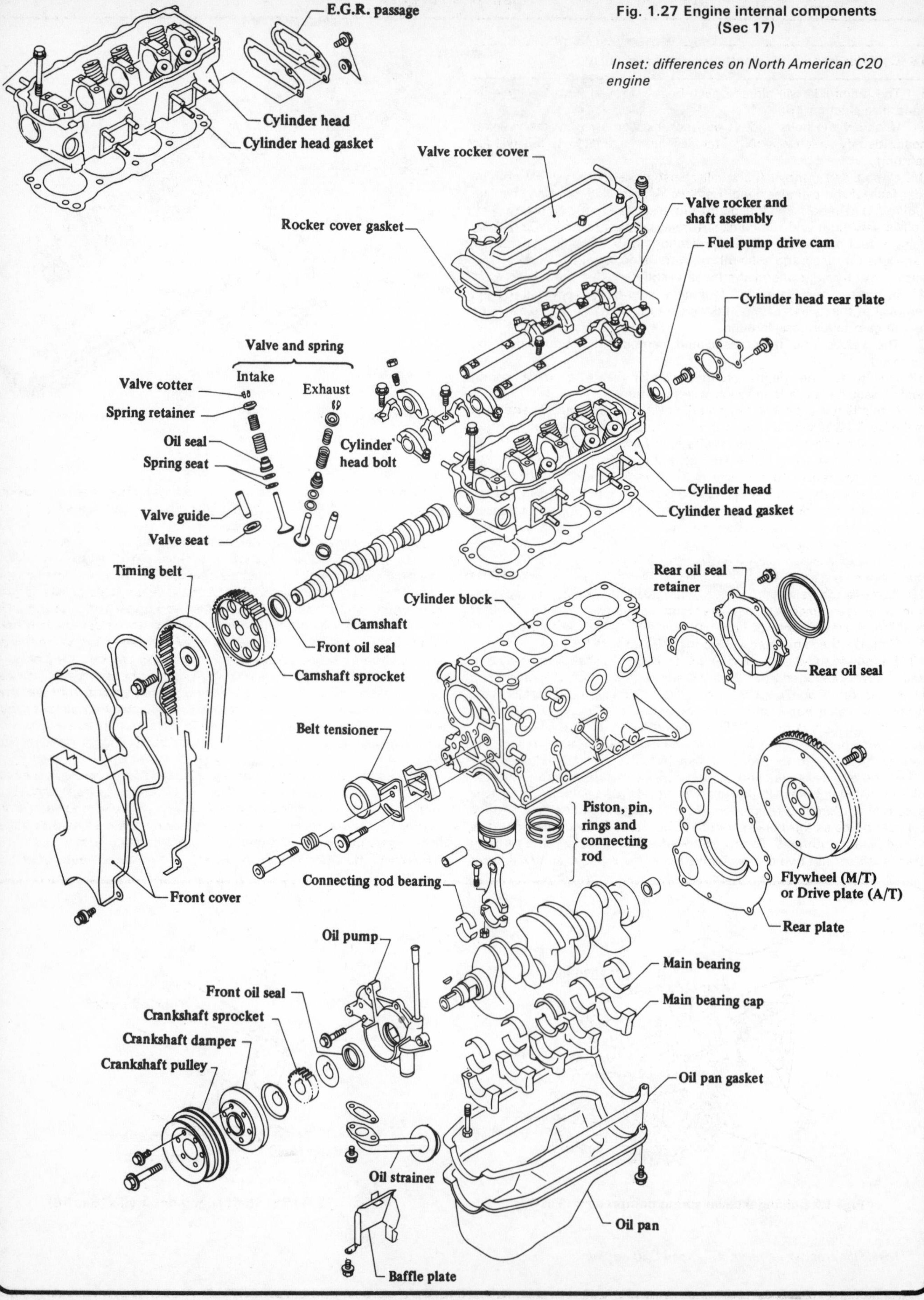

E.G.R. passage

Fig. 1.27 Engine internal components (Sec 17)

Inset: differences on North American C20 engine

Cylinder head

Cylinder head gasket

Valve rocker cover

Rocker cover gasket

Valve rocker and shaft assembly

Fuel pump drive cam

Cylinder head rear plate

Valve and spring

Intake

Exhaust

Valve cotter

Spring retainer

Oil seal

Spring seat

Cylinder head bolt

Valve guide

Valve seat

Cylinder head

Cylinder head gasket

Timing belt

Camshaft

Front oil seal

Camshaft sprocket

Cylinder block

Rear oil seal retainer

Rear oil seal

Belt tensioner

Piston, pin, rings and connecting rod

Connecting rod bearing

Flywheel (M/T) or Drive plate (A/T)

Rear plate

Front cover

Oil pump

Main bearing

Main bearing cap

Front oil seal

Crankshaft sprocket

Crankshaft damper

Crankshaft pulley

Oil pan gasket

Oil strainer

Oil pan

Baffle plate

18 Cylinder head – dismantling and decarbonising

1   The manifolds will already have been removed from the cylinder head (see Section 16).

2   Unscrew the bolts and lift the rocker assembly from the cylinder head. Identify which way round the assembly is located as this will aid refitting.

3   Unbolt and remove the small camshaft retaining plate from the rear face of the cylinder head. Remove the spark plugs. Unscrew the fuel pump cam bolt. The fuel pump cam also retains the camshaft. This bolt is very tight and the camshaft must be held stationary either by using a tool on the two square projections or by jamming one of the cam lobes by inserting a length of metal strip under it. Alternatively pass a rod through one of the holes in the camshaft sprocket.

4   Withdraw the camshaft (sprocket previously removed during removal of the cylinder head) taking care not to damage the bearings as the cam lobes pass through.

5   The valves and their associated components should now be removed.

6   Owing to the depth of the cylinder head, a valve spring compressor having a long reach will be required.

7   If this is not available, temporarily refit the rocker shafts and then make up a lever with a fork at one end to compress the valve spring by using the underside of the shafts as a fulcrum point.

8   Compress the first valve springs, extract the split cotters. If the valve springs refuse to compress, do not apply excessive force, but remove the compressor and place the end of a piece of tubing on the valve spring retainer. Strike it a sharp blow to release the collets from the valve stem. Refit the compressor and resume operations when the collets should come out.

9   Gently release the compressor, take off the spring retaining cap, the valve springs and the spring seat.

10   Remove the valve and keep it, with its associated components, in numbered sequence so that they can be refitted in their original position. A small box with divisions is useful for this purpose.

11   Remove the remaining valves in a similar way (photo).

12   Bearing in mind that the cylinder head is of light alloy construction and is easily damaged use a blunt scraper or rotary wire brush to clean all traces of carbon deposits from the combustion spaces and the ports. The valve head, stems and valve guides should also be freed from any carbon deposits. Wash the combustion spaces and ports down with paraffin and scrape the cylinder head surface free of any foreign matter with the side of a steel rule, or a similar article.

13   If the engine is installed in the car, clean the pistons and the top of the cylinder bores. If the pistons are still in the block then it is essential that great care is taken to ensure that no carbon gets into the cylinder bores as this could scratch the cylinder walls or cause damage to the piston and rings. To ensure this does not happen, first turn the crankshaft so that two of the pistons are at the top of their bores. Stuff

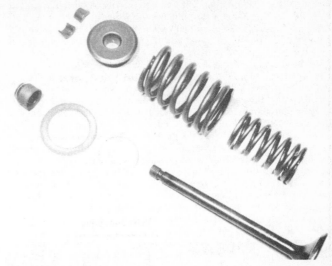

18.11 Valve components

rag into the other two bores or seal them off with paper and masking tape. The waterways should also be covered with small pieces of masking tape to prevent particles of carbon entering the cooling system and damaging the coolant pump.

14   Press a little grease into the gap between the cylinder walls and the two pistons which are to be worked on. With a blunt scraper carefully scrape away the carbon from the piston crown, taking great care not to scratch the aluminium. Also scrape away the carbon from the surrounding lip of the cylinder wall. When all carbon has been removed, scrape away the grease which will now be contaminated with carbon particles, taking care not to press any into the bores. To assist prevention of carbon build-up the piston crown can be polished with a metal polish. Remove the rags or masking tape from the other two cylinders and turn the crankshaft so that the two pistons which were at the bottom are now at the top. Place rag or masking tape in the cylinders which have been decarbonised, and proceed as just described.

15   Examine the head of the valves for pitting and burning, especially the heads of the exhaust valves. The valve seatings should be examined at the same time. If the pitting on the valve and seat is very slight, the marks can be removed by grinding the seats and valves together with coarse, and then fine, valve grinding paste.

16   Where bad pitting has occurred to the valve seats it will be

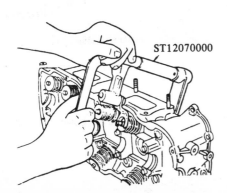

Fig. 1.28 Using a valve spring compressor (Sec 18)

ST12070000

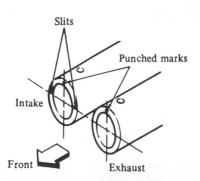

Fig. 1.29 Rocker shaft alignment marks (Sec 18)

Slits

Punched marks

Intake

Front

Exhaust

necessary to recut them and fit new valves. This latter job should be entrusted to the local agent or engineering works. In practice it is very seldom that the seats are so badly worn. Normally it is the valve that is too badly worn for refitting, and the owner can easily purchase a new set of valves and match them to the seats by valve grinding.

17 Valve grinding is carried out as follows. Smear a trace of coarse carborundum paste on the seat face and apply a suction grinder tool to the valve head. With a semi-rotary motion, grind the valve head to its seat, lifting the valve occasionally to redistribute the grinding paste. When a dull matt even surface is produced on both the valve seat and the valve, wipe off the paste and repeat the process with fine carborundum paste, lifting and turning the valve to redistribute the paste as before. A light spring placed under the valve head will greatly ease this operation. When a smooth unbroken ring of light grey matt finish is produced, on both valve and valve seat faces, the grinding operation is complete. Carefully clean away every trace of grinding compound, take great care to leave none in the ports or in the valve guides. Clean the valves and valve seats with a paraffin soaked rag, then a clean rag, and finally, if an air line is available, blow the valves, valve guides and valve ports clean.

18 Check that all valve springs are intact. If any one is broken, all should be renewed. Check the free height of the springs against new ones. If some springs are not within specifications, replace them all. Springs suffer from fatigue and it is a good idea to renew them even if they look serviceable.

19 Check that the oil supply holes in the rocker arm studs are clear.

20 The cylinder head can be checked for warping either by placing it on a piece of plate glass or using a straight-edge and feeler blades. If there is any doubt or if its block face is corroded, have it re-faced by your dealer or motor engineering works.

21 Examine the camshaft bearings for wear, scoring or pitting. If evident, then the complete cylinder head will have to be renewed as the bearings are machined directly in it.

22 The camshaft itself should show no marks or scoring on the journal cam lobe surfaces. Where evident, renew the camshaft or have it reprofiled by a specialist reconditioner.

23 Check the teeth of the distributor drivegear and the camshaft sprocket, renew if chipped or worn. The fuel pump eccentric cam should not show any sign of scoring or grooving. It is removable (one bolt).

24 Test the valves in their guides for side to side rock. If this is anything more than almost imperceptible, new guides must be fitted. This, as with valve seat renewal, is really a job for your dealer as the cylinder head must be warmed and the oil guide driven out towards the rocker cover side. New guides should be pressed in to protrude between 10.2 and 10.4 mm (0.402 and 0.409 in) above the cylinder head and then reamed to between 10.975 and 10.996 mm (0.4321 and 0.4329 in).

25 Renew the valve stem oil seal (photo).

26 Commence reassembly by oiling the stem of the first valve and pushing it into its guide (photo).

27 Fit the spring seat, the inner and outer springs so that their closer coils are towards the cylinder head and then the spring retaining cap (photos).

28 Compress the valve springs and locate the split cotters in the valve stem cut-out (photo).

29 Gently release the compressor, checking to see that the collets are not displaced.

30 Fit the remaining valves in the same way.

31 Tap the end of each valve stem with a plastic or copper-faced hammer to settle the components.

32 Lubricate the camshaft bearings and insert the camshaft into the cylinder head (photo).

33 Fit the fuel pump cam and tighten the bolt to the specified torque. Bolt on the camshaft end cover plate with a new gasket. Fit a new camshaft oil seal (photos).

34 Check that the camshaft sprocket dowel is in position at the end of the camshaft and then bolt on the sprocket aligning the marks made at dismantling (photos).

35 Before refitting the rocker gear, check the shafts for wear and the rocker arms for general condition. Renew any worn components, but make sure when reassembling that they are kept in their original order (photos).

36 The inlet valve rocker shaft is marked on its end face with two

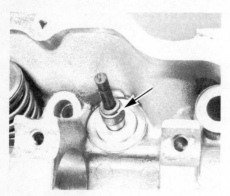

18.25 Valve stem oil seal

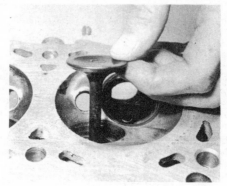

18.26 Fitting valve to cylinder head

18.27A Valve spring seat

18.27B Valve springs

18.27C Valve spring cap

18.28 Compressing a valve spring (split collets arrowed)

18.32 Fitting camshaft

18.33A Fuel pump cam and bolt

18.33B Camshaft end cover

18.33C Camshaft oil seal

18.34A Camshaft sprocket (dowel arrowed)

18.34B Camshaft sprocket bolt

18.35A Rocker arm retainers

18.35B Rocker arms correctly located

lines. This end of the shaft should be at the timing belt end. The exhaust valve rocker shaft is not marked in this way.

37 The punch marks on the ends of the shafts should be uppermost. These marks indicate the location of the rocker shaft oil holes.

38 The rocker arms are identical on both inlet and exhaust sides for cylinders 1 and 3 and cylinders 2 and 4, but the pairs of arms are marked 1 and 2 only.

39 Release the rocker arm adjuster screws fully and then bolt the rocker gear onto the cylinder head. Bolt the shafts down evenly in two or three stages and raise the cylinder head on wooden blocks while doing it as some of the valves will be forced open by the setting of the camshaft lobes.

40 Turn the camshaft sprocket so that the camshaft lobes for No. 1 cylinder are pointing away from the cylinder head.

41 Refit the spark plugs.

19 Examination and renovation

1 With the engine stripped and all parts thoroughly cleaned, every component should be examined for wear. The items listed in the Sections following should receive particular attention and where necessary be renewed or renovated.

2 So many measurements of engine components require accuracies down to tenths of a thousandth of an inch. It is advisable therefore to check your micrometer against a standard gauge occasionally to ensure that the instrument zero is set correctly.

3 If in doubt as to whether or nor a particular component must be renewed, take into account not only the cost of the component, but the time and effort which will be required to renew it if it subsequently fails at an early date.

Cylinder block and crankcase

4 Examine the casting carefully for cracks especially around the bolt holes and between the cylinders.

5 The cylinder bores must be checked for taper, ovality, scoring and scratching. Start by examining the top of the cylinder bores. If they are at all worn, a ridge will be felt on the thrust side. This ridge marks the upper limit of piston ring travel. The owner will have a good indication of bore wear prior to dismantling by the quantity of oil consumed and the emission of blue smoke from the exhaust especially when the engine is cold.

6 An internal micrometer or dial gauge can be used to check bore wear and taper against Specifications, but this is a pointless operation if the engine is obviously in need of reboring as indicated by excessive oil consumption.

7 Your engine reconditioner will be able to rebore the block for you and supply the correct oversize pistons to give the correct running clearance.

8 To rectify minor bore wear, it is possible to fit special oil control rings as described in Section 10.

9 A good way to test the condition of the engine is to have it at normal operating temperature with the spark plugs removed. Screw a compression tester (available from most motor accessory stores) into the first plug hole. Hold the throttle fully open and crank the engine on the starter motor for several revolutions. Record the reading. Zero the tester and check the remaining cylinders in the same way. All four compression figures should be approximately equal and within the tolerance given in Specifications.

10 If they are all low, suspect piston ring or cylinder bore wear. If only one reading is down, suspect a valve not seating.

Crankshaft and bearings

11 Examine the crankpin and main journal surfaces for signs of scoring or scratches, and check the ovality and taper of the crankpins and main journals. If the bearing surface dimensions do not fall within the tolerance ranges given in the Specifications at the beginning of this Chapter, the crankpins and/or main journals will have to be reground.

12 Big-end and crankpin wear is accompanied by distinct metallic knocking, particularly noticeable when the engine is pulling from low revs, and some loss of oil pressure.

13 Main bearing and main journal wear is accompanied by severe engine vibration rumble – getting progressively worse as engine revs increase – and again by loss of oil pressure.

14 If the crankshaft requires regrinding take it to an engine reconditioning specialist, who will machine it for you and supply the correct undersize bearing shells.

15 Inspect the big-end and main bearing shells for signs of general wear, scoring, pitting and scratches. The bearings should be matt grey in colour. With lead indium bearings, should a trace of copper colour be noticed, the bearings are badly worn as the lead bearing material has worn away to expose the indium underlay. Renew the bearings if they are in this condition or if there are any signs of scoring or pitting. **You are strongly advised to renew the bearings – regardless of their condition at time of major overhaul. Refitting used bearings is a false economy.**

16 The undersizes available are designed to correspond with crankshaft regrind sizes. The bearings are in fact, slightly more than the stated undersize as running clearances have been allowed for during their manufacture.

17 Main and big-end bearing shells can be identified as to size by the marking on the back of the shell. Standard size shell bearings are marked STD or .00, undersize shells are marked with the undersize such as 0.020 u/s (photo).

Connecting rods

18 Check the alignment of the connecting rods visually. If you suspect distortion, have them checked by your dealer or engine reconditioner on the special jig which he will have.

19 The gudgeon pin is an interference fit in the connecting rod small-end and removal, refitting of the pin or changing a piston is a job best left to your dealer or engine reconditioner owing to the need for a press and jig and careful heating of the connecting rod.

Pistons and piston rings

20 If the engine is rebored then new oversize pistons with rings and gudgeon pins will be supplied. Have the supplier fit the new pistons to

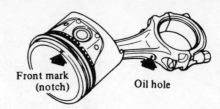

Fig. 1.30 Piston to connecting rod alignment (Sec 19)

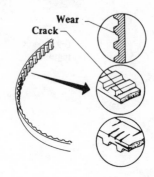

Fig. 1.31 Timing belt wear points (Sec 19)

19.17 Shell bearing marking

the rods making sure that the oil hole in the connecting rod is located as shown with reference to the front facing mark on the piston crown.

21 Removal and refitting of the piston rings is covered in Section 10.

Flywheel

22 Check the clutch mating surface of the flywheel. If it is deeply scored (owing to failure to renew a worn driven plate) then it may be possible to have it surface ground provided the thickness of the flywheel is not reduced by more than 0.3 mm (0.012 in) in thickness.

23 Where lots of tiny cracks are visible on the surface of the flywheel then this will be due to overheating caused by slipping the clutch or riding the clutch pedal.

24 With a pre-engaged type of starter motor, it is rare to find the teeth of the flywheel starter ring gear damaged or worn, but if they are, then the ring gear will have to be renewed.

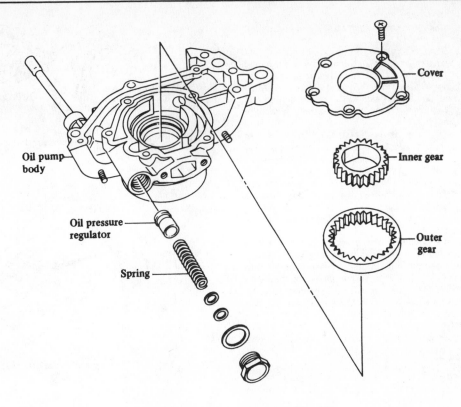

Fig. 1.32 Oil pump components (Sec 19)

25 To remove the ring gear, drill a hole between the roots of two teeth taking care not to damage the flywheel and then split the ring with a sharp cold chisel.
26 The new ring gear must be heated to between 180 and 220°C (356 and 428°F).
27 This is very hot so if you do not have facilities for obtaining these temperatures, leave the job to your dealer or engine reconditioner.

Driveplate (automatic transmission)
28 Should the starter ring gear on the driveplate require renewal, then the driveplate should be renewed complete.

Timing belt and tensioner
29 Examine the belt for cracking or fraying and tooth wear. If any of these conditions is evident, or if the belt has been in service for 80 000 km (50 000 miles), it is recommended that it is renewed.
30 The tensioner should not be noisy when turned and have a good spring action. Where these conditions are not satisfied renew the tensioner complete (photo).

Oil pump
31 Extract the screws (impact driver), remove the cover and check the following clearances with a feeler blade and compare with the specified tolerances.

Inner gear to crescent
Outer gear to crescent
Outer gear to body (photo)

32 If these clearances are satisfactory, now measure the gear endfloat using a feeler blade and a straight edge across the pump body. The endfloat must be within the specified tolerance (photo).
33 If any of the clearances are outside those specified, renew the components or complete oil pump as necessary.
34 The pressure regulator components are seldom found to be faulty,

19.30 Timing belt tensioner

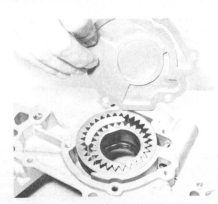
19.31A Oil pump cover removed

19.31B Checking inner gear to crescent clearance

19.31C Checking outer gear to crescent clearance

19.31D Checking outer gear to body clearance

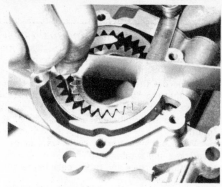

19.32 Checking oil pump gear endfloat

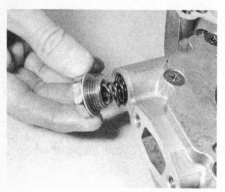

19.34A Oil pump pressure regulator cap

19.34B Oil pump pressure regulator plunger and spring

19.34C Prising out oil pump oil seal

19.34D Locating oil pump oil seal

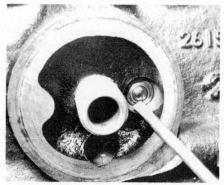

19.35 Oil pressure relief valve

but if they are, unscrew the end plug and renew all the valve components. Renew the pump oil seal (photos).
35 While the oil filter is removed at time of renewal, it is worth checking the pressure relief valve. If there is any indication of scoring or chipping of the ball valve, prise the valve from the oil filter mounting base and tap a new one into place with a piece of tubing (photo).

Cylinder head
36 This is covered in Section 18 during dismantling and decarbonising.

Oil seals and gaskets
37 It is recommended that all gaskets and oil seals are renewed at major engine overhaul. Sockets are useful for removing and refitting oil seals. On most seals, an arrow is moulded onto the rubber lip to

indicate the rotational direction of the component which it serves. Make sure that the seal is fitted the correct way round to comply with the arrow.

20 Engine – reassembly general

1 To ensure maximum life with minimum trouble from a rebuilt engine, not only must everything be correctly assembled, but everything must be spotlessly clean, all the oilways must be clear, locking washers and spring washers must always be fitted where indicated and all bearing and other working surfaces must be thoroughly lubricated during assembly.
2 Before assembly begins renew any bolts or studs, the threads of which are in any way damaged, and whenever possible use new spring washers.

21 Engine – reassembly

Crankcase, crankshaft and main bearings

1 Have the block standing on a flat surface with the crankcase uppermost and thoroughly clean internally.

2 Bolt the baffle plate into the crankcase (photo).

3 Wipe out the crankcase bearing shell seats and locate the shells noting that the flanged one which controls crankshaft endfloat is the centre one (photo).

4 Oil the shells liberally and then lower the crankshaft into them (photo).

5 Wipe out the bearing shell seats in the main bearing caps and locate the shells (photo).

6 Oil the journals and fit the caps in their numbered sequence (No.1 at timing belt end).

7 Screw in the cap bolts and tighten to the specified torque in the sequence shown (photo).

8 If new bearing shells have been fitted, then the crankshaft endfloat should be as specified, but it is worth checking at this stage. If the original shells are being used again then the endfloat should certainly be checked to ensure that wear on the centre bearing shell thrust flanges has not increased the crankshaft endfloat to the point where it is outside specified tolerance.

9 To check the end-float, tap the crankshaft fully in one direction and measure the gap between the thrust flange of the bearing shell and the machined face of the crankshaft (photo).

10 If the clearance is too large and new shells have been fitted, suspect a fault in re-grinding of the crankshaft.

11 Bolt the crankshaft rear oil seal retainer into position using a new oil seal and gasket (photos).

Flywheel or driveplate (automatic transmission)

12 Locate the engine rear plate on its dowels (photo).

13 Fit the flywheel onto its mounting flange.

14 Apply thread locking fluid to the flywheel bolts, screw them in and

21.2 Crankcase oil baffle

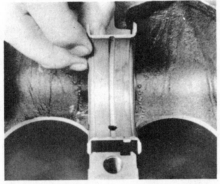
21.3 Centre main shell bearing with thrust flanges

21.4 Locating crankshaft

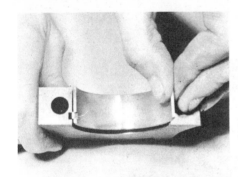
21.5 Connecting rod big-end cap shell bearing

21.7 Tightening a main bearing cap bolt

21.9 Checking crankshaft endfloat

21.11A Crankshaft rear oil seal

21.11B Fitting crankshaft rear oil seal/retainer

21.12 Engine rear plate

tighten to the specified torque. Lock the flywheel teeth as shown (photos).

15 Fit the piston/connecting rods as described in Section 10.

16 Tape the shoulder on the crankshaft to prevent damage to the oil pump oil seal and then fit the pump to the front face of the crankcase using a new gasket. Remove the tape (photo).

17 Push the timing belt inner guide disc onto the front end of the crankshaft. Fit the Woodruff key (photo).

18 Fit the crankshaft sprocket so that its timing mark is visible (photo).

19 Using a new gasket, bolt on the oil pick-up pipe and strainer (photo).

20 Fit the sump pan using a new gasket as described in Section 8.

21 Fit the cylinder head (Section 7).

22 Fit the timing belt and tensioner (Section 6).

23 Fit the timing belt outer guide disc (photo).

24 Fit the timing belt lower cover.

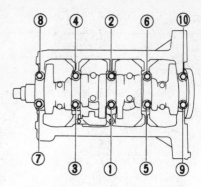

Fig. 1.33 Main bearing cap bolt tightening sequence (Sec 21)

21.14A Applying thread locking fluid to flywheel bolt

21.14B Tightening a flywheel bolt

21.14C Flywheel tooth locking device

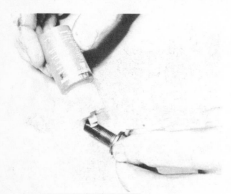

21.16A Crankshaft shoulder taped

21.16B Fitting oil pump

21.17 Timing belt inner guide

21.18 Timing belt crankshaft sprocket

21.19 Fitting oil pick-up pipe and strainer

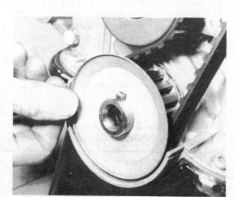

21.23 Timing belt outer guide

21.26 Crankshaft pulley bolt

21.28 Rocker cover screw with smaller diameter washer

21.30 Fitting intake manifold and carburettor

21.32 Exhaust manifold

21.34 Oil pressure switch

21.39 Engine stabiliser bar anchor strut

25 Fit the coolant pump using a new gasket. Locate the alternator adjuster link under one of the pump bolts.

26 Fit the crankshaft pulley and the belt upper cover. Lock the flywheel teeth and tighten the pulley bolt to the specified torque (photo).

27 Adjust the valve clearances (Section 5).

28 Fit the rocker cover complete with a new gasket. Note the smaller diameter washers under the fixing screws go at the timing cover end (photo).

29 Tap in the crankcase ventilation system oil separator.

30 If not already fitted at the time the cylinder head was installed, bolt on the inlet manifold with carburettor using a new gasket (photo).

31 Fit the inlet manifold support strut.

32 If not already fitted at the time the cylinder head was installed, bolt on the exhaust manifold using a new gasket (photo).

33 Bolt the hot air collector plate to the exhaust manifold (photo).

34 Screw in the oil pressure switch (photo).

35 Bolt on the coolant pump pulley.

36 Fit the drivebelt and tension as described in Chapter 2.

37 Fit the thermostat and housing cover.

38 Fit the coolant hose which runs between the base of the inlet manifold and the rear of the coolant pump.

39 Fit the engine stabiliser bar anchor strut to the timing cover end of the engine (photo).

22 Engine ancillary components – refitting

1 The operations are a reversal of removal. Refer to the Chapters indicated for precise details.

Alternator – Chapter 10
Distributor – Chapter 4
Fuel pump – Chapter 3
Clutch – Chapter 5

23 Engine/manual transmission – reconnection and refitting

1 Make sure that the clutch driven plate has been centralised as described in Chapter 5.

2 Offer the transmission to the engine not allowing its weight to hang upon the input shaft while the shaft is engaged in the hub of the driven plate.

3 Locate the metal coolant pipe and engine/transmission mounting brackets and then screw in and tighten the flywheel housing to engine connecting bolts (photos).

23.3A Engine mounting bracket at flywheel housing

23.3B Engine mounting bracket adjacent to speedometer drive cable

23.3C Engine mounting bracket at timing end of cylinder block

23.3D Gearchange stabiliser rod bracket

23.4 Flywheel housing lower cover plate

4   Bolt the flywheel housing cover plate into position (photo).

5   Fit the starter motor.

6   Attach the lifting gear and lift the engine/transmission over the engine compartment.

7   Pull the driveshafts outwards and then lower the power unit down into the engine compartment. Take care not to damage adjacent components within the compartment.

8   Connect the mounting bolts, but do not fully tighten them until the weight of the engine and transmission is fully on them with the lifting gear removed.

9   Remove the temporary retainers from the differential side gears and reconnect the driveshaft inboard ends to the transmission. It is recommended that new retaining circlips are used when refitting the shafts.

10 Check that the driveshafts are positively engaged and if necessary, drive them fully home by applying force to the rim of the slide joint cover using a rod and hammer.

11 Reconnect the suspension strut lower balljoints, using new nuts.

12 Tighten the strut upper mounting nuts to the specified torque.

13 Fit the roadwheels, lower the vehicle to the floor.

14 On North American vehicles, reconnect the emission control devices (Chapter 3).

15 Remove the plug and reconnect the hose to the fuel pump.

16 Reconnect the heater hoses.

17 Reconnect the brake servo vacuum hose.

18 Connect the leads to the oil pressure and coolant temperature switches.

19 Connect the leads to the reversing lamp switch.

20 Connect the leads to the starter motor.

21 Connect the ignition leads to the coil.

22 Connect the electrical leads to the carburettor.

23 Connect the throttle control cable to the carburettor.

24 Connect the speedometer drive cable to the transmission.

25 Connect the clutch operating cable and adjust as described in Chapter 5.

26 Reconnect the gearchange control rod and its support rod.

27 Reconnect the exhaust downpipe and front mounting.

28 If the vehicle is equipped with power-assisted steering, refit the steering pump and tension the drivebelt (Chapter 2).

29 If the vehicle is equipped with air conditioning, relocate the compressor and tension the drivebelt (Chapter 2).

30 Fit the radiator/cooling fan.

31 Refit the undershield.

32 Refit the air cleaner.

33 Refit and reconnect the battery and its support tray.
34 Refit the cooling system expansion tank.
35 With the help of an assistant, fit the bonnet.
36 Fill the cooling system with antifreeze mixture or corrosion inhibitor (Chapter 2).
37 Fill the engine with oil.
38 Check and top up the transmission oil.
39 Check for loose connecting leads, control cables and hoses. Make sure that all nuts and bolts have been tightened and all tools, rags and other items have been removed from the engine compartment.

24 Engine/automatic transmission – reconnection and refitting

1 Check that the torque converter is in full engagement with the fluid pump. To verify this, measure between the face of a connecting bolt boss on the torque converter and the surface of the torque converter housing mating flange. This should be in excess of 21.1 mm (0.831 in) to ensure full engagement (see Chapter 7).
2 Offer the transmission to the engine and make sure that the marks made at dismantling on the driveplate and the torque converter are in alignment.
3 Screw in the connecting bolts and tighten to the specified torque. The crankshaft will have to be turned to gain access to all the bolts.
4 Refitting the engine/transmission is very similar to the procedure described in the preceding Section, but ignore all reference to the clutch operating cable.
5 Reconnect the transmission fluid cooler lines.
6 Reconnect the speed selector control linkage.
7 Check and top up the transmission fluid as described in Chapter 7.

25 Engine – initial start-up after overhaul

1 Make sure the battery is fully charged and that all lubricants, coolant and fuel are replenished.
2 If the fuel system has been dismantled it will require several revolutions of the engine on the starter motor to pump the petrol up to the carburettor.
3 As soon as the engine fires and runs, keep it going at a fast tickover only (no faster), and bring it up to the normal working temperature.
4 As the engine warms up there will be odd smells and some smoke from parts getting hot and burning off oil deposits. The signs to look for are leaks of water or oil which will be obvious if serious. Check also the exhaust pipe and manifold connections, as these do not always 'find' their exact gastight position until the warmth and vibration have acted on them, and it is almost certain that they will need tightening further. This should be done, of course, with the engine stopped.
5 When normal running temperature has been reached adjust the engine idling speed, and check the ignition timing.
6 Stop the engine and wait a few minutes to see if any lubricant or coolant is dripping out when the engine is stationary.
7 Road test the car to check that the timing is correct and that the engine is giving the necessary smoothness and power. Do not race the engine – if new bearings and/or pistons have been fitted it should be treated as a new engine and run in at a reduced speed for the first 500 miles (800 km).
8 On vehicles equipped with air conditioning, if the system was discharged during overhaul, have it re-charged by your dealer or a competent refrigeration engineer.

26 Fault diagnosis – engine

Symptom	Reason(s)
Engine fails to turn when starter control operated	
No current at starter motor	Flat or defective battery
	Loose battery leads
	Defective starter solenoid or switch or broken wiring
	Engine earth strap disconnected
Current at starter motor	Jammed starter motor drive pinion
	Defective starter motor
Engine turns but will not start	
No spark at spark plug	Ignition leads or distributor cap damp or wet
	Ignition leads to spark plugs loose
	Shorted or disconnected low tension leads
	Dirty, incorrectly set, or pitted contact breaker points *
	Faulty condenser *
	Defective ignition switch
	Ignition leads connected wrong way round
	Faulty coil
	Contact breaker point spring earthed or broken *
No fuel at carburettor float chamber or at jets	No petrol in petrol tank
	Vapour lock in fuel line (in hot conditions at high altitude)
	Blocked fuel chamber needle valve
	Fuel pump or filter clogged
	Choked or blocked carburettor jets
	Faulty fuel pump
Engine stalls and will not restart	
Excess of petrol in cylinder or carburettor flooding	Too much choke allowing too rich a mixture or wet plugs
	Float damaged or leaking or needle not seating
	Float lever incorrectly adjusted
No spark at spark plug	Ignition failure – sudden
	Ignition failure – misfiring precedes total stoppage
	Ignition failure – in severe rain or after traversing water splash
No fuel at jets	No petrol in petrol tank
	Petrol tank breather choked
	Sudden obstruction in carburettor
	Water in fuel system

Symptom	Reason(s)
Engine misfires or idles unevenly	
Intermittent spark at spark plug	Ignition leads loose
	Battery leads loose on terminals
	Battery earth strap loose on body attachment point
	Engine earth lead loose
	Low tension leads on coil loose
	Low tension lead to distributor loose
	Dirty or incorrectly gapped plugs
	Dirty, incorrectly set, or pitted contact breaker points *
	Tracking across inside of distributor cover
	Ignition too retarded
	Faulty coil
	Slack timing belt
Fuel shortage at engine	Mixture too weak
	Air leak in carburettor
	Air leak at inlet manifold to cylinder head, or inlet manifold to carburettor
Lack of power and poor compression	
Mechanical wear	Burnt out valves
	Sticking or leaking valves
	Weak or broken valve springs
	Worn valve guides or stems
	Worn pistons and piston rings
Fuel/air mixture leaking from cylinder	Burnt out exhaust valves
	Sticking or leaking valves
	Worn valve guides and stems
	Weak or broken valve springs
	Blown cylinder head gasket (accompanied by increase in noise)
	Worn pistons and piston rings
	Worn or scored cylinder bores
Incorrect adjustments	Ignition timing wrongly set
	Contact breaker points incorrectly gapped *
	Incorrectly set spark plugs
	Carburation too rich or too weak
Carburation and ignition faults	Dirty contact breaker points *
	Fuel filter blocked
	Air cleaner blocked
	Distributor automatic advance and retard mechanisms not functioning correctly
	Faulty fuel pump giving top end fuel starvation
Excessive oil consumption	Excessively worn valve stems and valve guides
	Worn piston rings
	Worn pistons and cylinder bores
	Excessive piston ring gap allowing blow-by
	Piston oil return holes choked
Oil being lost due to leaks	Leaking oil filter gasket
	Leaking rocker cover gasket
	Leaking sump gasket
	Loose sump plug
Unusual noises from engine	
Excessive clearances due to mechanical wear	Worn valve gear (noisy tapping from rocker box)
	Worn big-end bearing (regular heavy knocking)
	Worn main bearings (rumbling and vibration)
	Worn crankshaft (knocking, rumbling and vibration)
Pinking on acceleration	Fuel octane rating too low
	Ignition timing over-advanced
	Carbon build-up in cylinder head
	Ignition timing incorrect
	Mixture too weak
	Overheating

* C16, C18 engines only

Chapter 2 Cooling, heating and air conditioning systems

Refer to Chapter 13 for specifications applicable to 1984 and later models

Contents

Specifications

System type .... Semi-sealed with radiator belt-driven pump and electric cooling fan. Fresh air type heater. Optional air conditioner

Radiator cap relief pressure .... 0.90 bar (13 lbf/in²)

Thermostat opening temperature .... 82°C (180°F)

Coolant
Type/specification .... Antifreeze to BS 3151, 3152 or 6580 (Duckhams Universal Antifreeze and Summer Coolant)

Capacity (including heater) .... 7.3 litres (12.8 Imp pints, 7.7 US qts)

Torque wrench settings

	Nm	lbf ft
Coolant pump bolts	20	15
Thermostat housing cover bolts	22	16
Air conditioner compressor bracket bolts	75	55
Drivebelt idler bracket bolt	55	41
Compressor to bracket bolts	50	37
Pipeline unions at compressor	7	5
Hose unions at condenser	7	5
High pressure pipeline unions	20	15
Low pressure pipeline unions	25	19

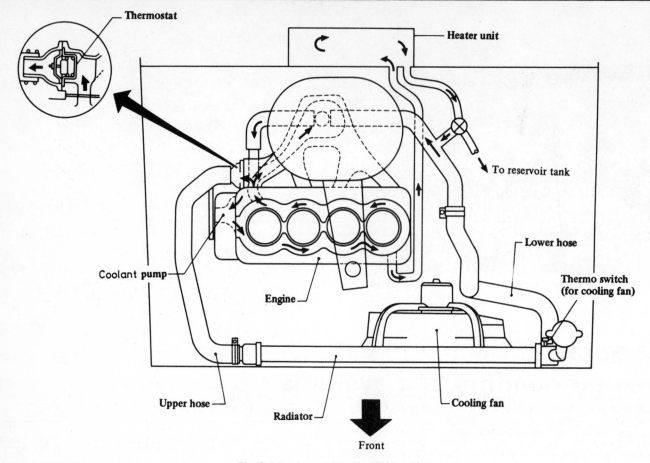

Fig. 2.1 Engine cooling circuit (Sec 1)

1 General description

The cooling system is of semi-sealed type incorporating an expansion tank. The radiator is front-mounted with a thermostatically-controlled electric cooling fan.

A thermostat is located at the end of the inlet manifold to prevent circulation of the coolant until the engine has warmed up. Once the thermostat has opened the coolant circulates by thermo-syphon action assisted by a belt-driven pump.

The engine coolant is used to heat the inlet manifold and the vehicle interior heater.

An air conditioner is available as an option.

2 Maintenance

1 At weekly intervals, check the coolant level in the expansion (reservoir) tank when the engine is cold.
2 The level should be between the MIN and MAX marks. If necessary, add coolant made up in the same proportions as the original anti-freeze mixture.
3 With this type of cooling system, the addition of coolant should only be required very infrequently. If regular additions of coolant are required check for a leaking hose or loose hose clip. If these are not evident the loss of coolant may be due to an engine internal leak in which case water will usually be observed on the engine oil dipstick.
4 Discolouration of the coolant in the expansion tank may be caused by a leaking cylinder head gasket.
5 Regularly check the condition and tension of the drivebelts (Section 9).

3 Cooling system – draining, flush and refilling

1 Allow the engine to cool before draining the coolant.
2 Set the heater control lever to HOT.
3 Release the radiator and expansion tank caps (photo).

3.3 Radiator pressure cap removed

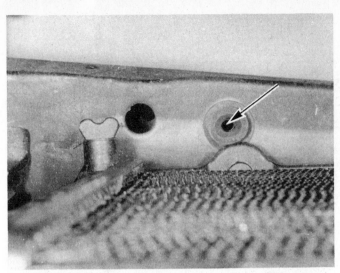

3.4 Radiator drain tap and a lower mounting grommet (arrowed)

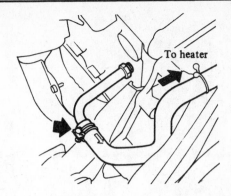

Fig. 2.2 Heater hose at rear of cylinder block (Sec 3)

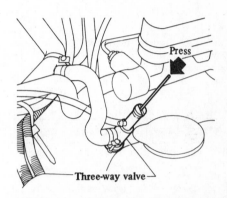

Fig. 2.3 Heat bleed screw (Sec 4)

4   Open the radiator drain tap, catching the coolant in a container if it is required for further use (photo).

5   Disconnect the heater inlet hose from the metal connecting pipe at the rear of the cylinder block.

6   If the coolant has been changed regularly there should be no evidence of rust and sediment and the system may be refilled immediately as described later in this Section.

7   If the system has been neglected, flush it through with a cold water hose until the water flows clear. In severe cases of corrosion or sediment accumulation, the radiator should be removed (Section 7) and both it and the cylinder block reverse flushed.

8   Allow the system to drain completely. Then tighten the radiator drain plug and reconnect the heater hose.

9   Using a coolant mixture made up as described in Section 5, pour it slowly into the radiator until it is full.

10 Using similar coolant, fill the expansion tank to the MAX mark.

11 Refit the radiator and expansion tank caps.

12 Start the engine and run it until it is hot enough for the radiator fan to switch on.

13 Switch off the engine and allow to cool.

14 Check the coolant level in the radiator and the expansion tank, top up if necessary.

4   Cooling system – bleeding

1   This operation will normally only be necessary if the heater hoses or matrix have been removed, drained and refitted.

2   With the cooling system filled as previously described, set the heater control to HOT.

3   Insert a 3.0 mm (0.12 in) diameter pin into the hole in the 3-way bleed valve. Press it in as far as it will go (photo).

4   With an assistant holding the pin depressed, remove the radiator cap and top up to replace the air being bled out of the system.

5   Remove the pin from the valve.

5   Coolant mixture

1   In these cars it is important to use an antifreeze mixture in the system all the year round. The mixture should be made up from clean, preferably soft, tap water (or rain water) and a good quality antifreeze liquid containing inhibitor. The proportions of water to antifreeze will depend on the degree of protection required.

2   25% of antifreeze should be regarded as the minimum proportion required to maintain good anti-corrosion characterisics and to protect against freezing down to -10°C (+14°F).

3   For absolute protection, use a 50% mixture.

4.3 Bleed valve

4   Before filling with fresh antifreeze, drain and flush the system as described in Section 3 and check that all the hoses are in good condition and that the clips are all tight. Antifreeze has a searching action and will leak more rapidly than plain water. Pour a couple of pints of water into the system and then add the correct quantity of antifreeze fluid. Complete the refilling as described in Section 3.

5   All future topping up should be done using mixed coolant of the correct proportions.

6   The antifreeze should be renewed every two years as the corrosion

6.2 Thermostat housing cover

6.5 Thermostat

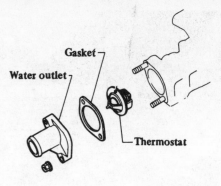

Fig. 2.4 Thermostat components (Sec 6)

inhibitor will then be of little use. Don't attempt to use the engine antifreeze in the windscreen wash system; it will attack the car's paintwork and will smear the windscreen. Finally remember that antifreeze is very poisonous and must be handled with due care.

7   In climates where antifreeze is not required, use a corrosion inhibitor in the cooling system water, never use plain water.

6   Thermostat – removal, testing and refitting

1   Unscrew the radiator drain tap and draw off about 1.5 litres of coolant.
2   Unbolt the thermostat housing cover and move it aside (photo).
3   Discard the gasket and withdraw the thermostat. If it is stuck tight do not lever it by its bridge piece, but cut around its edge using a sharp pointed knife.
4   The thermostat can be tested easily for correct functioning if this should be in doubt. Boil a pan of water and suspend the thermostat on a piece of cord. Lower the thermostat into the hot water and it should be seen to open on immersion. Remove the thermostat from the water and it should be seen to close. This is a simply functional test but it will identify a failed thermostat. With a thermometer you can check the correct opening temperature, see Specifications.
5   When renewing this component make sure that the replacement item is the correct one for your car as thermostats are made for a wide range of different models and conditions. You can drive without a thermostat in an emergency, no harm will result but the engine will not warm up properly (photo).

6   Clean the mating faces of the thermostat housing and its cover and use a new gasket.
7   Locate the thermostat so that the jiggle pin is uppermost.

7   Radiator – removal, repair and refitting

1   Drain the cooling system as described in Section 3.
2   Disconnect the coolant hoses, including the one to the expansion tank, from the radiator. On vehicles equipped with automatic transmission, disconnect the fluid hoses from the cooler and plug the hoses (photo).
3   Disconnect the electrical leads from the radiator thermostatic switch and the cooling fan motor (photo).
4   Unscrew the radiator upper fixing bolts and lift the radiator complete with fan from its lower insulators, taking care not to damage the condenser on vehicles equipped with air conditioning (photo).
5   Once the radiator is removed, the fan may be unbolted from it.
6   If the radiator was removed because of clogging causing overheating then try reverse flushing or, in severe cases, use a radiator cleanser strictly in accordance with the manufacturer's instructions.
7   A leaking radiator may be sealed using one of the many products available from motor accessory stores. To make a permanent repair by soldering is a job best left to a specialist radiator repairer.
8   Refit by reversing the removal operations making sure that the bottom fixings locate positively in the insulators.
9   The efficiency of the radiator pressure cap can be tested on a special gauge at your dealer or service station.

7.2 Radiator inlet hose

7.3 Electric fan thermostatic switch

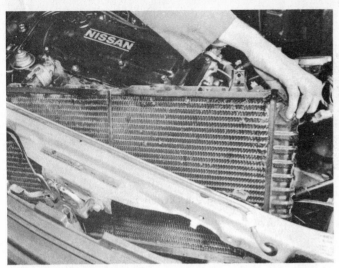

7.4 Removing radiator

8.3 Radiator cooling fan

10 On automatic transmission models, check the fluid level of the transmission and top up if necessary as described in Chapter 7.

8 Radiator cooling fan and switch – removal and refitting

1 Disconnect the battery.
2 Disconnect the electrical leads from the fan motor.

3 Remove the screws which hold the fan to the radiator frame and lift the assembly from the engine compartment (photo).
4 The thermostatically-operated fan control switch can be removed from the radiator having first drained the cooling system and disconnected the switch leads.
5 The switch is designed to operate the cooling fan when the coolant reaches a temperature of 85°C (185°F). The switch can be tested by connecting it to a bulb and battery and suspending it in

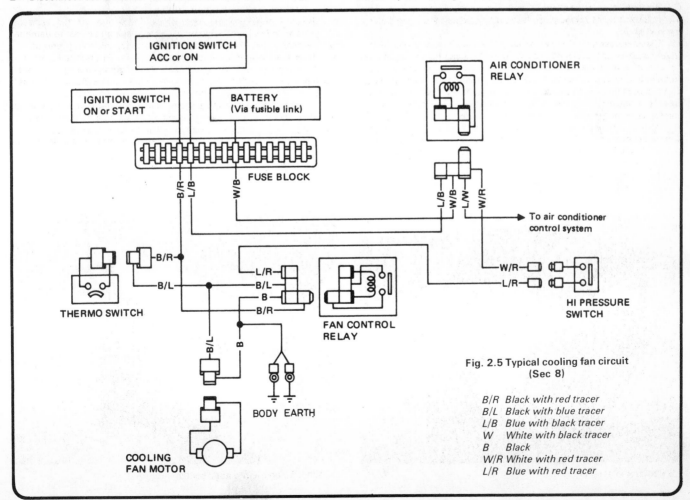

Fig. 2.5 Typical cooling fan circuit (Sec 8)

B/R Black with red tracer
B/L Black with blue tracer
L/B Blue with black tracer
W   White with black tracer
B   Black
W/R White with red tracer
L/R Blue with red tracer

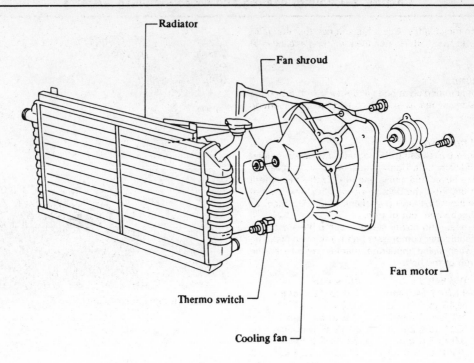

Fig. 2.6 Cooling fan components (Sec 8)

water which is being heated. When the water reaches the specified temperature level, the test bulb should come on.

6   Refitting of the components is a reversal of removal. Use a new sealing washer on the switch. Refill the cooling system as described in Section 3.

9   Drivebelts – removal, refitting and tensioning

1   The drivebelt configurations vary according to the accessories with which the engine is equipped.

2   On models without power-assisted steering or an air conditioner,

a single belt is used to drive the alternator and coolant pump pulley from the crankshaft pulley.

3   If power-assisted steering is fitted, a second belt runs from the dual groove in the crankshaft pulley over idler pulleys while a third belt takes the drive from the idler pulley to the power steering pump pulley.

4   Where air conditioning is fitted, the compressor for the system is substituted for the idler pulley.

5   Adjustment of the belts, so that their tension is as given in the table at the end of this Section, is carried out in the following way.

Alternator/coolant pump

6   Release the mounting and adjuster link bolts, but only enough to

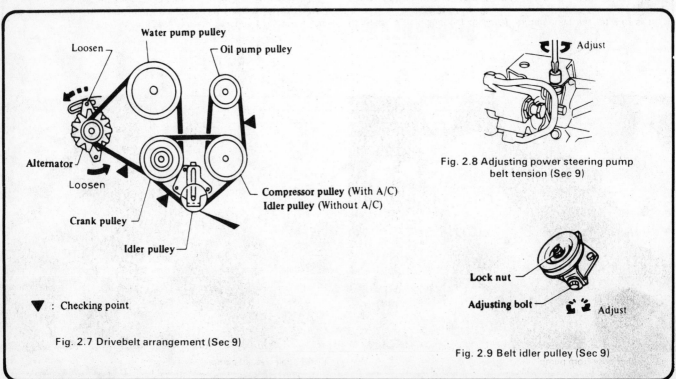

Fig. 2.7 Drivebelt arrangement (Sec 9)

Fig. 2.8 Adjusting power steering pump belt tension (Sec 9)

Fig. 2.9 Belt idler pulley (Sec 9)

permit the alternator to move stiffly. Use a bar to prise the alternator until the belt tension is as specified. Tighten the mounting and adjuster link bolts.

Power steering pump

7   Release the pump mounting pivot bolts and then turn the adjuster screw until the belt is tensioned as specified. Tighten the mounting bolts.

Air conditioner compressor

8   The belt is tensioned by releasing the locknut on the lower idler pulley and turning the adjuster bolt. Tighten the locknut on completion.
9   A drivebelt can be removed and a new one fitted if the adjustment is first slackened right off. Prise the belt over the pulley rims, do not use a tool especially without first having slackened the adjustment as the pulleys will probably be bent out of true.
10   Access to the alternator and power steering pump belts can only be obtained if the air conditioner compressor belt is removed first. The figures below apply when using moderate thumb pressure at the centre of the longest run of the belt.

Belt	Old belt	New belt
Alternator/coolant pump	11.0 to 14.0 mm (0.43 to 0.55 in)	9.0 to 12.0 mm (0.35 to 0.47 in)
Air conditioner compressor	4.0 to 6.0 mm (0.16 to 0.24 in)	3.0 to 5.0 mm (0.12 to 0.20 in)
Idler pulley (instead of air conditioner compressor)	6.0 to 9.0 mm (0.24 to 0.35 in)	5.0 to 7.0 mm (0.20 to 0.28 in)
Power steering pump	6.0 to 9.0 mm (0.24 to 0.35 in)	5.0 to 8.0 mm (0.20 to 0.31 in)

10.1 Coolant temperature switch

operation check the lead from the switch for broken insulation and earthing. If the gauge reads maximum, suspect the sender switch.
6   Access to the coolant temperature gauge is covered in Chapter 10.

10 Coolant temperature switch

1   This is screwed into the thermostat housing (photo).
2   If a fault develops, first check the wiring between the switch and the gauge.
3   The switch can only be tested satisfactorily using an ohmmeter or by substitution of a new unit.
4   Before the switch can be removed, partially drain the cooling system. Smear the threads of the union nut with sealant when refitting.
5   It is rare for the temperature gauge to fail, but if it is erratic in

11 Coolant pump – removal and refitting

1   Remove the drivebelt as described in Section 9.
2   Drain the cooling system and disconnect the coolant hoses from the pump (photo).
3   Unbolt and remove the pulley.
4   Unbolt the pump from the engine and remove it (photo).
5   The pump cannot be repaired as it is a sealed unit. Renew it complete if it is leaking or the bearing is rough or noisy.
6   Always use a new gasket when fitting the pump and make sure that the mating surfaces are perfectly clean.

2

11.2 Coolant hose from pump

11.4 Fitting coolant pump

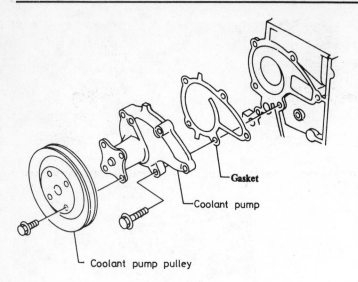

11.7 Alternator adjuster link attached to coolant pump

Fig. 2.10 Exploded view of coolant pump (Sec 11)

7　Tighten the pump bolts to the specified torque making sure to locate the alternator adjuster link (photo).
8　Fit and tension the drivebelt.
9　Fill the cooling system.

12 Heating and ventilation system – description

1　The heater utilises heat from the engine cooling system to warm the vehicle interior.
2　The system is of the fresh air type, air being drawn in through a grille at the base of the windscreen and passed over the heater matrix where it absorbs warmth from the coolant.
3　Control levers are provided to vary the air temperature and direction of flow, and permit the entry of fresh unheated air into the vehicle interior.
4　An electric booster fan is provided for use when the vehicle is moving slowly or stationary or when the heater is set to recirculate air only.
5　Stale air is exhausted through one-way flap valves either in the tailgate frame, door closure edge or just forward of the rear lamp clusters according to model.
6　The control panel for the heater varies according to model, either lever or push-button.

13 Heater controls – removal and refitting

Lever type controls
1　Extract the screws which are located one on either side of the heater control finisher plate and the three screws located under the hood over the radio receiver.
2　Remove the finisher plate.
3　Remove the cover from under the instrument panel.
4　Release the cable clamps at the heater control flap valves. To assist refitting, put a spot of quick drying paint on the cable on both sides of the clamp before disconnecting.
5　Remove the control panel fixing screws.
6　Withdraw the control panel far enough to be able to disconnect the wiring harness plug and the earth cable.
7　Refitting is a reversal of removal, but adjust the cables where necessary in the following way.

Air mix flap cable
8　Set the control lever to COLD.
9　Pull the outer cable away from the lever on the flap valve and secure with the clamp.

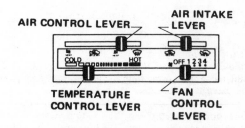

Fig. 2.11 Typical lever type heater controls (Sec 12)

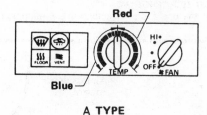

A TYPE

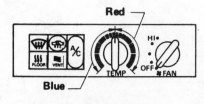

B TYPE

Fig. 2.12 Typical pushbutton heater controls (Sec 13)

A　Without air conditioner　　　B　With air conditioner

Fig. 2.13 Heater control cable clamp
(Sec 13)

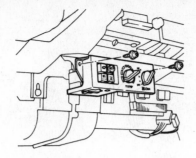

Fig. 2.14 Heater control panel screws
(Sec 13)

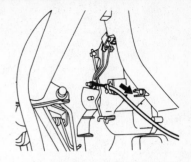

Fig. 2.15 Heater air mix flap valve cable
(Sec 13)

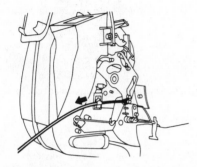

Fig. 2.16 Heater air control cable (Sec 13)

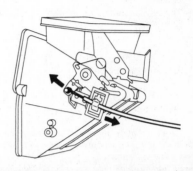

Fig. 2.17 Heater air intake control cable (Sec 13)

Air control cable

10 Set the control lever to VENT.
11 Pull the outer cable away from the lever on the flap valve and then clamp the cable.

Air intake control cable

12 This cable varies the source of air from fresh to recirculated.
13 Set the control lever to REC and the flap valve shut against the entry of fresh air.
14 Pull the outer cable away from the lever on the flap valve and then clamp it.

Push-button type controls

15 Carry out the operations described in paragraphs 1 to 3 of this Section.

16 Disconnect the air mix flap valve cable by prising off the clamp.
17 Extract the control panel fixing screws and withdraw the panel far enough to be able to disconnect the vacuum hose and the wiring plug.
18 The fan control switch cannot be removed from the control panel.

14 Heater matrix – removal, repair and refitting

1   Drain the cooling system as described in Section 3.
2   Working inside the vehicle, remove the pedal bracket mounting bolts, the steering column mounting bolts.
3   Disconnect the cable and pushrod from the pedal arms.
4   Push the steering column and the pedal bracket to the left-hand side.
5   Disconnect the control cable from the coolant valve and also release the control rod.

2

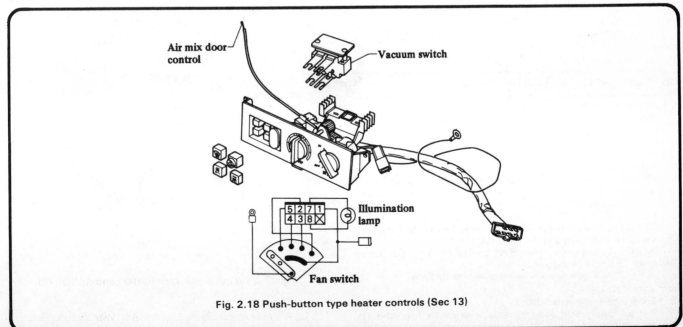

Fig. 2.18 Push-button type heater controls (Sec 13)

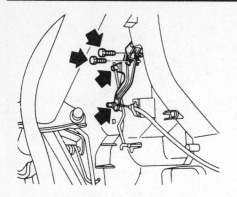

Fig. 2.19 Heater coolant valve control arm (Sec 14)

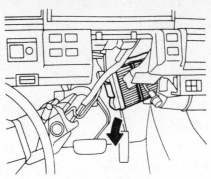

Fig. 2.20 Removing heater matrix and valve (Sec 14)

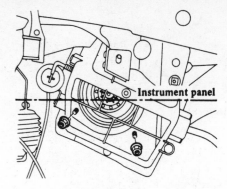

Fig. 2.21 Removing heater air intake box (Sec 15)

6   Extract the screw from the control arm and take off the arm.
7   Remove the heater matrix cover.
8   Disconnect the coolant hoses from the heater coolant valve.
9   Remove the heater matrix and valve downwards.
10 If the matrix is clogged, try clearing it with a cold water hose or the careful use of a radiator cleanser.
11 If the matrix is leaking, have it professionally repaired or exchange it for a new or reconditioned unit.
12 Refitting is a reversal of removal, fill the cooling system and bleed as described in Sections 3 and 4. It is recommended that a new O-ring seal is used when fitting the coolant valve.

15 Heater air intake box – removal and refitting

1   Remove the cover from under the right-hand side of the facia panel.
2   Extract the fixing screws from the fuse block.
3   Remove the right-hand heater floor duct.

4   Unscrew the air intake box mounting bolts and withdraw the box downwards.
5   Refitting is a reversal of removal.

16 Heater blower motor – removal and refitting

1   The blower motor is removed into the engine compartment.
2   Disconnect the blower cover upper fixing clamps and pull the cover away (photo).
3   Unscrew the blower motor fixing bolts.
4   Push the blower motor casing downwards and lift out the blower.
5   Refitting is a reversal of removal.

17 Heater unit (complete) – removal and refitting

1   Remove the facia panel as described in Chapter 12.
2   Drain the cooling system.

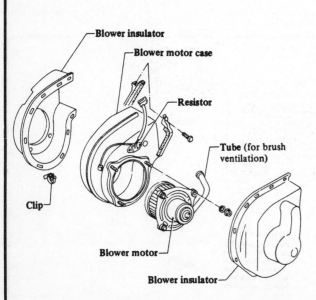

Fig. 2.22 Heater blower motor components (Sec 16)

- Blower insulator
- Blower motor case
- Resistor
- Tube (for brush ventilation)
- Clip
- Blower motor
- Blower insulator

16.2 Heater blower motor

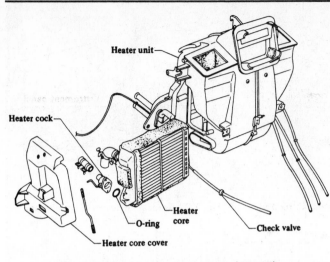

Fig. 2.23 Major heater components (Sec 17)

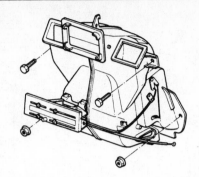

Fig. 2.24 Heater unit mounting bolts (Sec 17)

7   Refitting is a reversal of removal.
8   Refill the cooling system and bleed as described in Sections 3 and 4.

18 Air conditioner – description and maintenance

1   Air conditioning is an option available on North American models and for certain other territories.
2   Air is drawn into the system by the blower motor and wheel and passed through the evaporator (for cooling) or the heater matrix (for heating) and then enters the vehicle interior.
3   If the vehicle has been parked in the sun for a long period, drive

3   Disconnect the coolant hoses for the heater within the engine compartment also the vacuum pipe.
4   Remove the heater control panel as described in Section 13.
5   Unscrew and remove the heater unit mounting bolts and nuts.
6   Withdraw the heater downwards taking care not to damage the demister duct connections.

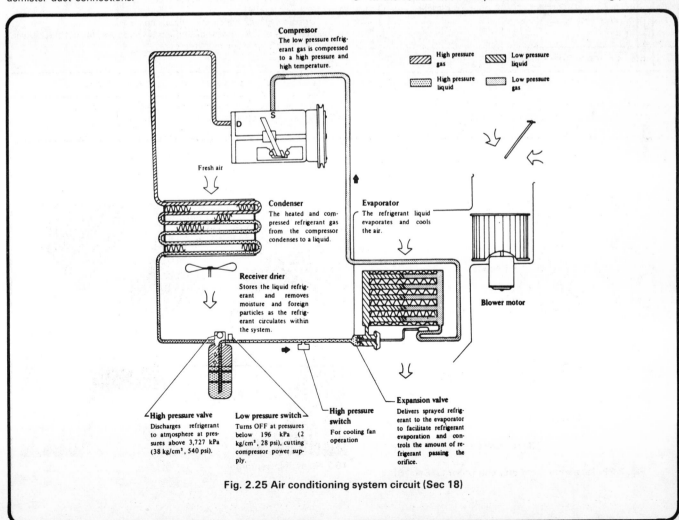

Fig. 2.25 Air conditioning system circuit (Sec 18)

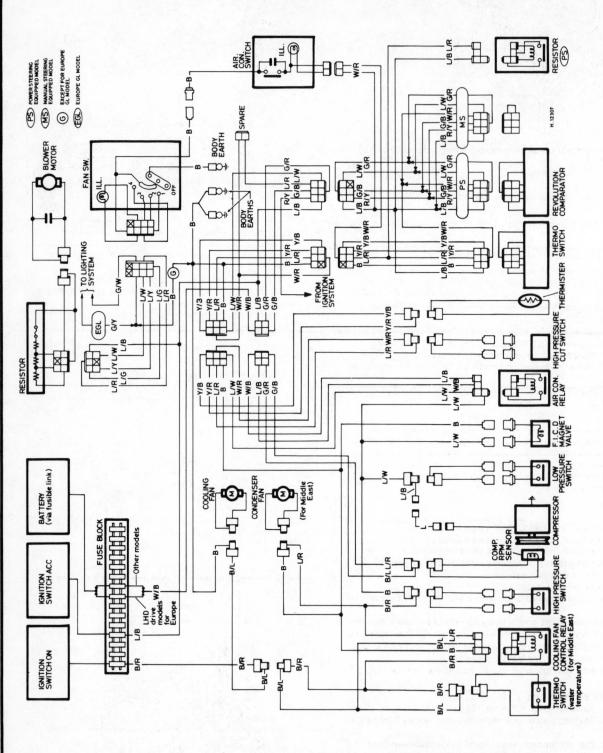

Fig. 2.26 Air conditioner wiring diagram (Sec 18)

PS POWER STEERING EQUIPPED MODEL
MS MANUAL STEERING EQUIPPED MODEL
G   EXCEPT FOR EUROPE GL MODEL
EGL EUROPE GL MODEL

B/R Black with red tracer	B Black	Y/R Yellow with red tracer	L/Y Blue with yellow tracer
L/B Blue with black tracer	B/L Black with blue tracer	Y/B Yellow with black tracer	W/R White with red tracer
W/B White with black tracer	L/R Blue with red tracer	L/G Blue with green tracer	R/Y Red with yellow tracer
	B/B Green with black tracer		
	G/R Green with red tracer		
	L/W Blue with white tracer		

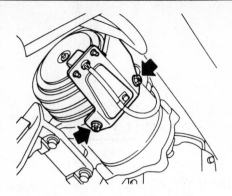

Fig. 2.27 Compressor revolution sensor fixing screws (Sec 19)

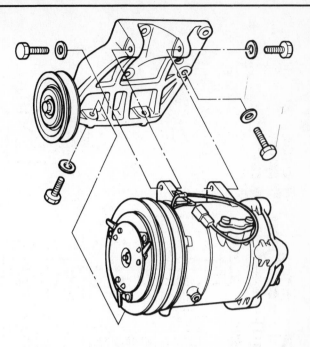

Fig. 2.28 Compressor mounting bracket and bolts (Sec 19)

for two or three minutes with all the windows open to exhaust the hot air.

4   For normal use, keep the windows closed when the air conditioner is in operation.

5   If the air conditioner has not been operated for a month, run the engine at idle speed and turn the air conditioner on for a few minutes.

6   During winter time it is recommended that the system is operated for a few minutes regularly each week in order to keep the compressor and seals lubricated.

7   Periodically inspect all the system flexible hoses for deterioration. Any which show signs of splitting or cracking must be renewed.

8   Keep the compressor drivebelt correctly tensioned and renew it immediately if it becomes frayed or shows signs of splitting (refer to Section 9).

9   Periodically clean flies and dirt from the condenser using a jet from a cold water hose.

---

19 Air conditioner – removal and refitting of major components

1   Before undertaking any of the following operations, the refrigerator system must be discharged (refer to Section 4, Chapter 1) and the battery disconnected.

Compressor
2   Raise the front of the vehicle and support securely.
3   Remove the engine compartment under shield.
4   Unbolt and remove the compressor revolution sensor.
5   Remove the compressor drivebelt as described in Section 9.
6   Disconnect the wiring harness.
7   Disconnect the flexible hoses.
8   Remove the mounting bolts and remove the compressor from the engine.
9   If the compressor is left on its side or inverted for more than ten minutes, oil will enter the low pressure chambers. This must be expelled by turning the compressor pulley several times by hand after the compressor has been installed.
10 Always use new O-rings when reconnecting the flexible hoses.

Condenser/receiver dryer
11 Remove the radiator grille (Chapter 12).
12 Remove the bonnet release lock mounting stay and the right-hand headlamp unit.
13 Disconnect the refrigerant lines from the condenser and the receiver dryer.
14 Unbolt and remove the condenser/receiver dryer from the vehicle.
15 Refitting is a reversal of removal.

Evaporator
16 Remove the air cleaner.
17 Disconnect the vacuum non-return valve fixing bolt which is located on the engine compartment rear bulkhead.

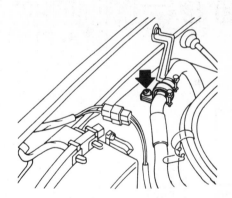

Fig. 2.29 Vacuum non-return valve fixing bolt (Sec 19)

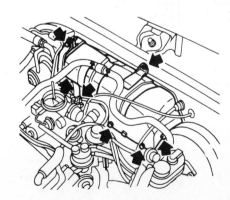

Fig. 2.30 Evaporator upper casing bolts (Sec 19)

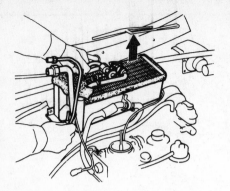

Fig. 2.31 Removing evaporator (Sec 19)

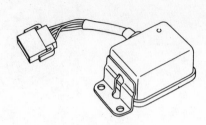

Fig. 2.32 Compressor revolution comparator (Sec 19)

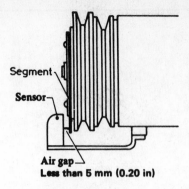

Fig. 2.33 Compressor revolution sensor setting (Sec 19)

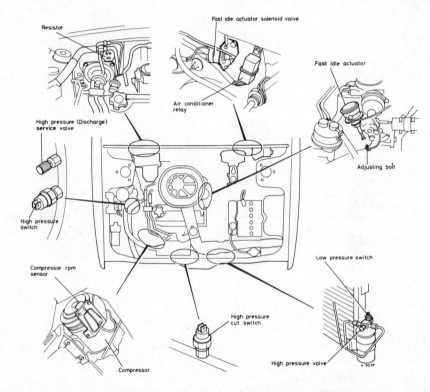

Fig. 2.34 Location of engine compartment electrical and vacuum air conditioning components (Sec 19)

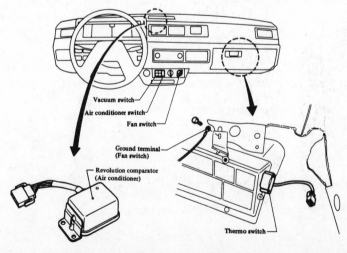

Fig. 2.35 Location of vehicle interior electrical and vacuum air conditioning components (Sec 19)

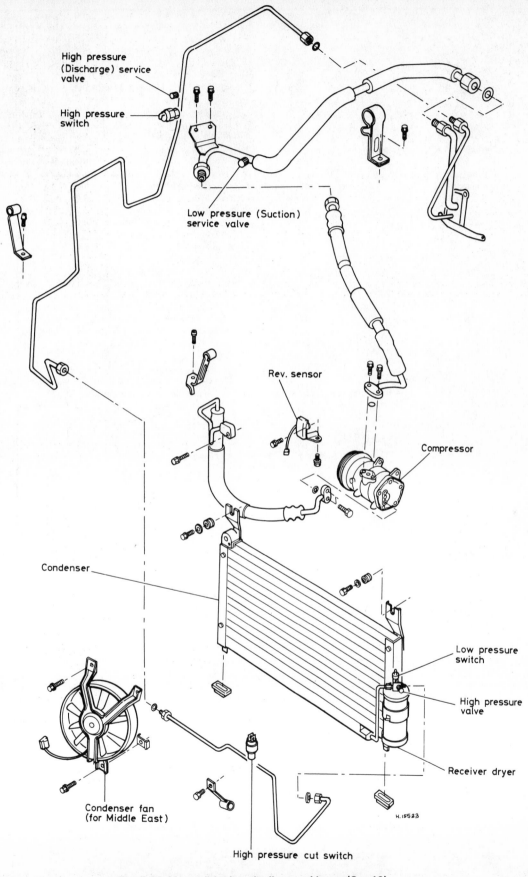

High pressure (Discharge) service valve

High pressure switch

Low pressure (Suction) service valve

Rev. sensor

Compressor

Condenser

Low pressure switch

High pressure valve

Receiver dryer

Condenser fan (for Middle East)

High pressure cut switch

Fig. 2.36 Air conditioning pipelines and hoses (Sec 19)

2

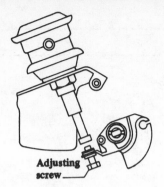

Fig. 2.37 Throttle fast idle vacuum actuator (Sec 19)

18 Still working under the bonnet, remove the fixing screws, cut around the sealing head and remove the evaporator upper casing.
19 Disconnect the pipelines from the evaporator and lift it out of the lower casing.
20 Refit by reversing the removal operations. Seal the joint between the upper and lower casing sections.

High and low pressure switches
21 The high pressure switch is located on the high pressure pipeline. The low pressure switch is located on the receiver drier.

22 Unscrew the switches from their adaptors by using two spanners.

Relay
23 The air conditioner relay is located on the engine compartment rear bulkhead and described more fully in Chapter 10.

Compressor protective comparator and sensor
24 These components are designed to monitor the compressor speed (revolutions) and disengage the compressor magnetic clutch in the event of a malfunction.
25 The revolution comparator is located on the air intake box.
26 The revolution sensor must be adjusted so that an air gap exists between the sensor and the segment of less than 5.0 mm (0.20 in).

Fast idle relay, solenoid and vacuum actuator
27 These components are designed to increase the idle speed to overcome the drag of the compressor when the air conditioner is switched on and to maintain the minimum compressor speed for efficient cooling.
28 The relay is located on the relay bracket within the engine compartment and is described more fully in Chapter 10.
29 The solenoid valve controls vacuum to the actuator which in turn moves the throttle lever through a pushrod.
30 With the engine at operating temperature and the air conditioner switched on, the engine speed should be 800 rev/min. If it is not, adjust the pushrod screw.

Refitting – general
31 Tighten all system nuts, bolts and pipeline unions to the specified torque. Have the system recharged by your dealer or a competent refrigeration engineer.

20 Fault diagnosis – cooling and heating system

Symptom	Reason(s)
Overheating	Insufficient coolant in system
	Pump ineffective due to slack drivebelt
	Radiator blocked either internally or externally
	Kinked or collapsed hose causing coolant flow restriction
	Thermostat not working properly
	Engine out of tune
	Ignition timing retarded or auto advance malfunction
	Cylinder head gasket blown
	Engine not yet run-in
	Exhaust system partially blocked
	Engine oil level too low
	Brakes binding
Engine running too cool	Faulty, incorrect or missing thermostat
Loss of coolant	Loose hose clips
	Hoses perished or leaking
	Radiator leaking
	Radiator pressure cap defective
	Blown cylinder head gasket
	Cracked cylinder block or head
	Leak into transmission fluid (automatic transmission)
Heater gives insufficient output	Engine overcooled (see above)
	Heater matrix blocked
	Heater controls maladjusted or broken
	Heater control valve jammed or otherwise defective

21 Fault diagnosis – air conditioner

Symptom	Reason(s)
Bubbles observed in sight glass of receiver drier	Leak in system Low refrigerant level
No cooling	No refrigerant
Expansion valve frosted over on evaporator	Faulty or clogged expansion valve Thermal bulb leaking
Insufficient cooling	Faulty expansion valve Air in refrigerant circuit Clogged condenser Receiver drier clogged Faulty compressor Compressor overfilled with oil

2

Chapter 3
Fuel, emission control and exhaust systems

Refer to Chapter 13 for specifications and information applicable to 1984 and later models

Contents

Specifications

System type .... Rear-mounted fuel tank, mechanical fuel pump and dual barrel carburettor

Fuel tank capacity .... 54.0 litres, 11.9 Imp gals, 14.3 US gals.

Carburettor
CA16 engine .... 21E series
CA18 engine .... 21E series
CA20 engine .... DCR series

Carburettor calibration and adjustments
C16 and C18 engines
Fast idle speed:
    Manual transmission .... 1600 to 2400 rev/min
    Automatic transmission .... 2000 to 2800 rev/min
Fast idle (valve plate clearance A):
    C16 manual transmission .... 0.53 to 0.67 mm (0.0208 to 0.0264 in)
    C18 manual transmission .... 0.57 to 0.71 mm (0.0224 to 0.0280 in)
    C18 automatic transmission .... 0.76 to 0.93 mm (0.0299 to 0.0365 in)
Vacuum break adjustment (clearance B between edge of choke valve plate and carburettor) .... 1.76 and 1.94 mm (0.0693 to 0.0763 in)
Choke unloader (clearance C between edge of choke valve plate and carburettor):
    Manual .... 3.30 to 3.36 mm (0.1299 to 0.1323 in)
    Automatic .... 3.13 to 3.19 mm (0.1232 to 0.1256 in)
Throttle interlock (clearance G1 between edge of primary throttle valve plate and carburettor) .... 7.33 to 7.43 mm (0.2886 to 0.2926 in)
Dashpot touch speed .... 1900 to 2100 rev/min
Dashpot pushrod to screw clearance .... 0.77 to 0.79 mm (0.0303 to 0.0311 in)
Idle speed:
    Manual .... 750 rev/min
    Automatic .... 850 rev/min (in N)
CO% at idle .... 0.5 to 1.5

C20 engine (North America)
Fast idle (valve plate clearance A) .... 0.66 to 0.80 mm (0.0260 to 0.0315 in)
Vacuum break (clearance B, edge of choke valve plate to carburettor) .... 3.12 to 3.72 mm (0.1228 to 0.1465 in)

Throttle interlock (clearance between edge of primary throttle plate and carburettor)	7.38 to 8.38 mm (0.2906 to 0.3299 in)
Idle speed	550 to 750 rev/min
CO% at idle	0.5 to 1.5

Torque wrench settings

	Nm	lbf ft
Exhaust manifold nuts	24	18
Intake manifold bolts and nuts	20	15
Fuel tank mounting bolts	18	13
Exhaust downpipe flange nuts	30	22
Exhaust bracket to clutch housing	40	30
Fuel cut-off solenoid valve	30	22
Carburettor mounting nuts	18	13
Thermal vacuum valve	20	15
Catalytic converter bolts	40	30
Vacuum reservoir tank screws	5	4
EGR vacuum control valve screw	5	4
VVT valve mounting screw	5	4

1 General description

The fuel system consists of a rear-mounted fuel tank, a fuel pump, mechanically operated from the camshaft and a dual barrel carburettor which has an automatic choke.

Being of crossflow design, the inlet and exhaust manifolds are located on opposite sides of the cylinder head. The inlet manifold is coolant heated.

Some form of emission control system is fitted to all models, but those destined for operation in North America and certain other territories have a comprehensive system as described later in this Chapter.

2 Air cleaner – servicing, removal and refitting

1   At the intervals specified in Routine Maintenance, the air cleaner element should be renewed.

2   Take off the air cleaner cover, lift out and discard the element. Wipe out the interior of the casing.
3   Fit the new element and replace the lid (photo).
4   The air cleaner can be removed from the carburettor in the following way after first taking out the element.
5   Unscrew and remove the two bolts which hold the air cleaner support struts to the rocker cover.
6   Disconnect the hoses from the air cleaner casing and remove the air intake ducting (photos).
7   Lift the air cleaner from the engine (photo).
8   Refitting is a reversal of removal.

3 Air cleaner – testing

1   The air cleaner is of the temperature controlled type drawing in and mixing both cold and warm air (from around the exhaust manifold) to provide air of optimum temperature at the carburettor intake.

3

2.3 Air cleaner element

2.6A Air cleaner cold air intake

2.61B Cold air intake at left-hand wing valance

2.6C Cold air intake trunking fixing screw

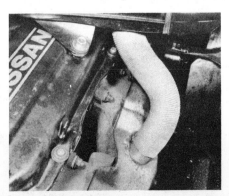

2.6D Air cleaner hot air intake

2.7 Removing air cleaner

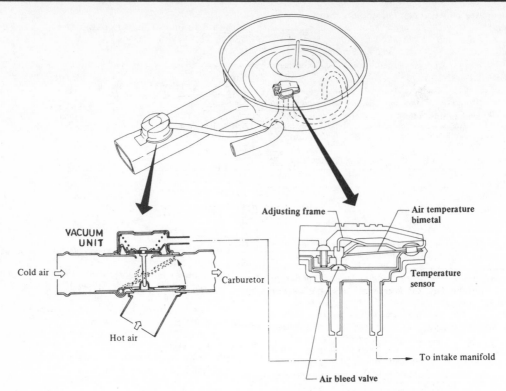

VACUUM UNIT

Cold air

Hot air

Carburetor

Adjusting frame

Air temperature bimetal

Temperature sensor

To intake manifold

Air bleed valve

Fig. 3.1 Temperature controlled air cleaner (Sec 3)

Fig. 3.2 Checking air cleaner flap valve with a mirror (Sec 3)

2   The air cleaner incorporates a vacuum capsule and a temperature sensor.
3   The volume of cold and warm air is varied according to engine vacuum and temperature by the operation of the two devices.
4   If it is suspected that the air cleaner is not functioning correctly use a mirror to look up the intake spout. If the engine is cold, the flap valve should be closed against cold air and if the engine is hot, closed against hot air.

5   If the flap valve does not move at all, then check the vacuum hose for a split or renew the vacuum capsule.
6   If the vacuum hose and capsule are in good order, renew the temperature sensor.

---

4   Fuel filter – renewal

1   The fuel filter is of the in-line disposable type. It should be renewed at the specified intervals (photo).
2   Disconnect the hoses from the filter, discard it and fit the new one. Make sure that the arrow on the filter points towards the fuel pump.

---

5   Fuel pump – removal and refitting

1   The fuel pump is of sealed type, no provision being made for cleaning.
2   To remove the pump, disconnect the fuel hoses and plug the inlet hose (photo).
3   Unbolt and remove the pump from the cylinder head (photo).
4   When refitting, use a new gasket at the mounting flange.

4.1 Fuel filter

5.2 Fuel pump

5.3 Removing fuel pump

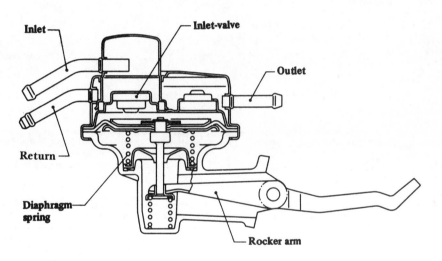

Fig. 3.3 Sectional view of fuel pump without fuel return (C16, C18 engines) (Sec 5)

Fig. 3.4 Sectional view of fuel pump with fuel return (C20 engine) (Sec 5)

3

Fig. 3.5 Releasing fuel level transmitter lockplate (Sec 6)

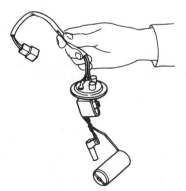

Fig. 3.6 Fuel level transmitter (Sec 6)

Fig. 3.7 Fuel level transmitter O-ring (Sec 6)

6 Fuel level transmitter – removal and refitting

1 Disconnect the battery.
2 Remove the rear seat cushion as described in Chapter 12.
3 Extract the two screws and remove the cover plate.
4 Disconnect the wiring harness plug from the transmitter unit.
5 Using two screwdrivers or a piece of flat metal as a lever, rotate the transmitter cover plate until it releases.
6 Carefully withdraw the transmitter unit taking care not to bend the float or float arm.
7 Refitting is a reversal of removal but use a new O-ring.

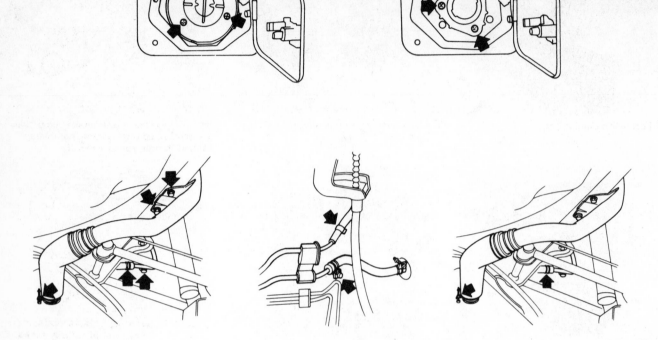

Fig. 3.8 Fuel tank filler pipe and hose connections (Sec 7)

7 Fuel tank – removal and refitting

1   Disconnect the battery.
2   Remove the fuel tank drain plug and drain the fuel into a sealed container (photo).
3   Working under the vehicle, disconnect and plug the fuel lines. Disconnect the fuel filler and breather hoses. Plug the tank filler opening with a piece of rag (photo).
4   Remove the fuel tank protective plate.
5   Working inside the vehicle, remove the rear seat cushion and then the tank transmitter unit cover plate.
6   Disconnect the wiring harness plug from the tank transmitter.
7   Working under the vehicle, remove the tank fixing screws, lower the tank slowly until the wiring harness can be unclipped. Remove the tank (photo).
8   If the tank contains sediment, remove the tank transmitter unit as described in the preceding Section. Pour in some paraffin and shake the tank vigorously. Repeat with fresh paraffin until clean.

9   If the tank was removed for permanent repair, this should be left to a specialist repairer (often radiator repairers) as the tank must be steamed out thoroughly before any attempt is made to solder or weld it.
10 Various products are available for repairing holes in fuel tanks caused by rust and can be applied without the need to remove the tank.

8 Carburettor – description

1   The carburettor is of dual barrel downdraught type with the primary main system based on the Stromberg principal.
2   The carburettor incorporates the following devices:

Electrically-heated automatic choke (photo)
Accelerator pump (photo)
Fuel cut-off (anti-diesel) solenoid valve
Valve (choke) break diaphragm

7.2 Fuel tank drain plug

7.3A Fuel outlet pipe at tank

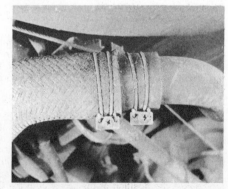

7.3B Fuel filler pipe

7.7 Fuel tank mounting bolt

8.2A Carburettor – automatic choke side

8.2B Carburettor – accelerator pump side idle mixture screw – (capped) arrowed (A) and throttle speed screw (B)

8.2C Carburettor – BCDD side

8.2D Carburettor – float chamber sight glass side

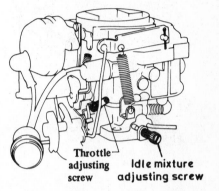

Fig. 3.9 Carburettor adjusting screws (Sec 9)

Vacuum diaphragm secondary throttle switch over
Boost controlled deceleration device (see Section 21) (photo)
Idle compensator for additional air bleed at high engine compartment temperatures (photo)

3   On carburettors designed for the North American market, the following additional devices are fitted to the carburettor.
  Idle speed control system to provide additional fuel to maintain the specified idle speed when major ancillaries are switched on.
  Altitude compensator to weaken the air/fuel mixture ratio when the mixture is enriched at high altitudes due to the air being of lower density.

KV10108300

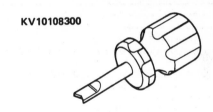

Fig. 3.10 Special tool for adjusting carburettor mixture screw (Sec 9)

9 Carburettor – idle speed and mixture adjustment

Except North America
1   The fuel/air mixture is set during production and normally it is only the idle speed which may require alteration.
2   Have the engine at operating temperature with the valve clearances and the ignition correctly set. On vehicles with an air conditioner, make sure that it is switched off. On models without a tachometer, such an instrument should be connected in accordance with the maker's instructions.
3   Turn the throttle speed screw until the idle speed is as specified.
4   If the mixture must be adjusted due to a change in engine characteristics (carbon build up, bore wear etc) or after major overhaul of the carburettor, the engine must be at normal operating temperature and idling at specified speed with an exhaust gas analyser connected in accordance with the maker's instructions.
5   Break off the mixture screw tamperproof cap and using the special tool, adjust the position of the screw until the CO percentage level is within specified tolerance.
6   Adjust the idle speed if necessary as previously described.

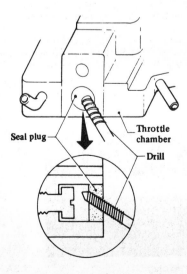

Fig. 3.11 Removal of mixture screw tamperproof plug (Sec 9)

North America
7   The operations are similar to those just described except that the front roadwheels must be set in the straight-ahead position if the vehicle is equipped with power steering.
8   The mixture screw is sealed with a metal plug which must be removed by drilling a hole in it and prising it out with a thin screwdriver.
9   After adjustment, fit a new plug.

10 Carburettor (21E Series) – in-car adjustments

1   The following adjustments can be carried out without having to remove the carburettor from the engine.

Fast idle
2   With the engine warm, remove the air cleaner and then set the choke valve plate in the fully open position and the fast idle lever on the second step of the fast idle cam.
3   Start the engine and check that the reading on the tachometer is at the specified level according to transmission fitted.
4   Where it is not possible to bring the fast idle within tolerance, more extensive adjustment will be required as described in Section 13.

Vacuum break
5   Remove the air cleaner and the cover from the automatic choke.
6   Hold the choke valve plate closed with a rubber band.
7   Apply finger pressure to the vacuum unit pushrod and then check that the clearance B between the edge of the choke valve plate and the carburettor wall is as specified. If it is not, bend the adjusting tongue.

Choke unloader
8   Remove the air cleaner and the cover from the automatic choke.
9   Close the choke valve plate and hold it in this position using a rubber band.
10 Open the primary throttle valve plate fully and check the clearance C between the choke valve plate and the carburettor body. If it is not as specified at an ambient temperature of 20°C (68°F) bend the unloader tongue.

Throttle interlock
11 Rotate the throttle arm until the adjuster plate contacts the lock lever at point A. Now check the clearance G1 between the primary throttle valve and the inner wall of the carburettor. If the clearance is outside that specified, bend the tongue on the throttle arm.

Dashpot (automatic transmission models)
12 With the engine at operating temperature, turn the throttle valve lever with the engine idling, then increase the engine speed until the dashpot just makes contact with the stop lever. Check the engine speed on a tachometer. If the speed is not within specified limits, turn the adjuster screw on the dash pot and repeat the test.

11 Carburettor (DCR Series) – in-car adjustments

1   The following adjustments can be carried out without having to remove the carburettor from the engine.

Cam follower lever adjustment
2   Remove the air cleaner and close the choke valve plate with the fingers. Now turn the adjuster screw until the clearance between the cam follower lever and the fast idle cam is eliminated.

Vacuum break
3   Remove the air cleaner and close the choke valve plate fully. Hold it closed using a rubber band.

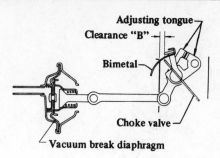

Fig. 3.12 Vacuum break adjustment diagram (Sec 10)

For B see Specifications

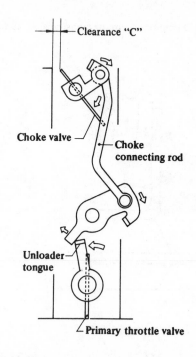

Fig. 3.13 Choke unloader setting diagram (Sec 10)

For C see Specifications

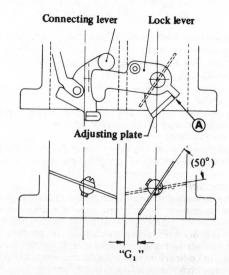

Fig. 3.14 Throttle interlock setting diagram (Sec 10)

For G1 see text

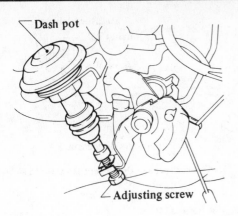

Fig. 3.15 Dashpot (automatic transmission) (Sec 10)

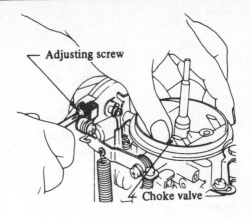

Fig. 3.16 Cam follower lever adjustment screw (Sec 11)

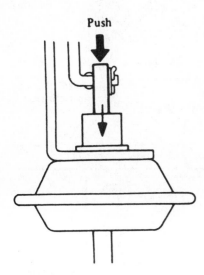

Fig. 3.17 Vacuum break diaphragm pushrod (Sec 11)

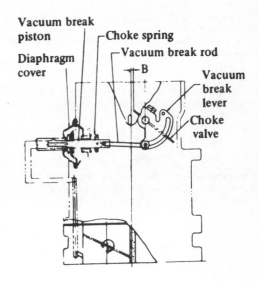

Fig. 3.18 Vacuum break setting diagram (Sec 11)

4   Push the vacuum break pushrod into the diaphragm. Check the clearance between the edge of the choke valve plate and the carburettor body. Adjust as necessary by bending the vacuum unit mounting bracket.

Choke unloader
5   Remove the air cleaner and close the choke valve plate completely. Hold it closed using a rubber band.
6   Pull the throttle lever fully open.
7   Check the clearance between the edge of the valve plate and the carburettor body is as specified. If it is not, bend the unloader tongue.

Throttle interlock
8   When the following throttle settings are made the movements should be as described. If necessary, bend the connecting link to achieve this.
9   Open the primary throttle plate through 50° when the adjust plate should be in contact with the return plate at A, Fig. 3.19.
10 Now open the primary throttle plate further when the locking arm B should release from the secondary throttle arm.
11 The linkage between the throttle arms will function correctly if the gap between the edge of the primary throttle plate and the carburettor wall is between 7.38 and 8.38 mm (0.2906 and 0.3299 in).

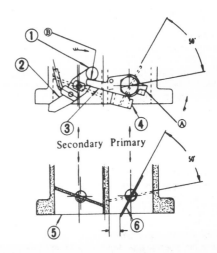

Fig. 3.19 Throttle interlock setting diagram (Sec 11)

1	Roller	4	Adjuster plate
2	Connecting lever	5	Throttle valve block
3	Return plate	6	Throttle valve

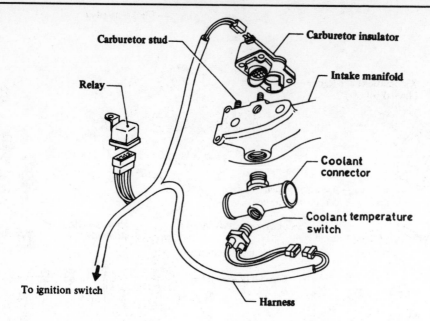

Fig. 3.20 Components of the mixture heating system (Sec 11)

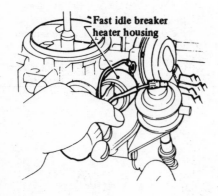

Fig. 3.21 Fast idle breaker heater housing (Sec 11)

Fast idle actuator

12 This device is used in conjunction with an air conditioner where fitted. Refer to Chapter 2, Section 19 for full details.

13 The following devices cannot be adjusted, but if a malfunction occurs, first check the wiring and connectors and if in order renew the component concerned.

Idle speed control
Fuel cut-off solenoid
Mixture heating system
Fast idle breaker heater

12 Carburettor – removal and refitting

1 Remove the air cleaner as described in Section 2.
2 Disconnect the fuel hoses and plug them.
3 Disconnect the throttle linkage.
4 Disconnect the electrical leads from the fuel cut-off valve and the automatic choke on the carburettor.
5 Disconnect the distributor vacuum hose.
6 Unscrew the four mounting nuts and remove the carburettor from the intake manifold.
7 Refitting is a reversal of removal, but use a new mounting flange gasket.

13 Carburettor (21E Series) – overhaul

1 It is rare for the carburettor to require complete dismantling; indeed, normally where this is required then it would probably be more economical to renew the complete unit.
2 It will usually be found that the first few operations described in the following paragraphs to remove the cover will be sufficient to enable cleaning of the jets and carburettor float chamber to be carried out.
3 With the carburettor removed, clean away external dirt.
4 Disconnect the linkage between the top cover and body, remove the securing screws. Lift the cover from the carburettor body.
5 Mop out the fuel from the float chamber and then remove all the jets and air bleeds. Take care to identify each jet and its location as it is removed.
6 Clean the jets with air from a tyre pump, on no account probe them with wire or their calibration will be ruined.
7 The vacuum units, dashpot, automatic choke housing and solenoid valve may all be removed if essential for renewal.
8 Examine the float and fuel inlet needle valve in the top cover. If the carburettor has seen considerable service it is worthwhile renewing the needle valve even if it does not appear to be worn.
9 If the throttle block is to be detached from the main carburettor body, extract the securing screws from the lower face of the throttle block.
10 If the throttle valve plates or spindles are worn, do not attempt to renew them, but rather obtain a new or factory reconditioned carburettor.
11 With the carburettor dismantled and worn parts renewed, obtain a repair kit which will contain all the necessary new gaskets and other renewable items.
12 Reassembly is a reversal of dismantling, but as work progresses, carry out the following checks and adjustments.

Float setting

13 Invert the carburettor top cover so that the float hangs under its own weight.
14 Measure the distance H between the nearest point of the float and the surface of the cover. This should be 6.0 mm (0.24 in). If it is not, bend the float seat.
15 Now check the float drop (h). This should be 46.0 mm (1.81 in). If it is not, bend the float stop.

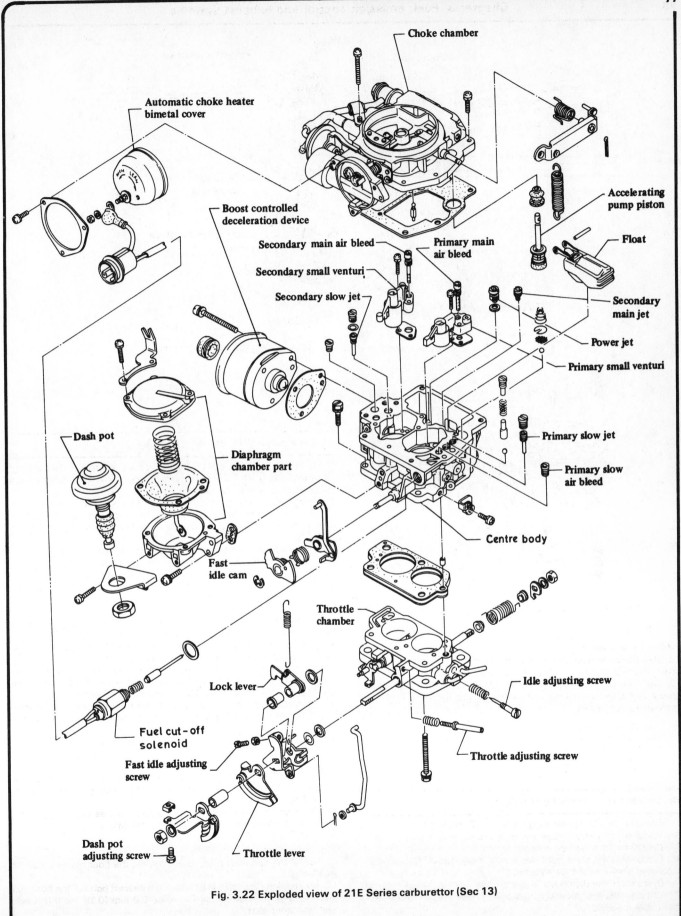

Choke chamber

Automatic choke heater
bimetal cover

Boost controlled
deceleration device

Secondary main air bleed

Primary main
air bleed

Accelerating
pump piston

Secondary small venturi

Float

Secondary slow jet

Secondary
main jet

Power jet

Primary small venturi

Dash pot

Diaphragm
chamber part

Primary slow jet

Primary slow
air bleed

Centre body

Fast
idle cam

Throttle
chamber

Lock lever

Idle adjusting screw

Fuel cut-off
solenoid

Throttle adjusting screw

Fast idle adjusting
screw

Dash pot
adjusting screw

Throttle lever

3

Fig. 3.22 Exploded view of 21E Series carburettor (Sec 13)

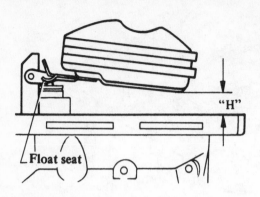

Fig. 3.23 Float setting diagram (Sec 13)

H = 6.0 mm (0.24 in)

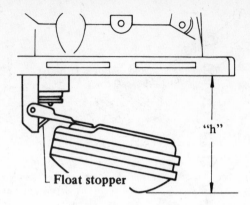

Fig. 3.24 Float drop setting diagram (Sec 13)

h = 46.0 mm (1.81 in)

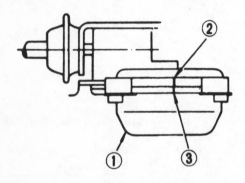

Fig. 3.25 Automatic choke setting diagram (Sec 13)

1 Cover
2 Housing
3 Central index marks

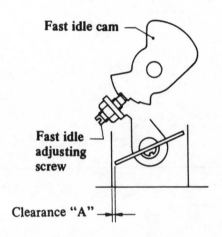

Fig. 3.26 Fast idle (basic setting) (Sec 13)

Automatic choke

16 Set the automatic choke housing cover so that the centre index marks are in alignment.

Fast idle (basic setting)

17 Set the fast idle arm on the second step of the fast idle cam. Check the clearance A Fig. 3.26 between the edge of the primary throttle valve and the carburettor wall. If it is not as specified, turn the fast idle screw.
18 After the carburettor has been fitted to the engine, check the fast idle speed as described in Section 10.

14 Carburettor (DCR Series) – overhaul

1 These carburettors, which are fitted to North American models, operate on similar principles and are overhauled in a similar manner to the carburettors described in Section 12, but there are considerable differences in detail design and construction.
2 Refer to paragraphs 1, 2 and 3 of Section 12.
3 Disconnect the linkage between the carburettor top cover and the main body. This includes the accelerator pump rod, the choke connecting rod, throttle return spring, and pull off the vacuum break unit hose.
4 Extract the four screws which hold the top cover to the main body and remove the top cover.

5 Repeat the operations described in Section 12, paragraphs 5 to 7.
6 Remove the fuel level sight glass and its frame. Examine the float and the fuel inlet needle valve. If the carburettor has seen considerable service, it is worthwhile renewing the needle valve even if it does not appear to be worn.
7 Repeat the operations described in paragraphs 9 to 11 of Section 12.
8 Reassembly is a reversal of dismantling, but as work progresses, carry out the following checks and adjustments.

Float setting

9 Before fitting the fuel level sight glass and its frame, invert the carburettor body so that the float rests on the needle valve under its own weight.
10 Measure the distance H, Fig. 3.28 which should be 7.2 mm (0.283 in). If it is not, bend the float seat.
11 Now check that the dimension (h) between the float seat and the end of the needle valve is between 1.3 and 1.7 mm (0.051 and 0.067 in). If not, bend the float stop.

Fast idle

12 Position the fast idle screw on the second step of the cam.
13 Measure the gap A between the edge of the throttle valve plate and the carburettor. A twist drill is useful for doing this. If the gap is not between 0.66 and 0.80 mm (0.0260 and 0.0315 in) turn the fast idle screw.

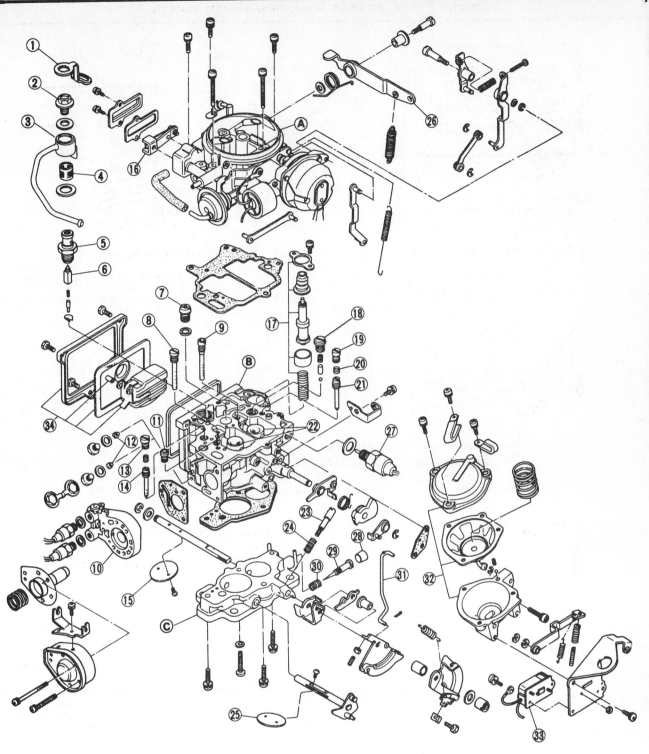

Fig. 3.27 Exploded view of DCR Series carburettor (Sec 14)

1 Lock lever	11 Secondary slow air bleed	21 Primary slow jet	29 Idle mixture screw
2 Banjo union bolt	12 Secondary main jet	22 Primary and secondary	30 Spring
3 Banjo union	13 Plug	small venturi	31 Choke link rod
4 Filter gauze	14 Secondary slow jet	23 Throttle speed screw	32 Diaphragm chamber
5 Fuel inlet valve body	15 Primary throttle valve	24 Spring	33 Throttle valve switch
6 Needle valve	16 Idle compensator	25 Secondary throttle valve	34 Float and sight glass
7 Power valve	17 Accelerator pump	26 Accelerator pump lever	A Top cover
8 Secondary main air bleed	18 Plug	27 Fuel cut-off valve	B Main body
9 Primary main air bleed	19 Plug	28 Tamperproof plug	C Throttle block
10 BCDD (emission control)	20 Spring		

3

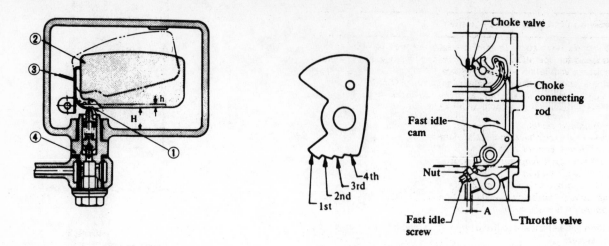

Fig. 3.28 Float setting diagram (Sec 14)

1	Float seat	$H = 7.2$ mm (0.283 in)
2	Float	$h = 1.3$ to 1.7 mm (0.051 to 0.067 in)
3	Float chamber	
4	Needle valve	

Fig. 3.29 Fast idle cam and adjustment diagram (Sec 14)

For A see Specifications

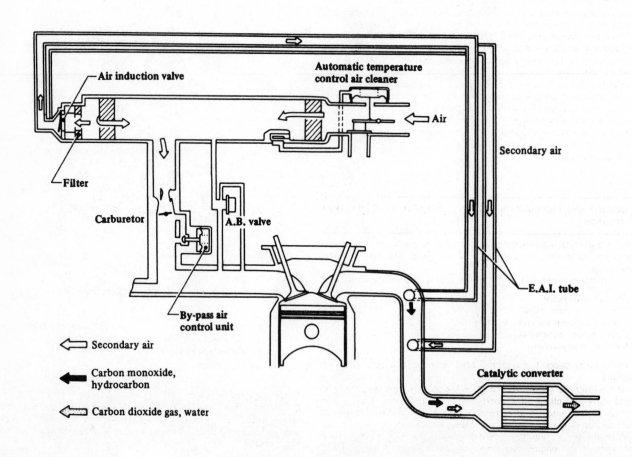

Fig. 3.30 Air inductive system (Sec 16)

15 Emission control systems – general

1   All models have some form of emission control, but on vehicles not produced for operation in North America this is usually limited to the crankcase ventilation system (Chapter 1, Section 3) and in certain territories a boost controlled deceleration device (BCDD).
2   In North America, the engine is equipped with complex emission control systems which may include the following:

Air induction system
Exhaust gas recirculation control system
Spark timing control system
Spark plug switching control system
Fuel shut-off system
Boost controlled deceleration device
High altitude emission control system
Evaporative emission control system

3   Californian vehicles are fitted with a catalytic converter in the exhaust system.
4   It must be appreciated that the carburettor, ignition system and engine condition all contribute to the volume of noxious gases emitted from the exhaust and these items should always be kept in adjustment and tune.

16 Air induction system – description, testing and maintenance

1   This system is designed to send secondary air to the exhaust manifold to dilute the CO and HC content in the exhaust gas.
2   The air is drawn into the exhaust manifold in proportion to the vacuum created by the pulsating of the exhaust pressure caused by the opening and closing of the exhaust valves.
3   The main components of the system are an air induction valve and filter, and anti-backfire valve.
4   Check the system hoses periodically and renew if necessary.
5   At the intervals specified in Routine Maintenance renew the filter which is located in the air cleaner casing.
6   The anti-backfire valve can be checked if the engine is first run to operating temperature. Disconnect the hose from the valve and place a finger over the valve opening.
7   Run the engine at 3000 rev/min and release the throttle sharply. A suction should be felt on the finger proving that the valve is operating correctly.

17 Exhaust gas recirculation system – description, testing and maintenance

1   With this system, a proportion of the exhaust gas is returned to the combustion chamber as a means of lowering the spark flame temperature.
2   The major components of the system include the following:

EGR control valve
Thermal vacuum valve
Venturi vacuum transducer valve
EGR vacuum control valve
Vacuum delay valve

3   Periodically check the system hoses for condition and renew as necessary.
4   At the intervals specified in Routine Maintenance remove the EGR control valve and clean off deposits using a wire brush.
5   If a fault occurs in the system, check the entire system or individual components using the following procedure.
6   With the engine idling, place a finger on the EGR control valve diaphragm. If the engine has only just started and is below 15°C (59°F) check that the control valve, or both valves on Californian models do not operate when the engine speed is raised to between 3000 and 3500 rev/min.
7   If the engine temperature is above 60°C (140°F) and idling, the valves should operate when the engine speed is increased to between 3000 and 3500 rev/min.

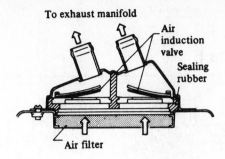

Fig. 3.31 Air induction valve (Sec 16)

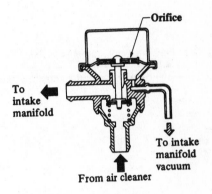

Fig. 3.32 Anti-backfire valve (Sec 16)

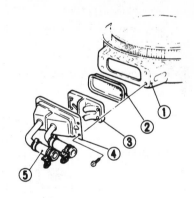

Fig. 3.33 Air induction system filter (Sec 16)

1	Air cleaner	4	Valve casing
2	Air induction filter	5	Hose
3	Air induction valve		

EGR control valve
8   Remove the valve from the engine and apply suction with the mouth to the hose stub. The valve should move to the fully operational position and remain in this position for 30 seconds after the suction has ceased.

Thermal vacuum valve
9   This is attached to the thermostat housing and monitors the temperature of the engine coolant.
10 To check the operation of the valve, first partially drain the cooling system and remove the valve. Apply suction with the mouth to the

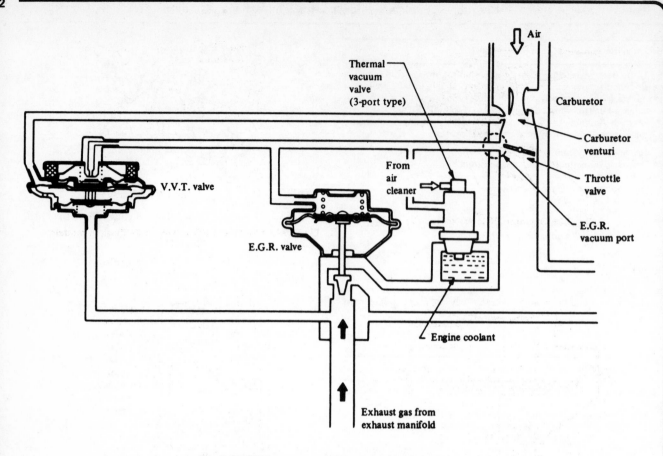

Fig. 3.34 EGR system excluding California (Sec 17)

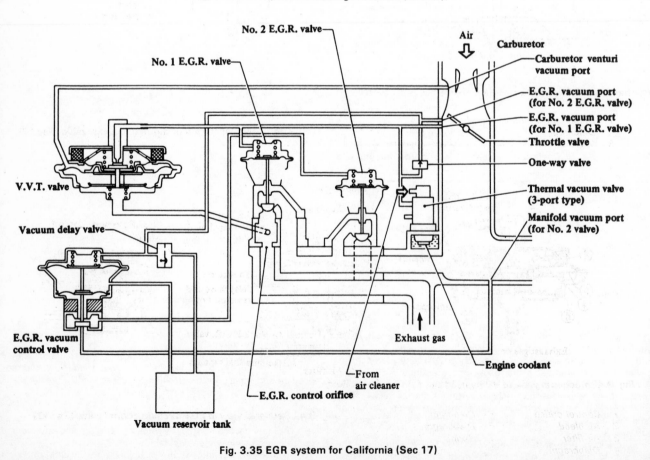

Fig. 3.35 EGR system for California (Sec 17)

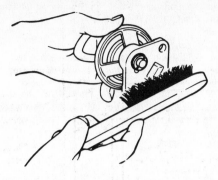

Fig. 3.36 Cleaning EGR valve (Sec 17)

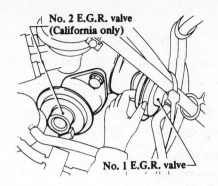

Fig. 3.37 Location of EGR valves on Californian models
(Sec 17)

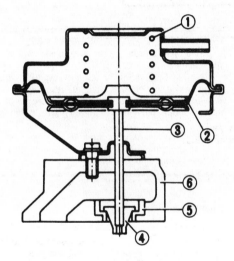

Fig. 3.38 Sectional view of EGR control valve (Sec 17)

1 Diaphragm spring   4 Valve
2 Diaphragm   5 Valve seat
3 Valve spindle   6 Valve chamber

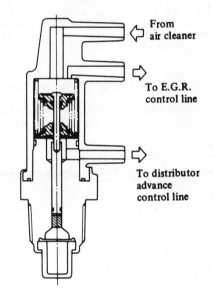

Fig. 3.39 Sectional view of thermal vacuum valve (Sec 17)

3

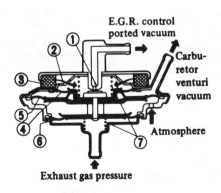

Fig. 3.40 Sectional view of VVT valve (Sec 17)

1 Control orifice   5 Diaphragm
2 Air bleed   6 Diaphragm
3 Air filter   7 Spring
4 Diaphragm

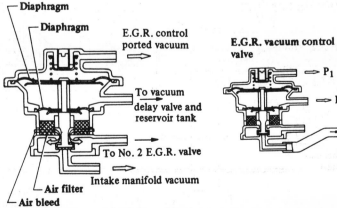

Fig. 3.41 Sectional view of EGR vacuum control valve (Sec 17)

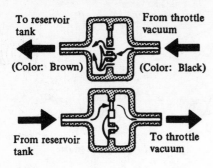

Fig. 3.42 Vacuum delay valve (Sec 17)

13 Now apply vacuum to the side stub when no leakage should be felt at the top stub. If it is, renew the valve.

EGR vacuum control valve

14 Fitted to Californian models, this valve monitors the throttle vacuum and the vacuum in the reservoir tank. The valve controls the intake manifold vacuum in order to actuate No 2 EGR valve.

15 To test the valve, apply suction to the stubs P1 and P2 in turn and check for leakage. Apply suction to the bottom stub and check that the valve operates.

Vacuum delay valve

16 This valve provides a slight delay in the operation of the vacuum control valve. If the valve is removed or a new one fitted, make sure that it is fitted the right way round as indicated by its colour coding.

17 If air is blown through the valve, resistance to its passage should be greater when blowing into the stub on the brown coloured side. If it is not, renew the valve.

middle pipe stub of the valve. If the temperature of the valve is below 60°C (140°F) the valve should be open. If the valve is then heated in hot water to a higher temperature, it should close. Take care not to allow water to enter the valve openings, either fit caps or lengths of tubing to project above the surface of the water.

Venturi vacuum transducer (VVT)

11 This valve monitors the pressure of the exhaust gas which actuates the diaphragm (6) Fig. 3.40, also the venturi vacuum which actuates the diaphragms (4) and (5). The valve therefore controls the carburettor throttle vacuum which is required to operate the EGR control valve.

12 To test the valve apply pressure to the bottom hose stub of the valve. No air should be felt to leak from the top stub.

18 Spark timing control system – description, testing and maintenance

1   This system is designed to control the distributor vacuum advance under varying driving conditions in order to keep the emission of exhaust gas pollutants to a minimum.

2   Periodically inspect the system hoses and renew if necessary.

3   The system can be checked for satisfactory operation in the following way. With the engine cold and a stroboscopic timing lamp connected in accordance with the maker's instructions, check the ignition timing.

4   Allow the engine to warm up until the needle on the coolant gauge is mid-way between the cold and hot positions. Check that the timing has advanced from its earlier position.

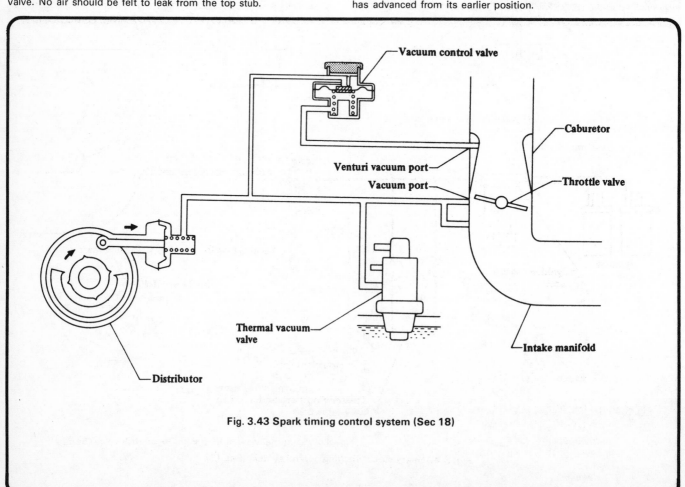

Fig. 3.43 Spark timing control system (Sec 18)

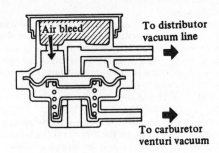

Fig. 3.44 Spark timing vacuum control valve (Sec 18)

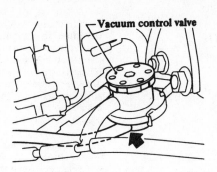

Fig. 3.45 Hose detachment point on vacuum control valve for testing (Sec 18)

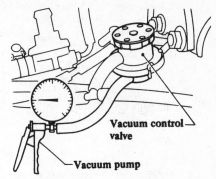

Fig. 3.46 Vacuum pump and gauge connected to vacuum control valve (Sec 18)

5   No change in the advance indicates the need for a new thermal vacuum valve.

Thermal vacuum valve
6   The testing of this valve is as described in Section 16.

Vacuum control valve
7   This valve is attached to the exhaust air induction tube support and connected into the distributor vacuum line. When the carburettor venturi vacuum exceeds a predetermined value air is bled into the distributor vacuum line to retard the ignition advance.
8   The valve can be tested if the venturi-vacuum hose is disconnected at the control valve end. If a vacuum or suction pump is now connected to the valve as soon as vacuum is created, the ignition should retard when the engine is idling. If it does not, renew the valve.

19 Spark plug switching control system – description and testing

1   This system is designed to switch from the two spark plug per cylinder arrangement on NAP-X type engines to single plug operation when the engine is under heavy load in order to reduce engine noise.
2   The ignition is advanced simultaneously at the moment of switchover.
3   Major components of the system consist of a control unit attached to the distributor, a vacuum switch and neutral and clutch switches.
4   Periodically check the condition of the system wiring and hoses.

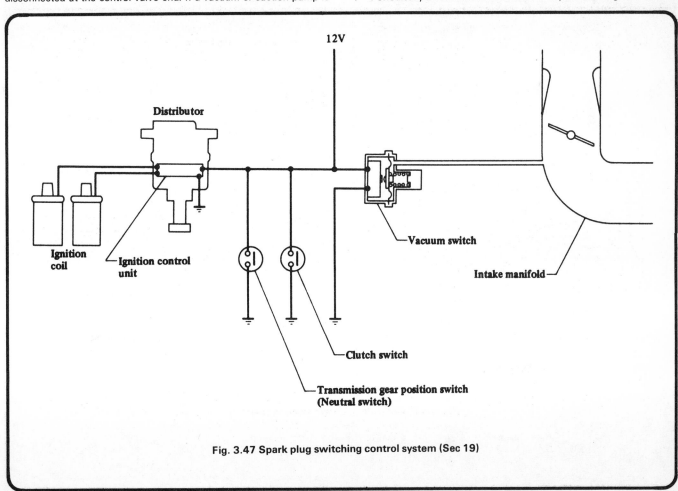

Fig. 3.47 Spark plug switching control system (Sec 19)

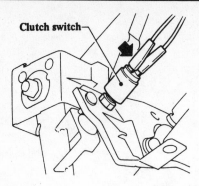

Fig. 3.48 Clutch switch (spark plug switching control system)
(Sec 19)

20 Fuel shut-off system – description and testing

1   This system operates when the engine is running in excess of 2200 rev/min on the overrun with the throttle valve closed.
2   Use is made of the fuel cut-off solenoid valve (provided to prevent running on when the ignition is switched off) with the addition of an engine revolution switch and a throttle valve switch.

3   To check the system for satisfactory operation, disconnect the wiring plug at the carburettor.
4   Using two short lengths of wire, bridge the red and black male and female terminals of the plugs.
5   Start the engine and increase its speed to between 2000 and 2500 rev/min. The engine should cut out and stop. If it does not and the connecting wires are in order, renew the engine revolution switch.
6   The throttle switch can be checked if with the connector plug disconnected at the carburettor, there is continuity between the black wire terminal on the plug and the carburettor body when the accelerator pedal is depressed and released.

21 Boost controlled deceleration device (BCDD)

1   This device is designed to reduce the emission of HC and engine oil vapour during deceleration on the overrun with the throttle valve closed. During the period of high intake manifold vacuum, the system operates to admit additional mixture to ensure complete combustion.
2   To check operation of the system, connect a vacuum gauge to the intake manifold.
3   Remove the dashpot adjusting screw.
4   Start the engine and note the vacuum gauge reading while alternately depressing the accelerator pedal fully and then releasing it sharply. The vacuum reading should rise above -85.3 kPa (-25.2 in Hg) and then slowly decrease to -81.3 kPa (-24.02 in Hg) eventually dropping to its idle boost.
5   If the vacuum readings do not conform to the pattern described adjust the control unit in the following way.

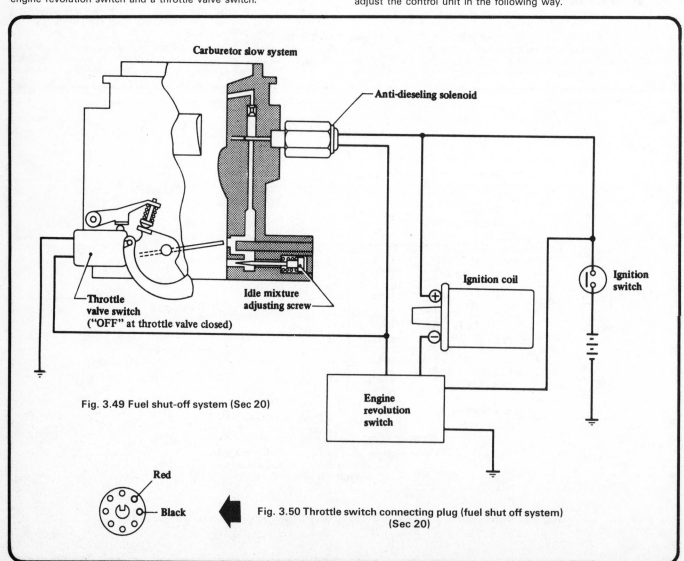

Fig. 3.49 Fuel shut-off system (Sec 20)

Fig. 3.50 Throttle switch connecting plug (fuel shut off system)
(Sec 20)

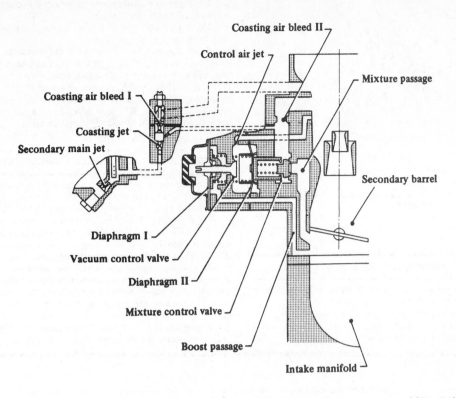

Fig. 3.51 Boost controlled deceleration device (BCDD) (21E Series carburettor) (Sec 21)

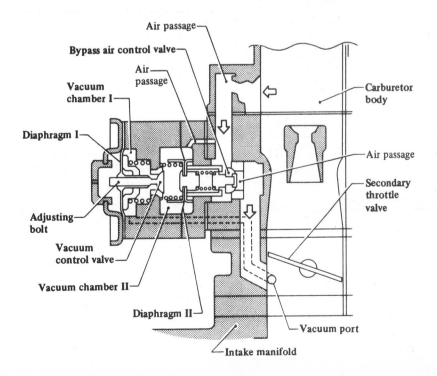

3

Fig. 3.52 Boost controlled deceleration device (BCDD) (DCR Series carburettor) (Sec 21)

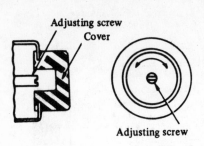

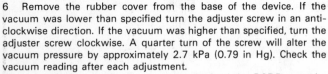

Fig. 3.53 BCDD cover and adjuster screw (Sec 21)

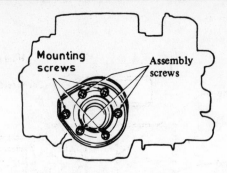

Fig. 3.54 BCDD cover and mounting screws (Sec 21)

6   Remove the rubber cover from the base of the device. If the vacuum was lower than specified turn the adjuster screw in an anti-clockwise direction. If the vacuum was higher than specified, turn the adjuster screw clockwise. A quarter turn of the screw will alter the vacuum pressure by approximately 2.7 kPa (0.79 in Hg). Check the vacuum reading after each adjustment.

7   If satisfactory readings cannot be obtained the BCDD must be renewed. When removing the unit make sure that the fixing screws and not the body screws are undone.

22 High altitude emission control system – description

1   In order to offset the effects of thinner air at high altitudes, vehicles operating under these conditions will have an altitude

compensator (see Section 8) and a canister to reduce vapour emission from the carburettor float chamber.

23 Fuel evaporative emission control system – description

1   This system employs a sealed fuel tank from which fuel vapour is vented and stored in a canister filled with activated charcoal. Once the engine is started, the vapour is drawn from the canister into the engine where it is burned during the normal combustion process.

2   Under normal circumstances, the only maintenance required is to check the security and condition of all the system hoses at periodic intervals.

3   The fuel tank filler cap incorporates a vacuum relief valve to admit air should vacuum conditions occur in the tank as the result of

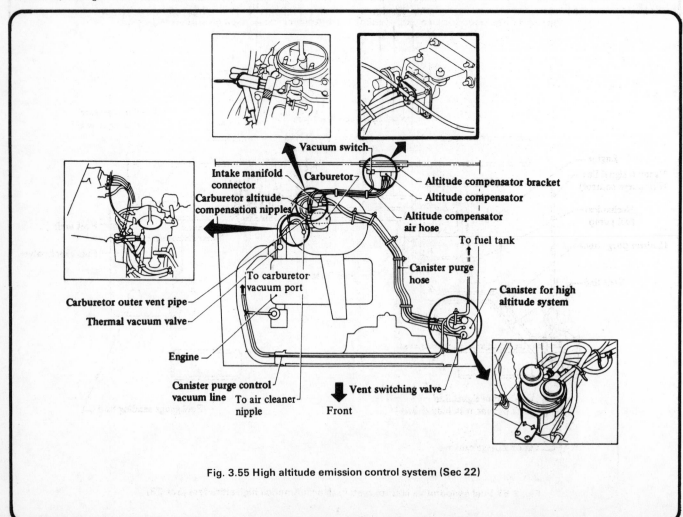

Fig. 3.55 High altitude emission control system (Sec 22)

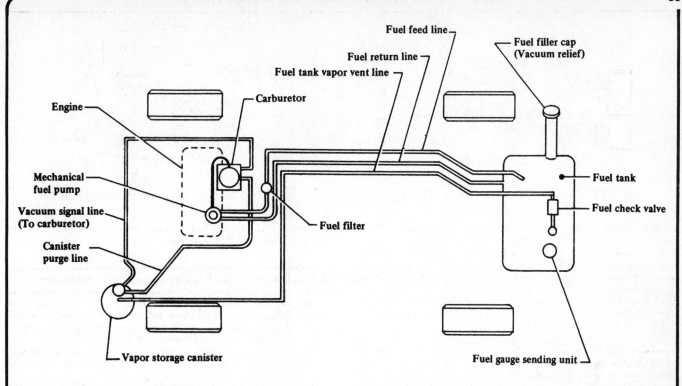

Fig. 3.56 Fuel evaporative control system (North America excluding high altitudes) (Sec 23)

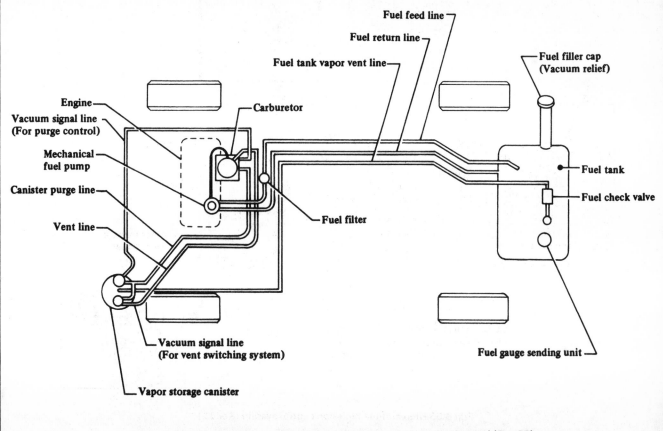

Fig. 3.57 Fuel evaporative control system (North America high altitudes) (Sec 23)

3

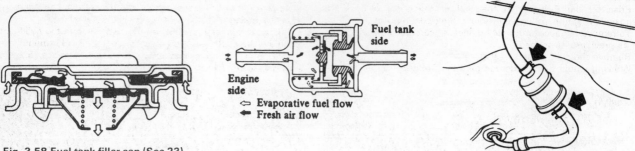

Fig. 3.58 Fuel tank filler cap (Sec 23)

Evaporative fuel flow
Fresh air flow

Fig. 3.59 Fuel evaporative control system non-return valve (Sec 23)

withdrawal of fuel vapour. Check the operation of the valve regularly. Apply suction to the valve housing in the cap using the mouth. A slight resistance should be felt and then as the suction is increased the resistance should disappear and the valve heard to 'click'.

4   If the filler cap valve does not behave in this way, renew the cap complete.

5   The fuel check (non-return) valve can be removed and tested by blowing through it from the fuel tank side. Considerable resistance should be felt with only a slight air bleed through the valve.

6   Now blow from the opposite direction and there should be no resistance or obstruction to the air flow at all.

24 Catalytic converter

1   This device is fitted into the exhaust system on North American versions. It is basically a container of catalyst beads through which the exhaust gases pass to change their hydrocarbon (HC) and carbon

monoxide (CO) content into harmless carbon dioxide (CO_2) and water (H_2O).

2   Take care not to damage the catalytic converter by careless jacking.

3   Expect high underfloor temperatures during the descent of long down gradients with the throttle closed or if there is an ignition or carburation fault.

4   Avoid parking a vehicle with a catalytic converter over long grass owing to the danger from fire.

25 Accelerator pedal and cable – removal, refitting and adjustment

1   To remove the pedal, first take off the cover from under the facia panel.

2   Pull the end fitting on the cable towards you until the cable can be slipped out of the slit in the pedal arm. If the cable is not slack enough

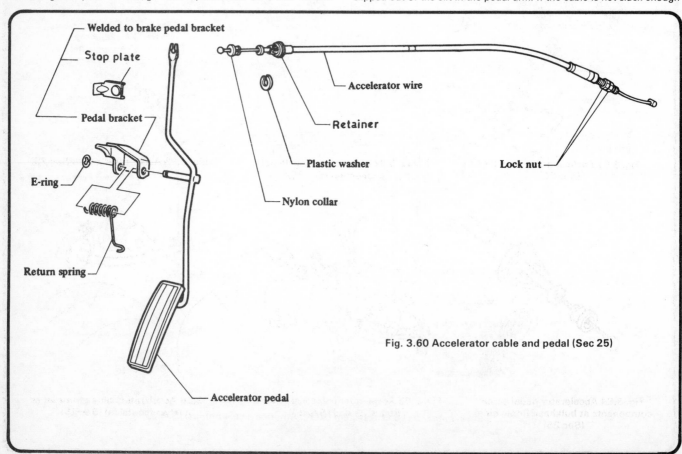

Fig. 3.60 Accelerator cable and pedal (Sec 25)

to be able to do this, slacken the cable adjuster at the carburettor.

3   Prise off the E-ring from the end of the pedal pivot shaft, disengage the return spring and remove the pedal (photo).
4   To remove the accelerator cable, release the cable from the pedal arm as previously described.
5   Remove the split plastic washer.
6   Working within the engine compartment, remove the air cleaner

and release the cable adjuster locknuts. Unscrew the nuts until the cable nipple can be released from the quadrant on the carburettor. Note the wiring plug clip held by the cable nut (photo).
7   Squeeze the retaining tabs on the cable bush at the bulkhead and withdraw the cable assembly into the engine compartment.
8   Refitting is a reversal of removal, but apply grease to the cable ends and to the pedal pivot. Adjust the cable in the following way.

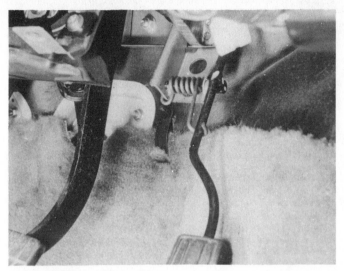

25.3 Accelerator pedal spring

25.6 Wiring connector plug at throttle cable bracket

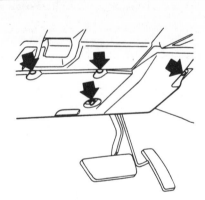

Fig. 3.61 Facia panel lower cover
(Sec 25)

Fig. 3.62 Accelerator pedal/cable
connection (Sec 25)

Fig. 3.63 Accelerator pedal (Sec 25)

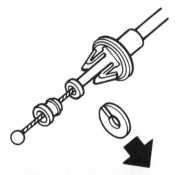

Fig. 3.64 Accelerator pedal cable
components at bulkhead (inner side)
(Sec 25)

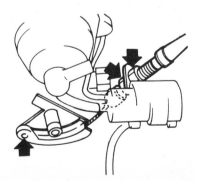

Fig. 3.65 Accelerator cable locknuts at
carburettor end (Sec 25)

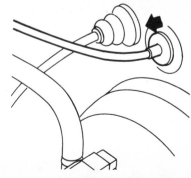

Fig. 3.66 Accelerator cable grommet at
bulkhead (outside) (Sec 25)

3

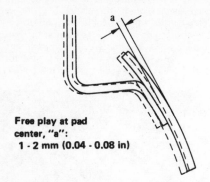

Fig. 3.67 Accelerator pedal adjusting diagram (Sec 25)

9   Using the fingers, open the throttle lever on the carburettor and
then set the choke valve plate in the fully open position.
10 Adjust the accelerator cable by means of the end fitting locknuts
until there is a free play measured at the centre of the upper surface
of the pedal pad of between 1.0 and 2.0 mm (0.04 and 0.08 in).

26 Manifolds and exhaust system

1   The intake and exhaust manifolds are located on opposite sides of
the cylinder head as it is of crossflow design.
2   The intake manifold is coolant heated and before the manifold can
be removed, the cooling system must be partially drained.
3   The exhaust manifold has the hot air collector plate attached to it
which is the source of warm air for the temperature-controlled air
cleaner (photo).
4   When removing or refitting a manifold, always use a new gasket
and tighten nuts and bolts to the specified torque.
5   The exhaust system used on vehicles not destined for operation in
North America incorporates single or dual downpipes according to
engine size, a flexible joint to absorb engine movement and an
expansion box and silencer (photo).
6   The exhaust system on North American models will normally
incorporate a catalytic converter ahead of the silencer. Take great care
not to damage this device when working on the system.
7   If the complete system is to be renewed, position the vehicle over
an inspection pit. If this is not possible, jack the vehicle up as high as
possible and secure it on axle stands.
8   Cutting through the connecting pipes will make removal in
sections easier than attempting to withdraw the complete exhaust
assembly.

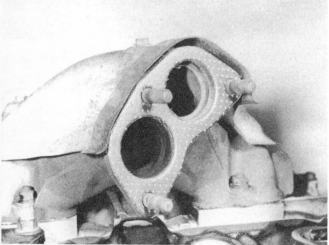

26.3 Exhaust downpipe flange gasket

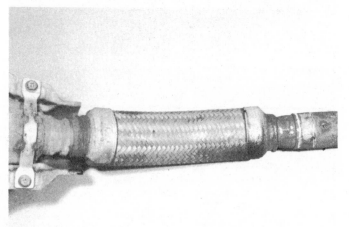

26.5 Exhaust pipe flexible section

26.10A Exhaust rubber mounting

26.10B Exhaust rubber mounting

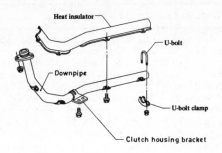

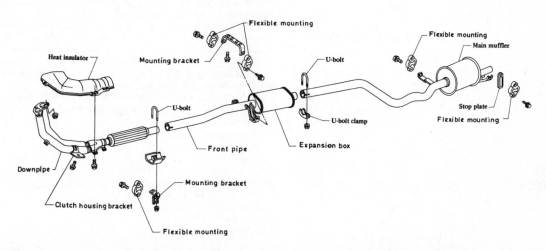

Fig. 3.68 Typical exhaust system (excluding North America) (Sec 26)

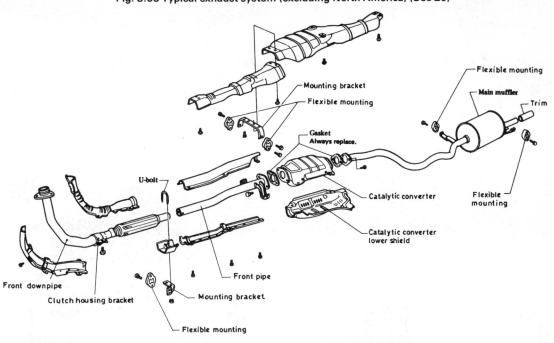

Fig. 3.69 Typical exhaust system (North America) (Sec 26)

9   If only one section is to be renewed, make quite sure that you have left an adequate overlap of original pipe to fit into the new section before cutting the old section out. Failure to do this will prevent a gastight joint being achieved at the coupling.
10 The exhaust system is flexibly mounted. Renew any mounting components which are deformed or have deteriorated. Always renew clamps (photos).

11 When connecting a new section of pipe, expansion box or silencer, remove burrs from the socket joints and apply a little grease before connecting. Fit the clamps only finger tight at first until the alignment of the system has been checked and adjusted.
12 Make sure that no component of the system is likely to touch adjacent parts of the bodyframe or suspension when deflected within the full extent of movement of its flexible mounting.

27 Fault diagnosis – fuel system

Unsatisfactory engine performance and excessive fuel consumption are not necessarily the fault of the fuel system or carburettor. In fact they more commonly occur as a result of ignition and timing faults. Before acting on the following it is necessary to check the ignition system first. Even though a fault may lie in the fuel system it will be difficult to trace unless the ignition is correct. The faults below, therefore, assume that this has been attended to first (where appropriate).

Symptom	Reason(s)
Smell of petrol when engine is stopped	Leaking fuel lines or unions Leaking fuel tank
Smell of petrol when engine is idling	Leaking fuel line unions between pump and carburettor Overflow of fuel from float chamber due to wrong level setting, ineffective needle valve or punctured float
Excessive fuel consumption for reasons not covered by leaks or float chamber faults	Worn jets Over-rich setting Sticking mechanism Dirty air cleaner element Sticking air cleaner thermostat mechanism
Difficult starting, uneven running, lack of power, cutting out	One or more jets blocked or restricted Float chamber fuel level too low or needle valve sticking Fuel pump not delivering sufficient fuel Faulty solenoid fuel shut-off valve Induction leak
Difficult starting when cold	Automatic choke maladjusted Automatic choke not cocked before starting Incorrect fast idle setting Faulty fuel cut-off solenoid valve Fuel filter clogged
Difficult starting when hot	Automatic choke malfunction Accelerator pedal pumped before starting Vapour lock (especially in hot weather or at high altitude) Faulty fuel cut-off solenoid valve Fuel filter clogged
Engine does not respond properly to throttle	Faulty accelerator pump Blocked jet(s) Slack in accelerator cable
Engine idle speed drops when hot	Defective temperature compensator Overheated fuel pump
Engine runs on	Faulty fuel cut-off valve

28 Fault diagnosis – emission control system

Symptom	Reason(s)
Fumes escaping from engine	Seized PCV valve Split or collapsed system hoses
Fuel odour or rough engine running	Choked carbon canister Fuel filler cap valve not operating
Rough idling	Faulty or dirty EGR valve Collapsed system hoses
Fume emission from exhaust	Catalytic converter fault Faulty idle compensator in air cleaner Fault in BCDD Faulty EGR valve
Backfire	Defective air cleaner intake valve Faulty EGR valve Faulty spark timing control system
Engine noisy under load	Faulty spark plug switching control system

Chapter 4 Ignition system

Refer to Chapter 13 for specifications and information applicable to 1984 and later models

Contents

Specifications

System type – except N. America .... Battery, coil, mechanical breaker distributor

Distributor
Type (1598 cc) D409-81
Type (1809 cc)
    Manual transmission D408-57
    Automatic transmission D408-59
Rotor rotation .... Anti-clockwise
Contact points gap .... 0.45 to 0.55 mm (0.018 to 0.022 in)
Dwell angle .... 49° to 55°
Cap carbon brush wear limit .... 10.0 mm (0.39 in)
Firing order .... 1–3–4–2 (No. 1 at timing belt end of engine)

Ignition timing (at idle, vacuum hose disconnected)
(1598 cc) CA16 .... 3° BTDC
(1809 cc) CA18 .... 5° BTDC

Ignition coil
Type C6R-206
Primary resistance (at 20°C - 68°F) .... 1.35 to 1.65 ohm
Secondary resistance (at 20°C - 68°F) .... 6.8 to 10.2 kohm

Spark plugs
Type .... NGK BPR6ES
Electrode gap .... 0.8 to 0.9 mm (0.031 to 0.035 in)

System type – N. America .... Breakerless ignition

Distributor
Type D4N80-29
Rotor rotation .... Anti-clockwise
Air gap .... 0.3 to 0.5 mm (0.012 to 0.020 in)
Cap carbon brush wear limit .... 10.0 mm (0.39 in)
Firing order .... 1-3-4-2 (No. 1 at timing belt end of engine)

Ignition timing
    (at idle, vacuum hose disconnected) .... 2° BTDC to 2° ATDC

4

Ignition coils
Type .... CIT 49
Primary resistance (20°C - 68°F) .... 0.84 to 1.02 ohm
Secondary resistance (20°C - 68°F) .... 8.2 to 12.4 kohm

Spark plugs
Intake side BPR6ES-11
Exhaust side BPR5ES-11
Electrode gap .... 1.0 to 1.1 mm (0.039 to 0.043 in)

Torque wrench settings
	Nm	lbf ft
Distributor clamp bolt	6	4
Spark plug	20	15

1 General description

On all models except North American versions fitted with a NAPS-X engine (120.45 cu in) the ignition system is of conventional type with a mechanical breaker distributor.

The NAPS-X engine is equipped with electronic ignition using a breakerless distributor, two coils and dual spark plugs at each cylinder.

Mechanical breaker ignition

In order that the engine can run correctly it is necessary for an electrical spark to ignite the fuel/air mixture in the combustion chamber at exactly the right moment in relation to engine speed and load. The ignition system is based on feeding low tension voltage from the battery to the coil where it is converted to high tension voltage. The high tension voltage is powerful enough to jump the spark plug gap in the cylinders many times a second under high compression, providing that the system is in good condition and that all adjustments are correct.

The ignition system is divided into two circuits, low tension and high tension.

The low tension circuit (sometimes known as the primary) consists of the battery, lead to the ignition switch, lead from the ignition switch to the low tension or primary coil windings, and the lead from the low tension coil windings to the contact breaker points and condenser in the distributor.

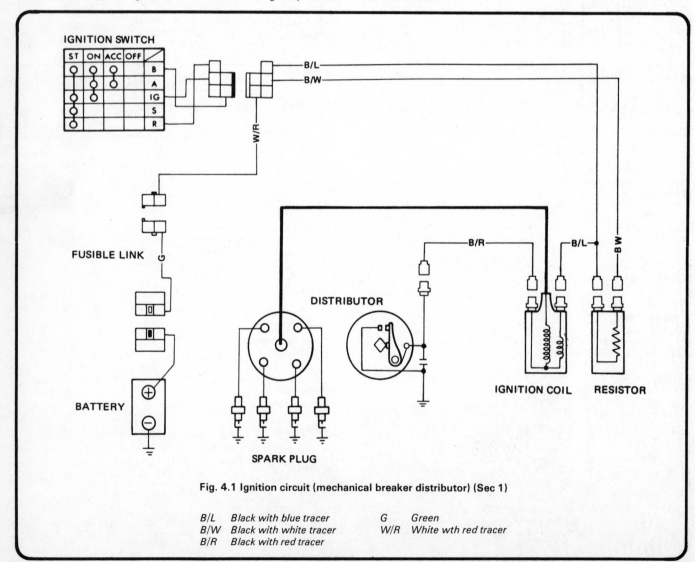

Fig. 4.1 Ignition circuit (mechanical breaker distributor) (Sec 1)

B/L   Black with blue tracer   G   Green
B/W   Black with white tracer   W/R   White wth red tracer
B/R   Black with red tracer

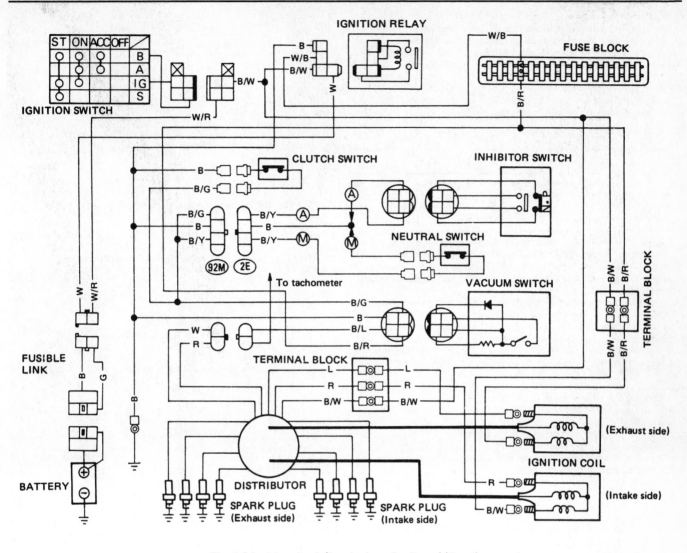

Fig. 4.2 Ignition circuit (breakerless distributor) (Sec 1)

W	White	G	Green	B/Y	Black with yellow tracer	R	Red
W/R	White with red tracer	B/W	Black with white tracer	B/G	Black with green tracer	L	Blue
B	Black	W/B	White with black tracer				

The high tension circuit consists of the high tension or secondary coil winding, the heavy ignition lead from the centre of the coil to the centre of the distributor cap, the rotor arm, and the spark plug leads and spark plugs.

The system functions in the following manner. Low tension voltage is changed in the coil into high tension voltage by the opening and closing of the contact breaker points in the low tension circuit. High tension voltage is then fed via the carbon brush in the centre of the distributor cap to the rotor arm of the distributor cap, and each time it comes in line with one of the four metal segments in the cap, which are connected to the spark plug leads, the opening and closing of the contact breaker points causes the high tension voltage to build up, jump the gap from the rotor arm to the appropriate metal segment and so via the spark plug lead to the spark plug, where it finally jumps the spark plug gap before going to earth.

The ignition is advanced and retarded automatically, to ensure that the spark occurs at just the right instant for the particular load at the prevailing engine speed.

The ignition advance is controlled both mechanically and by a vacuum operated system. The mechanical governor consists of two weights, which move out from the distributor shaft as the engine speed rises due to centrifugal force. As they move outwards they rotate the cam relative to the distributor shaft, and so advance the

spark. The weights are held in position by two light springs and it is the tension of the springs which is largely responsible for correct spark advancement.

The vacuum control consists of a diaphragm, one side of which is connected via a small bore tube to the carburettor, and the other side to the contact breaker plate. Depression in the inlet manifold and carburettor, which varies with engine speed and throttle opening, causes the diaphragm to move, so moving the contact breaker plate, and advancing or retarding the spark. A resistor is built into the primary circuit.

During low speed operation when primary current flow is high, the temperature of the resistor rises to increase resistance and so reduce current flow. This prolongs the life of the contact points. During high speed operation, when primary current is low, the resistor cools to permit greater current flow which is needed for high speed operation. When the starter is operated, the ballast resistor is bypassed to allow full battery voltage through the ignition primary circuit.

Breakerless ignition

The main difference between this system and the mechanical breaker type is in the distributor, where the contact breaker is replaced by an armature and magnetic pick-up unit.

When the ignition is switched on, the primary circuit is energized.

When the high points on the reluctor approach the pick-up unit, a voltage is induced which turns off the primary current and creates high voltage in the coil secondary winding. This is conducted to the distributor rotor where it is directed to the appropriate spark plug. The process is repeated for each power stroke of the engine.

Timing and mechanical and vacuum advance are as for mechanical breaker systems.

With a breakerless ignition system, the voltages are very high, take care not to touch HT leads or connections when the engine is running.

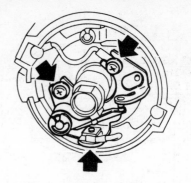

Fig. 4.3 Contact breaker detachment points (Sec 2)

2 Mechanical contact breaker – points servicing

1 At the intervals specified in Routine Maintenance, remove the distributor cap by prising down the two securing clips, remove the rotor.

2 Prise open the contact breaker points with the thumb nail and examine the faces. If they are severely eroded or a large 'pip' and crater are visible, the points should be renewed, dressing the original points on an oilstone or abrasive paper is not recommended.

3 If the points are in reasonably good condition, but have been in service for some time, check the dwell angle and adjust if necessary as described later in this Section.

4 If the points must be renewed, proceed in the following way.

5 Extract the screw from the LT terminal on the distributor body.

6 Extract the screws which hold the fixed contact arm to the baseplate. Note the small earth lead under one of the screws.

7 Remove the contact set and discard it. On some contact sets, the spring arm is held to its pivot by an E-ring. This arm can be removed separately if required.

8 Fit the new contact points, but only just tighten the fixing screws. Reconnect the LT and earth leads.

9 Turn the crankshaft until the heel of the spring contact arm is on one of the high points of the cam.

10 Lever the fixed arm using a screwdriver against the fulcrum pin provided until a feeler blade (0.45 to 0.55 mm – 0.018 to 0.022 in) is a sliding fit between the points faces. Tighten the screws (photo).

11 Fit the rotor and the distributor cap.

12 Apply two or three drops of oil to the screw head or felt pad on the top of the distributor shaft.

13 Apply a smear of high melting point grease to the high spots on the distributor shaft cam.

14 Check the condition of the carbon brush in the distributor cap. If it is worn down, renew the cap.

15 Check the rotor arm contact and distributor cap contacts for erosion and renew the components where necessary.

16 Setting the contact breaker points gap using feeler gauges must be regarded as a basic adjustment only. For optimum engine performance the dwell angle must be checked. The dwell angle is the number of degrees through which the distributor cam turns during the period between the instants of closure and opening of the contact breaker points.

17 Checking and adjusting the dwell angle not only gives a more accurate setting of the contact breaker points gap, but also evens out any variations in the gap which could be caused by wear in the distributor shaft or its bushes or difference in height of any of the cam peaks.

18 The dwell angle should be checked with a dwell meter connected in accordance with the maker's instructions. Refer to Specifications for the correct dwell angle.

19 If the dwell angle is found to be too large, increase the points gap and then recheck. If too small, reduce the points gap.

20 The dwell angle should always be adjusted before checking and adjusting the ignition timing. The ignition timing must always be checked after adjusting the dwell angle.

2.10 Checking contact points gap

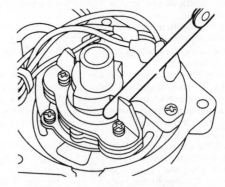

Fig. 4.4 Checking air gap (Sec 3)

3 Breakerless distributor – air gap adjustment

1 This should only require adjustment if an engine fault indicates the need after reference to Fault diagnosis, Section 13.

2 Remove the distributor cap (three screws) and rotor and loosen the stator fixing screws.

3 Move the stator until a feeler blade 0.3 to 0.5 mm (0.012 to 0.020 in) is a sliding fit between a high point on the reluctor and the pick-up point on the stator.

4 Tighten the stator screws, refit the rotor and the distributor cap.

4 Ignition timing

1 It is necessary to time the ignition when it has been upset due to overhauling or dismantling. Also, if maladjustments have affected the engine performance it is very desirable, although not always essential,

5° A.T.D.C. (White)
T.D.C. (Orange)
20° B.T.D.C. (White)
10° B.T.D.C. (White)

Fig. 4.5 Timing marks (Sec 4)

to reset the timing starting from scratch. In the following procedures it is assumed that the intention is to obtain standard performance from the standard engine which is in reasonable condition. It is also assumed that the recommended fuel octane rating is used.

2   Set the transmission to neutral and remove all four spark plugs.

3   Place a thumb over No 1 cylinder spark plug hole and rotate the engine clockwise by means of the crankshaft pulley bolt until pressure is felt building up in No 1 cylinder. This indicates that the No 1 cylinder piston is approaching top dead centre (tdc) on the firing stroke.

4   Continue to rotate the crankshaft until the notch in the pulley is directly opposite the timing pointer as appropriate (see Specifications).

5   In this position, the timing is set at the specified BTDC number of degrees **not** TDC.

6   Slacken the distributor clamp bolt or nut and rotate the distributor body until the contact breaker points are just opening and then tighten the clamp bolt or nut.

7   Difficulty is sometimes experienced in determining exactly when the contact breaker points open. This can be ascertained most accurately by connecting a 12V bulb in parallel with the contact breaker points (one lead to earth and the other from the distributor low tension terminal). Switch on the ignition and turn the distributor body until the bulb lights up, indicating that the points have just opened.

8   If it was found impossible to align the rotor arm correctly the distributor cam assembly has been incorrectly fitted on the driveshaft. To rectify this, it will be necessary to partially dismantle the distributor and check the position of the cam assembly on the centrifugal advance mechanism; it may be 180° out of position.

9   As a final check on the ignition timing the best method is to use a strobe lamp.

10   Put a spot of white paint on the notch in the crankshaft pulley and the timing pointer and connect the strobe light into the No 1 cylinder HT circuit following the maker's instructions. Disconnect and plug the distributor vacuum pipe.

11   Run the engine at idling speed and point the strobe lamp at the timing marks. At idling speed the white paint marks should appear to be immediately opposite each other; open the throttle slightly and check that as the engine revolutions rise the spot on the crankshaft will move away from the pointer. This indicates the centrifugal advance mechanism is operating correctly.

12   If the timing marks do not line up under the strobe light, slightly slacken the distributor clamp bolt and carefully turn the distributor in its location to bring the marks into line and retighten the clamp bolt.

13   Reconnect the distributor vacuum pipe and check that a small advance occurs to the ignition timing, indicating that the vacuum unit is operating correctly.

5   Condenser (mechanical breaker distributor)

1   The purpose of the condenser (sometimes known as the capacitor) is to ensure that when the contact breaker points open there is no sparking across them which would waste voltage and cause wear.

2   On this distributor the condenser is mounted on the outside of the distributor body. If it develops a short-circuit it will cause ignition failure as the points will be prevented from interrupting the low tension circuit.

3   If the engine becomes very difficult to start or begins to miss after several miles running and the breaker points show signs of excessive

burning, then the condition of the condenser must be suspect. A further test can be made by separating the points by hand with the ignition switched on. If this is accompanied by a strong blue flash it is indicative that the condenser has failed in the open circuit mode.

4   Without special equipment the only sure way to diagnose condenser trouble is to replace a suspected unit with a new one and note if there is any improvement.

6   Distributor – removal and refitting

1   On mechanical breaker type distributors, prise down the spring clips and move the distributor cap complete with HT leads to one side. On breakerless units, the cap is held by screws.

2   Remove the distributor clamp plate screw and pull the distributor out of the cylinder head (photo).

3   To fit the distributor turn the crankshaft until No. 1 piston is at TDC on its compression stroke. To do this, remove No. 1 cylinder spark plug and place a finger over the hole to feel the compression being generated as the crankshaft pulley bolt is being turned. As soon as compression is felt, continue to turn until the TDC mark is in alignment with the timing pointer on the front of the crankcase.

4   Align the punch marks on the distributor gear and shaft housing and then push the distributor into position while holding it so that the vacuum unit is at the correct angle to the top surface of the rocker cover (photos).

6.2 Distributor clamp bolt

4

6.4 Distributor driveshaft alignment marks

Cylinder head
Mark
Distributor shaft
Drive gear

Fig. 4.6 Distributor gear to body punch marks (Sec 6)

90°
ROCKER COVER

H.12304.

Fig. 4.7 Distributor installation position (Sec 6)

6.5 Rotor aligned with No 1 contact in distributor cap

Cap assembly

Carbon point assembly

Rotor head

Contact set

Earth wire

Breaker plate

Cam set assembly

Governor weight

Governor spring

Shaft assembly

Housing

Thrust washer

Lead wire

Terminal assembly

Vacuum control assembly

Condenser assembly

Fixing plate

Pinion set

Fig. 4.8 Components of the mechanical breaker distributor (Sec 7)

5   Check that the contact end of the rotor is in alignment with No. 1 contact in the distributor cap (as if fitted) (photo).
6   Turn the distributor until the points are just about to open (mechanical breaker) or a high point on the reluctor is aligned with the pick-up point on the stator.
7   Tighten the distributor clamp plate.
8   Check and adjust the ignition timing (Section 4).

7   Distributor (mechanical breaker type) – overhaul

1   With the distributor removed as described in the preceding Section, remove the rotor.
2   Extract the two screws and remove the vacuum unit. Tilt the unit as it is withdrawn to unhook the link from the pin on the baseplate.
3   Remove the contact breaker as described in Section 2.
4   Extract the fixing screws and remove the baseplate assembly.
5   If the fixed and moveable baseplates are separated, take care not to lose the balls.
6   Remove the driven gear by knocking out the pin.
7   Remove the screw from the upper end of the distributor shaft.
8   Mark the relationship of the cam assembly to the shaft with quick-drying paint or a spirit marker and remove the cam.
9   If the centrifugal advance components must be dismantled, note the precise location of the weights and the two springs, the latter are not interchangeable.
10 Clean, inspect and renew components as necessary.
11 Oil the components as reassembly progresses.
12 Reassembly is a reversal of dismantling, but observe the following points.
13 The rotor locating flat on the cam must face towards the counterweight which has the spring with the circular hook connected to it.
14 The pin for the spring with the circular hook engages in the longer cut-out of the cam plate.
15 Fit the gear to the shaft using a new pin and make sure that the gear and distributor body punch marks are in alignment when the contact end of the rotor is in alignment with No. 1 contact in the distributor cap when it is fitted.
16 Set the points gap using a feeler blade.
17 When the distributor has been refitted to the engine, check the dwell angle and the ignition timing.

8   Distributor (breakerless type) – overhaul

1   With the distributor removed as described in Section 6, remove the rotor.
2   Release the wiring harness from the distributor body.
3   Extract the pivot screw from the vacuum capsule link and remove the unit.
4   Using two screwdrivers, carefully prise the reluctor from the distributor shaft.
5   Remove the roll pin from the reluctor.
6   Extract the screws and remove the baseplate and the control unit.
7   Separate the magnet, stator and setter from the baseplate if necessary.
8   Remove the distributor clamp plate.
9   Drive out the roll pin and remove the gear from the distributor shaft.
10 Extract the felt pad from the top of the distributor shaft, remove the screw and take the upper shaft from the main distributor shaft.
11 Note the relationship of the counterweights and springs and then dismantle the mechanical advance components.
12 Clean and examine all components and renew any that are worn or damaged.
13 Oil the components as reassembly progresses and apply a little grease to the balls which are located between the fixed and moveable baseplates.
14 Reassembly is a reversal of dismantling, but observe the following points.
15 Fit the gear to the shaft using a new pin and make sure that the gear and distributor body punch marks are in alignment when the contact end of the rotor is in alignment with No. 1 contact in the distributor cap when it is fitted.

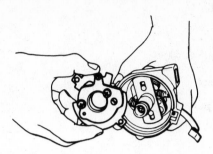

Fig. 4.9 Removing baseplate from mechanical breaker distributor (Sec 7)

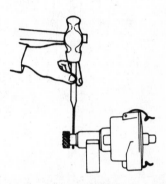

Fig. 4.10 Removing distributor gear pin (Sec 7)

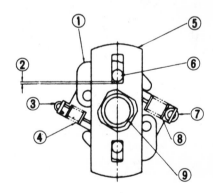

Fig. 4.11 Advance mechanism on mechanical breaker distributor (Sec 7)

1	Counterweight	6	Pivot pin
2	Clearance	7	Circular spring hook
3	Rectangular spring hook	8	Spring
4	Spring	9	Rotor positioning flat
5	Camplate		

16 When fitting the roll pin to the reluctor, note the fitted direction of the pin slit.
17 Make sure that the marks on the baseplate and the distributor body are in alignment.
18 When connecting the wiring leads, note that they are connected correctly as shown in Fig. 4.18.
19 Adjust the air gap as described in Section 3.

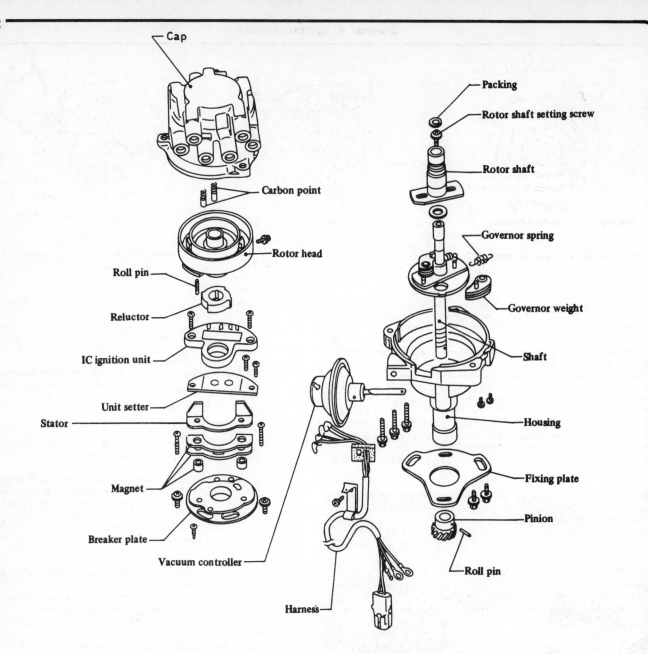

Fig. 4.12 Components of the breakerless distributor (Sec 8)

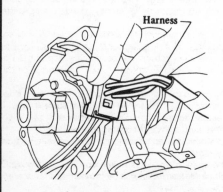

Fig. 4.13 Wiring harness (breakerless distributor) (Sec 8)

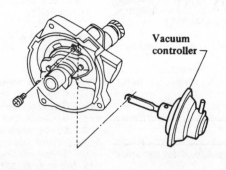

Fig. 4.14 Vacuum unit (breakerless distributor) (Sec 8)

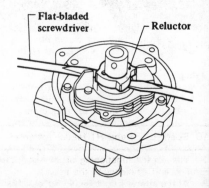

Fig. 4.15 Removing reluctor (breakerless distributor) (Sec 8)

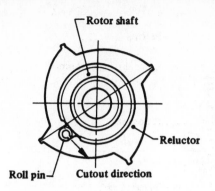

Fig. 4.16 Reluctor roll pin setting (Sec 8)

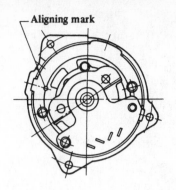

Fig. 4.17 Baseplate/body alignment marks (breakerless distributor) (Sec 8)

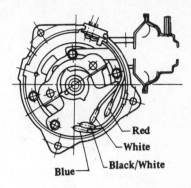

Fig. 4.18 Wiring lead connections (breakerless distributor) (Sec 8)

9 Ignition coil – general

1   The coil is an auto-transformer and has two sets of windings wound around a core of soft iron wires. The resistance of the primary winding is given in Specifications at the beginning of this Chapter (photo).

2   If the coil is suspect then the resistance may be checked by an auto electrician and if faulty it may readily be renewed after undoing the mounting bolts.

9.1 Ignition coil

10 Spark plugs and HT leads – general

1   The correct functioning of the spark plugs is vital for the correct running and efficiency of the engine.

2   At the intervals specified in Routine Maintenance the plugs should be removed, cleaned and regapped.

3   To remove the plugs, first open the bonnet and pull the HT leads from them. Grip the rubber end fitting not the lead otherwise the lead connection may be fractured.

4   Brush out any accumulated dirt or grit from the spark plug recess in the cylinder head otherwise it may drop into the combustion chamber when the plug is removed.

5   Unscrew the spark plugs with a deep socket or a box spanner. Do not allow the tool to tilt otherwise the ceramic insulator may be cracked or broken.

6   Examination of the spark plugs will give a good indication of the condition of the engine.

7   If the insulator nose of the spark plug is clean and white with no deposits, this is indicative of a weak mixture, or too hot a plug (a hot plug transfers heat away from the electrode slowly, a cold plug transfers heat away quickly).

8   The plugs fitted as standard are specified at the beginning of this Chapter. If the top and insulator nose are covered with hard black-looking deposits, then this is indicative that the mixture is too rich. Should the plug be black and oily, then it is likely that the engine is fairly worn, as well as the mixture being too rich.

9   If the insulator nose is covered with light tan to greyish brown deposits, then the mixture is correct and it is likely that the engine is in good condition.

10   If there are any traces of long brown tapering stains on the outside of the white portion of the plug, then the plug will have to be renewed, as this shows that there is a faulty joint between the plug body and the insulator, and compression is being allowed to leak away.

11   Before cleaning a spark plug, wash it in petrol to remove oily deposits.

12   Although a wire brush can be used to clean the electrode end of the spark plug this method can cause metal conductance paths across the nose of the insulator and it is therefore to be preferred that an abrasive powder cleaning machine is used. Such machines are available quite cheaply from motor accessory stores or you may prefer to take the plugs to your dealer who will not only be able to clean them, but also to check the sparking efficiency of each plug under compression.

13   The spark plug gap is of considerable importance, as, if it is too large or too small, the size of the spark and its efficiency will be seriously impaired. For the best results the spark plug gap should be set in accordance with the Specifications at the beginning of this Chapter.

14   To set it, measure the gap with a feeler gauge, and then bend open, or close, the outer plug electrode until the correct gap is achieved. The centre electrode should never be bent as this may crack the insulation and cause plug failure if nothing worse.

15   Special spark plug electrode gap adjusting tools are available from most motor accessory stores.

16   Before refitting the spark plugs, wash each one thoroughly again in fuel in order to remove all trace of abrasive powder and then apply a trace of grease to the plug threads.

17   Screw each plug in by hand. This will make sure that there is no chance of cross-threading.

18   Tighten to the specified torque. If a torque wrench is not available, just nip up each plug. It is better to slightly undertighten rather than over do it and strip the threads from the light alloy cylinder head.

4

10.19 Distributor cap lead sequence

19 When reconnecting the spark plug leads, make sure that they are refitted in their correct order, 1-3-4-2. No. 1 cylinder being at the timing belt end of the engine.
20 The plug leads require no routine attention other than being kept clean and wiped over regularly. At intervals of 6000 miles (10 000 km), however, pull each lead off the plug in turn and remove it from the distributor. Water can seep down into the joints giving rise to a white corrosive deposit which must be carefully removed from the end of each cable.

11 Ignition switch – removal and refitting

1   The ignition switch may be removed independently of the steering column lock to which it is attached (see Chapter 11).
2   Disconnect the battery.
3   Remove the lower shroud from the upper end of the steering column.
4   Disconnect the ignition switch wiring plug.
5   Extract the switch fixing screws and withdraw the switch from the steering column lock housing.
6   Refitting is a reversal of the removal procedure.

12 Fault diagnosis (mechanical breaker ignition)

Symptom	Reason(s)
Engine fails to start	Loose battery connections
	Discharged batttery
	Oil on contact points
	Disconnected ignition leads
	Faulty condenser
Engine starts and runs but misfires	Faulty spark plug
	Cracked distributor cap
	Cracked rotor arm
	Worn advance mechanism
	Incorrect spark plug gap
	Incorrect contact points gap
	Faulty condenser
	Faulty coil
	Incorrect timing
	Poor engine/transmission earth connections
Engine overheats, lacks power	Seized distributor weights
	Perforated vacuum pipe
	Incorrect ignition timing
Engine 'pinks'	Timing too advanced
	Advance mechanism stuck in advanced position
	Broken distributor weight spring
	Low fuel octane
	Upper cylinder oil used in fuel
	Excessive oil vapour from crankcase ventilation system (worn piston rings)

13 Fault diagnosis (breakerless ignition)

Symptom	Reason(s)
Starter turns but engine will not start	Faulty or disconnected leads
	Faulty spark plug
	Air gap incorrect
	Fault in ignition coil
	Fault in pick-up/starter unit
Engine starts but runs erratically	Incorrect timing
	Fouled spark plug
	Incorrectly connected HT leads
	Crack in distributor cap or rotor
	Poor battery, engine and earth connections

Common spark plug conditions

NORMAL
Symptoms: Brown to grayish-tan color and slight electrode wear. Correct heat range for engine and operating conditions.
Recommendation: When new spark plugs are installed, replace with plugs of the same heat range.

WORN
Symptoms: Rounded electrodes with a small amount of deposits on the firing end. Normal color. Causes hard starting in damp or cold weather and poor fuel economy.
Recommendation: Plugs have been left in the engine too long. Replace with new plugs of the same heat range. Follow the recommended maintenance schedule.

CARBON DEPOSITS
Symptoms: Dry sooty deposits indicate a rich mixture or weak ignition. Causes misfiring, hard starting and hesitation.
Recommendation: Make sure the plug has the correct heat range. Check for a clogged air filter or problem in the fuel system or engine management system. Also check for ignition system problems.

ASH DEPOSITS
Symptoms: Light brown deposits encrusted on the side or center electrodes or both. Derived from oil and/or fuel additives. Excessive amounts may mask the spark, causing misfiring and hesitation during acceleration.
Recommendation: If excessive deposits accumulate over a short time or low mileage, install new valve guide seals to prevent seepage of oil into the combustion chambers. Also try changing gasoline brands.

OIL DEPOSITS
Symptoms: Oily coating caused by poor oil control. Oil is leaking past worn valve guides or piston rings into the combustion chamber. Causes hard starting, misfiring and hesitation.
Recommendation: Correct the mechanical condition with necessary repairs and install new plugs.

GAP BRIDGING
Symptoms: Combustion deposits lodge between the electrodes. Heavy deposits accumulate and bridge the electrode gap. The plug ceases to fire, resulting in a dead cylinder.
Recommendation: Locate the faulty plug and remove the deposits from between the electrodes.

TOO HOT
Symptoms: Blistered, white insulator, eroded electrode and absence of deposits. Results in shortened plug life.
Recommendation: Check for the correct plug heat range, over-advanced ignition timing, lean fuel mixture, intake manifold vacuum leaks, sticking valves and insufficient engine cooling.

PREIGNITION
Symptoms: Melted electrodes. Insulators are white, but may be dirty due to misfiring or flying debris in the combustion chamber. Can lead to engine damage.
Recommendation: Check for the correct plug heat range, over-advanced ignition timing, lean fuel mixture, insufficient engine cooling and lack of lubrication.

HIGH SPEED GLAZING
Symptoms: Insulator has yellowish, glazed appearance. Indicates that combustion chamber temperatures have risen suddenly during hard acceleration. Normal deposits melt to form a conductive coating. Causes misfiring at high speeds
Recommendation: Install new plugs. Consider using a colder plug if driving habits warrant.

DETONATION
Symptoms: Insulators may be cracked or chipped. Improper gap setting techniques can also result in a fractured insulator tip. Can lead to piston damage.
Recommendation: Make sure the fuel anti-knock values meet engine requirements. Use care when setting the gaps on new plugs. Avoid lugging the engine.

MECHANICAL DAMAGE
Symptoms: May be caused by a foreign object in the combustion chamber or the piston striking an incorrect reach (too long) plug. Causes a dead cylinder and could result in piston damage.
Recommendation: Repair the mechanical damage. Remove the foreign object from the engine and/or install the correct reach plug.

Chapter 5 Clutch

Refer to Chapter 13 for specifications and information applicable to 1984 and later models

Contents

Specifications

Type	Single dry plate, diaphragm spring with cable actuation
Clutch diameter	200.0 mm (7.87 in)
Clutch pedal height	
Left-hand drive	149.5 to 155.5 mm (5.89 to 6.12 in)
Right-hand drive	164.5 to 170.5 mm (6.48 to 6.71 in)
Pedal free movement	11.0 to 16.0 mm (0.43 to 0.63 in)
Release lever plug	2.0 to 3.0 mm (0.08 to 0.12 in)

Torque wrench settings	Nm	lbf ft
Clutch cover bolts	20	15

1 General description

The clutch is of single dry plate type with a diaphragm spring.

The clutch is cable operated and the release bearing is of sealed ball type.

The clutch driven plate is located between the flywheel and the clutch pressure plate and it can slide on splines on the gearbox input shaft. When the clutch is engaged, the diapragm spring forces the pressure plate to grip the driven plate against the flywheel and drive is transmitted from the crankshaft through the driven plate to the gearbox input shaft. On disengaging the clutch the pressure plate is lifted to release the driven plate with the result that the drive to the gearbox is disconnected.

The clutch is operated by a foot pedal suspended under the facia and a cable connected to the clutch release lever mounted on the clutch bellhousing. Depressing the pedal causes the release lever to move the thrust bearing against the release fingers of the diaphragm spring in the pressure plate assembly. The spring is sandwiched between two rings which act as fulcrums. As the centre of the spring is moved in, the periphery moves out to lift the pressure plate and disengage the clutch. The reverse takes place when the pedal is released.

As wear takes place on the driven plate with usage, the foot pedal free movement will increase. Adjust periodically as described in the next Section.

2 Clutch – adjustment

1   At the intervals specified in Routine Maintenance check the clutch pedal and cable adjustment in the following way.

2   First check the height of the top surface of the pedal above the metal surface of the floor. This should be as shown in Specifications at the beginning of this Chapter according to LH or RH steering.

3   Where adjustment is required, alter the position of the pedal stop bolt after releasing its locknut.

4   Now gently depress the pedal with the fingers until the pedal becomes hard to depress indicating that the release bearing is in contact with the fingers of the diaphragm spring. Measure this free movement. If it is not approximately 12.7 mm (0.5 in) turn the cable adjuster at the engine compartment rear bulkhead (photo).

3 Clutch cable – renewal

1   Slacken the clutch cable by turning the cable adjuster on the bulkhead until the cable can be detached from the end of the release lever (photo).

2   Working inside the vehicle, remove the facia panel lower cover to give access to the pedals.

3   Remove the heater duct.

4   Disconnect the clutch cable from the pedal arm.

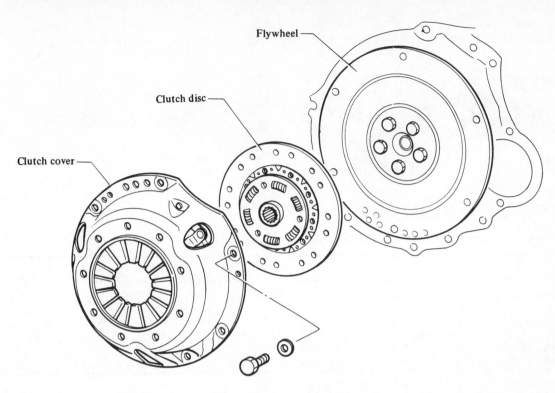

Flywheel

Clutch disc

Clutch cover

Fig. 5.1 Clutch components (Sec 1)

2.4 Clutch cable adjuster at engine bulkhead

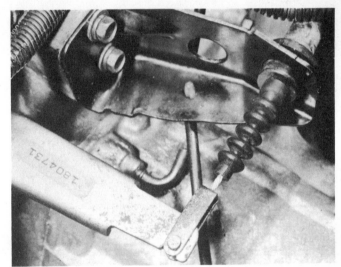

3.1 Clutch cable at release lever

5   Remove the two screws which hold the cable adjuster plate to the engine compartment bulkhead and then remove the cable by withdrawing it through the hole in the bulkhead.
6   Refit the new cable by reversing the removal operations.
7   Apply grease to both cable end fittings.
8   Adjust as described in the preceding Section.

6   Tap out the shaft, lower the pedal and disconnect the return spring.
7   The pedal bushes can be renewed.
8   Reassembly and refitting are reversals of removal and dismantling. Apply grease to the pivot shaft and cable end fitting and adjust as described in Section 2.

4   Clutch pedal – removal and refitting

1   Slacken the clutch cable by turning the bulkhead adjuster.
2   Remove the facia panel lower cover.
3   Remove the heater duct.
4   Disconnect the cable from the clutch pedal.
5   Remove the pin and nut from the pedal pivot shaft.

5   Clutch – removal

1   Overhaul of the clutch will normally be indicated as imminent when slipping is noticed (see Fault diagnosis).
2   Unless the complete engine/transmission is being removed for major overhaul, access to the clutch is obtained by removing the transmission (Chapter 6) leaving the engine in place.

5

7.3 Clutch release bearing

Fig. 5.2 Clutch release bearing (Sec 7)

3   With the transmission removed, unscrew the clutch cover bolts, one half turn at a time working in diametrically opposite sequence.
4   As soon as the point is reached where the bolts can be unscrewed with the fingers, support the cover and then remove the bolts completely.
5   Withdraw the cover and catch the driven plate. There is only need to mark the relationship of the cover to the flywheel if the cover is to be used again.

6   Clutch – inspection

1   In the normal course of events, clutch dismantling and reassembly involves simply fitting a new clutch pressure plate, driven plate and release bearing. Under no circumstances should the diaphragm spring clutch unit be dismantled. If a fault develops in the pressure plate assembly, a new or exchange replacement unit must be fitted.
2   Do not attempt to reline a driven plate yourself, it is just not worth it but obtain a new component. The necessity for renewing the plate will be apparent if the lining material has worn down to the rivets or the linings are oil stained. If the latter, rectify the faulty engine or transmission oil seal which must be the cause. The driven plate may also have broken torsion springs or worn hub splines.
3   If a new clutch is being fitted, it is false economy not to renew the release bearing at the same time (see Section 7). This will preclude having to replace it at a later date.
4   Check the machined faces of the flywheel and the pressure plate. If either is badly grooved it should be machined until smooth, or replaced with a new item. If the pressure plate is cracked or split it must be renewed.

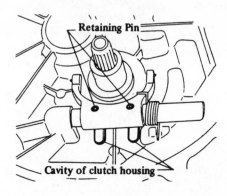

Fig. 5.3 Release fork retaining pins (Sec 8)

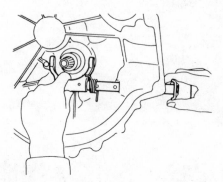

Fig. 5.4 Removing release shaft (Sec 8)

7   Clutch release bearing – renewal

1   Prise off the release bearing spring clips and pull the bearing from its guide sleeve.
2   Apply molybdenum disulphide grease to the groove in the bearing sleeve.
3   Make sure that the spring clips are in position on the bearing and then push the bearing fully home on its sleeve until the clips are heard to 'click' (photo).

8   Clutch release fork and shaft – removal and refitting

1   Remove the release bearing as previously described.
2   Turn the release shaft until the fork retaining pins can be driven out into the small recesses in the face of the clutch housing. Drive out the pins.

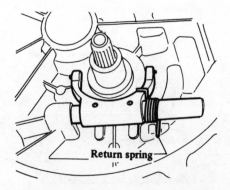

Fig. 5.5 Release fork return spring (Sec 8)

8.3 Fitting clutch release lever to bellhousing

8.4A Clutch release fork outer roll pin

8.4B Clutch release fork inner roll pin

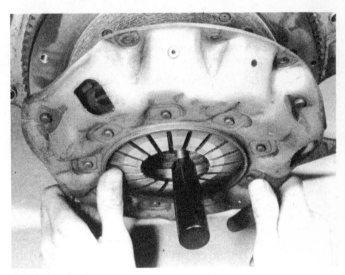

9.6 Fitting clutch cover

9.7 Clutch driven plate aligned

3   Withdraw the shaft from the fork and take off the return spring (photo).

4   Refitting of the components is a reversal of removal. Apply grease to the cross-shaft bushes and make sure that the return spring is correctly located. Use new double roll pins (photos).

9   Clutch – refitting

1   Make sure that the friction faces of the flywheel and pressure plate are clean. Use solvent to remove any protective grease.

2   Hold the driven plate against the flywheel so that the greater projecting boss is towards the flywheel, and the spring hub assembly faces away from the flywheel.

3   Offer up the clutch cover and locate it on its dowels.

4   Screw in the clutch cover screws evenly, but only finger tight at this stage.

5   The clutch driven plate must now be centralised in order that the transmission input shaft will be able to pass through the splined hub of the plate when the transmission is being connected to the engine.

6   Although the front end of the gearbox input shaft is not supported in the bush in the centre of the flywheel mounting flange, the bush can be used to engage a clutch alignment tool (photo).

7   Pass the clutch alignment tool through the splined hub of the driven plate and engage the end of the tool in the pilot bearing in the

end of the crankshaft flange. This will have the effect of sliding the driven plate sideways and so centralising it so that the transmission input shaft will pass through it without obstruction.

8   Clutch alignment tools can be purchased from motor accessory stores or one can be made up from a length of dowelling or rod using tape wound around it to match the diameter of the splined hole in the hub of the driven plate.

9   Once the alignment tool is an easy sliding fit in the hub, tighten the clutch cover bolts to the specified torque. Remove the tool (photo).

10   Refit the transmission as described in Chapter 6.

10   Fault diagnosis – clutch

Symptom	Reason(s)
Judder when taking up drive	Loose engine or gearbox mountings Badly worn friction surfaces or contaminated with oil Worn splines on gearbox input shaft or driven plate hub
*Clutch spin (failure to disengage) so that gears cannot be meshed	Incorrect release bearing to diaphragm spring finger clearance Driven plate sticking on input shaft splines due to rust. May occur after vehicle standing idle for long period Damaged or misaligned pressure plate assembly
Clutch slip (increase in engine speed does not result in increase in vehicle road speed – particularly on gradients)	Incorrect release bearing to diaphragm spring finger clearance Friction surfaces worn out or oil contaminated
Noise evident on depressing clutch pedal	Dry, worn or damaged release bearing Insufficient pedal free travel Weak or broken pedal return spring Weak or broken clutch release lever return spring Excessive play between driven plate hub splines and input shaft splines
Noise evident as clutch pedal released	Distorted driven plate Broken or weak driven plate cushion coil springs Insufficient pedal free travel Weak or broken clutch pedal return spring Weak or broken release lever return spring Distorted or worn input shaft Release bearing loose on retainer hub

*This condition may also be due to the driven plate being rusted to the flywheel or pressure plate. It may be possible to free it by applying the handbrake, engaging top gear, depressing the clutch pedal and operating the starter motor. If really badly corroded, then the engine will not turn over, but in the majority of cases the driven plate will free. Once the engine starts, increase its speed and slip the clutch several times to clear the rust deposits.

Chapter 6 Manual transmission

Refer to Chapter 13 for specifications and information applicable to 1984 and later models

Contents

Specifications

Type .... Transversely mounted with four-or five-speeds and reverse. Synchromesh on all forward gears, floor-mounted gearchange

Designation
Four-speed RN4F31A
Five-speed RS5F31A

Ratios (except N. America)
1st .... 3.333 : 1
2nd .... 1.955 : 1
3rd .... 1.286 : 1
4th .... 0.902 : 1
5th .... 0.733 : 1
Reverse .... 3.417 : 1
Final drive .... 3.650 : 1

Ratios (N. America)
1st .... 3.063 : 1
2nd .... 1.826 : 1
3rd .... 1.207 : 1
4th .... 0.902 : 1
5th .... 0.733 : 1
Reverse .... 3.417 : 1
Final drive .... 3.550 : 1

Lubrication
Type/specification .... Hypoid gear oil, viscosity SAE 80W/90, to API GL4 (Duckhams Hypoid 80)

Capacity:
  Four-speed .... 2.6 litres, 4.6 Imp pts, 2.7 US qts
  Five-speed .... 2.7 litres, 4.8 Imp pts, 2.8 US qts

Torque wrench settings

	Nm	lbf ft
Clutch bellhousing to engine	20	15
Clutch bellhousing to casing	20	15
Circular cover plate to transmission casing	8	6
Input shaft bearing retainer	20	15
5th/reverse detent plug	24	18
Crownwheel bolts	85	62
Oil filler/level plug	32	24
Oil drain plug	32	24
Reverse lamp switch	28	21
Neutral switch	28	21
Left-hand mounting bracket to body frame	50	37
Rear mounting bracket to bodyframe	50	37
Rear mounting to transmission	35	26
Gearchange support rod to transmission	30	22
Gearchange control rod to transmission	8	6
Front mounting bracket to bodyframe	50	37
Front suspension top mounting nuts	23	17
Suspension lower balljoint to track control arm	60	44
Roadwheel nuts	95	70

1 General description

The manual transmission is of four or five-speed type, depending upon the model. On both transmissions, top gear is of overdrive type.

Synchromesh is provided on all forward gears and gear selection is by means of a floor-mounted control lever.

The transmission is mounted transversely in line with the engine. Power is transmitted from the clutch through an input shaft and mainshaft to the final drive/differential which is incorporated within the transmission casing.

The four and five-speed units are so similar that their overhaul is not described separately in this Chapter as it is assumed that owners of four-speed models will be able to ignore reference to a 5th speed gear in the operations listed.

2 Maintenance

1   At the intervals specified in Routine Maintenance check the transmission oil level. Do this by removing the filler/level plug using a $\frac{1}{2}$ in drive extension (photo).

2   If oil just starts to dribble out then the oil level is correct. If it does not, pour oil of the specified type into the hole to raise the level. Refit the plug (photo).

3   Although the manufacturers only advise changing the transmission oil if the vehicle is used for trailer towing or particularly arduous duties, it is recommended that the oil is renewed at the intervals specified in Routine Maintenance. This will ensure that metal particles which are held in suspension in the oil are removed. The original oil will also have lost much of the effectiveness of its additives.

4   The transmission oil should be drained hot by removing both the drain plug and the filler/level plug. Wipe the metal particles from the magnetic drain plug (photos).

3 Gear lever – removal, refitting and adjustment

1   Remove the gear lever knob. Do this by covering the knob with a piece of thick rag and then hold it with an adjustable pair of grips and twist and pull.

2   Working under the vehicle, remove the exhaust pipe shield.

3   Disconnect both the gearchange control rod and the support rod from the transmission.

4   Remove the control bracket bolts and then remove the gear lever.

5   Refit by reversing the removal operations, but on completion, carry out the following adjustment.

6   Release the stop plate bolts and select 1st gear.

7   Adjust the clearance between the control rod and the stop plate until a 1.0 mm (0.039 in) feeler blade is a sliding fit.

8   Push the gear lever knob onto the lever having applied some quick setting adhesive to hold it in position.

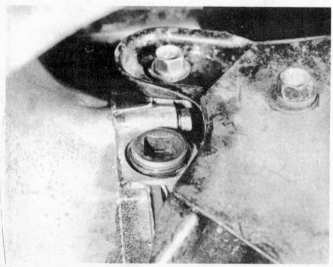
2.1 Transmission filler/level plug

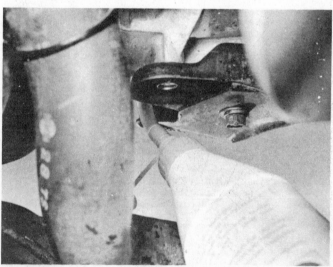
2.2 Filling transmission

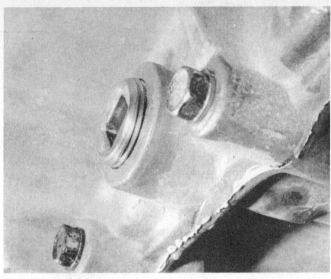

2.4A Transmission drain plug

2.4B Drain plug magnet

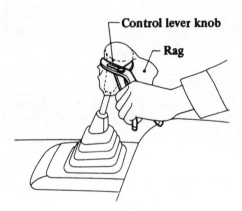

Fig. 6.1 Removing gear lever knob (Sec 3)

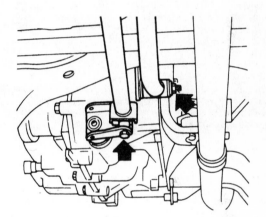

Fig. 6.2 Gearchange support rod and control rod bolts at transmission (Sec 3)

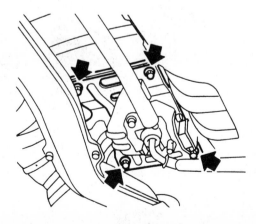

Fig. 6.3 Control bracket bolts (Sec 3)

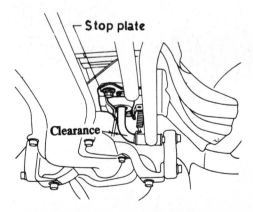

Fig. 6.4 Gearchange control rod to stop plate clearance (Sec 3)

6

114

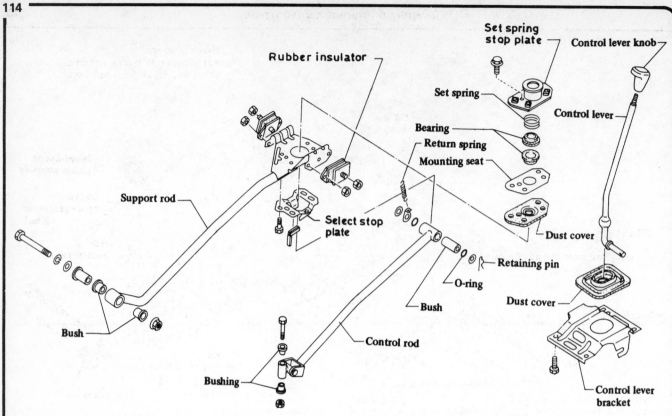

Fig. 6.5 Gearchange linkage components (Sec 4)

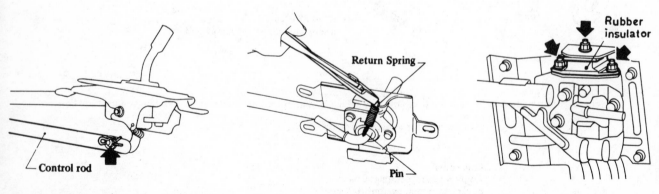

Fig. 6.6 Gearchange control rod pivot pin (Sec 4)

Fig. 6.7 Disconnecting return spring (Sec 4)

Fig. 6.8 Control lever bracket nuts (Sec 4)

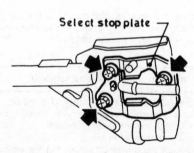

Fig. 6.9 Stop plate bolts (Sec 4)

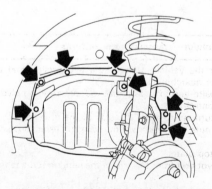

Fig. 6.10 Inner wing shield screws (Sec 5)

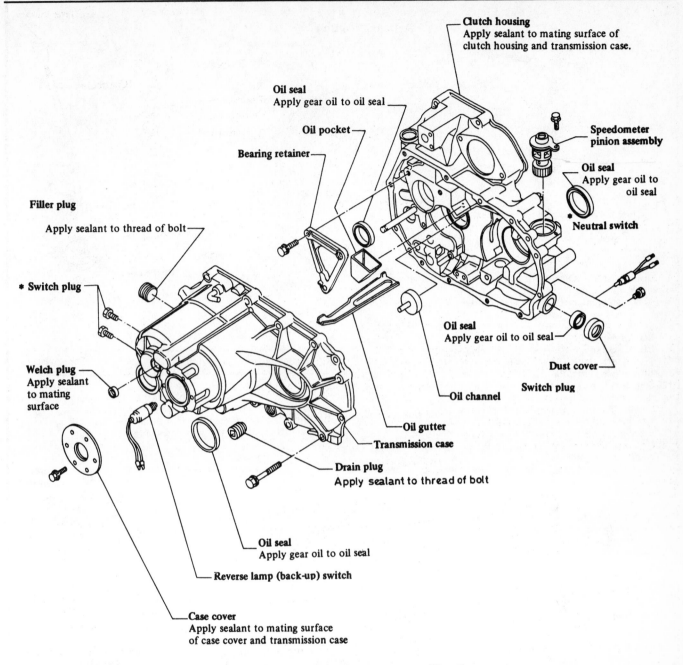

Clutch housing
Apply sealant to mating surface of
clutch housing and transmission case.

Oil seal
Apply gear oil to oil seal

Oil pocket

Bearing retainer

**Speedometer
pinion assembly**

Oil seal
Apply gear oil to
oil seal

Neutral switch

Filler plug

Apply sealant to thread of bolt

* **Switch plug**

Welch plug
Apply sealant
to mating
surface

Oil seal
Apply gear oil to oil seal

Dust cover

Switch plug

Oil channel

Oil gutter

Transmission case

Drain plug
Apply sealant to thread of bolt

Oil seal
Apply gear oil to oil seal

Reverse lamp (back-up) switch

Case cover
Apply sealant to mating surface
of case cover and transmission case

Fig. 6.11 Transmission casing components (Sec 6)

4 Gearchange linkage – removal and refitting

1 Working under the vehicle, remove the pin, washer and O-ring from the end of the gearchange control rod.
2 From the opposite end of the control rod unscrew the pivot bolt.
3 Remove the control rod.
4 Detach the return spring from the side of the stop plate.
5 Unscrew the nuts and remove the control lever bracket and insulator.
6 Remove the stop plate.
7 Remove the pivot bolt from the end of the support rod and remove the rod.
8 Check all components for wear and renew if necessary.
9 The flexible bush can be renewed by pressing the old one out of the control rod and pressing in the new. Alternatively, use a bolt, nut, washers and distance piece to draw out the old bush and insert the new one.

10 Refitting is a reversal of removal, but apply grease to all friction surfaces and make sure that the control rod retaining pin has its looped end towards the front of the vehicle.

5 Transmission – removal and refitting

1 Disconnect the battery, remove the holding clamp and lift the battery from the engine compartment. Remove the support tray.
2 Remove the coolant expansion tank.
3 Drain the transmission oil.
4 Disconnect the driveshafts from the transmission as described in Chapter 1, Section 13, paragraphs 25 to 28.
5 Extract the screws and remove the protective panel from the lower part of the inner wing.
6 Disconnect the gearchange control and support rods at the transmission end.

6

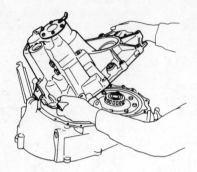

Fig. 6.12 Withdrawing transmission casing (Sec 6)

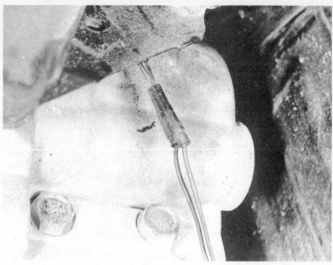

5.11 Reversing lamp wire connector

7   Disconnect the exhaust downpipe from the manifold and the exhaust system front mounting.
8   Unbolt and remove the cover plate from the front lower face of the flywheel housing.
9   Refer to Chapter 5 and disconnect the clutch operating cable from the clutch release lever.
10   Disconnect the speedometer drive cable from the transmission.
11   Disconnect the electrical leads from the reversing lamp and neutral switches (photo).
12   Support the engine on a jack placed under the sump pan using a wooden block as an insulator.
13   Support the transmission in a similar way.
14   Disconnect the leads and unbolt and remove the starter motor.
15   Disconnect the transmission mounting bolts.
16   Unscrew and remove the bolts which connect the flywheel housing flange to the engine.
17   Withdraw the transmission from the engine in a downward direction not allowing its weight to hang upon the input shaft while it is engaged in the clutch driven plate hub.
18   Refitting is a reversal of removal, but if the clutch has been dismantled, make sure that the driven plate has been centralised as described in Chapter 5 before offering up the transmission.
19   Adjust the clutch and refill the transmission with the specified oil.
20   Tighten the transmission mountings to the specified torque after the weight of the engine and transmission are on them.

6   Transmission – dismantling

1   With the transmission removed from the vehicle, clean away external dirt using a water-soluble solvent or paraffin and a stiff brush. Remove the mounting brackets, noting their location.
2   Drain the transmission oil if not drained previously.
3   With the unit standing on the flange of the clutch bellhousing, unscrew the casing to bellhousing bolts and withdraw the casing from the bellhousing. On five-speed units, tilt the casing slightly as it is withdrawn, to prevent the selector fork jamming inside the casing. If the casing is stuck, tap it off carefully, to break the joint, using a plastic hammer.

Transmission casing
4   Unscrew and remove the reverse lamp switch also neutral switch (N. American models).
5   Remove the oil trough.
6   If the input shaft rear bearing is to be renewed, remove the very

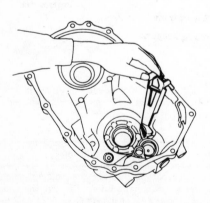

Fig. 6.13 Removing the oil trough (Sec 6)

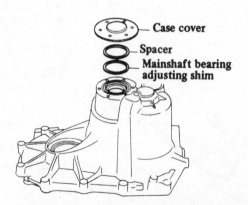

Case cover
Spacer
Mainshaft bearing adjusting shim

Fig. 6.14 Mainshaft bearing adjusting components (Sec 6)

6.6A Input shaft rear bearing welch plug

6.6B Input shaft bearing

6.8 Differential bearing outer track

small welch plug from the transmission casing. Do this by drilling a hole in the plug and then screw in a self-tapping screw. The screw will probably force out the plug or its head can be used to lever it out (photo).

7   Unbolt the circular cover from the casing and take out the spacer and the mainshaft bearing adjusting shim. If the mainshaft bearing is to be renewed, drive out the old outer track and fit the new one.

8   If the differential side bearings are to be renewed, drive the bearing outer track from the transmission casing. A new oil seal will be required (photo).

Clutch housing

9   The clutch housing will have been left standing with the geartrains projecting from it when the transmission casing was drawn off.

10   Withdraw the selector shaft out of the 3rd, 4th and 5th selector forks. Extract the coil spring from the end of the shaft.

11   Remove the 5th, 3rd and 4th selector forks. Retain the plastic slides from the forks. Do not lose the rectangular bushes located in the fork arm cut-outs.

12   Remove the control bracket with 1st/2nd selector fork. Take care not to lose the small 5th speed detent ball and spring. Extract the

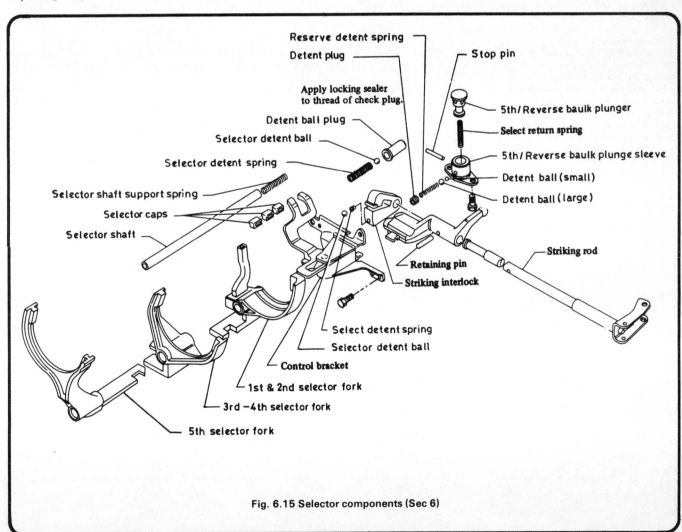

Fig. 6.15 Selector components (Sec 6)

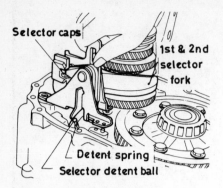

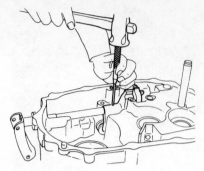

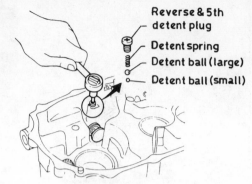

Fig. 6.16 Control bracket and 1st/2nd selector fork (Sec 6)

Fig. 6.17 Removing selector dog roll pin (Sec 6)

Fig. 6.18 Unscrewing 5th/reverse detent plug (Sec 6)

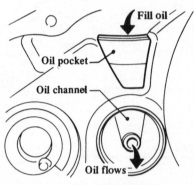

Fig. 6.19 Removing 5th/reverse interlock plunger (Sec 6)

Fig. 6.20 Plastic oil channel and pocket (Sec 6)

larger coil spring, sleeve and ball from the remote control selector rod hole (photo).

13 Remove the screws from the triangular-shaped bearing retainer. One of these screws may be of Torx type and will require a special bit to unscrew it. Hold the reverse idler gear up while the screw is undone. Remove the spacer from the reverse idler shaft. The bearing retainer can only be removed if the input shaft bearing is first removed.

14 Turn the clutch housing on its side and remove the mainshaft assembly. Remove the input shaft assembly by tapping the end of the shaft with a plastic-faced or copper hammer. The reverse idler gear will come off its shaft as the input shaft is released. Note the tooth leads are at the top.

15 Take out the final drive/differential.

16 If the plastic oil pocket must be removed then the bearing outer

track which retains it must first be drawn out using a suitable extractor which has thin claws. Extract the small retaining bolt and remove the speedometer drivegear.

17 Drive the roll pin from the selector rod dog then withdraw the rod, dog and interlock. When removing the rod, take care not to damage the oil seal lips.

18 Unscrew 5th/reverse detent plug which will require a Torx type bit and then extract the spring and ball.

19 Remove 5th/reverse baulk plunger assembly the screws again being of Torx type. Extract the smaller detent ball. The O-ring seal should be renewed at reassembly (photo).

20 Remove the clutch release shaft, bearing and lever as described in Chapter 5.

21 Remove the plastic oil channel from the transmission casing.

6.12 Control bracket

6.19 Extracting 5th/reverse baulk plunger screw

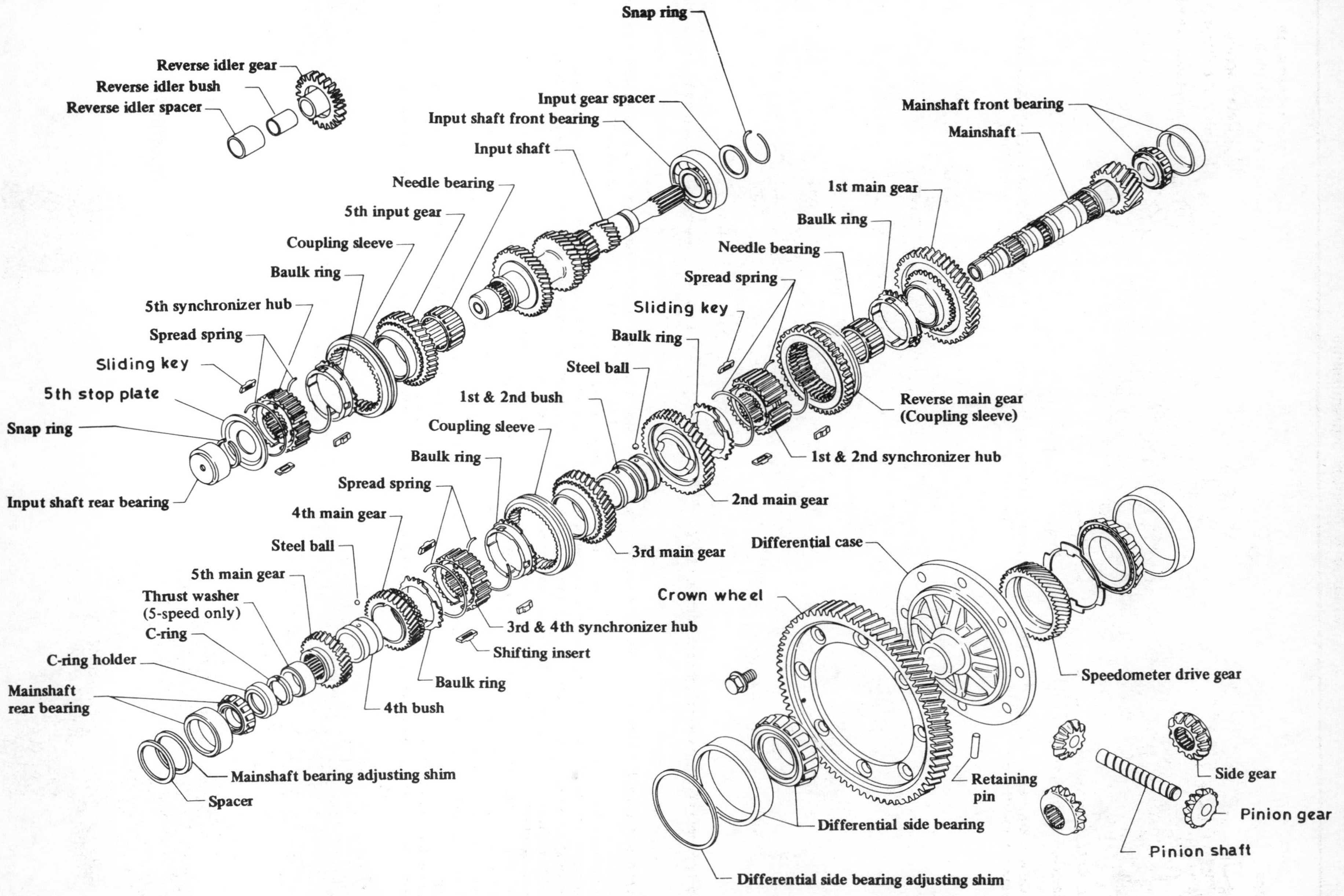

Fig. 6.21 Geartrain components (Sec 6)

6

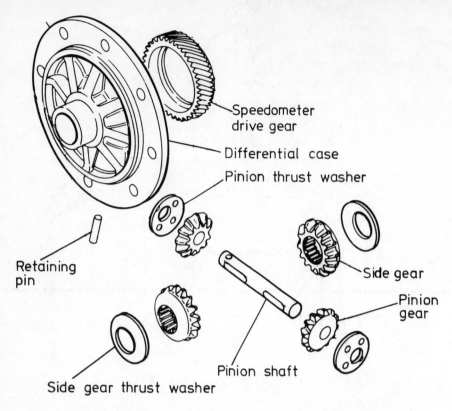

Speedometer drive gear

Differential case

Pinion thrust washer

Retaining pin

Side gear

Pinion gear

Side gear thrust washer

Pinion shaft

Fig. 6.22 Later type differential components showing gear thrust washers (Sec 6)

5th stop plate

Snap ring

Fig. 6.23 Extracting 5th speed gear circlip (Sec 6)

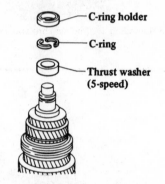

C-ring holder

C-ring

Thrust washer (5-speed)

Fig. 6.24 Mainshaft (5th speed gear) thrust washer and C-rings (Sec 6)

Input shaft

22 On 5th speed units, measure and record the input shaft 5th speed gear endfloat. Extract the circlip and 5th speed gear stop plate.
23 Remove the 5th speed gear with synchroniser and the split needle bearing from inside the gear.
24 The input shaft cannot be dismantled further except to draw off the front bearing after having first extracted the retaining circlip and taken off the spacer. If a bearing puller is not available, support the bearing and drive the shaft from it (photos).

Mainshaft

25 Before dismantling the mainshaft, check and record the endfloat of the gears.
26 Remove the bearing inner races from the front and rear ends of the shaft. Use either a two-legged puller or press the shaft out of the bearings.

27 On five-speed units, remove the C-ring retainer, the C-rings and the thrust washer. Remove the 5th speed gear, a puller will be required for this (photo).
28 Remove 4th speed gear, the gear bush and steel locking ball.
29 Remove the baulk ring.
30 Remove the 3rd/4th synchro unit.
31 Remove 3rd speed gear.
32 Remove 2nd and 3rd gear bush.
33 Remove the steel locking ball.
34 Remove the 2nd speed gear.
35 Remove the baulk ring.
36 Remove 1st/2nd synchro unit with reverse gear (straight cut teeth on synchro sleeve) together with 1st speed gear as an assembly. The synchro hub is tight on the shaft and the best way to remove the assembly is to support under 1st speed gear and drive the shaft downward using a copper-faced hammer (photo).
37 Remove 1st speed gear split needle bearing (photo).

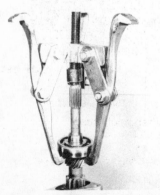

6.24A Drawing off input shaft front bearing

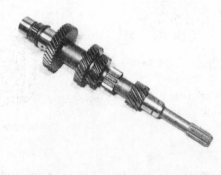

6.24B Input shaft stripped

6.27 Removing mainshaft 5th speed gear

6.36 Removing 1st/2nd synchro and 1st speed gear

6.37 Mainshaft stripped

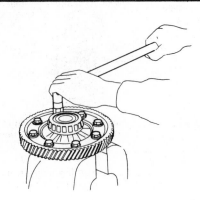

Fig. 6.25 Unscrewing a crownwheel bolt (Sec 6)

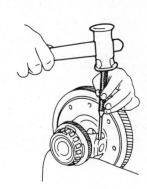

Fig. 6.26 Removing pinion shaft roll pin (Sec 6)

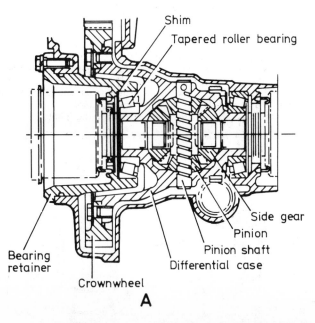

Shim
Tapered roller bearing

Side gear
Pinion
Pinion shaft
Differential case

Bearing retainer
Crownwheel

A

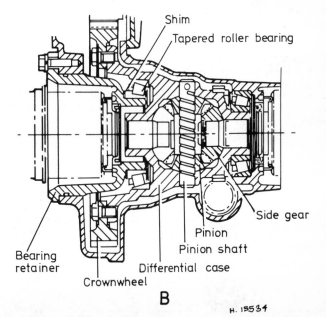

Shim
Tapered roller bearing

Side gear
Pinion
Pinion shaft
Differential case

Bearing retainer
Crownwheel

B

H. 15534

Fig. 6.27 Differential side gear taper roller bearing angle (Sec 6)

A   Earlier models   B   Later models

6

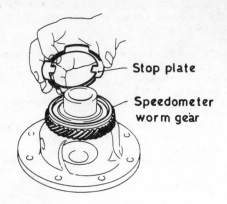

Fig. 6.28 Speedometer drivegear and stop plate (Sec 6)

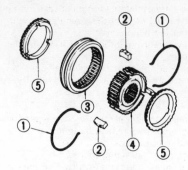

Fig. 6.29 Synchroniser components (Sec 7)

1	Spring	4	Hub
2	Sliding key	5	Baulk ring
3	Sleeve		

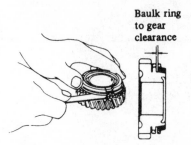

Fig. 6.30 Checking synchro baulk ring to cone clearance (Sec 7)

Differential/final drive

38 Unbolt the crownwheel from the differential case.

39 Using a punch, drive out the pinion shaft lock pin and withdraw the shaft.

40 Remove the pinion and side gears.

41 Draw off the differential side bearing races, noting exactly how the taper of the rollers is set.

42 Remove the speedometer drivegear stop plate and the gear.

7 Transmission components – inspection

1 With the transmission completely dismantled, clean all components and inspect them for wear or damage.

2 Check the gears for chipped teeth and their bushes for wear.

3 Check the shafts for scoring or grooving.

4 Check the bearings for wear by spinning them with the fingers. If they shake or rattle then they must be renewed.

5 Wear in the synchronisers will usually be suspected before dismantling as a result of noisy gear changing, or to the fact that the synchro-action could be easily 'beaten' during rapid gearchanging.

6 Even if the synchro is operating quietly, it is worthwhile checking the units in the following way at time of major overhaul.

7 Extract the spreader springs (1), remove the sliding keys (2) and then push the hub (4) from the sleeve (3), but not before having marked the components with quick drying paint to ensure that their relative position to each other is maintained at reassembly.

8 Check the synchro components for wear or deformation. Place the baulk ring on its cone and twist it to ensure good contact between the surfaces. Using a feeler blade, check that the gap between gear and baulk ring is not less than 0.7 mm (0.028 in). If it is, renew the baulk ring.

9 When reassembling the synchro units, make sure that the spreader springs run in opposite directions when viewed from each side of the synchro and that the spring ends do not engage in the same sliding key.

10 It is recommended that all oil seals are renewed at time of major overhaul. These include those for the clutch cross-shaft, differential side bearings, gearchange remote control rod and the input shaft.

11 The oil seals for the differential side bearings and the gearchange remote control rod can be renewed without having to remove the transmission from the vehicle, should anything more than the slightest seepage of oil be observed during normal operation of the vehicle (photo).

Fig. 6.31 Fitted direction of synchro springs – (Sec 7)

8 Transmission – reassembly

Differential/final drive

1 Fit the speedometer worm drivegear and its stop plate to the differential case.

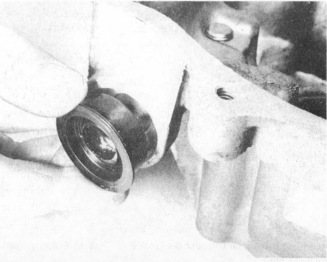

7.11 Gearchange remote control oil seal

2   Press on the differential bearing inner races (photo).
3   Into the differential case fit the pinion gears with thrust washers (later models) and the pinion shaft.
4   Drive in a new pinion shaft roll pin, making sure that it is flush with the differential case.
5   Clean the threads of the crownwheel bolts and apply thread locking fluid, then screw them in and tighten to the specified torque.

Mainshaft
6   Oil all components liberally as they are reassembled.
7   Fit 1st speed gear needle bearing (photo).
8   Fit 1st speed gear (photo).
9   Fit 1st speed gear baulk ring (photo).
10 Fit 1st/2nd synchro unit with reverse. Tap the synchro hub down the mainshaft using a piece of tubing, but hold the synchro together with the hand in case the vibration makes it fall apart (photo).

11 Locate the steel lock ball in its hole in the shaft. On no account place the ball in the hole in the shaft groove (photo).
12 Fit 2nd speed gear baulk ring.
13 Fit 2nd speed gear.
14 Fit 2nd/3rd speed gear bush, turning it slowly to engage its cut-out with the lockball (photo).
15 Fit 3rd speed gear (photo).
16 Fit the baulk ring (photo).
17 Fit 3rd/4th synchro unit so that the engraved dashes on the sleeve are visible (photo).
18 Using thick grease, stick the second (4th gear bush) lock ball in its shaft hole (not the hole in the shaft groove) (photo).
19 Fit the baulk ring.
20 Fit 4th speed gear bush, turning it slowly to engage its cut-out with the lock ball (photo).
21 Fit 4th speed gear (photo).

8.2 Differential bearing inner race

8.7 Mainshaft 1st speed gear split needle bearing

8.8 1st speed gear fitted to mainshaft

8.9 Mainshaft 1st speed gear baulk ring

8.10 1st/2nd synchro, with reverse fitted to mainshaft

8.11 Gear bush locking ball

8.14 2nd speed gear and bush being fitted to mainshaft

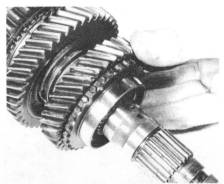
8.15 Fitting 3rd speed gear to mainshaft

8.16 3rd speed gear baulk ring fitted to mainshaft

6

8.17 3rd/4th synchro fitted to mainshaft

8.18 4th speed gear locking ball fitted to mainshaft

8.20 Fitting 4th speed gear bush

8.21 Fitting 4th speed gear

8.22 Fitting 5th speed gear

8.23 Fitting thrust washer to 5th speed gear

8.24 C-rings

8.25 C-ring retainer

8.26 Mainshaft bearing inner race

8.27 Checking gear endfloat

8.28 Input shaft split needle roller bearing

8.29 Fitting input shaft 5th speed gear

8.30 Input shaft 5th speed gear baulk ring

8.31 Input shaft 5th speed gear synchro

8.32A Input shaft synchro stop plate

8.32B Input shaft circlip

8.33A Input shaft bearing and retainer

8.33B Input shaft bearing and circlip

8.34A Oil channel

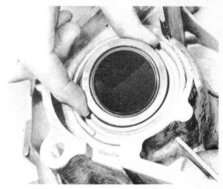

8.34B Oil pocket

8.35A Differential bearing oil seal

22 If the transmission is of five-speed type, fit 5th speed gear. Drive it carefully onto the mainshaft using a piece of tubing (photo).

23 On five-speed models only, fit the thrust washer (photo).

24 Fit the C-rings. These are supplied in various thicknesses to correct gear endfloat (photo).

25 Fit the C-ring retainer (photo).

26 Press on new bearing inner races to both ends of the mainshaft (photo).

27 Using a feeler blade check that the gear endfloat is as recorded at dismantling or within the following tolerances (photo).

1st speed gear	*0.18 to 0.31 mm*
	(0.0071 to 0.0122 in)
2nd, 3rd, 4th speed gear	*0.20 to 0.40 mm*
	(0.0079 to 0.0157 in)
5th speed gear	*0.18 to 0.41 mm*
	(0.0071 to 0.0161 in)

Input shaft

28 Fit the split type needle roller bearing (photo).

29 Fit 5th speed gear (photo).

30 Fit the baulk ring (photo).

31 Fit the synchro unit so that the engraved 'dashes' on the sleeve are visible (photo).

32 To the synchro unit fit the stop plate and the circlip. The circlips are available in various thicknesses to eliminate endfloat (photos).

33 Locate the triangular bearing retainer on the shaft then press on a new shaft front bearing, fit the spacer and use a new circlip (photos).

Clutch housing

34 Fit a new oil channel so that its relieved area is towards the oil pocket when installed (photos).

35 Press or drive in the differential and mainshaft bearing outer tracks into their seats. Fit new differential bearing oil seals (photos).

8.35B Differential bearing outer track and oil seal

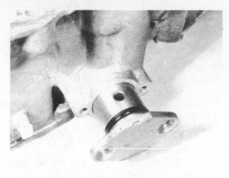

8.37 5th/reverse baulk plunger with O-ring

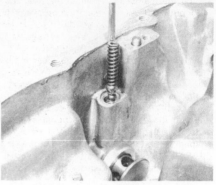

8.38A 5th/reverse baulk plunger balls and spring

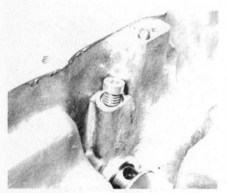

8.38B 5th/reverse baulk plunger screw plug

8.41A Remote control rod outer roll pin

8.41B Remote control rod inner roll pin

8.41C Striking lever and interlock

8.42A Speedometer drivegear pinion

8.42B Speedometer pinion lockbolt

36 Remember that the mainshaft bearing outer track retains the oil pocket, so align the pocket correctly before fitting the bearing track.
37 Fit the 5th/reverse baulk assembly and tighten the Torx type fixing screws. A new O-ring should be used (photo).
38 Fit reverse/5th baulk plunger balls (small one first), the spring and the plug (photos).
39 The force of the reverse baulk plunger should now be checked using a spring balance. On four-speed models, the pull required to move against the detent should be between 5.4 and 7.7 kg (12 to 17 lb). On five-speed models the pull should be between 7.2 and 9.1 kg (16 to 20 lb).
40 The detent force may be increased by changing the detent plug for one of greater length.
41 Using new double roll pins, refit the remote control rod so that the detent notch is downward. Fit the striking lever and interlock (photos).

42 Refit the speedometer drivegear and then screw in the lockbolt (photos).
43 Fit the side gears into the differential case (tapping with a hardwood drift may be required) and retain them with a wire clip or piece of wooden dowel. Some later models have side gear thrust washers (photos).
44 Lower the differential/final drive into position (photo).
45 Fit the input shaft and reverse idler gear simultaneously. The idler gear (marked before removal) should be refitted in its original position. Use a plastic-faced or copper hammer to tap the input shaft fully home in the clutch housing (photo).
46 Fit the spacer to the reverse idler shaft.
47 Fit the triangular-shaped bearing retainer. Apply thread locking fluid to the screw threads and tighten them as tightly as possible (photo).

48 Fit the mainshaft, carefully meshing the gear teeth with those of the input shaft. As the operation proceeds, push both synchro sleeves down and hold' the reverse idler gear up (photo).

49 Fit the bush, the ball and the large coil spring to the hole in the remote control rod housing (photos).

50 Locate 1st/2nd selector fork under the control bracket which itself incorporates reverse selector fork. As the control bracket is bolted into place, make sure that 5th speed detent spring and ball are in the hole in the remote control interlock (photos).

51 Locate the remaining selector forks. The 2nd/3rd fork is the lower one and the 4th/5th fork the upper one. Make sure that the plastic slides are in position in the fork arm cut-outs also the rectangular-shaped metal bushes are in the selector dog cut-outs (photos).

52 Pass the selector shaft through the forks making sure that the coil spring is located in the recess at the lower end of the shaft (photos).

Transmission casing

53 If the differential side bearings were renewed, fit the new bearing outer track now with a new oil seal.

54 If the mainshaft bearing was renewed, fit the new track into the casing now.

55 If the input shaft rear bearing was renewed, tap a new small welch plug into the hole in the casing.

56 Fit the plastic oil trough (photo).

57 Screw in the reverse lamp switch and the neutral switch (where fitted).

58 With the clutch housing standing on the bench with the geartrains vertical, apply jointing compound to the mating faces of the transmission casing and clutch housing.

59 Lower the casing into position over the geartrains. On five-speed units, tilt the casing as necessary to clear the selector fork (photo).

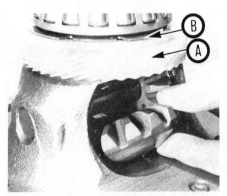

8.43A Fitting differential side gear
A   Speedometer worm gear
B   Lockplate

8.43B Side gear retained with dowel

8.44 Differential/final drive installed

8.45 Fitting input shaft and reverse idler gear

8.47 Bearing retainer (arrowed)

8.48 Fitting mainshaft assembly

8.49A Remote control rod housing bush

8.49B Remote control rod detent spring and ball

8.50A 1st/2nd selector fork

6

8.50B Control bracket located

8.50C 5th speed detent spring and ball

8.50D Control bracket selector fork on reverse idler gear

8.50E 5th speed detent ball (arrowed) held by control bracket

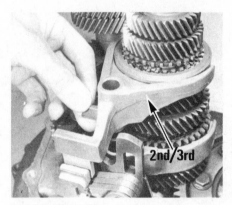

8.51A 2nd/3rd selector fork

8.51B 4th/5th selector fork

8.51C Selector fork arm cut-outs and plastic slides (arrowed)

8.52A Selector shaft and coil spring

8.52B Selector shaft installed

8.56 Plastic oil trough in transmission casing

8.59 Lowering transmission casing into position

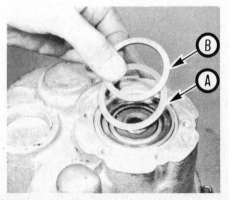

8.61 Mainshaft adjusting shim A and spacer B

60 Fit the connecting bolts and tighten to specified torque.
61 If the mainshaft bearing has not been changed, fit the original adjusting shim and the spacer. If a new bearing has been fitted, refer to Section 10 for details of mainshaft bearing preload adjustment (photo).
62 Apply jointing compound to the edges of the circular cover and bolt it into position on the transmission casing (photo).

9 Final drive – adjustment

1 If any of the following components of the transmission have been renewed during overhaul than you have to take the assembly to your dealer for the final drive to be adjusted to ensure correct crownwheel to pinion meshing and specified bearing preload.

Differential case
Differential side bearing
Clutch housing
Transmission casing

Owing to the need for special tools, this work is not within the scope of the home mechanic.

8.62 Transmission casing circular cover

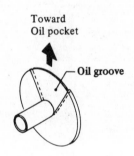

Fig. 6.32 Oil channel (Sec 8)

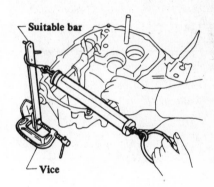

Fig. 6.33 Checking reverse detent torque (Sec 8)

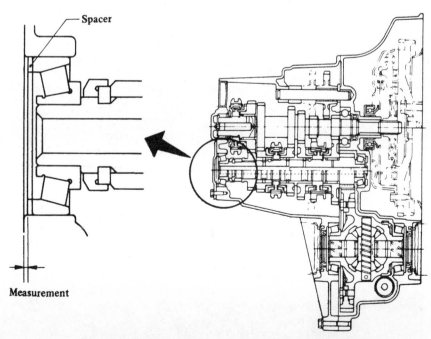

Fig. 6.34 Mainshaft bearing adjustment diagram (Sec 10)

10 Mainshaft bearing preload – adjustment

1   If any of the following components have been renewed during overhaul, then the mainshaft bearing preload must be checked and adjusted.

  Mainshaft
  Mainshaft bearings
  Clutch housing
  Transmission casing

2   Remove the circular cover from the transmission. To carry out the adjustment, measure between the machined face of the transmission casing and the surface of the spacer. A shim should now be selected which is 0.2 mm (0.008 in) thicker than the dimension just taken.
3   Fit the spacer, the selected shim and the cover and check that the input shaft turns smoothly with 4th gear selected. A special tool is available at Datsun/Nissan dealers (KV 38105900) which engages in the side gears and gives a torque reading for rotation of the final drive when 4th gear is selected.
4   The correct turning torque should be between 7.4 and 10.8 Nm (65 to 95 lbf in).

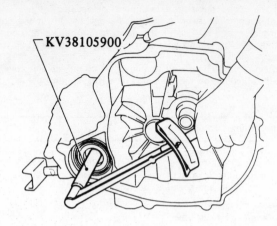

Fig. 6.35 Using special tool to check final drive rotational torque (Sec 10)

11 Fault diagnosis – manual transmission

Symptom	Reason(s)
Weak or ineffective synchromesh	Synchro baulk rings worn, split or damaged Synchromesh units worn, or damaged
Jumps out of gear	Gearchange mechanism worn Synchromesh units badly worn Selector fork badly worn
Excessive noise	Incorrect grade of oil in gearbox or oil level too high Gearteeth excessively worn or damaged Intermediate gears or bushes worn allowing excessive end play Worn bearings
Difficulty in engaging gears	Clutch pedal adjustment incorrect
Noise when cornering	Wheel bearing or driveshaft fault Differential fault

Note: *It is sometimes difficult to decide whether it is worthwhile removing and dismantling the gearbox for a fault which may be nothing more than a minor irritant. Gearboxes which howl, or where the synchromesh can be 'beaten' by a quick gearchange, may continue to perform for a long time in this state. A worn gearbox usually needs a complete rebuild to eliminate noise because the various gears, if re-aligned on new bearings, will continue to howl when different wearing surfaces are presented to each other. The decision to overhaul therefore, must be considered with regard to time and money available, relative to the degree of noise or malfunction that the driver has to suffer.*

two

Chapter 7 Automatic transmission

Refer to Chapter 13 for specifications and information applicable to 1984 and later models

Contents

Specifications

Type .... RN3F01A, three element hydraulic torque converter with two planetary gear sets and final drive and differential

Ratios
1st	2.826 : 1
2nd	1.543 : 1
3rd	1.000 : 1
Reverse	2.364 : 1
Final drive	3.36 : 1

Transmission fluid
Type/specification	Dexron type ATF (Duckhams D-Matic)
Capacity	6.0 litres, 5.25 Imp pints, 6.3 US qts

Torque wrench settings
	Nm	lbf ft
Driveplate to torque converter	100	74
Torque converter housing to engine	55	41
Oil pan bolts	7	5
Brake band adjuster locknut	22	16
Control valve fixing bolts	9	7
Oil filter screw bolts	7	5
Governor shaft fixing bolt	6	4
Fluid cooler pipe union to transmission casing	45	33
Torque converter housing cover plate	20	15

1 General description

The automatic transmission is of fully automatic type and incorporates a three element hydraulic torque converter, two planetary geartrains and the final drive/differential.

Cooling of the hydraulic fluid is carried out by running it through a cooler in the radiator bottom tank.

2 Maintenance

1 Keep the outside of the transmission casing free from dirt and grease.
2 Check the fluid level regularly in the following way.
3 Make sure that the vehicle is standing on a level surface, start the engine and allow it to idle for ten minutes.

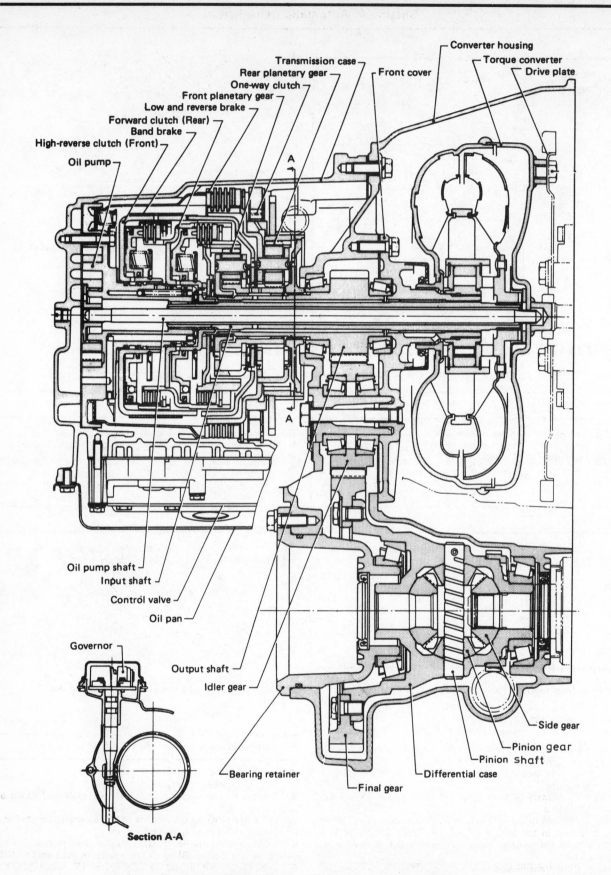

Fig. 7.1 Sectional view of the automatic transmission (Sec 1)

AMBIENT TEMPERATURE	UNIT : mm (in)
30-50°C (86-122°F)	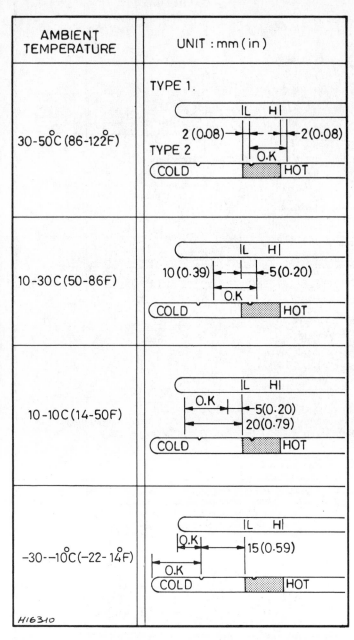
10-30°C (50-86°F)	
10-10°C (14-50°F)	
-30--10°C (-22-14°F)	

H16310

Fig. 7.2 Fluid level range at various ambient temperatures (Sec 2)

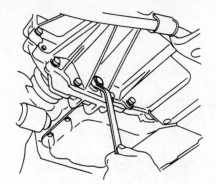

Fig. 7.3 Automatic transmission drain plug (Sec 2)

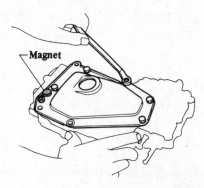

Fig. 7.4 Removing filter screen (Sec 2)

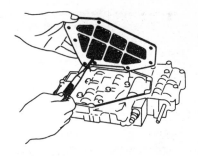

Fig. 7.5 Underside of filter screen (Sec 2)

7

4   With the engine still idling, withdraw the dipstick, wipe it clean, re-insert it and withdraw it for the second time. .
5   The oil level mark should be as shown in the diagram according to ambient temperature.
6   Top up as necessary by pouring oil into the dipstick guide tube. Switch off the engine.
7   Further operations to the automatic transmission should be limited to those described in the following Sections. More extensive work should be left to your dealer as special equipment is needed to overhaul the unit.
8   Renewal of the transmission fluid is not specified by the manufacturers, but if it must be renewed for any reason, remove the drain plug to drain the fluid which should be cool to avoid scalding.
9   Unbolt and remove the oil pan.
10 Inspect the filter screen. If it is clogged or dirty, do not clean it but renew it.
11 Refit the drain plug, oil pan with new gasket and refill with fluid.

3   Automatic transmission – in car adjustment

Kickdown cable
1   Remove the air cleaner.
2   Release the locknuts on the kickdown cable end fitting at the carburettor.
3   Move the cable quadrant to its fully open position and check that the throttle valve plate is also fully open.
4   Now move the end fitting (Q) Fig. 7.7 in the direction (T) and then gently run the locknut (B) up to the bracket in the direction (U).
5   Unscrew the nut (B) and then tighten nut (A), keeping the throttle in the fully open position.
6   The kickdown cable movement can be checked by marking the exposed inner cable with a spot of quick-drying paint and then moving the throttle from the idle to the full throttle position. The paint mark should move through a distance of between 27.4 and 31.4 mm (1.079 and 1.236 mm).

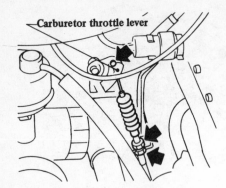

Fig. 7.6 Kickdown cable locknuts at carburettor (Sec 3)

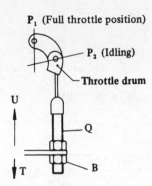

Fig. 7.7 Kickdown cable adjustment diagram (Sec 3)

For key see text

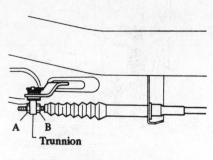

Fig. 7.8 Speed selector control cable at transmission (Sec 3)

A   *Locknut*   B   *Locknut*

	1	2	3	4
N and P ranges	o─o			
P ranges			o─o	

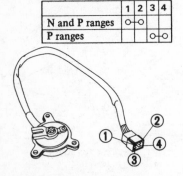

Fig. 7.9 Starter inhibitor switch (Sec 3)

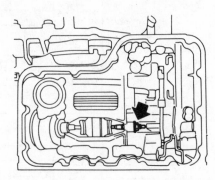

Fig. 7.10 Control valve assembly bolts (Sec 3)

Fig. 7.11 Brake band adjuster and locknut (Sec 3)

Speed selector cable

7   Move the hand control lever to P.
8   Release the locknuts at the transmission end of the cable and then check that the selector lever on the transmission is fully locked in the P detent.
9   Tighten both locknuts at the trunnion on the selector without moving the setting of the lever.
10 Check the adjustment by moving the hand control lever to all positions with the engine running.

Inhibitor switch

11 The inhibitor switch controls the reverse lamps when the selector lever is moved to R and prevents operation of the starter motor unless the selector lever is in N or P.
12 If the inhibitor switch wiring harness plug is disconnected, use a continuity tester to check that there is only continuity when the speed selector lever is in N, P or R.
13 If the test is unsatisfactory, release the switch mounting screws and turn the switch slightly, tighten the screws and re-test. Continue the readjustment until operation is satisfactory. It will be found that with the selector lever in N, the switch setting is correct when a position is found where if the switch is rotated through 1° 30' in either direction, current flows.

Brake band

14 This will only be necessary if indicated after reference to Fault Diagnosis, Section 9.
15 Drain the transmission fluid.
16 Unbolt the oil pan and guard.
17 Unbolt and remove the control valve assembly.
18 An accurate torque wrench will be required to carry out the adjustment satisfactorily.
19 Release the locknut on the brake band adjuster screw and tighten the screw to between 4 and 6 Nm (2.9 and 4.3 lbf ft).
20 Unscrew the adjuster screw $2\frac{1}{2}$ turns exactly and then re-tighten the locknut without moving the screw.

4   Speed selector control cable – removal and refitting

1   Set the selector linkage in P.
2   Pull out the spring pin and disconnect the control cable from the lever on the side of the transmission.
3   Unbolt the cable bracket from the transmission casing.
4   Pull out the spring pin and disconnect the control cable from the base of the hand control lever.
5   Refit by reversing the removal operations, apply grease to the cable end pivot pins and make sure that the spring retaining pins are positioned as shown in the illustration (Fig. 7.13).

5   Kickdown cable – renewal

1   Drain the transmission (Section 2).
2   Remove the guard and oil pan and unbolt the valve control assembly (Section 3).
3   Disconnect the kickdown cable from the carburettor.
4   Disconnect the kickdown cable from the lever within the transmission after unscrewing the gland nut.
5   Fit the new cable by reversing the removal operations and adjust as described in Section 3.
6   Refill the transmission.

6   Governor shaft – removal and refitting

1   This will only be required if after reference to Fault Diagnosis, a fault is indicated in the governor assembly.
2   Disconnect and remove the battery.
3   Release the coolant expansion tank and move it aside.
4   Unbolt and remove the battery mounting bracket.
5   From the transmission, prise off the spring retainer and cap with breather hose and sealing ring.

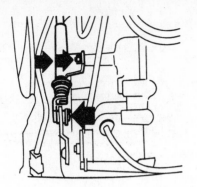

Fig. 7.12 Speed selector cable bracket (Sec 4)

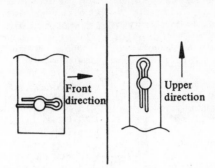

Fig. 7.13 Speed selector cable pivot pin clips (Sec 4)

A   At hand control lever
B   At transmission

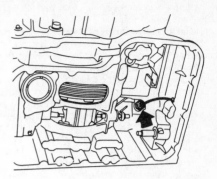

Fig. 7.14 Kickdown cable in transmission (Sec 5)

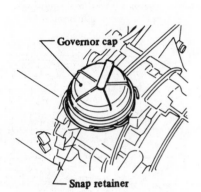

Fig. 7.15 Governor cap and spring retainer (Sec 6)

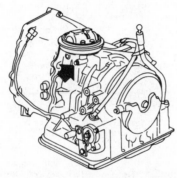

Fig. 7.16 Governor fixing bolt (Sec 6)

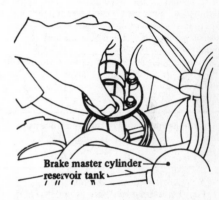

Fig. 7.17 Withdrawing governor (Sec 6)

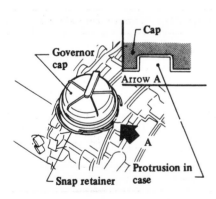

Fig. 7.18 Alignment of governor cap (Sec 6)

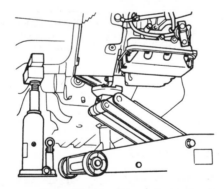

Fig. 7.19 Engine and transmission supported on separate jacks (Sec 8)

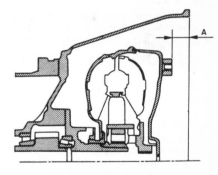

Fig. 7.20 Torque converter 'fully installed' diagram (Sec 8)

A = In excess of 21.1 mm (0.831 in)

6   Unscrew and remove the governor shaft retaining bolt.
7   Withdraw the governor shaft assembly.
8   Refitting is a reversal of removal, but make sure that the notch in the cap is opposite the projection on the casing.

7   Differential bearing oil seals – renewal

1   The oil seals at the differential bearings into which the driveshafts engage can be renewed without removing the transmission.
2   Disconnect the driveshaft as described in Chapter 1, Section 13, paragraphs 25 to 28.
3   Using a suitable claw-type extractor withdraw the oil seal.

4   Apply transmission fluid to the lips of the new seal and drive it squarely into position using a piece of tubing.
5   Reconnect the driveshaft as described in Chapter 1, Section 23, paragraphs 9 to 12.

8   Automatic transmission – removal and refitting

1   Disconnect the battery, raise the vehicle and remove the road-wheels.
2   Drain the transmission fluid and unbolt and remove the engine compartment undershield.
3   Disconnect the driveshafts from the transmission as described in Chapter 1, Section 13, paragraphs 25 to 28.

4   Unbolt and remove the cover plate from the base of the torque converter housing.
5   Mark the relationship of the torque converter to the driveplate with quick-drying paint and then unscrew the converter to driveplate connecting bolts. The crankshaft will have to be turned by means of the crankshaft pulley bolt to bring the connecting bolts into view within the aperture left by removal of the cover plate.
6   Disconnect the speedometer drive cable from the transmission.
7   Disconnect the kickdown cable from the carburettor.
8   Disconnect the speed selector cable from the transmission.
9   Unbolt and remove the shield from the inboard side of the left-hand front wing.
10 Disconnect the exhaust downpipe from the manifold and the transmission bracket.
11 Unbolt and remove the starter motor.
12 Disconnect the oil cooler hoses and plug or cap them.
13 Support the transmission on a trolley jack and unscrew and remove the bolts which connect the torque converter housing to the engine. Support the engine on a second jack.
14 Disconnect the transmission mounting bolts, lower the jack slightly and withdraw the transmission from the engine. Keep the torque converter in full engagement with the fluid pump by pressing it into the torque converter housing during withdrawal of the transmission.
15 Refitting is a reversal of removal, but observe the following points.
16 Check that the torque converter is in full engagement with the fluid pump by measuring between the face of a connecting bolt boss on the torque converter and the surface of the torque converter housing mating flange. This should be in excess of 21.1 mm (0.831 in) to ensure full engagement.
17 Offer the transmission to the engine and make sure that the marks made at dismantling on the driveplate and the torque converter are in alignment.
18 Screw in the driveplate/torque converter connecting bolts and tighten to the specified torque. The crankshaft will have to be turned to gain access to each bolt in turn.
19 Screw in the torque converter housing flange bolts.
20 Raise the jack slightly until the flexible mountings can be connected.
21 Reconnect the fluid cooler hoses.
22 Bolt the starter motor into position.
23 Reconnect the exhaust pipe.
24 Refit the front wing shield.
25 Reconnect the speed selector cable, the speedometer drive cable and the kickdown cable.
26 Fit the cover plate to the base of the torque converter housing.
27 Reconnect the driveshafts as described in Chapter 1, Section 23, paragraphs 9 to 12.
28 Refit the engine compartment undershield.
29 Refit the roadwheels.
30 Connect the battery.
31 Refill the transmission.
32 Check the adjustment of the kickdown cable and the speed selector cable.

9 Fault diagnosis – automatic transmission

Symptom	Reason(s)
Starter operates in other than N or P positions	Incorrectly adjusted inhibitor switch
No drive in R only forward speed ranges	Low fluid level Incorrectly adjusted speed selector cable
No forward drive but operates in R	Low fluid level Incorrectly adjusted speed selector cable Internal fluid passage leak
Excessive creep	Idle speed too high
No creep at all	Low fluid level Incorrectly adjusted speed selector cable Idle speed too low Fluid pump fault
No upshift	Incorrectly adjusted throttle cable or kickdown cable or detent valve Faulty governor Brake band servo fault Brake band requires adjustment
1st to 3rd upshift omitting 2nd	Faulty governor Brake band fault Internal oil passage leak
Shock when upshifting	Incorrectly adjusted kickdown cable Brake band requires adjustment Clutch fault
Slip when upshifting	Low fluid level Incorrectly adjusted throttle or kickdown cable Brake or clutch fault
Poor acceleration or restricted maximum speed	Low fluid level Throttle cable incorrectly adjusted Brake band or clutch fault Fluid pump fault
No downshift	Incorrectly adjusted throttle cable Faulty governor Brake or clutch fault Brake band requires adjustment

Symptom	Reason(s)
No kickdown in 3rd	Kickdown cable incorrectly adjusted or faulty detent valve Faulty governor Brake band requires adjustment Internal fluid passage leak
No drive in any range	Low fluid level Incorrectly adjusted throttle cable Faulty fluid pump Internal fluid passage leak Fault in Park mechanism

7

Chapter 8 Driveshafts, hubs, roadwheels and tyres

Refer to Chapter 13 for specifications and information applicable to 1984 and later models

Contents

Specifications

Type	Open type driveshafts with joint at each end, tapered roller bearings at hubs and pressed steel or light alloy roadwheels
Roadwheel size	5J – 13
Tyre size	165 SR 13 or 185/70 SR 13
Spare tyre (certain territories)	T 125/70 D16
Tyre pressures (cold)	
Front and rear	1.77 bar (26 lbf/in^2)
Hub bearings	
Lubricant type/specification	Multi-purpose lithium-based grease, to NLGI No 2 (Duckhams LB 10)

Torque wrench settings

	Nm	lbf ft
Roadwheel nut	95	70
Lower balljoint nuts	60	44
Driveshaft nut	196 to 275	145 to 203
Hub to disc bolts	50	37
Caliper bolts	95	70
Clamp bolts (strut to stub axle carrier)	100	74
Tie-rod end balljoint nut	35	26
Front strut upper mounting nuts	23	17

1 General description

The driveshafts are of open, tubular type with a spider type joint at the roadwheel end and a sliding type joint at the inboard end (photo).

The front hubs incorporate inner and outer tapered roller bearings. A spacer is used to obtain the specified bearing preload.

The rear hubs are also supported on inner and outer tapered roller bearings, but the bearing preload is adjusted by the setting of the stub axle nut.

The roadwheels may be of pressed steel or light alloy construction depending upon model.

Tyres on all models are of tubeless, radial ply construction.

2 Maintenance

1 Regularly examine the driveshaft bellows. If splits are evident or lubricant is leaking from them, then they must be renewed immediately.

2 At specified intervals, check the driveshaft joints for wear. Do this by gripping the driveshaft near each joint in turn and twisting the shaft. Then push and pull it in all directions. Any movement between the

1.1 Driveshaft

tubular section of the shaft and the joint or shaft splined section will indicate wear in the joint components, see Sections 5 and 6.

3 At the intervals specified in Routine Maintenance, check the rear hub bearing preload and adjust if necessary as described in Section 8.

4 The pressed steel type of roadwheel should be checked for rim damage caused by kerbing. Any rust on either the inside or the outside of the roadwheels should be treated with anti-rust paint and then refinished to the original colour.

5 Check the tyres as described in Routine Maintenance for both damage and wear.

3 Driveshaft – removal and refitting

1 Raise the front of the vehicle and support it securely.

2 Remove the roadwheel.

3 Disconnect the front suspension lower balljoint by unscrewing the three bolts which hold it to the track control arm.

4 Unscrew, but do not remove the three nuts on the suspension strut top mounting. This is to provide geater flexibility (photo).

5 Extract the split pin and remove the nut lock from the end of the driveshaft.

6 Using a long knuckle bar, unscrew the driveshaft nut. In order to prevent the driveshaft from turning, either have an assistant apply the

3.4 Front suspension strut top mounting nuts

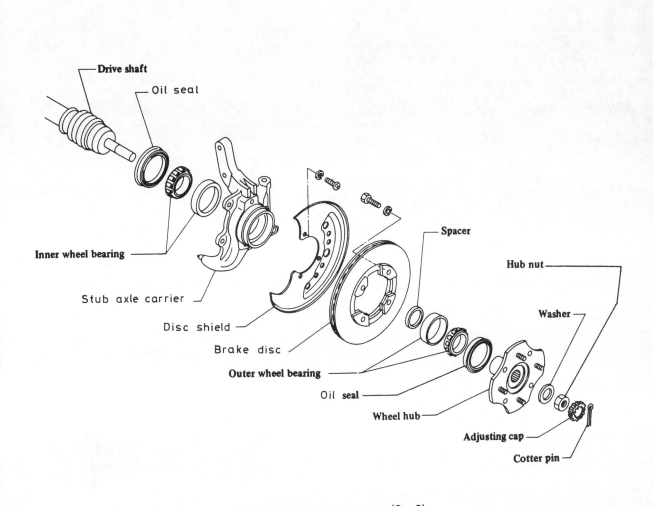

Fig. 8.1 Front hub components (Sec 3)

8

3.6A Roadwheel centre cap

3.6B Unscrewing driveshaft nut

3.7 Releasing driveshaft from transmission

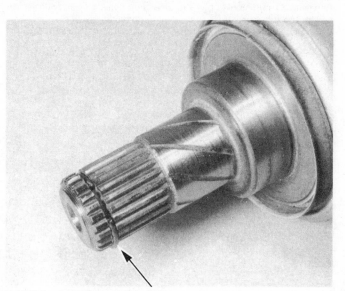

3.12 Driveshaft inboard stub circlip

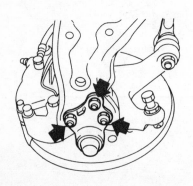

Fig. 8.2 Front suspension lower balljoint nuts (Sec 3)

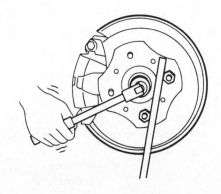

Fig. 8.3 One method of releasing driveshaft nut (Sec 3)

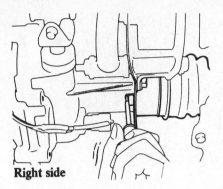

Right side

Fig. 8.4 Driveshaft release point (Sec 3)

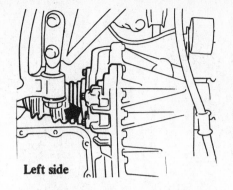

Left side

Fig. 8.5 Driveshaft release point (Sec 3)

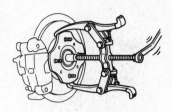

Fig. 8.6 Pressing driveshaft from stub axle carrier (Sec 3)

footbrake hard or temporarily fit two wheel nuts and place a lever between them. Take care not to damage the stud threads. Alternatively refit the roadwheel, lower the vehicle and prise out the centre cap (photo).

7   Using a lever inserted between the inboard joint of the driveshaft and the transmission casing, prise the shaft against the resistance of the circlip until it is released from the transmission (photo).

8   Insert a dummy bar or U-shaped piece of wire into the hole in the transmission left by removal of the driveshaft. This is to prevent the differential side gears from being displaced.

9   Now press the splined end of the driveshaft out of the stub axle carrier. If it is tight, use a two or three-legged puller. Remove the driveshaft.

10   To refit a driveshaft, insert its splined end into the stub axle carrier.

11   Remove the temporary tube or clip from the differential side gear and engage the inboard end of the shaft with the transmission. Take care not to damage the oil seal.

12   It is recommended that a new retaining circlip is used when refitting the shaft (photo).

13   Check that the driveshaft is positively engaged in the transmission and if necessary drive it fully home by applying force to the rim of the slide joint cover using a rod and hammer.

14   Reconnect the suspension strut lower balljoint using new nuts.

15   Tighten the strut upper mounting nuts to the specified torque.

16   Tighten the driveshaft nut to the specified torque. If the original hub bearings and spacer are being used, the bearing preload will be set by the torque of the driveshaft nut. If new components are being fitted then the preload must be set as described in Section 7.

17   Fit the nut lock and insert a new split pin.

18   Refit the roadwheel.

19   Lower the vehicle and then check and top up the transmission oil if required.

---

4   Driveshaft bellows – renewal

1   The bellows can be removed after withdrawal of the joint spiders as described in the following Sections.

---

5   Driveshaft inboard joint – overhaul

1   With the driveshaft removed from the vehicle, grip it securely in a vice.

8

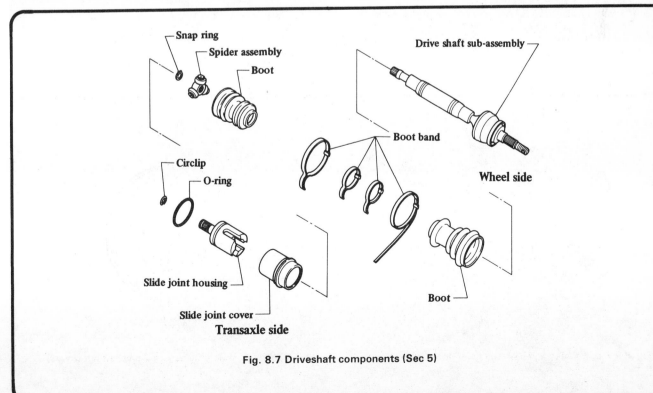

Fig. 8.7 Driveshaft components (Sec 5)

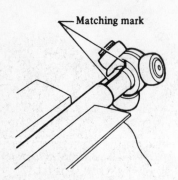

Fig. 8.8 Joint and shaft alignment marks (Sec 5)

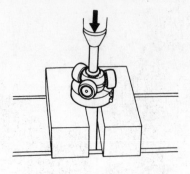

Fig. 8.9 Pressing driveshaft from spider (Sec 5)

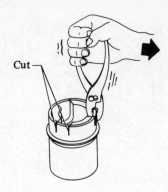

Fig. 8.10 Bending slide joint cover (Sec 5)

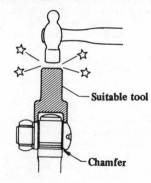

Fig. 8.11 Fitting spider to driveshaft (Sec 5)

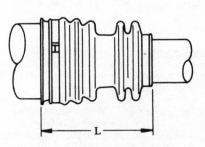

Fig. 8.12 Driveshaft bellows setting diagram (inboard joint) (Sec 5)

$L = 113.0\ mm\ (4.45\ in)$

2 Cut off the bellows securing bands.
3 Pull the slide joint housing from the shaft.
4 Clean the grease from the spider and mark the relative position of the spider to the shaft using quick-drying paint.
5 Extract the circlip and remove the spider from the shaft using a press or a small three-legged extractor (photo).
6 Slide off the bellows.
7 Make several cuts on the edge of the slide joint cover. Bend the sections between the saw cuts until the cover can be removed.
8 Remove the O-ring.

9 Renew the spider complete also the slide joint cover. The needles cannot be separated from the spider.
10 Reassemble by reversing the dismantling operations, use a new circlip and O-ring.
11 Peen the edge of the slide cover all around its edge and seal it with a bead of suitable sealant (photo).
12 Slide on the bellows.
13 Drive on the spider using a piece of tubing as a drift. Note that the chamfer on the spider is towards the shaft. The alignment marks made at dismantling should be correctly located if the original components

5.5 Extracting spider circlip

5.11 Driveshaft joint slide cover

5.15 Driveshaft joint lubricant

5.16A Driveshaft bellows larger clip

5.16B Driveshaft bellows smaller clip

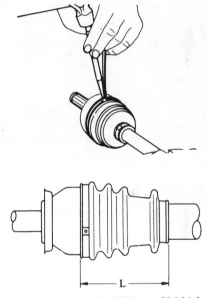

Length "L": 120.5 mm (4.74 in)

Fig. 8.13 Lock the driveshaft bellows band securely with a punch, then set the bellows length before installing the smaller band

are being refitted. If new parts are being assembled, make sure that the spider is in a similar attitude (zero phase) to the one at the roadwheel end of the driveshaft.

14 Fit a new spider retaining circlip, making sure that the round edge of the circlip is towards the spider.

15 Pack the joint with 185g (6.52 oz) of specified grease (photo).

16 Set the overall length of the bellows to the dimension shown (Fig. 8.12) and then fit new securing bands. Bend over the band retaining tabs (photos).

6 Driveshaft outboard joint — inspection and bellows replacement

Caution: *The outboard joint spider assembly is of a non-disassembling design, and other than bellows replacement no overhaul procedures are possible. In the event of damage to the outboard joint replacement of the driveshaft with a new or factory reconditioned unit is required.*

1 With the driveshaft removed from the vehicle, grip it securely in a vice.

2 Remove the inboard joint spider assembly as detailed in the previous Section.

3 Cut off the outboard joint bellows securing bands.

4 Draw off the bellows over the inboard joint.

5 Thoroughly clean the grease from the driveshaft assembly with solvent.

6 Check the driveshaft for twist or cracks, and replace if the shaft is deformed or damaged.

7 The spider assembly on the wheel side is of a non-disassembling design and no dismantling beyond this point is possible. If replacement is required a new axleshaft will have to be secured.

8 When the inspection has been completed, pack the driveshaft with approximately 290 g (10.15 oz) of the specified grease.

9 Install the new bellows, using caution not to damage the bellows on the edge of the driveshaft.

10 Install a new larger diameter bellows band.

11 Wrap the band twice around the bellows, then use a screwdriver to hold the band while pulling on the free end with pliers to tighten. When tight bend the free end of the band up at approximately 90 degrees.

12 Lock the band securely with a punch, securing it by bending it back

8

over itself.

13 Set the bellows length to 120.5 mm (4.74 in) as shown in the accompanying illustration and install the new smaller diameter bellows band.

14 Check to insure that the joint moves smoothly over its entire range without binding.

15 Reinstall the inboard joint spider assembly and bellows and refit the driveshaft.

7 Front hub bearings – renewal and adjustment

1 Wear in the front hub bearings can usually be detected if the roadwheel is raised off the floor and the tyre gripped at top and bottom and an attempt made to 'rock' it on its bearings.

2 If movement is evident and the driveshaft nut is fully tight then the bearings are worn and must be renewed.

3 Remove the roadwheel and the shaft protective cap (photo).

4 Extract the split pin and remove the nut lock from the driveshaft.

5 Loosen, but do not remove the driveshaft nut. Hold the hub against rotation using one of the methods described in Section 3 (photo).

6 Unbolt the brake caliper and tie it up out of the way. There is no need to disconnect the hydraulic flexible hose.

7 Unscrew the nut from the tie-rod end balljoint taper pin and then using a suitable tool disconnect the balljoint from the steering arm on the stub axle carrier.

8 Disconnect the suspension lower balljoint by unscrewing the three nuts which hold it to the track rod arm. Use new nuts at reassembly.

9 Remove the bolts from the clamp which holds the stub axle carrier to the base of the suspension strut (photo).

10 Slide the stub axle carrier downwards out of the strut clamp.

11 Disconnect the driveshaft from the transmission as described in Section 3.

12 Remove the driveshaft nut and press the shaft out of the stub axle carrier. If it is tight, use a two or three-legged puller.

13 Remove the hub/disc from the stub axle carrier. This will usually come out with the bearing race attached. Use a press for this job or a slide hammer (photo).

14 The disc can be separated from the hub by unscrewing the connecting bolt (photo).

15 Prise out the oil seal and drive out the bearing outer tracks. Always renew bearings as a complete set, inner and outer.

16 Thoroughly clean the bearing recess in the stub axle carrier and then drive in the two bearing outer tracks. Use a brass drift to drive in the tracks.

17 Apply grease liberally to the inner bearing race and locate it in the stub axle carrier (photo).

18 Drive a new inner oil seal squarely into position and apply grease to its lips (photo).

19 Fit the original spacer and then apply grease liberally to the outer bearing race and then insert it into the stub axle carrier (photo).

20 Drive a new outer oil seal squarely into position and apply grease to its lips.

21 If the brake disc was separated from the hub, refit it now and tighten the bolts to the specified torque.

22 Push the hub/disc into the bearing in the stub axle carrier.

23 Grip the driveshaft in a vice and fit the stub axle carrier/hub to it. Fit the washer and screw on the nut.

24 Tighten the hub nut to the specified minimum torque. In order to prevent the driveshaft from turning in the vice jaws, screw on two roadwheel nuts and place a lever between them.

25 Move the position of the assembly in the vice so that the stub axle carrier is gripped and the driveshaft hangs free.

26 Using a spring balance attached to one of the roadwheel studs, check the pull required to start the hub turning. This should be within the range of 1.4 to 4.9 kg (3.1 to 10.8 lb).

27 If the pull required is too small or there is evidence of endfloat, then the spacer will have to be changed for a thinner one. Should the bearing preload be greater than specified, change the spacer for a thicker one.

28 If dismantling was carried out for the purpose of renewing the stub axle carrier, a new spacer will be needed, the calculation of its thickness being as described in Chapter 11.

29 Fit the nut lock (slots in alignment with split pin hole) and insert a new split pin. Bend the ends around the nut lock (photo).

30 Remove the temporary tube or clip from the differential side gear and offer the driveshaft into the hole.

31 Push the driveshaft fully into engagement so that the circlip snaps into its groove.

32 Push the stub axle carrier upwards into the strut clamp and insert and tighten the bolts to the specified torque.

33 Reconnect the suspension lower balljoint.

34 Reconnect the tie-rod end balljoint.

35 Bolt the brake caliper to the stub axle carrier, tightening the bolts to the specified torque.

36 Refit the roadwheel, lower the vehicle to the floor.

37 Check and top up the transmission oil.

38 The stub axle carriers are fitted with steering lock stop bolts. These should not normally need adjustment, but if new components have been fitted, adjust the stop bolts so that dimension A is 34.0 mm (1.33 in) (photo).

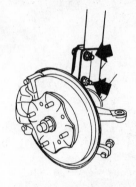

Fig. 8.14 Stub axle to strut clamp bolts (Sec 7)

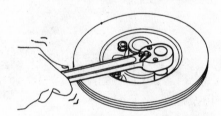

Fig. 8.15 Unscrewing a brake disc to hub connecting bolt (Sec 7)

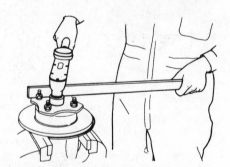

Fig. 8.16 Tightening driveshaft nut (Sec 7)

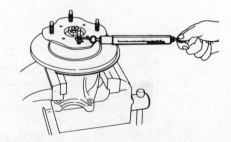

Fig. 8.17 Checking front hub bearing preload (Sec 7)

7.3 Shaft protective cap

7.5 Driveshaft nut

7.9 Front strut lower clamp bolt

7.13 Hub/disc separated from stub axle carrier

7.14 Front hub components

7.17 Hub inner bearing

7.18 Hub inner oil seal

7.19 Front hub bearing spacer

7.29 Driveshaft nut retainer and split pin

7.38A Steering lock stop bolt

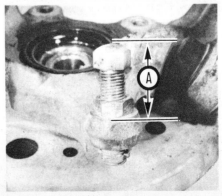
7.38B Steering lock stop bolt setting

8

8.2 Prising off rear hub grease cap

8.8 Fitting rear hub grease cap. Note O-ring seal

Fig. 8.18 Direction of bending split pin ends (Sec 8)

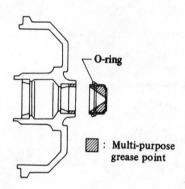

Fig. 8.19 Rear hub grease cap with O-ring (Sec 8)

8 Rear hub bearings – adjustment

1   Raise the roadwheel off the floor and remove the roadwheel. Release the handbrake.
2   Prise off the hub cap (photo).
3   Extract the split pin and take off the nut lock.
4   Tighten the stub axle nut to a torque of 40 Nm (30 lbf ft) while turning the brake drum.
5   Unscrew the nut through a quarter of a turn and then retighten it with moderate finger pressure only.
6   Check that the hub turns smoothly and freely without any hint of endfloat.
7   Fit the nut lock so that two cut-outs are in alignment with the split pin hole. Insert a new split pin and bend its ends around the nut lock, not over the end.
8   Check the O-ring in the grease cap, half fill the cap with grease and tap it squarely into position (photo).

9 Rear hub bearings – renewal

1   The need to renew the rear hub bearings will be indicated if they become noisy on turning a corner or if it is found impossible to eliminate endfloat or 'rock' after having correctly adjusted the bearings as described in the preceding Section.
2   Raise the rear of the vehicle and support it securely. Remove the roadwheel.
3   Release the handbrake.
4   Using a screwdriver, prise off the grease cap.

5   Extract the split pin, take off the nut lock.
6   Unscrew and remove the stub axle nut and take off the thrust washer (photo).
7   Withdraw the brake drum, taking care to retain the bearing as it will come out with the drum (photo).
8   Prise out the hub inner seal and discard it.
9   Remove the inner bearing race.
10 Drive out the bearing outer tracks. Cut-outs are provided in the hub to permit use of a drift to remove them.
11 Clean the inside of the hub and then fit the new bearing tracks. It is recommended that they are pressed or drawn into position using a bolt, nut and washers rather than driving them into position as they may crack.
12 Apply grease liberally to the inner bearing race and locate it in the hub.
13 Tap a new oil seal squarely into place and apply grease to its lips.
14 Offer the hub/drum onto the stub axle and then push the outer bearing race (liberally greased) into the hub.
15 Fit the thrust washer and nut and then adjust the bearings as described in the preceding Section, paragraphs 4 to 8.
16 Check that the grease cap O-ring is in good order, half fill the cap with grease and tap it squarely into position.
17 Fit the roadwheel and lower the vehicle.

10 Roadwheels and tyres

1   Whenever the roadwheels are removed, it is a good idea to clean the insides of the wheels to remove accumulations of mud and in the case of the front ones, disc pad dust.

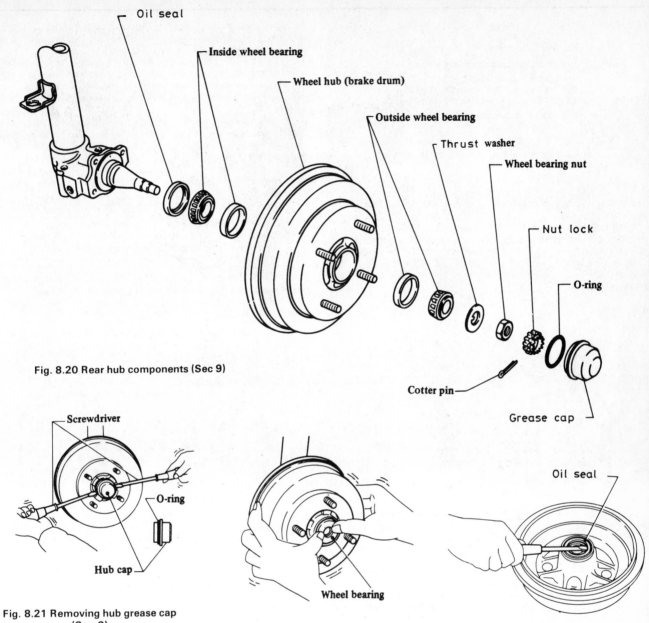

Oil seal

Inside wheel bearing

Wheel hub (brake drum)

Outside wheel bearing

Thrust washer

Wheel bearing nut

Nut lock

O-ring

Cotter pin

Grease cap

Fig. 8.20 Rear hub components (Sec 9)

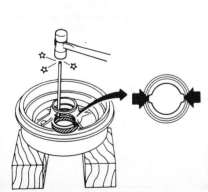

Screwdriver

O-ring

Hub cap

Fig. 8.21 Removing hub grease cap
(Sec 9)

Wheel bearing

Fig. 8.22 Removing brake drum (Sec 9)

Oil seal

Fig. 8.23 Prising out hub grease seal
(Sec 9)

Fig. 8.24 Removing rear hub outer track
(Sec 9)

9.6 Removing rear hub nut

9.7 Removing rear hub outer bearing

8

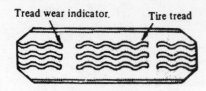

Fig. 8.25 Tyre tread wear indicator (Sec 10)

2   Check the condition of the wheel for rust and repaint if necessary (pressed steel type).
3   Examine the wheel bolt holes. If these are tending to become elongated, or the dished recesses in which the nut seats have worn or become overcompressed, then the wheel will have to be renewed.
4   With a roadwheel removed, pick out any embedded flints from the tread and check for splits in the sidewalls or damage to the tyre carcass generally.
5   Where the depth of tread pattern is 1 mm or less, the tyre must be renewed.

6   Moving of the roadwheels to even out wear may be a worthwhile idea if the wheels have been balanced off the car. Include the spare wheel in the rotational pattern.
7   Due to the fact that radial ply tyres are fitted, move the wheels from front to rear on the same side of the vehicle not from side to side.
8   It is recommended that wheels are rebalanced halfway through the life of the tyres to compensate for the loss of tread rubber due to wear.
9   Finally, always keep the tyres (including the spare) inflated to the recommended pressures and always refit the dust caps on the tyre valves. Tyre pressures are best checked first thing in the morning when the tyres are cold.
10   On vehicles destined for operation in North America and certain other territories, the spare tyre is of T type and should be used in an emergency only.
11   Certain precautions are necessary with this type of tyre:

Maintain its pressure at 4.12 bar (60 lbf/ft²)
Restrict road speed to 80 km/h (50 mph) when fitted
Do not use an automatic car wash when the tyre is in use
Do not use snow chains on this type of tyre

12   The tyres fitted as original equipment incorporate wear indicators in the tread. Renew the tyres as soon as these appear.
13   The appearance of the surface of the tyre tread will indicate the condition of the suspension and steering (Fig. 8.26).

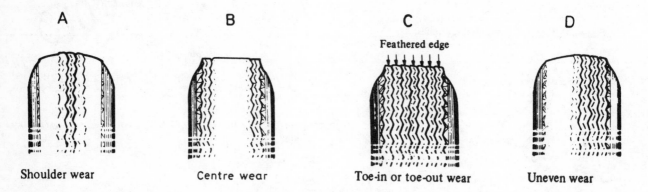

Fig. 8.26 Appearance and causes of uneven tread wear (Sec 10)

A Shoulder wear caused by under-inflation or incorrect camber	D One sided tread wear caused by incorrect camber or castor, unbalanced wheel, worn suspension bushes or shock absorber
B Centre wear caused by over-inflation	
C Feathered edge caused by incorrect roadwheel alignment (toe)	

11 Fault diagnosis – driveshafts and hub bearings

Symptom	Reason(s)
Vibration	Driveshaft bent Worn shaft joints Out-of-balance roadwheels
'Clonk' on taking up drive or on overrun	Worn shaft joints Worn splines on shaft, hub carrier or differential side gears Loose driveshaft nut Loose roadwheel bolts
Noise or roar especially when cornering	Worn hub bearings Incorrectly adjusted hub bearings

Chapter 9 Braking system

Refer to Chapter 13 for specifications and information applicable to 1984 and later models

Contents

Specifications

System type ....

Four wheel hydraulic, dual circuit with pressure regulator and servo assistance. Handbrake mechanical on rear (self-adjusting) shoes

Brake fluid
Type/specification ....

Hydraulic fluid to FMVSS 116 DOT 3 (Duckhams Universal Brake and Clutch Fluid)

Disc brakes
Disc diameter	232.0 mm (9.13 in)
Minimum refinishing or wear limit:	
Unventilated disc	10.0 mm (0.39 in)
Ventilated disc	16.0 mm (0.63 in)
Maximum run-out	0.15 mm (0.0059 in)
Pad (friction material) minimum thickness	2.0 mm (0.08 in)

Drum brakes
Drum internal diameter	203.2 mm (8.0 in)
Maximum internal diameter after refinishing	204.5 mm (8.05 in)
Maximum out-of-round	0.02 mm (0.0008 in)
Lining (friction material) minimum thickness on bonded shoes	1.5 mm (0.059 in)

Brake pedal adjustment
Height (h) – top face of pedal pad to metal surface of floor:
LHD – manual transmission	149.5 to 155.5 mm (5.89 to 6.12 in)
LHD – automatic transmission	151.5 to 157.5 mm (5.96 to 6.20 in)
RHD – manual transmission	164.5 to 170.5 mm (6.48 to 6.71 in)
RHD – automatic transmission	166.5 to 172.5 mm (6.56 to 6.79 in)
Pedal free play at pedal pad (a)	1.0 to 5.0 mm (0.04 to 0.20 in)

Torque wrench settings
	Nm	lbf ft
Pipeline unions	18	13
Hose banjo bolt	20	15
Bleed screw	9	7
Pedal cross-shaft nut	40	30
Vacuum servo fixing nuts	11	8
Master cylinder fixing nuts	11	8
Disc caliper mounting bolts	90	66
Caliper to bracket fixing bolts	20	15
Disc to hub bolts	50	37
Rear backplate bolts	25	18
Rear wheel cylinder bolts	8	6
Caliper guide and lockpins	35	26
Disc shield bolts	11	8
Roadwheel nuts	95	70

1 General description

The braking system is of four wheel, hydraulic dual circuit type. The dual circuits are of diagonal configuration – front right and rear left and front left and rear right.

All models are fitted with a vacuum servo unit (booster).

A pressure regulator valve is used to prevent rear wheel lock up during heavy applications of the foot pedal.

The rear brakes are of self-adjusting type.

The handbrake is cable-operated to the rear wheels only.

2 Maintenance and adjustment

1   At weekly intervals check the level of fluid in the master cylinder reservoir.

2   Top up if necessary to maintain the level between the MIN and MAX marks.

3   Additions of hydraulic fluid should only be required very infrequently. The fluid level will normally drop very slowly just enough to compensate for wear in the brake friction material.

4   At the intervals specified in Routine Maintenance check all hydraulic hoses, pipelines and unions for leaks. Examine the condition of the hoses as described in Section 11.

5   Also at the specified intervals, check the wear in the disc pads and brake shoe linings as described in Sections 3 and 4.

3 Disc pads – inspection and renewal

1   Raise the front of the vehicle and support it securely.

2   Remove the roadwheels.

3   Remove the caliper lock pin.

4   Release the caliper guide pin.

5   Swivel the caliper bracket upwards to expose the disc pads.

6   If the thickness of the friction material has worn down to 2.0 mm (0.079 in) or less then the pads must be renewed as an axle set.

7   Prise out the pad retaining clips, grip the pad backplates with a pair of pliers and withdraw them together with the anti-squeal shims (photos).

8   Brush out all dust from the caliper. *Take care not to inhale the dust.*

9   Do not touch the brake pedal while the pads are out of the caliper.

10 In order to accommodate the new thicker pads, the caliper piston must be depressed fully into its cylinder. Doing this will cause the fluid level in the master cylinder reservoir to rise. Anticipate this by syphoning off some of the fluid with a clean old battery hydrometer or poultry baster.

3.7A Prising out disc pad retaining clip

3.7B Disc pad anti-squeal shim

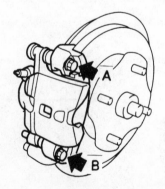

Fig. 9.1 Caliper guide pin (A) and lock pin (B) (Sec 3)

Fig. 9.2 Caliper swivelled upwards to remove pad retaining springs (Sec 3)

3.11 Disc pads

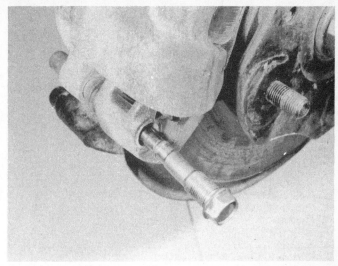

3.13 Caliper lockpin

11 Apply just a smear of high melting point brake grease to the backing plates of the new disc pads and locate them in the caliper making sure that the friction side is against the disc. Fit the anti-squeal shims (photo).
12 Fit the pad retainers.
13 Swivel the caliper downwards and insert the lockpin. Tighten the guide pin and lockpin to specified torque (photo).
14 Repeat the operations on the opposite wheel.
15 Refit the roadwheels and lower the vehicle.
16 Apply the footbrake hard to position the pads against the disc.
17 Check the fluid level in the master cylinder reservoir and top up if necessary.

4 Rear shoe linings – inspection and renewal

1 Raise the rear of the vehicle and support it securely. Remove the roadwheels.
2 Remove the brake drums as described in Chapter 8, Section 9 (photo).
3 Brush away dust from the shoes and the interior of the drum. *Take care not to inhale any dust* (photo).
4 If the shoe friction lining has been reduced to 1.5 mm (0.059 in) on bonded type linings or down to the rivet heads, the shoes must be renewed as an axle set. Obtain factory re-lined shoes. Attempting to reline them yourself is not satisfactory.
5 Remove the shoe steady springs. Do this by gripping the rim of the spring cup, depressing it and turning it through 90° and then slowly

releasing it so that the T of the steady pin passes through the cup (photo).
6 Note the location of the leading and trailing shoes and how the lining does not extend to the end of the shoes. Note also in which holes in the shoe web the return springs engage. Sketch the original fitting if necessary as a reminder when refitting.
7 Disconnect the shoe upper return spring.
8 Pull the upper ends of the shoes apart and disengage the automatic adjuster. If for any reason the adjuster must be removed then the handbrake cable will have to be detached from it.
9 Prise the shoes apart to expand the lower return spring and lift the bottom of the shoes over and off the fixed anchor block. Do not touch the brake pedal while the shoes are removed.
10 Turn the nut on the automatic adjuster to fully contract the adjuster strut.
11 Clean the brake backplate and apply a smear of high melting point brake grease to the high points on the backplate and to the ends of the pistons and shoe anchor block which contact the shoes. Apply grease sparingly to the threads of the automatic adjuster.
12 Arrange the shoes on the bench so that the leading and trailing shoes are correctly located. Engage the lower return spring.
13 Fit the shoes to the backplate by levering the bottom ends over and into the fixed anchor block.
14 Engage the automatic adjuster and connect the upper springs.
15 Fit the shoe steady pins, springs and cups.
16 Refit the brake drum (Chapter 8, Section 9) and adjust the bearings, Chapter 8, Section 8.
17 Apply the handbrake several times to bring the shoes into close adjustment through the automatic adjuster.

4.2 Brake drum removed

4.3 View of rear shoe layout

4.5 Removing shoe steady spring cup

9

Fig. 9.3 Shoe steady spring and pin (Sec 4)

Fig. 9.4 Shoe arrangement (Sec 4)

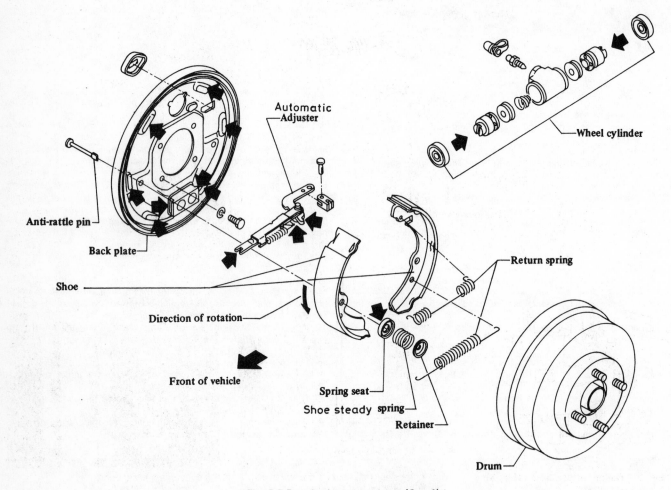

Fig. 9.5 Rear brake components (Sec 4)

5 Caliper – removal, overhaul and refitting

1 Remove the disc pads as described in Section 3.
2 Disconnect the brake hose at the caliper by unscrewing the banjo union hollow bolt. Note the sealing washer on each side of the union.
3 Unscrew and remove the caliper mounting bolts and withdraw the caliper off the disc (photo).
4 Clean away all external dirt.
5 Separate the caliper cylinder and bracket.
6 Remove the piston by ejecting it with air pressure applied with a tyre pump at the fluid entry port. Only low pressure is required.
7 Examine the surfaces of piston and cylinder and if they are scored or corroded, then they must be renewed complete. If the components are in good condition then continue the overhaul by removing and discarding the piston seal and dust excluder.
8 Wash the components in clean brake fluid or methylated spirit – nothing else.
9 Obtain a repair kit which will contain the new seals and other renewable items.
10 Fit the new seal into the cylinder groove using the fingers only to manipulate it into position.
11 Dip the piston in clean hydraulic fluid and insert it squarely into the cylinder.
12 Fit the dust excluder and its retaining ring.

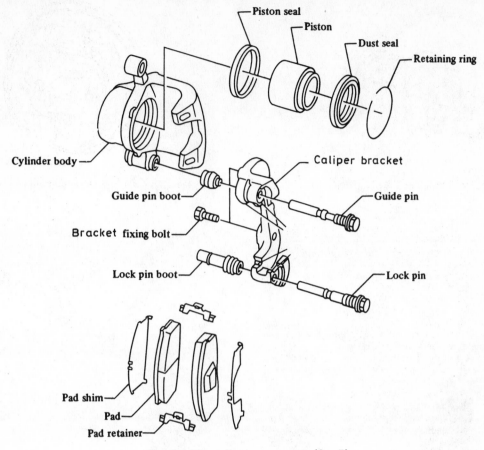

Fig. 9.6 Disc caliper components (Sec 5)

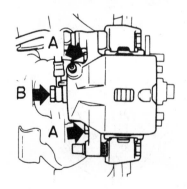

Fig. 9.7 Caliper attachments (Sec 5)

A   Mounting bolts
B   Hydraulic hose banjo bolt

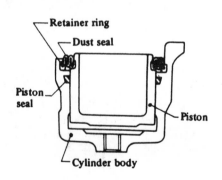

Fig. 9.8 Sectional view of caliper cylinder and piston (Sec 5)

5.3 Caliper mounting bolts

9

13 Reconnect the caliper bracket to the cylinder by applying rubber grease to the sliding surface of the guide pin and having fitted its boot, screw it in finger tight.
14 Bolt the caliper to the stub axle carrier, tightening to the specified torque.
15 Fit the disc pads (Section 3) and their retaining clips.
16 Reconnect the hydraulic hose union.
17 Swivel the caliper cylinder downwards and screw in the lockpin, having applied rubber grease to its sliding surface. Make sure that the boot is in position.
18 Tighten the guide pin and lockpin to the specified torque.
19 Bleed the appropriate hydraulic circuit as described in Section 12.

6   Disc – inspection, renovation or renewal

1   Whenever the disc pads are being inspected, check the disc for deep scoring. Light scoring is normal, but heavy scoring can only be remedied by fitting a new disc or by surface grinding the original one provided its thickness is not reduced below the minimum specified.
2   If it is suspected that the disc is distorted, it can be checked for run-out using a dial gauge or feeler blades between the disc and a fixed point while the disc is being rotated.
3   Removal and refitting of the disc is described in Chapter 8, Section 7.

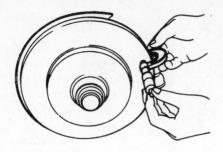

Fig. 9.9 Measuring brake disc thickness (Sec 6)

Fig. 9.10 Checking brake disc run-out (Sec 6)

7 Rear wheel cylinder – removal, overhaul and refitting

1   Remove the brake shoes as described in Section 4.
2   Disconnect the hydraulic brake line from the wheel cylinder.
3   Remove the wheel cylinder from the backplate.
4   Clean away external dirt and pull off the dust excluders.
5   Pull out the pistons and springs.
6   Examine the surface of the pistons and cylinder bores and if scored or corroded, the complete cylinder must be renewed.
7   If the components are in good condition however, remove and discard the seals and wash the other parts in clean hydraulic fluid or methylated spirit – nothing else.
8   Obtain a repair kit which will contain the new seals and other renewable components. It should be noted that both NABCO and TOKICO wheel cylinders are fitted during production. Make sure that you obtain the correct kit for your vehicle as they are not interchangeable.
9   Fit the new seals using the fingers only to manipulate them onto the pistons. Note that the seal lips are towards the spring.
10 Dip the pistons in clean hydraulic fluid and insert them into the cylinder with the spring between them.
11 Fit the dust excluders having packed some rubber grease inside them.
12 Refit the wheel cylinders to the backplate.
13 Fit the brake shoes as described in Section 4.
14 Bleed the appropriate hydraulic circuit as described in Section 12.

8 Brake drum – inspection, renovation or renewal

1   Whenever the brake drum is removed to inspect the linings, take the opportunity to check the drum itself.
2   If it is scored internally or has been stepped or grooved by the brake shoes, it may be possible to refinish it provided the internal diameter is not increased beyond the specified limit, otherwise the drum must be renewed.
3   If as the result of reference to Fault Diagnosis, the drum is suspected of being out of round, it can be measured using an internal micrometer and if confirmed, the drum will probably require renewing.

9 Master cylinder – removal, overhaul and refitting

1   Disconnect the leads from the fluid reservoir cap.
2   Disconnect the hydraulic pipelines from the master cylinder. Allow the fluid to drain into a suitable container.
3   Unscrew the nuts which hold the master cylinder to the front face of the servo unit and remove the master cylinder (photo).
4   Clean away external dirt and using circlip pliers, extract the circlip from the end of the master cylinder body. The primary piston assembly will be ejected.
5   Using a thin rod, depress the secondary piston slightly against its spring pressure and holding it in this position, unscrew and remove the stop bolt from the side of the cylinder body.
6   The secondary piston assembly will then be ejected.

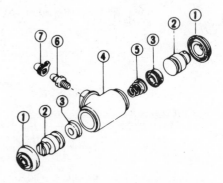

Fig. 9.11 Exploded view of rear wheel cylinder (Sec 7)

1 Dust excluder	5 Coil spring
2 Piston	6 Bleed nipple
3 Seal	7 Dust cap
4 Cylinder body	

9.3 Master cylinder and servo

7   Examine the surfaces of the pistons and cylinder bore. If they are scored or show signs of corrosion then the master cylinder must be renewed complete.
8   If these items are in good condition, remove the seals, noting the direction in which the lips face, and discard them.
9   Obtain a repair kit which will contain all the necessary new seals and other renewable items. Make sure that you obtain the correct kit for your master cylinder, two makes are used in production, NABCO and TOKICO, parts are not interchangeable.

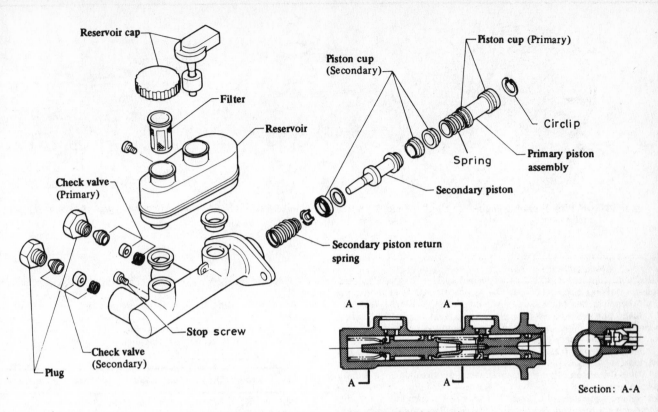

Fig. 9.12 Master cylinder components (NABCO) (Sec 9)

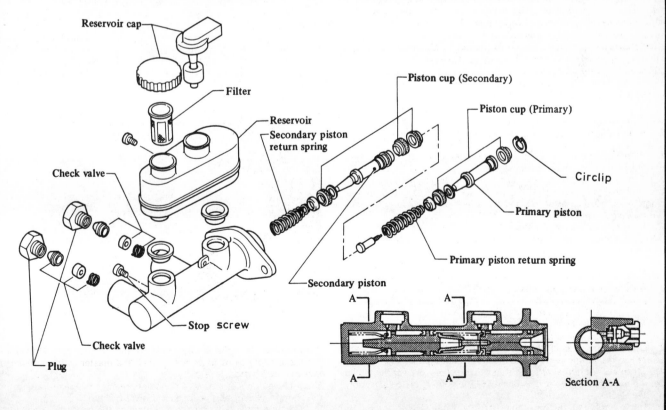

Fig. 9.13 Master cylinder components (TOKICO) (Sec 9)

9

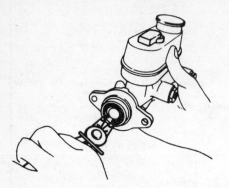

Fig. 9.14 Extracting master cylinder circlip (Sec 9)

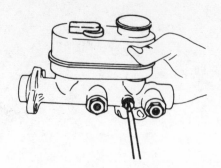

Fig. 9.15 Removing master cylinder secondary piston stop bolt (Sec 9)

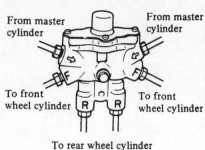

From master cylinder

From master cylinder

To front wheel cylinder

To front wheel cylinder

To rear wheel cylinder

Fig. 9.16 Pressure differential valve (Sec 10)

10 Clean the pistons and cylinder in hydraulic fluid or methylated spirit – nothing else, and fit the new ones manipulating them into position using the fingers only.

11 Insert the spring into the cylinder and then dip the secondary piston in clean hydraulic fluid and insert it into the cylinder bore.

12 Hold the cylinder depressed while the stop bolt is screwed in.

13 Dip the primary piston in clean hydraulic fluid and insert it into the cylinder.

14 Hold the piston slightly depressed while the circlip is fitted into its groove.

15 Where necessary, the check valves may be unscrewed and the internal parts renewed. Retighten to the specified torque.

16 If the fluid reservoir must be detached exert a pull and at the same time apply a rocking motion until the stubs on the reservoir release from the rubber sealing collars.

17 Refit the master cylinder to the front face of the servo unit, reconnect the pipelines and the warning switch electrical leads.

18 Fill the reservoir with clean hydraulic fluid and then bleed the complete system as described in Section 12.

10 Pressure regulating valve – removal and refitting

1 The pressure regulating or dual proportioning valve is located within the engine compartment on the rear bulkhead (photo).

2 The valve cannot be dismantled, but if a fault is suspected, renew it complete.

3 Note the location of the connecting pipelines and disconnect them.

4 Remove the fixing screw from the centre of the valve and remove the valve.

5 Fit the new valve and reconnect the pipelines.

6 Bleed the entire system as described in Section 12.

11 Flexible and rigid hydraulic lines – inspection and renewal

1 Periodically, inspect the condition of the flexible brake hoses. If they appear swollen, chafed or when bent double with the fingers tiny cracks are visible, then they must be renewed.

2 Always uncouple the rigid pipe from the flexible hose first, then release the end of the flexible hose from the support bracket. To do this, pull out the lockplate using a pair of pliers.

3 Now unscrew the flexible hose from the caliper or connector. On calipers, a banjo type hose connector is used. When installing the hose, always use a new sealing washer.

4 When installation is complete, check that the flexible hose does not rub against the tyre or other adjacent components. Its attitude may be altered to overcome this by pulling out the clip at the support bracket and twisting the hose in the required direction by not more than one quarter turn.

5 Bleed the hydraulic system (Section 12).

6 At regular intervals wipe the steel brake pipes clean and examine them for signs of rust or denting caused by flying stones (photo).

10.1 Pressure regulating valve

11.6 Brake and fuel pipeline clamp

7 Examine the fit of the pipes in their insulated securing clips and bend the tongues of the clips if necessary to ensure a positive fit.

8 Check that the pipes are not touching any adjacent components or rubbing against any part of the vehicle. Where this is observed, bend the pipe gently away to clear.

9 Any section of pipe which is rusty or chafed should be renewed. Brake pipes are available, to the correct length and fitted with end unions, from most dealers and can be made to pattern by many accessory suppliers. When installing the new pipes use the old pipes as a guide to bending and do not make any bends sharper than is necessary.

10 The system will of course have to be bled when the circuit has been reconnected.

12 Hydraulic system – bleeding

1 If the master cylinder or the pressure regulating valve have been disconnected and reconnected then the complete system (both circuits) must be bled.

2 If a component of one circuit has been disturbed then only that particular circuit need be bled.

3 Bleed one rear brake and its diagonally opposite front brake. Repeat in this sequence on the remaining circuit if the complete system is to be bled.

4 Unless the pressure bleeding method is being used, do not forget to keep the fluid level in the master cylinder reservoir topped up to prevent air from being drawn into the system which would make any work done worthless.

5 Before commencing operations, check that all system hoses and pipes are in good condition with all unions tight and free from leaks.

6 Take great care not to allow hydraulic fluid to come into contact with the vehicle paintwork as it is an effective paint stripper. Wash off any spilled fluid immediately with cold water.

7 If the system incorporates a vacuum servo, destroy the vacuum by giving several applications of the brake pedal in quick succession.

Bleeding – two man method

8 Gather together a clean glass jar and a length of rubber or plastic tubing which will be a tight fit on the brake bleed screws.

9 Engage the help of an assistant.

10 Push one end of the bleed tube onto the first bleed screw and immerse the other end in the glass jar which should contain enough hydraulic fluid to cover the end of the tube.

11 Open the bleed screw one half a turn and have your assistant depress the brake pedal fully then slowly release it. Tighten the bleed screw at the end of each pedal downstroke to obviate any chance of air or fluid being drawn back into the system.

12 Repeat this operation until clean hydraulic fluid, free from air bubbles, can be seen coming through into the jar.

13 Tighten the bleed screw at the end of a pedal downstroke and remove the bleed tube. Bleed the remaining screws in a similar way.

Bleeding – using one way valve kit

14 There is a number of one-man, one-way brake bleeding kits available from motor accessory shops. It is recommended that one of these kits is used wherever possible as it will greatly simplify the

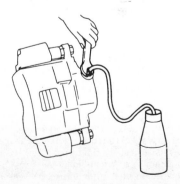

Fig. 9.17 Bleeding a caliper (Sec 12)

bleeding operation and also reduce the risk of air or fluid being drawn back into the system quite apart from being able to do the work without the help of an assistant.

15 To use the kit, connect the tube to the bleedscrew and open the screw one half a turn.

16 Depress the brake pedal fully and slowly release it. The one-way valve in the kit will prevent expelled air from returning at the end of each pedal downstroke. Repeat this operation several times to be sure of ejecting all air from the system. Some kits include a translucent container which can be positioned so that the air bubbles can actually be seen being ejected from the system.

17 Tighten the bleed screw, remove the tube and repeat the operations on the remaining brakes.

18 On completion, depress the brake pedal. If it still feels spongy repeat the bleeding operations as air must still be trapped in the system.

Bleeding – using a pressure bleeding kit

19 These kits too are available from motor accessory shops and are usually operated by air pressure from the spare tyre.

20 By connecting a pressurised container to the master cylinder fluid reservoir, bleeding is then carried out by simply opening each bleed screw in turn and allowing the fluid to run out, rather like turning on a tap, until no air is visible in the expelled fluid.

21 By using this method, the large reserve of hydraulic fluid provides a safeguard against air being drawn into the master cylinder during bleeding which often occurs if the fluid level in the reservoir is not maintained.

22 Pressure bleeding is particularly effective when bleeding 'difficult' systems or when bleeding the complete system at time of routine fluid renewal.

All methods

23 When bleeding is completed, check and top up the fluid level in the master cylinder reservoir.

24 Check the feel of the brake pedal. If it feels at all spongy, air must still be present in the system and further bleeding is indicated. Failure to bleed satisfactorily after a reasonable repetition of the bleeding operation may be due to worn master cylinder seals.

25 Discard brake fluid which has been expelled. It is almost certain to be contaminated with moisture, air and dirt making it unsuitable for further use. Clean fluid should always be stored in an airtight container as it absorbs moisture readily (hygroscopic) which lowers its boiling point and could affect braking performance under severe conditions.

13 Vacuum servo unit (booster) – description

1 The unit operates in series with the master cylinder to provide assistance to the driver when the brake pedal is depressed. This reduces the effort required by the driver to operate the brake under all braking conditions. The unit operates by vacuum, obtained from the intake manifold and basically consists of a booster diaphragm and control valve assembly.

2 The servo unit and hydraulic master cylinder are connected together so that the servo unit piston rod (valve rod) acts as the master cylinder pushrod. The driver's braking effort is transmitted through another pushrod, to the servo unit piston and its built-in control system. The servo unit piston is attached to a rolling diaphragm, which ensures an airtight seal between the two major parts of the servo unit casing. The forward chamber is held under vacuum conditions created in the intake manifold of the engine and during periods when the brake pedal is not in use, the controls open a passage to the rear chamber, so placing it under vacuum conditions as well. When the brake pedal is depressed, the vacuum passage to the rear chamber is cut off and the chamber opened to atmospheric pressure. The consequent pressure difference across the servo piston pushes the piston forward in the vacuum chamber and operates the main pushrod to the master cylinder.

3 The controls are designed so that assistance is given under all conditions and, when the brakes are not required, vacuum in the rear chamber is established when the brake pedal is released.

4 No maintenance is required except occasionally to check the security and condition of the vacuum connecting pipe and check valve.

5 Should a fault develop in the servo unit, do not attempt to overhaul it, but renew it complete.

9

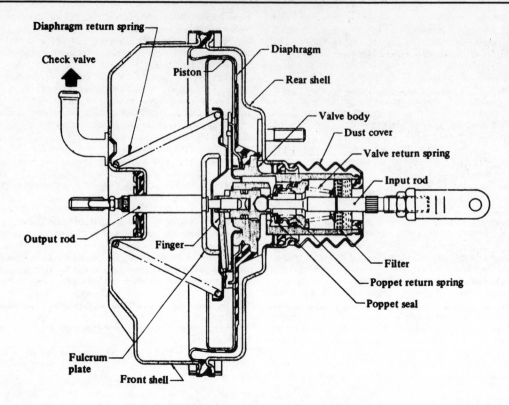

Fig. 9.18 Sectional view of the vacuum servo unit (Sec 13)

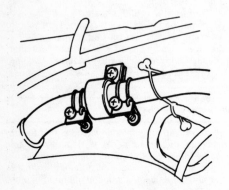

Fig. 9.19 Vacuum servo non-return
(check) valve (Sec 13)

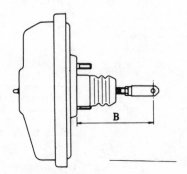

Fig. 9.20 Servo pushrod setting diagram
(Sec 14)

$B = 130.0 \ mm \ (5.12 \ in)$

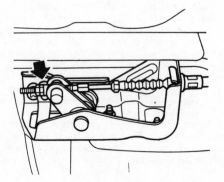

Fig. 9.21 Handbrake cable adjusting nuts
(Sec 15)

14 Vacuum servo unit – removal and refitting

1   Remove the master cylinder as described in Section 9.
2   Disconnect the vacuum hose from the servo unit.
3   Working inside the vehicle, disconnect the pushrod from the brake
pedal by either removing the spring clip (earlier models) or the plastic
snap washer (later models) and then withdrawing the clevis pin.
4   Still working inside the vehicle, unscrew the servo unit mounting
nuts and remove the unit from the engine compartment.
5   Refit the new servo by reversing the removal operations, but
before installing, adjust the length of the pushrod as shown in Fig.
9.20.
6   Refit the master cylinder and bleed the entire hydraulic system as
described in Section 12.

15 Handbrake – adjustment

1   Although the handbrake is self-adjusting by virtue of the automatic
adjuster on the rear shoes, the cable may stretch after a high mileage.
This will become evident when the handbrake lever moves over more
than five or six notches to lock the rear wheels.
2   Release the nuts on the threaded cable end fitting at the intermediate lever just forward of the fuel tank under the rear of the vehicle.
Turn the adjuster as necessary (photo).
3   Tighten the locknut on completion.
4   Check the operation of the handbrake ON warning switch. The
warning lamp should come on when the handbrake lever is moved over
the first notch, but go out when the lever is returned to the fully off
position.

15.2 Handbrake cable equaliser

5   If adjustment is required, remove the centre console and bend the switch plate.
6   Supplementary cable adjustment is provided at the cable attachment to the hand control lever, access being obtained by removing the centre console.

16 Handbrake cables – renewal

Primary cable
1   The primary cable is removed together with the handbrake lever.
2   Remove the centre console (Chapter 12).
3   Disconnect the wiring plug from the handbrake ON switch.
4   Unscrew the handbrake lever mounting bolts and the cable bracket screw.
5   Working under the vehicle, disconnect the primary cable from the intermediate lever by removing the clip and clevis pin.
6   Withdraw the cable into the vehicle interior.
7   The primary cable may be separated from the handbrake lever after grinding off the connecting rivet. A clevis pin and cotter pin are supplied with a new cable.

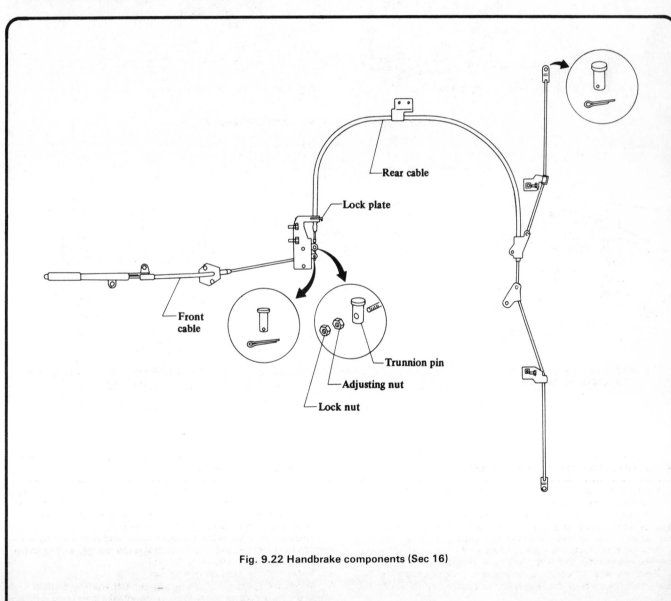

Fig. 9.22 Handbrake components (Sec 16)

9

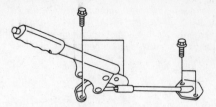

Fig. 9.23 Handbrake lever and primary cable bracket fixing bolts (Sec 16)

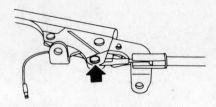

Fig. 9.24 Handbrake cable rivet (Sec 16)

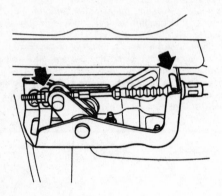

Fig. 9.25 Handbrake secondary cable fixing clip (Sec 16)

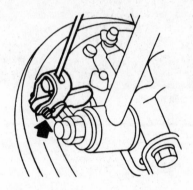

Fig. 9.26 Handbrake connection to backplate lever (Sec 16)

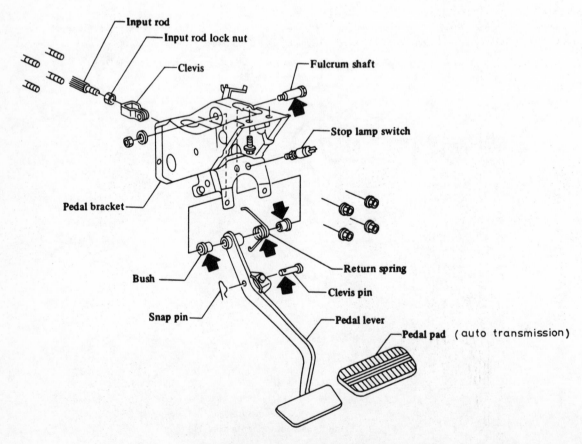

Fig. 9.27 Brake pedal components (Sec 17)

Secondary cable

8   Unscrew the adjusting nuts at the cable threaded end fitting at the intermediate lever so that the cable can be detached once the retaining spring clip is withdrawn.

9   Pull out the split pins and clevis pin and disconnect the cables from the levers at the brake backplates.

10 Remove the cable guides and withdraw the cable assembly from the vehicle.

11 Refitting is a reversal of removal. Apply grease to the contact points and oil the clevis pins. Adjust as described in the preceding Section.

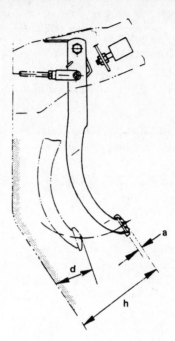

17 Brake pedal – removal and refitting

1   Remove the cover from under the facia panel.

2   Remove the heater duct.

3   Disconnect the pushrod from the brake pedal arm.

4   Remove the pin and unscrew the nut from the pedal cross-shaft and then withdraw the brake pedal.

5   Refit by reversing the removal operations, but smear the cross-shaft with grease first.

6   Check the pedal height (h). This must be as specified in Specifications Section otherwise adjust by means of the stop lamp switch.

7   Once this has been correctly adjusted, check the pedal free play (a). If this requires adjustment, make the alteration by means of the pushrod.

8   If the brake pedal is now depressed, the distance (d) must not be less than 60.0 mm (2.36 in) for LHD models or 70.0 mm (2.76 in) for RHD models. If it is, then suspect air in the hydraulic system.

Fig. 9.28 Pedal setting diagram – (Sec 17). For dimensions (a), (d) and (h) refer to Specifications

Fault diagnosis overleaf

9

18 Fault diagnosis – braking system

Before diagnosing faults from the following chart, check that any braking irregularities are not caused by:
> *Uneven and incorrect tyre pressures*
> *Wear in the steering mechanism*
> *Defects in the suspension and shock absorbers*
> *Misalignment of the bodyframe*

Symptom	Reason(s)
Pedal travels a long way before the brakes operate	Incorrect pedal adjustment Brake shoes set too far from the drums (seized adjusters)
Stopping ability poor, even though pedal pressure is firm	Linings, discs or drums badly worn or scored One or more wheel hydraulic cylinders seized, resulting in some brake shoes not pressing against the drums (or pads against disc) Brake linings contaminated with oil Wrong type of linings fitted (too hard) Brake shoes wrongly assembled Servo unit not functioning
Car veers to one side when the brakes are applied	Brake pads or linings on one side are contaminated with oil Hydraulic wheel cylinder on one side partially or fully seized A mixture of lining materials fitted between sides Brake discs not matched Unequal wear between sides caused by partially seized wheel cylinders
Pedal feels spongy when the brakes are applied	Air is present in the hydraulic system
Pedal feels springy when the brakes are applied	Brake linings not bedded into the drums (after fitting new ones) Master cylinder or brake backplate mounting bolts loose Severe wear in brake drums causing distortion when brakes are applied Discs out of true
Pedal travels right down with little or no resistance and brakes are virtually non-operative	Leak in hydraulic system resulting in lack of pressure for operating wheel cylinders If no signs of leakage are apparent the master cylinder internal seals are failing to sustain pressure
Binding, juddering, overheating	One or a combination of reasons given above Shoes installed incorrectly with reference to leading and trailing ends Broken shoe return spring Disc out-of-round Drum distorted Incorrect pedal adjustment
Lack of servo assistance	Vacuum hose disconnected or leaking Non-return valve defective or incorrectly fitted Servo internal defect

Chapter 10 Electrical system

Refer to Chapter 13 for information applicable to 1984 and later models

Contents

Specifications

System type .... 12 volt, negative earth alternator, battery and pre-engaged starter motor

Battery .... 60 Ah

Alternator .... 50A or 60A output depending upon territory and model (Type LR 150 or LR 160)
Regulated voltage (output) .... 14.4 to 15.1 volt
Brush wear limit .... 7.0 mm (0.28 in)

Independent type voltage regulator
Regulator voltage at 20°C (68°F) .... 14.4 to 15.1 volt
Regulator core gap .... 0.6 to 1.0 mm (0.024 to 0.039 in)
Point gap .... 0.35 to 0.45 mm (0.0138 to 0.0177 in)

Charge relay
Core gap .... 0.8 to 1.0 mm (0.031 to 0.039 in)
Point gap .... 0.4 to 0.6 mm (0.016 to 0.024 in)

10

Starter motor

Type ....
S114-319 – CA 16 engine
S114-320 – CA 18 engine
S114-320 – CA 20 engine
S114-322 – CA 20 engine (North America) special reduction gear type for cold climates

Output ....
0.8kW – S114-319
1.0kW – S114-320
1.2kW – S114-322

Brush wear limit .... 11.0 mm (0.43 in)

Bulbs

Headlamp (sealed beam type)	Sealed beam 65/35
Headlamp (bulb type):	
Halogen	60/65
Standard	75/60
Front direction indicator lamp:	
Except North America	21
North America	27
Front parking lamp	5
Front side marker lamp	8
Rear side marker lamp	3.4
Rear direction indicator lamp:	
Except North America	21
North America	27
Stop/tail lamp:	
Except North America	21/5
North America	27/8
Reversing lamps:	
Except North America	21
North America	27
Rear foglamp	21
Interior lamp	10
Luggage compartment lamp	5
Rear number plate lamp:	
Except North America	5 or 10*
North America	8 or 10*
*Depending upon type of lamp	
Front foglamp	55
Warning and indicator bulbs	3.4

Torque wrench settings

	Nm	lbf ft
Alternator adjuster link bolt	20	15
Alternator mounting bolt	55	41
Starter motor bolt	38	28

1 General description

1 The system is of 12 volt negative earth type with battery, alternator and pre-engaged starter motor.
2 All vehicles in the range are well equipped with electrical accessories and certain models have a power-operated sunroof, electric door locking, power-operated windows and a headlamp wash-wipe system.

2 Battery – maintenance and charging

1 A maintenance-free type of battery is fitted as standard equipment on many models (photo).
2 With this type of battery no topping up is required. Provided the indicator on the top cover is blue in colour then the battery is in good condition with a satisfactory charge.
3 If the battery indicator appears as a colourless disc then the battery is discharged and it should be charged overnight using a trickle charger. If after charging the battery indicator has not turned blue then the battery has reached the end of its life and must be renewed.
4 If a conventional type of battery is fitted, either in production or subsequently, then the electrolyte level should be kept topped up to the bottoms of the filler tubes in the cells, or if the battery case is of translucent type keep the level between the marks on the case.

2.1 Battery

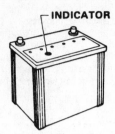

Fig. 10.1 Location of battery condition indicator (Sec 2)

Fig. 10.2 Significance of battery condition indicator (Sec 2)

5   The battery should only require very infrequent topping up, any requirement for large quantities of water will indicate overcharging due to a fault in the alternator regulator.

6   For topping up the battery only use distilled water or melted ice condensate from a refrigerator.

7   A battery should never need the addition of acid unless a spillage of electrolyte has occurred in which case leave anything to do with acid mixing and replenishment to your dealer or service station.

8   Inspect the battery terminals and battery platform for corrosion. This usually takes the form of white fluffy deposits. If evident, neutralise them with household ammonia or a paste made up from sodium bicarbonate and water. When dry, clean thoroughly and apply anti-corrosive paint (photo).

9   Keep the battery terminals smeared with petroleum jelly to prevent further corrosion occurring, do not use grease.

10   A conventional battery may be checked for its state of charge using a hydrometer. Compare the readings with the following table and charge from the mains if necessary.

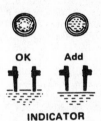

Fig. 10.3 Conventional type battery filler tubes (Sec 2)

Fully discharged	Electrolyte temperature	Fully charged
1.098	38°C (100°F)	1.268
1.102	32°C (90°F)	1.272
1.106	27°C (80°F)	1.276
1.110	21°C (70°F)	1.280
1.114	16°C (60°F)	1.284
1.118	10°C (50°F)	1.288
1.122	4°C (40°F)	1.292
1.126	-1.5°C (30°F)	1.296

Fig. 10.4 Electrolyte level markings on translucent battery case (Sec 2)

11   A battery in good condition should not require charging from an external source such is the efficiency of the alternator. It is possible however for the battery to become discharged if in the winter months only very short journeys are made with much use of the starter motor, lighting and electrical accessories. In this event, a charge from the mains using a trickle charger once or twice a week will keep matters right.

12   Before using a charger, disconnect both battery leads from their terminals.

3   Battery – removal and refitting

1   The battery is located on the left-hand side within the engine compartment.

2   Disconnect the leads from the battery terminal.

3   Unbolt the battery retaining clamp.

4   Remove the battery, keeping it level to avoid spillage of electrolyte.

5   Refitting is a reversal of removal. Make sure that the leads are connected securely to the correct terminals.

4   Alternator – description, maintenance and precautions

1   The alternator generates alternating current which is rectified by diodes into direct current which is needed to charge the battery.

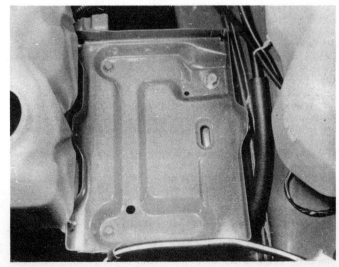

2.8 Battery tray

10

2   Main components consist of a stator and a rotor with diode rectifier.
3   The current is generated in the stator windings with the rotor carrying the field.
4   The field brushes carry only a light current and run on slip rings.
5   The alternator is driven by a belt from the crankshaft pulley. A fan is located behind the alternator pulley for cooling purposes.
6   Maintenance consists of periodically checking the security of the electrical connections, wiping the outside free from dirt and grease and keeping the drivebelt correctly tensioned as described in Chapter 2.
7   If there are indications that the charging system is malfunctioning in any way, care must be taken when diagnosing faults otherwise damage of a serious and expensive nature may occur to parts which are in fact quite serviceable. The following basic requirements must be observed at all times, therefore, if damage is to be prevented.
8   All alternator systems use a negative earth. Even the simple mistake of connecting the battery the wrong way round could burn out the alternator diodes quickly.
9   Before disconnecting any wires in the system the engine and ignition circuits should be switched off. This will minimise the risk of short-circuits in the system.
10 The engine must never be run with the alternator output wire (red wire on the positive terminal) disconnected.
11 Always disconnect the battery leads from the car's electrical system if an outside charging source is being used.
12 Do not use test wire connections that could move accidentally and short-circuit against nearby terminals. Short-circuits may not only blow fuses – they can also burn out diodes and transistors.
13 Always disconnect the battery cables and alternator output wires before any electric arc-welding work is done on the car body.

5   Alternator (independent voltage regulator type) – in vehicle test

1   A good quality voltmeter must be used for this test.
2   Disconnect the leads from the terminals on the rear of the alternator.
3   Using a bridging wire, connect the BAT terminal to the F terminal.
4   Place the positive probe of the voltmeter on the BAT terminal. Connect the other probe to earth. The voltmeter should register battery voltage.
5   Turn on the headlamps and switch to high beam.
6   Start the engine and gradually increase the engine speed to about 1100 rev/min.

7   Check the voltmeter reading. If it is less than 12.5v then the alternator is faulty. If it is in excess of 12.5v then the alternator is in good condition.
8   Do not increase the engine speed beyond 1100 rev/min while the test is being carried out.
9   Remember that the ignition (charge warning) lamp must be on when the ignition is switched on and go out as soon as the engine is started. If this does not happen, check the bulb and drivebelt. If these are in order, then the alternator or voltage regulator must be faulty.

6   Alternator (integral voltage regulator type) – in vehicle test

1   Ensure that the battery is fully charged. A 30v voltmeter must be available.
2   With the engine idling, place the positive probe of the voltmeter on the B terminal of the alternator and the negative probe on the L terminal. If more than 0.5v is indicated then a fault (not in the voltage regulator circuit) is indicated in the alternator.
3   Increase the engine speed to 1500 rev/min and switch on the headlamps. If the voltage exceeds 15.5v then the integral voltage regulator is faulty.
4   Remember that the ignition (charge warning) lamp must be on when the ignition is switched on and go out as soon as the engine is started. If this does not happen, check the bulb and drivebelt. If these are in order then the alternator must have an internal fault.

7   Alternator – removal and refitting

1   Disconnect the battery.
2   Disconnect the leads from the terminals on the rear of the alternator.
3   Slacken the mounting and adjuster link bolts and push the alternator in towards the engine so that the drivebelt can be slipped off the pulleys.
4   Remove the plastic shield from the right-hand inner wing.
5   Raise the front of the vehicle so that the right-hand roadwheel and driveshaft hang free. Support the car securely.
6   Remove the alternator mounting and adjuster link bolts and withdraw the unit from under the right-hand front wing (photo).
7   Refitting is a reversal of removal, tension the drivebelt.

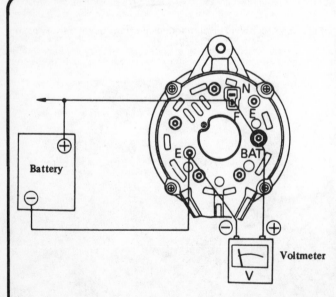

Fig. 10.5 Alternator (independent voltage regulator type) terminals and test circuit (Sec 5)

7.6 Alternator mounting bolt lockplate

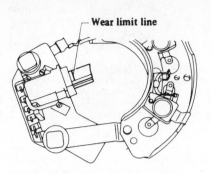

Fig. 10.6 Alternator brush wear limit line (Sec 8)

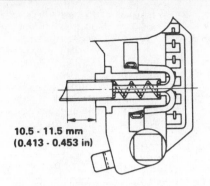

10.5 - 11.5 mm
(0.413 - 0.453 in)

Fig. 10.7 Alternator brush fixing diagram (Sec 8)

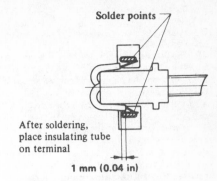

Solder points

After soldering, place insulating tube on terminal

1 mm (0.04 in)

Fig. 10.8 Alternator brush soldering diagram (Sec 8)

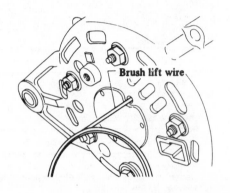

Brush lift wire

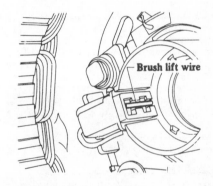

Brush lift wire

Fig. 10.9 Method of raising alternator brushes (Sec 8)

8 Alternator brushes – renewal

1   Remove the alternator.
2   Unscrew and remove the terminal nuts and screws from the rear cover (photo).
3   Unscrew and remove the tie-bolts and withdraw the rear cover.
4   The brush holder is now accessible and the brush length can be checked for wear. Most brushes incorporate a wear limit line which, if visible, indicates that the brush must be renewed as it will have worn down to 7.0 mm (0.28 in) which is the minimum length.
5   Unsolder the brush leads using the minimum amount of heat. Work quickly so that the heat from the soldering iron does not transfer to adjacent components. Take particular care not to damage the integral type voltage regulator on alternators where this arrangement is fitted (photo).
6   Make sure that the new brushes slide freely in their holders and solder the new leads so that the brush projects from its holder by between 10.5 and 11.5 mm (0.413 and 0.453 in) Fig. 10.7. Note the method of soldering the brush bared ends to the terminals. Fit the insulating covers to the terminals.
7   Before refitting the alternator rear cover, the brush must be held in the raised position so that it will pass over the slip ring. Do this by inserting a piece of thin rod or wire through the small hole in the rear cover (photo).
8   Fit the rear cover and screw in the tie-bolts.

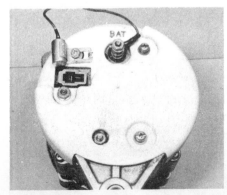

8.2 Alternator terminals

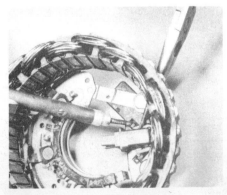

8.5 Unsoldering alternator brush leads

8.7 Alternator brush lift pin

10

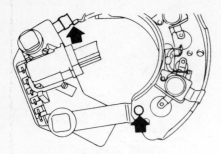

Fig. 10.10 Alternator integral type regulator disconnection points (Sec 9)

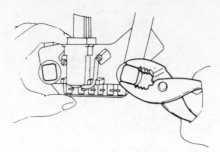

Fig. 10.11 Unscrewing regulator/brush holder fixing bolt (Sec 9)

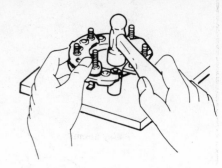

Fig. 10.12 Peening alternator regulator rivet (Sec 9)

9 Alternator voltage regulator (integral type) – removal and refitting

1   With the alternator removed from the vehicle, unscrew the tie-bolts and withdraw the rear cover.
2   Drill out the regulator plate rivet and unsolder the lead, Fig. 10.10 (photo).

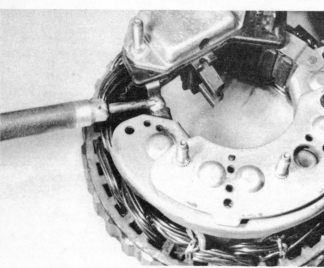

9.2 Unsoldering alternator regulator lead

3   Pull out the regulator/brush holder fixing pegs, unsolder the brush lead.
4   When reassembling the new regulator and brush holder, press the pegs into place and carefully peen a new rivet into position.

10 Alternator – overhaul

1   It will be found that renewal of the alternator brushes is really the only economical operation worth carrying out to an alternator. If anything more extensive requires dismantling, consider the purchase of a new or factory-reconditioned unit.
2   For those wishing to undertake complete dismantling, the sequence of operations is given in the following paragraphs.
3   With the alternator removed, clean away external dirt.
4   Unscrew and remove the tie-bolts.
5   Separate the front and rear covers by carefully inserting a screwdriver in the cut-outs provided.
6   Unscrew the pulley nut. In order to prevent the rotor from rotating on some alternators, a socket is provided in the end of the rotor shaft. An Allen key can be inserted to hold the shaft still. If such a socket is not provided, place an old drivebelt in the pulley groove and grip its ends as close as possible to the pulley in the jaws of a vice.
7   Remove the bearing retainer screws.
8   Unscrew the nuts on the rear cover and take it off to expose the stator (photo).
9   If the rotor bearing must be removed, use a puller or press the rotor shaft from it.
10   The diode can be removed once the stator coil leads have been unsoldered.
11   The brushes and integral type voltage regulator can be removed as described in Sections 8 and 9.

10.6 Releasing alternator pulley nut

10.8 Alternator stator

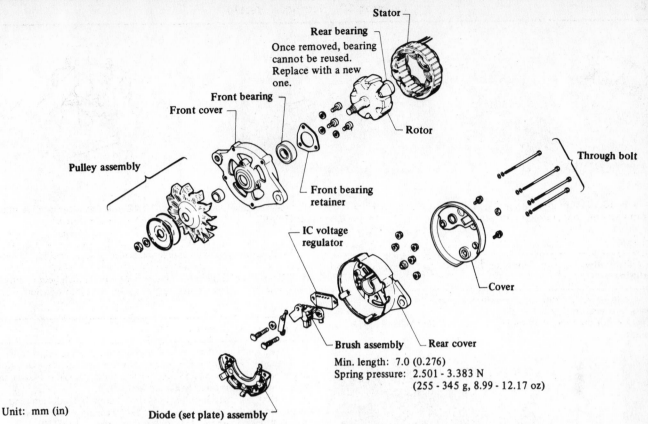

Stator

Rear bearing
Once removed, bearing
cannot be reused.
Replace with a new
one.

Front bearing

Front cover

Rotor

Through bolt

Pulley assembly

Front bearing
retainer

IC voltage
regulator

Cover

Brush assembly   Rear cover
Min. length: 7.0 (0.276)
Spring pressure: 2.501 - 3.383 N
(255 - 345 g, 8.99 - 12.17 oz)

Unit: mm (in)

Diode (set plate) assembly

Fig. 10.13 Type LR 160 alternator components (Sec 10)

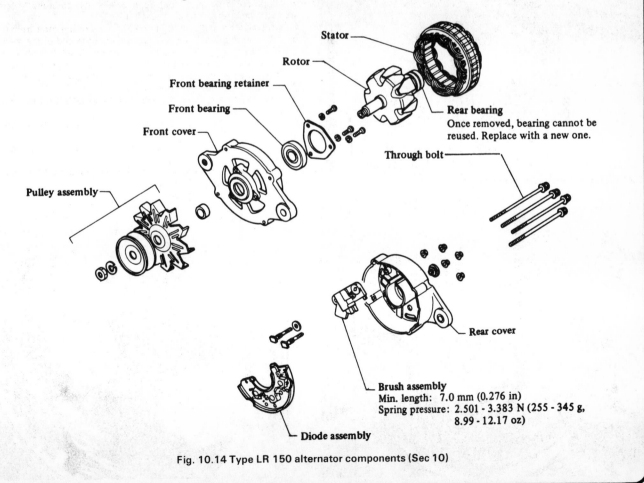

Stator

Rotor

Front bearing retainer

Front bearing

Front cover

Rear bearing
Once removed, bearing cannot be
reused. Replace with a new one.

Through bolt

Pulley assembly

Rear cover

10

Brush assembly
Min. length: 7.0 mm (0.276 in)
Spring pressure: 2.501 - 3.383 N (255 - 345 g,
8.99 - 12.17 oz)

Diode assembly

Fig. 10.14 Type LR 150 alternator components (Sec 10)

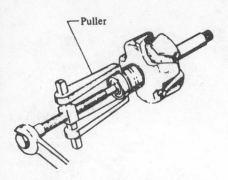

Fig. 10.15 Removing a rotor bearing (Sec 10)

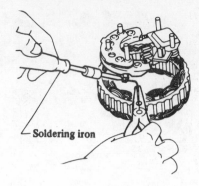

Fig. 10.16 Unsoldering stator coil leads (Sec 10)

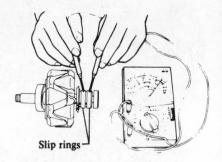

Fig. 10.17 Testing rotor slip rings for continuity (Sec 10)

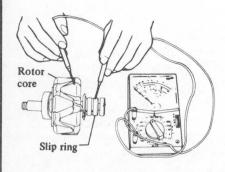

Fig. 10.18 Testing rotor for insulation breakdown (Sec 10)

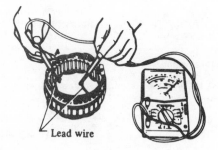

Fig. 10.19 Checking stator for continuity (Sec 10)

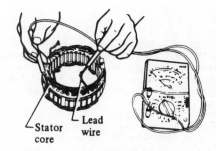

Fig. 10.20 Checking stator insulation (Sec 10)

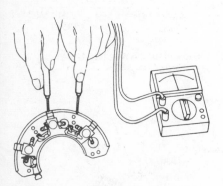

Fig. 10.21 Checking positive diode (Sec 10)

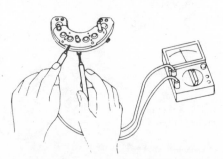

Fig. 10.22 Checking negative diode (Sec 10)

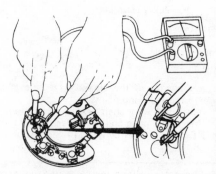

Fig. 10.23 Checking sub-diode (Sec 10)

10.12A Alternator rotor slip rings

10.12B Stator removal

12 If a suitable tester is available, the following tests may be carried out to major components:

Rotor, check for continuity by placing one tester probe on each of the slip rings. If there is no continuity, renew the rotor. The slip rings may be cleaned with solvent or fine glass paper. Check the insulation as shown in Fig. 10.18. If continuity exists, renew the rotor.

Stator, check for continuity by placing a tester probe on each lead. If there is no continuity, renew the stator. Check the insulation by placing one tester probe on a lead and the other on the stator core. If continuity exists, renew the stator (photo).

13 If an ohmmeter is available, use it to test the diodes in both directions. The results should be as shown in the table.

14 Some ohmmeters use reverse polarity in which case the continuity shown in the table will be directly opposite.

Tester positive probe	Tester negative probe	Continuity
(+) plate Holder plate	Diode terminal	Exists
Diode terminal	(+) plate Holder plate	None
(–) plate Rear cover	Diode terminal	None
Diode terminal	(–) plate Rear cover	Exists

15 Reassembly of the alternator is a reversal of dismantling, but observe the following points.

16 Renew the rotor shaft bearing if removed.

17 Grease the drive end cover bearing before fitting the retainer.

18 Fit the end cover by raising the brush as described in Section 9.

11 Alternator voltage regulator (independent type) – testing and adjustment

1 To test this type of regulator, a DC voltmeter and a DC ammeter will be required. A resistor should also be included in the circuit which should be as shown in Fig. 10.24.

2 Switch off all electrical components and connect a jump lead between the side terminal of the fusible link and the negative terminal of the ammeter.

3 Start the engine and run it at 2500 rev/min for several minutes. With a fully charged battery, the ammeter should indicate less than 5A.

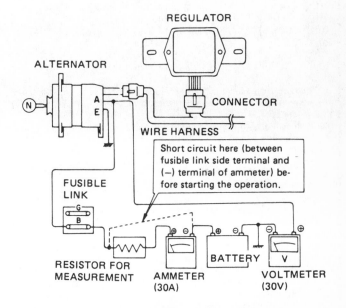

Fig. 10.24 Independent voltage regulator test circuit (Sec 11)

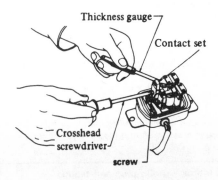

Fig. 10.25 Setting voltage regulator core gap (Sec 11)

10

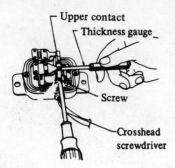

Fig. 10.26 Setting voltage regulator points gap (Sec 11)

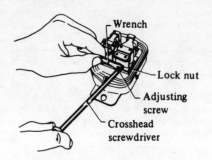

Fig. 10.27 Adjusting regulating voltage (Sec 11)

4   Allow the engine to return to idle and then increase its speed to 2500 rev/min while observing the voltmeter. If the reading is compatible with the temperature of the voltage regulator as shown in the following table then the regulator is in good order. If not, adjust as described in the following paragraphs or where such adjustment does not rectify matters, renew the unit.

Temperature	Voltage
–10°C (14°F)	14.7 to 15.25v
0°C (32°F)	14.6 to 15.2v
10°C (50°F)	14.5 to 15.15v
20°C (68°F)	14.4 to 15.1v
30°C (86°F)	14.3 to 15.05v
40°C (104°F)	14.2 to 15.0v

5   Extract the two screws and remove the cover.
6   Inspect the regulator contact faces. If they are rough, burnish with fine glasspaper.
7   Adjust the core gap and the point gap in that order.
8   Loosen the screw which holds the contact set to the yoke. Move the contact set up or down to achieve a core gap of between 0.6 and 1.0 mm (0.024 and 0.039 in) measured with a feeler gauge. Tighten screw.
9   Now adjust the point gap by releasing the screw on the upper contact and moving it to achieve a point gap of between 0.35 and 0.45 mm (0.014 and 0.018 in) using a feeler gauge to check the gap.
10   The regulating voltage may be adjusted to bring it within the tolerance given in the table (paragraph 4) by releasing the adjuster screw locknut and turning the screw clockwise to increase the voltage or anti-clockwise to decrease it.
11   Normal relay voltage is between 8 and 10v measured at the alternator A terminal. To test this, arrange a test circuit as shown using a DC voltmeter.
12   Connect the positive probe of the voltmeter to the N contact of the wiring harness plug.
13   Connect the negative probe of the voltmeter to earth.
14   Start the engine and allow it to idle.
15   Record the reading on the voltmeter.
16   If no reading is indicated, check for continuity between the N terminals of the regulator and the alternator. If continuity exists, then the alternator is faulty.
17   If the voltmeter indicates less than 5.2v and the ignition warning lamp remains on, first check that the alternator drivebelt is correctly tensioned and then carry out the adjustments previously described in this Section.
18   If the voltmeter indicates more than 5.2v, with the ignition warning lamp on, the voltage regulator is faulty and should be renewed.
19   If the voltmeter indicates more than 5.2v, but the warning lamp is out, then it can be assumed that the voltage regulator is in good order.

12 Starter motor – description and testing

1   The starter motor is of two brush, pre-engaged type.
2   If the starter motor does not turn at all, when the ignition switch

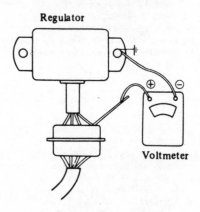

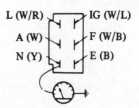

Fig. 10.28 Regulating voltage test circuit (Sec 11)

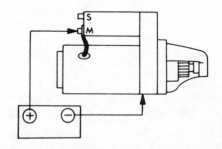

Fig. 10.29 Test circuit for starter motor bypassing solenoid (Sec 12)

is turned, then either the battery is flat or the battery terminals are corroded or the starter motor leads are loose or disconnected.
3   If when the ignition key is turned, the starter relay and the solenoid can be heard 'clicking' but the starter does not crank the engine, suspect a fault in the starter motor drive.
4   Remove the starter motor as described in Section 13 and connect a lead from the battery (+) terminal to the M terminal of the starter motor. Then connect a lead between the battery (–) terminal and the body of the starter motor. If the motor turns then check the solenoid. If the motor does not turn then the starter motor armature, field coil or brush are faulty.

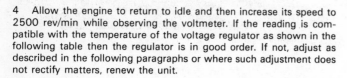

5   Should the situation occur where the starter motor keeps running when the ignition key is released then this will be due to a fault in the key switch, starter relay or solenoid switch.

13 Starter motor – removal and refitting

1   Disconnect the battery.
2   Disconnect the leads from the starter motor.
3   Unscrew the starter motor mounting bolts and remove the unit from the front face of the bellhousing. Remove the starter upwards.
4   Refitting is a reversal of removal.

14 Starter motor – overhaul

1   With the unit removed from the vehicle, clean away external dirt.
2   Disconnect the leads from the solenoid terminals and then extract the two screws which hold the solenoid to the drive end housing. Withdraw the solenoid (photos).
3   Prise off the small centre cap from the rear cover (photo).
4   Prise off the E-ring and remove the thrust washers (photo).
5   Unscrew the tie-bolts and fixing screws and remove the rear cover (photo).

14.2A Removing starter motor solenoid

14.2B Starter motor shift lever

14.3 Removing rear cover cap

14.4 Starter motor E-ring and thrust washers

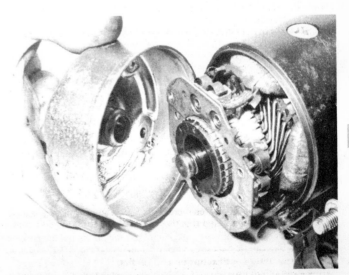

14.5 Starter motor rear cover

10

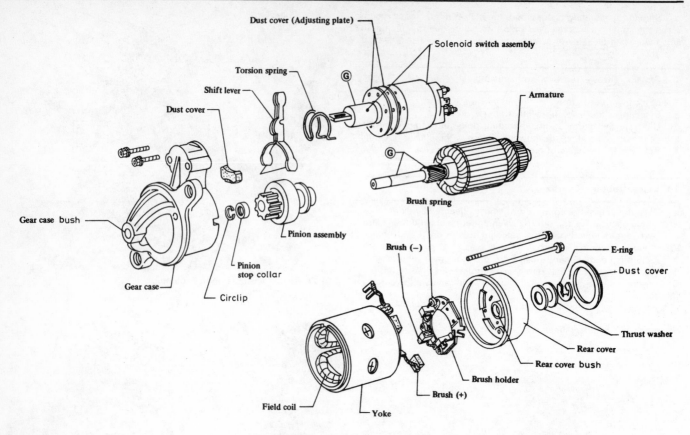

Fig. 10.30 Starter motor components (Sec 14)

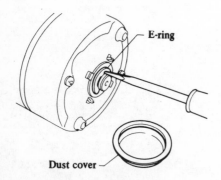

Fig. 10.31 Removing E-ring from starter motor shaft (Sec 14)

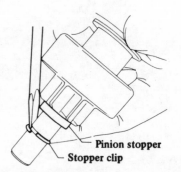

Fig. 10.32 Starter motor pinion stop clip and ring (Sec 14)

6   Extract the screws and remove the brush holder.
7   Withdraw the yoke, armature and shift lever.
8   If the starter drive must be removed, tap the pinion stop collar down the shaft to expose the circlip. Remove the circlip, the stop collar and pull the drive assembly from the armature shaft.
9   Inspect all components for wear and damage and renew as necessary.
10 If the commutator is discoloured, clean it with a fuel moistened rag or burnish with fine glasspaper.
11 If the mica separators of the commutator are not below the copper segments then they must be undercut as shown in Fig. 10.33 using a hacksaw or other suitable tool.
12 The armature may be tested if an ohmmeter is available by placing the probes on adjacent segments and working round the commutator. If there is no continuity, renew the armature.

13 Now check for continuity between each segment of the commutator in sequence and the armature shaft. Continuity here will indicate the need to renew the armature.
14 Check the brushes for wear. If they have worn down to 11.0 mm (0.43 in) or less then they must be renewed. When unsoldering the old brushes and soldering the new ones in place, work quickly and grip the brush lead with a pair of pliers to act as a heat sink and so prevent heat travelling down to the field coil. Take great care not to allow solder to run down the brush lead or its flexibility will be ruined.
15 The field coils can be checked if the ohmmeter is connected between the (+) terminal of the field coil and the positive brush. If there is no continuity, renew the field coil. This is a job best left to your dealer or auto-electrician as a pressure screwdriver will be needed.
16 Now check the insulation between the field coil positive terminal and the yoke. If continuity exists, then the field coils must be renewed.

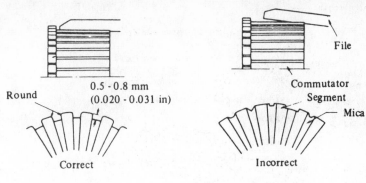

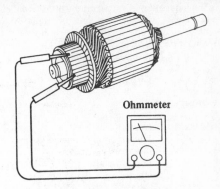

Fig. 10.33 Starter motor armature undercutting diagram (Sec 14)

Fig. 10.34 Checking for continuity (Sec 14)

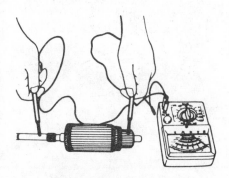

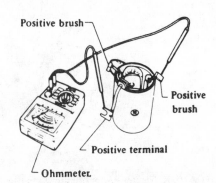

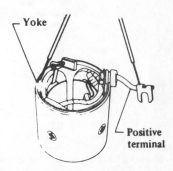

Fig. 10.35 Checking insulation (Sec 14)

Fig. 10.36 Checking starter field coils for continuity (Sec 14)

Fig. 10.37 Checking starter field coils for insulation (Sec 14)

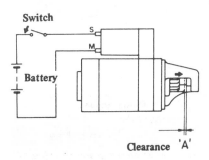

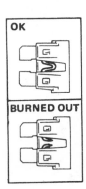

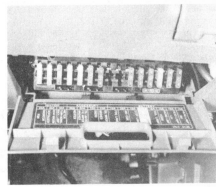

Fig. 10.38 Circuit for testing starter motor pinion stop clearance (Sec 14)

Fig. 10.39 Fuse condition (Sec 15)

15.1 Fuse box

10

17 Check that the drive pinion clutch is operating correctly. It should lock when turned in the drive direction and turn smoothly in the reverse direction.

18 Reassembly is a reversal of dismantling. Apply a smear of grease to the shift lever and drive pinion friction surfaces and to the armature shaft bushes.

19 Having fitted the drive pinion stop collar and circlip to the armature shaft, draw the stop collar over the circlip using a small two-legged puller.

20 Once the starter motor is reassembled, energise the solenoid and check that the clearance A between the end face of the pinion and the stop plate is between 0.3 and 2.5 mm (0.012 and 0.098 in). If adjustment is required, change the thickness of the shims which are located between the solenoid and the drive end housing. The shims are available in two thicknesses, 0.5 mm (0.020 in) and 0.8 mm (0.031 in).

15 Fuses and fusible links

Fuses

1 The fuse block is located under the facia glove compartment (photo).

2 Up to sixteen electrical circuits may be protected according to the particular model.

3   The fuse rating is shown on the translucent cover of the fuse block. Never renew a fuse with one of higher rating and if it blows immediately it is renewed, check the wiring of that particular circuit as the insulation is probably at fault.
4   A typical fuse arrangement is:

Fuse (numbering left to right)	Circuit protected	Rating - amps
1	Radiator fan	20
2	Heated rear window	20
3	Instruments, reversing lamps, direction indicators	10
4	Ignition coil	10
5	Heater	20
6	Cigar lighter, windscreen wiper/ washer	20
7	Radio/cassette player	10
8	Rear wiper/washer	10
9	Air conditioner	20
10	Stop-lamps, luggage compartment lamp	10
11	Clock, interior lamp	10
12	Tail lamp, rear number plate front parking lamp, instrument panel illumination	10
13	Horn, hazard warning lamps	10
14	Left-hand headlamp	10
15	Right-hand headlamp	10

Fusible links

5   Two fusible links are used and are located adjacent to the battery terminal. The green wire protects the ignition system, starting system and the radio while the black one protects the charging and lighting circuits and other accessories (photo).
6   Should a fusible link melt this will probably be due to a major short circuit, rectify immediately. Never bind the leads of the fusible link with insulating tape or attempt a makeshift repair, only renew.

16 Relays, circuit breakers, limit switches and sensors

1   The number and purpose of the relays will depend upon the particular model, operating territory and the accessories with which the vehicle is equipped.
2   The majority of relays are located either on the relay bracket within the engine compartment or on the fuse block, but other relays and their positions are described in the following paragraphs.

3   On the relay bracket in the engine compartment are mounted:

Horn relay
Automatic choke relay
Lighting relay
Wiper (intermittent) relay – except N. America
Carburettor heater relay
Idle-up relay for air conditioner (photo)

4   On the fuse block within the vehicle are located:

Ignition relay
Accessory relay
ASCD relay

5   On the engine compartment rear bulkhead are located:

Air conditioner relay
Wiper (intermittent) relay – N. America

6   The radiator fan relay is located on the fan shroud.
7   Behind the facia panel within the vehicle are located:

Direction indicator flasher relay
Hazard warning flasher relay
Warning buzzer (photo)

15.5 Fusible links at battery terminal

16.3 Engine compartment relay bracket

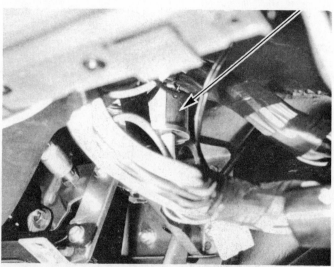

16.7 Direction indicator flasher unit

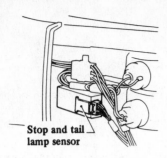

Stop and tail
lamp sensor

Fig. 10.40 Typical stop/tail lamp bulb failure sensor (Sec 16)

8   On the side panels adjacent to the front footwells are located:

Headlamp sensor
Interior lamp timer
Electric window amplifier and circuit breaker
Central door lock timer
Electric sunroof circuit breaker
Seat belt timer
ASCD controller
Engine revolution switch

9   A safety relay for the sunroof is mounted above the windscreen under the roof lining.
10 A stop and tail lamp sensor is located within the luggage compartment.
11 A resistor is fitted under the front right-hand wing and integrated into the tachometer wiring circuit.
12 Should a fault develop, the relay or other item described in this Section must be renewed complete, no repair being possible.

17 Steering column switch – removal and refitting

1   Refer to Chapter 11 and remove the steering wheel. Disconnect the battery.
2   Extract the screws and remove the steering column shrouds (photos).
3   Disconnect the switch wiring harness plugs.

4   Remove the retaining screw and lift the switch from the column.
5   Refitting is a reversal of removal, but make sure that the pip on the switch engages in the hole in the column.

18 Rocker type switches – removal and refitting

1   To remove this type of switch, reach behind the panel and compress the retaining tabs with the fingers (photo).
2   Withdraw the switch and disconnect the wiring plug.

19 Courtesy lamp switch – removal and refitting

1   These plunger type switches are located at the base of the centre pillar by means of a single screw (photo).
2   Extract the screw and withdraw the switch.
3   If the leads are to be disconnected from the switch, tape them to the bodywork to prevent them from slipping inside the pillar.
4   It is recommended that petroleum jelly is applied to the switch before fitting as a means of reducing corrosion.

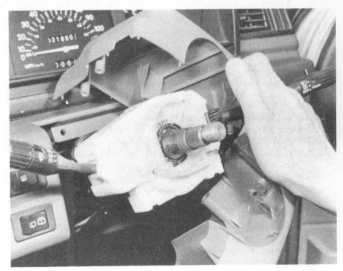

17.2 Removing steering column shroud

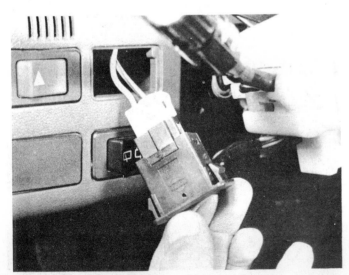

18.1 Removing a rocker switch

19.1 Courtesy lamp switch

10

19.5 Luggage compartment lamp switch at tailgate

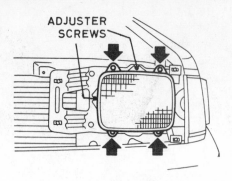

Fig. 10.41 Headlamp retaining ring screws (Sec 20)

5   Similar switches are used for the luggage and engine compartment lamps (photo).

20 Headlamp sealed beam unit – renewal

1   Rotate the clips which hold the front grille through 45° and remove the grille (Chapter 12).
2   Release the screws which hold the headlamp retaining ring and withdraw the headlamp. Do not disturb the beam adjusting screws.
3   Pull the wiring connecting plug from the rear of the headlamp.
4   Fit the new unit into its retaining ring and reconnect the plug.
5   Screw the headlamp unit into position.
6   Provided the beam adjusting screws have not been altered, the alignment of the headlamp beams should be as originally set.

21 Headlamp – bulb renewal

1   Working within the engine compartment, pull the wiring plug from the rear of the bulbholder.
2   Pull off the rubber cover (photo).
3   Prise back the bulbholder retainer and withdraw the holder (photo).

4   Remove the bulb and fit the new one without touching the glass with the fingers (photo).
5   Refit the bulbholder.
6   Refit the rubber cover so that the word TOP is uppermost.
7   Reconnect the wiring plug.

22 Headlamp beam – adjustment

1   The headlamp beams are adjustable and can be altered by turning the screws one of which is located at centre top of the lamp and the other on the centre of the inboard rim (photo).
2   It is recommended that headlamp adjustment is left to your dealer or service station where optical setting equipment will be available. In an emergency however, adjust in the following way.
3   During the hours of darkness set the vehicle square to, and 5.0 m (16.4 ft) from a wall or screen.
4   Mark the positions of the centres of the headlamps by measuring their height from the floor and the distance of the centre point of each lamp from the centre line of the vehicle.
5   Switch the headlamps to dipped beam and adjust so that the brightest spots of the light pattern coincide with the marks made on the wall.

23 Exterior lamps – bulb renewal

Front parking lamp
1   Extract the three securing screws and remove the lens. The bayonet fitting type bulb can then be removed and a new one fitted (photos).

21.2 Headlamp rear rubber cover

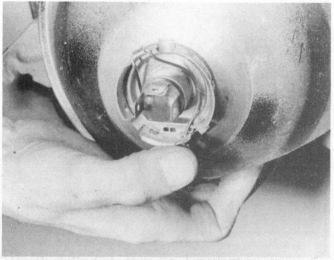

21.3 Headlamp bulb retaining springs

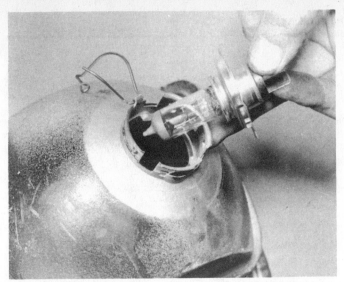
21.4 Removing bulbholder

22.1 Headlamp beam adjusting screw

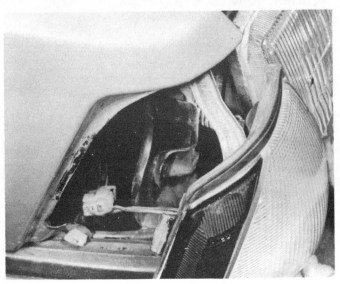
23.1A Front parking lamp lens unit removed

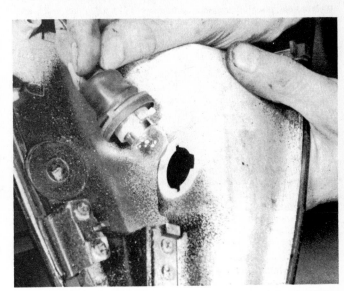
23.1B Front parking lamp bulbholder

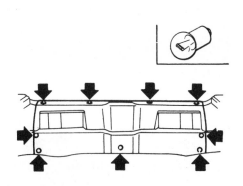
Fig. 10.42 Access panel for rear number plate lamps (Sec 23)

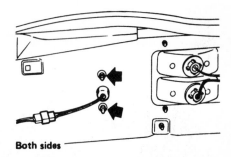
Both sides

Fig. 10.43 Rear number plate lamp fixing nuts (Sec 23)

23.2A Front direction indicator lens screw

23.2B Front direction indicator bulb

Front direction indicator lamp

2   Extract the two retaining screws and remove the lens. Renew the bayonet fiitting type bulb (photos).

Front side marker lamp

3   Unscrew the lens and pull out the wedge base type bulb. Refit the new bulb and screw on the lens.

Rear side marker lamp

4   The bulb is accessible from inside the vehicle.
5   Rock the bulbholder out of the lamp body.

Rear lamp

6   On hatchback versions, prise off the small cover panels and twist the bulbholder to remove (photos).
7   On saloon models, pull the bulbholder from the rear panel.

Rear number plate lamp

8   Where the lamps are located in the rear bumper, simply prise the lamps out of the bumper and then separate the lens for access to the bulb (photos).
9   On models where the lamps are located on the rear panel, then access to the lamp fixing nuts is obtained after first detaching the trim panel from the rear of the luggage area.

23.6A Rear lamp cluster bulb

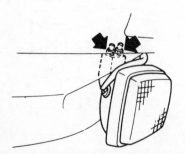

Fig. 10.44 Front foglamp fixing bolts (Sec 23)

Fig. 10.45 Front foglamp lens frame fixing screws (Sec 23)

Fig. 10.46 Front foglamp sections separated (Sec 23)

23.6B Rear lamp cluster bulb

23.8A Rear number plate lamp

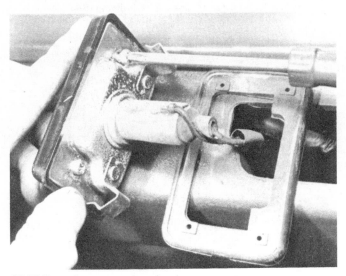

23.8B Extracting rear number plate lens screw

23.8C Rear number plate lamp bulb

Rear foglamp

10 Access to these lamps for bulb renewal is obtained after removal of the trim panel at the rear of the luggage area.

Front foglamp

11 To reach the bulb in this lamp, first withdraw the lamp by unscrewing the bracket bolts.
12 Separate the lens and body by unscrewing the pinch screws.
13 Unclip the bulbholder and remove it.

24 Interior lamps – bulb renewal

Interior lamp

1   Depending upon the type of lamp, either unscrew the lamp lens or prise it off (photo).
2   Pull the festoon type bulb from its spring contacts..

Luggage compartment lamp

3   The lens is secured by two screws. Remove these and the lens for access to the festoon type bulb (photo).

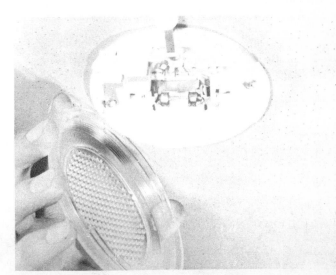

24.1 Interior lamp

10

24.3 Luggage compartment lamp

Fig. 10.47 Square type of interior lamp (Sec 24)

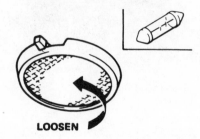

Fig. 10.48 Circular type of interior lamp (Sec 24)

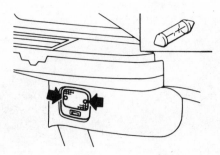

Fig. 10.49 Luggage compartment lamp (Sec 24)

Indicator and warning lamps

4   Withdraw the instrument panel as described in Section 26, until the bulbholders can be twisted from the panel. The bulbs are of wedge base type.

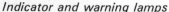

25 Headlamp – removal and refitting

1   Disconnect the wiring plug from the rear of the headlamp. Pull off the rubber dust cover.
2   Remove the sidelamp (three screws).
3   Remove the radiator grille (Chapter 12).
4   Release the spring from the out-board side of headlamp (photo).
5   Pull headlamp from base ball socket and slide sideways off adjuster screws (photo).
6   Refitting is a reversal of removal.

26 Instrument panel – removal and refitting

1   Disconnect the battery and then on tilt-type steering columns, release the adjusting lever and lower the column as far as it will go.
2   On non-tilt type columns, remove the column lower shroud and unbolt the column brackets. Lower the column and remove the upper shroud.
3   Extract the two fixing screws from the lower edge of the instrument panel hood (photo).
4   Pull the lower part of the hood forward and disengage the securing tabs. Disconnect the wiring plug and remove the hood (photo).

5   Unscrew the instrument panel fixing screws which are now exposed (photo).
6   Pull the instrument panel towards you while an assistant feeds the speedometer drive cable through the bulkhead grommet.
7   As soon as there is enough space to insert the hand behind the panel, disconnect the speedometer cable by depressing the grooved thumbpiece of the connector and pulling the cable from the speedometer head (photos).
8   Continue to withdraw the panel until the wiring plugs can be disconnected and the panel withdrawn.
9   Extract the instrument lens screws, unclip the lens and remove it.
10 The individual instruments may be unclipped and removed for renewal (photos).
11 Refitting is a reversal of removal.

25.4 Headlamp unit coil spring

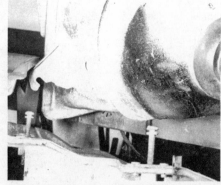

25.5 Headlamp adjuster screws and retainer bracket

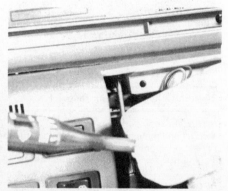

26.3 Extracting instrument panel hood screw

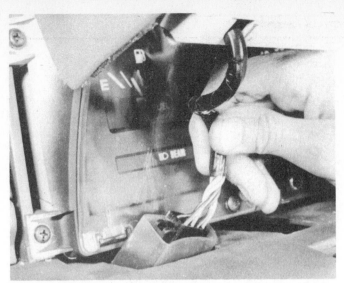

26.4 Instrument panel hood wiring plug

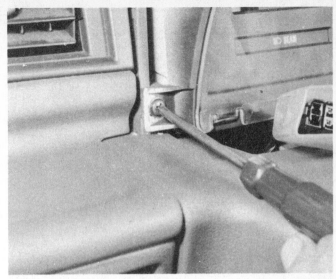

26.5 Extracting instrument panel screw

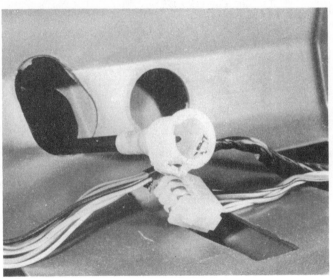

26.7A Speedometer cable connector

26.7B Speedometer cable disconnected from head

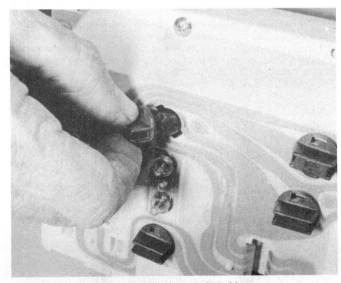

26.10A Instrument panel warning lamp bulb holders

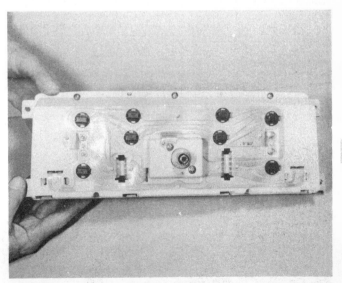

26.10B Rear view of instrument panel

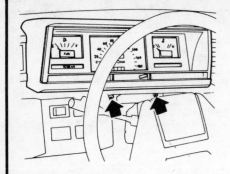

Fig. 10.50 Instrument hood screws (Sec 26)

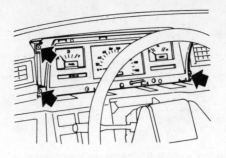

Fig. 10.51 Instrument panel screws (Sec 26)

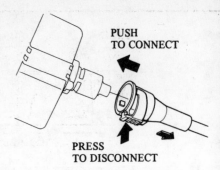

PUSH TO CONNECT

PRESS TO DISCONNECT

Fig. 10.52 Speedometer drive cable connection (Sec 26)

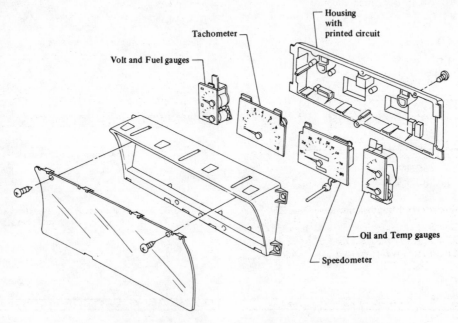

Tachometer

Housing with printed circuit

Volt and Fuel gauges

Oil and Temp gauges

Speedometer

Fig. 10.53 Instrument panel with tachometer (Sec 26)

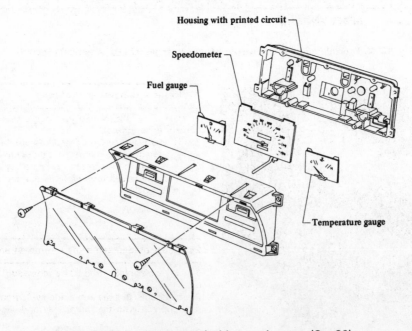

Housing with printed circuit

Speedometer

Fuel gauge

Temperature gauge

Fig. 10.54 Instrument panel without tachometer (Sec 26)

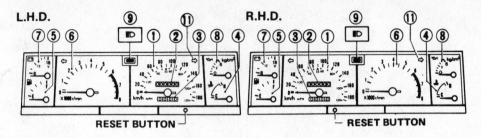

Fig. 10.55 Instruments including tachometer and warning lamps (Sec 26)

1 Speedometer	4 Coolant temperature gauge	7 Battery condition indicator (voltmeter)	9 Main beam warning lamp
2 Mileage recorder	5 Fuel contents gauge		11 Direction indicator/ hazard warning lamp
3 Trip mileage recorder	6 Tachometer	8 Oil pressure gauge	

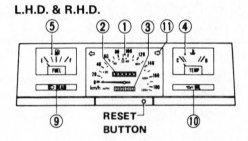

Fig. 10.56 Instrumentation without tachometer (Sec 26)

Key as in Fig. 10.55 except for
10 Oil pressure warning lamp

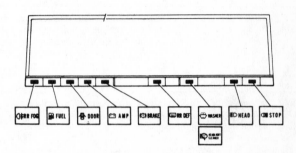

Fig. 10.57 Typical indicator and warning lamp arrangement (except N. America) (Sec 26)

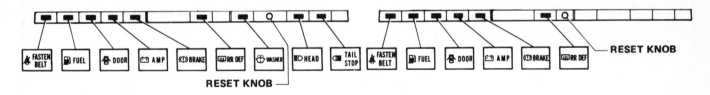

Fig. 10.58 Typical indicator and warning lamp arrangement (N. America) (Sec 26)

27.1 Location of horns

27 Horns – removal and refitting

1   The horns are located just to the rear of the lower edge of the radiator grille (photo).
2   The horn switches are fitted into the hub or spokes of the steering wheel and access to them may be obtained by extracting the screws and removing the spoke rear covers or by prising off the hub cover.
3   If the horns fail to operate, check the security of the wiring and connections.

28 Wiper blades and arms – removal and refitting

1   The wiper blades should be renewed if they fail to wipe the glass clean.
2   To do this, pull the arm/blade away from the glass, prise down the retaining clip with the thumb nail and slide the blade from the arm (photo).
3   Complete blades or rubber inserts are available. Changing the rubber inserts only should be carried out in accordance with the manufacturer's instructions.

10

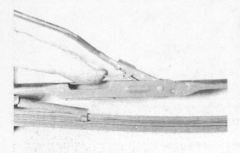

28.2 Releasing wiper blade catch

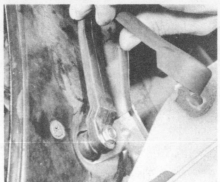

28.4 Lifting wiper arm cover

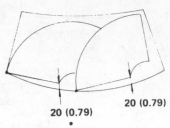

Fig. 10.59 Windscreen wiper arm setting diagram (Sec 28)

4   To remove the wiper arm, flip up the cover from the securing nut, unscrew the nut and pull the arm from the splined spindle (photo).
5   When refitting, check that the arms are set in accordance with the diagram, Fig. 10.59.

6   Remove the wiper mounting bolts and lift the motor from the tailgate (photo).
7   Refitting is a reversal of removal. Fit the arm to the splined spindle so that it takes up the position shown in the diagram when in the parked position.

29 Windscreen wiper and linkage – removal and refitting

1   Remove the wiper blade/arm assemblies.
2   Disconnect the battery.
3   Unscrew and remove the nuts which secure the drive spindles to the scuttle.
4   Working within the engine compartment, disconnect the wiring plug from the wiper motor. Extract the screws and remove the protective cover from the linkage (Chapter 12) (photo).
5   Unscrew the wiper motor mounting bolts and withdraw the motor with linkage.
6   The linkage may be separated from the motor by disconnecting the crankarm.
7   Refitting is a reversal of removal.

30 Tailgate wiper motor – removal and refitting

1   Disconnect the battery.
2   Open the tailgate fully and remove the trim panel from its lower part.
3   Partially close the tailgate and remove the wiper arm/blade assembly (photo).
4   Unscrew the nut which holds the drive spindle to the tailgate.
5   Fully open the tailgate again and disconnect the wiring plug from the wiper motor.

31 Windscreen/tailgate washer

1   This is a combined system having a fluid reservoir located adjacent to the battery.
2   The electric washer pump is mounted on the reservoir.
3   It is recommended that special windscreen washer fluid additive is used, not household detergent as the foaming action could damage the pump.
4   In very cold weather, add some methylated spirit to the fluid to prevent freezing. *Do not use cooling system antifreeze as this will damage the paintwork.*
5   The wash pattern on the glass may be adjusted by inserting a needle in the jets and moving them to obtain the specified jet striking points as shown in the diagrams.
6   The windscreen washer hoses are attached to the underside of the bonnet (photo).

32 Headlamp wash/wipe system

1   The wiper arm/blade assembly is removed in a similar way to the windscreen wiper.
2   Remove the radiator grille for access to the motor.
3   The electric pump and reservoir are located beneath the right-hand front wing, but the filler is within the engine compartment.
4   When refitting the headlamp wiper arm, set the blade as shown in the diagram.

29.4 Windscreen wiper motor linkage

30.3 Tailgate wiper viewed through glass

30.6 Tailgate wiper motor

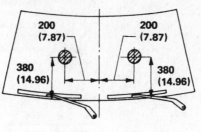

Nozzle
15 (0.59)
250 (9.84)
Unit: mm (in)
Washer adjustment

Fig. 10.60 Tailgate wiper arm setting
diagram (Sec 30)

200 (7.87)   200 (7.87)
380 (14.96)   380 (14.96)
Unit: mm (in)

Fig. 10.61 Windscreen washer jet
striking points (Sec 31)

31.6 Windscreen washer pipe attached to
underside of bonnet

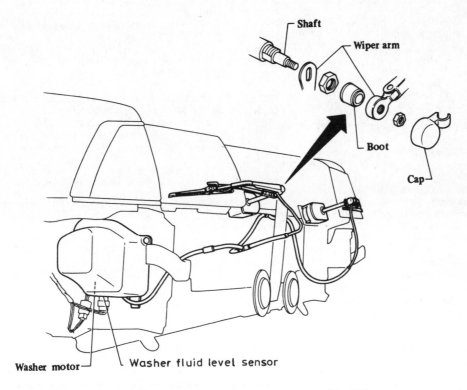

Shaft
Wiper arm
Boot
Cap

Washer motor   Washer fluid level sensor

Fig. 10.62 Headlamp wash/wipe arrangement (Sec 32)

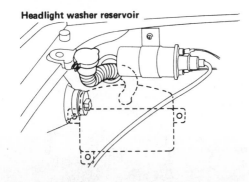

Headlight washer reservoir

Fig. 10.63 Headlamp washer fluid reservoir (Sec 32)

Headlamp
13 mm (0.51 in)

Fig. 10.64 Headlamp wiper arm setting diagram (Sec 32)

10

33 Heated rear glass – treatment and repair

1   The heater elements are fragile and the following precautions should be observed. Do not allow luggage or other items to rub against the inside surface of the glass.

   Do not stick labels over the elements
   Avoid scratching the elements when cleaning with rings on the fingers
   Clean the glass with water and detergent only and rub in the direction of the elements

2   Should an element be damaged so that the current is interrupted, a repair can be made using one of the conductive silver paints available from motor accessory stores.

34 Warning systems – description

1   Depending upon the model, one or all of the following systems may be fitted.

Seat belt warning system

2   A warning lamp and chime are actuated for a six second period if the ignition is switched on without the driver's seat belt having been fastened.

Anti-theft system

3   A warning chime sounds if the driver's door is opened from the inside with the ignition key in the steering column lock.

Door closure warning system

4   A warning lamp comes on when the engine is run and one door is not properly closed.

Stop/tail warning lamp

5   This lamp comes on if a stop/tail lamp bulb has blown when the engine is running and the brake pedal is depressed or the lighting switch is on. The lamp should glow if the bulbs are in good order when the ignition is switched on before starting the engine.

Washer fluid level warning lamp

6   This lamp comes on if the fluid level falls below one quarter full when the engine is running. The lamp should glow when the ignition is switched on before starting the engine.

Fuel level warning lamp

7   This lamp comes on when the engine is running if the fuel in the tank falls to a very low level (7.0 litres, 1.5 Imp gal, 1.88 US gal).

Brake system warning lamp

8   This lamp covers both the handbrake ON and low fluid level monitoring. The lamp should glow when the ignition is switched on before starting the engine. The lamp will remain on when the engine is running and the handbrake is applied.

9   If the engine is running and the handbrake is off, the lamp will only come on if the fluid level in the master cylinder reservoir is dangerously low.

10   When a fault develops in any system first check for a blown warning lamp bulb and then for disconnected or damaged wiring.

35 Radio and cassette player – removal and refitting

1   Extract the five fixing screws and remove the finisher cover.
2   Extract the screws which secure the radio or cassette player and withdraw the units until the power, aerial, speaker and earth leads can all be disconnected.
3   Refitting is a reversal of removal.
4   If the radio or aerial have been changed, then the aerial must be trimmed in the following way.
5   Fully extend the aerial and switch on the radio.
6   Tune in to a very weak station around 1400kHz.
7   Insert a thin screwdriver into the trim adjuster hole and turn the screw not more than half a turn in either direction until reception is at its best (loudest).

36 Power-operated windows

1   The electric motors for this system are located within the door cavities and are accessible after removal of the trim panels (Chapter 12).
2   The window control panel incorporates a one-touch switch which operates the driver's window only, moving it all the way up or down unless the switch is touched again.
3   A lock switch enables the driver to lock all the window switches except the one touch or normal switch for the driver's window.

37 Power-operated sunroof

1   As a safety feature, when the switch is depressed to close the sunroof, the roof will only close to a point 100.0 m (3.94 in) from the fully closed position. The switch button must then be released and depressed again to fully close the roof.
2   A safety relay is located at the forward end of the sunroof aperture and limit switches are used to control the opening and closing modes.
3   Should a fault develop in the electrical circuit, the sunroof may be closed manually using the handle stored in the glove compartment.

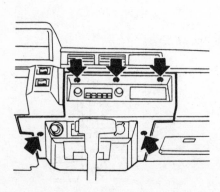

Fig. 10.65 Radio finisher screws (Sec 35)

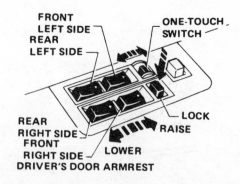

Fig. 10.66 Power-operated window controls (Sec 36)

4   Take off the cap just to the rear of the interior mirror to expose the motor shaft.

5   Engage the handle in the hexagonal socket in the end of the motor shaft and rotate clockwise to close the shaft.

38 Speedometer drive cable – renewal

1   Disconnect the cable from the speedometer as described in Section 26.

2   Disconnect the speedometer cable from the transmission by removing the bolt and lockplate.

3   Withdraw the cable through the bulkhead grommet.

4   The new cable is supplied as an assembly.

5   Fit the new cable by reversing the removal operations, do not make any curves more acute than the original ones.

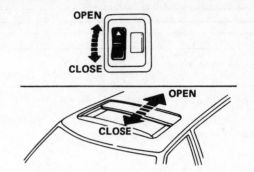

Fig. 10.67 Power-operated sunroof control switch (Sec 37)

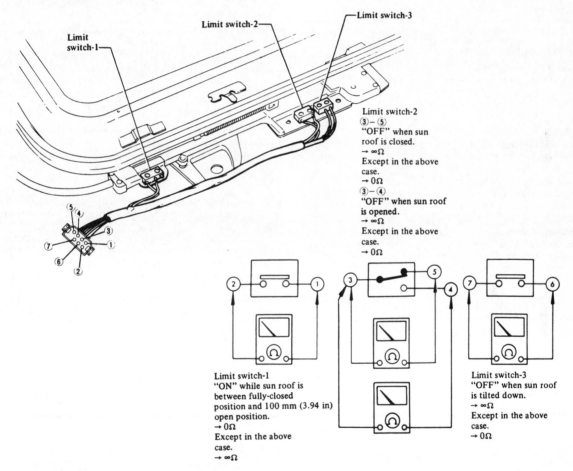

Fig. 10.68 Sunroof limit switches (Sec 37)

Fig. 10.69 Sunroof cranking shaft cover (Sec 37)

Fig. 10.70 Manually cranking the sunroof (Sec 37)

39 Fault diagnosis – electrical system

Symptom	Reason(s)
No voltage at starter motor	Battery discharged Battery defective internally Battery terminals loose or earth lead not securely attached to body Loose or broken connections in starter motor circuit Starter motor switch or solenoid faulty
Voltage at starter motor – faulty motor	Starter brushes badly worn, sticking, or brush wires loose Commutator dirty, worn or burnt Starter motor armature faulty Field coils earthed
Electrical defects	Battery in discharged condition Starter brushes badly worn, sticking, or brush wires loose Loose wires in starter motor circuit Dirt or oil on drivegear
Starter motor noisy or rough in engagement	Pinion or flywheel gear teeth broken or worn Starter drive main spring broken Starter motor retaining bolts loose
Alternator not charging	Drivebelt loose and slipping, or broken Brushes worn, sticking, broken or dirty Brush springs weak or broken
Battery will not hold charge for more than a few days	Battery defective internally Electrolyte level too low or electrolyte too weak due to leakage Plate separators no longer fully effective Battery plates severely sulphated Drivebelt slipping Battery terminal connections loose or corroded Alternator not charging properly Short in lighting circuit causing continual battery drain Integral regulator unit not working correctly
Ignition light fails to go out, battery runs flat in a few days	Drivebelt loose and slipping, or broken Alternator faulty

Failure of individual electrical equipment to function correctly is dealt with alphabetically below

Symptom	Reason(s)
Fuel gauge gives no reading (refer also to Chapter 3)	Fuel tank empty! Electric cable between tank sender unit and gauge earthed or loose Fuel gauge case not earthed Fuel gauge supply cable interrupted Fuel gauge unit broken
Fuel gauge registers full all the time	Electric cable between tank unit and gauge broken or disconnected
Horn operates all the time	Horn push either earthed or stuck down Horn cable to horn push earthed
Horn fails to operate	Blown fuse Cable or cable connection loose, broken or disconnected Horn has an internal fault
Horn emits intermittent or unsatisfactory noise	Cable connections loose Horn incorrectly adjusted Blown fuse
Lights do not come on	If engine not running, battery discharged Light bulb filament burnt out or bulbs broken Wire connections loose, disconnected or broken Light switch shorting or otherwise faulty Fusible link melted
Lights come on but fade out	If engine not running, battery discharged
Lights give very poor illumination	Lamp glasses dirty Reflector tarnished or dirty Lamps badly out of adjustment Incorrect bulb with too low wattage fitted Existing bulbs old and badly discoloured Electrical wiring too thin not allowing full current to pass

Symptom	Reason(s)
Lights work erratically, flashing on and off, especially over bumps	Battery terminals or earth connections loose Lights not earthing properly Contacts in light switch faulty
Wiper motor fails to work	Blown fuse Wire connections loose, disconnected or broken Brushes badly worn Armature worn or faulty Field coils faulty
Wiper motor works very slowly and takes excessive current	Commutator dirty, greasy or burnt Drive to spindles too bent or unlubricated Drive spindle binding or damaged Armature bearings dry or unaligned Armature badly worn or faulty
Wiper motor works slowly and takes little current	Brushes badly worn Commutator dirty, greasy or burnt Armature badly worn or faulty
Wiper motor works but wiper blades remain static	Linkage disengaged or faulty Drive spindle damaged or worn Wiper motor gearbox parts badly worn
Heated rear window not operating	Blown fuse Broken filament Faulty relay

10

WIRE NUMBER:

For identification, all wires are numbered and generally, numbers are classified by system.

100 ~ 199 . . . . Engine electrical system
200 ~ 299 . . . . Headlamp system
300 ~ 399 . . . . Meter, gauges and Warning system
400 ~ 499 . . . . Signal system
500 ~ 599 . . . . Accessory system
600 ~ 899 . . . . Supplemental numbers
900 ~ 999 . . . . Ground wire (Earth)

COLOR:

W . . . . White   LG . . . . Light green
B . . . . . Black   OR . . . Orange
R . . . . . Red   P . . . . Pink
Y . . . . . Yellow   PU . . . . Purple
G . . . . Green   GY . . . Gray
L . . . . Blue   SB . . . . Sky blue
BR . . . . Brown

In the case of two-tone color wires, the wire colors are indicated as follows.

B/R . . . . Black with Red stripe
L/OR . . . Blue with Orange stripe

Indicates that No. 406 wire is found only in harness of GL models.

NISSAN
MAIN HARNESS

NO.	FROM	TO	REMARKS
203	HEADLAMP	INST H	
204	HEADLAMP	INST H	
406	HORN	408	GL
408	HORN	INST H	
910	HEADLAMP	INST H	

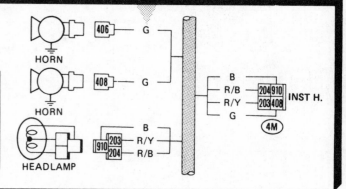

Indicates that No. 406 wire stems from the horn and is connected to No. 408 wire.

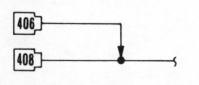

This harness diagram indicates harnesses and connectors to be used with all optional, as well as standard, equipment.

Fig. A Reading guide and colour code for N. American model wiring diagrams

Fig. 10.71A Key to Fig. 10.71

NO	FROM	TO
100	ENGINE ELECTRICAL SYSTEM	
101	ENG H NO2	F/BLOCK
102	ENG H NO2	101
103	F/LINK	101
104	F/BLOCK	101
110	F/LINK	IGN SW
111	IGN SW	IGN RELAY
112	IGN RELAY	101
113	IGN RELAY	F/BLOCK
114	IGN SW	AC RELAY
115	IGN SW	ENG H NO2
117	ACC RELAY	101
118	ACC RELAY	F/BLOCK
119	F/BLOCK	114
120	INHIBITOR RELAY	115
121	INHIBITOR RELAY	ENG H NO2
124	INHIBITOR RELAY	301
125	INHIBITOR RELAY	SPARE CONNECTOR
128	MOLD RESISTOR	DISB H
131	TERMINAL BLOCK	111
132	F/BLOCK	TERMINAL BLOCK
135	TERMINAL BLOCK	131
136	BOOST SW	751
137	BOOST SW	132
138	BOOST SW	125
139	ENG H NO2	138
140	CLUTCH SW	138
155	CAB HEATER RELAY	164
156	ENG H NO2	CAB HEATER RELAY
157	HEATER RELAY	102
158	HEATER	CAB HEATER RELAY
161	AUTO-CHOKE RELAY	132
162	AUTO-CHOKE RELAY	307
163	AUTO-CHOKE RELAY	132
164	CARB	AUTO-CHOKE RELAY
165	CARB	164
171	CARB	132
172	CARB	ENG REV SW
173	CARB	171
174	CARB	ENG REV SW
175	CARB	744
176	CARB	ENG REV SW
177	321	ENG REV SW
179	222	ENG REV SW
180	ENG REV SW	132
181	ENG REV SW	568
182	P/S SW	ENG REV SW
183	P/S SW	132
184	ENG REV SW	IDLE-UP RELAY
185	IDLE-UP RELAY	132
190	IDLE-UP RELAY	560
191	IDLE-UP RELAY	HEATER CONTROL
200	LIGHTING SYSTEM	
200	F/BLOCK	101
201	F/BLOCK	COMB SW(LAMP)
202	COMB SW(LAMP)	F/BLOCK
203	H/LAMP SENSOR	COMB SW(LAMP)
204	H/LAMP SENSOR	COMB SW(LAMP)
205	LIGHTING RELAY	HEADLAMP RH
206	HEADLAMP LH	205
207	LIGHTING RELAY	HEADLAMP RH
208	HEADLAMP LH	207
210	COMB SW (LAMP)	LIGHTING RELAY
211	H/LAMP SENSOR	HEADLAMP RH
212	H/LAMP SENSOR	HEADLAMP LH
218	INST H	211
219	INST H	205
221	COMB SW (LAMP)	F/BLOCK
222	COMB SW	S/COMB LAMP RH
223	S/COM LAMP LH	222
225	BODY H	222
229	INST H	222
234	AT INDICATOR LAMP	222
235	AT INDICATOR LAMP	276
239	DIODE	222
248	ROOM LAMP TIMER	547
250	ROOM LAMP H	547
257	ROOM LAMP H	ROOM LAMP TIMER
258	ROOL LAMP TIMER	308
261	BODY H	308
262	DOOR H FR LH	445
263	DOOR H FR LH	308
264	DOOR H FR RH	262
265	DOOR H FR RH	308
266	DOOR H RR RH	264
267	DOOR H RR RH	308
268	DOOR H RR LH	262

NO	FROM	TO
269	DOOR H RR LH	308
275	HEATER CONT	222
276	HEATER CONT	INST H
278	ROOM LAMP H	547
286	BODY H	445
300	METER, GAUGES AND WARNINIG SYSTEM	
301	F/BLOCK	INST H
302	INST H	HAND BRAKE SW
303	BRAKE LEVEL SW	302
304	ENG H NO2	INST H
305	INST H	ENG H NO2
306	INST H	BODY H
307	INST H	ENG H NO2
308	INST H	BODY H
321	MOLD RESISTOR	INST H
324	SEAT BELT SW	336
325	SEAT BELT SW	INST H
326	KEY SW	221
327	KEY SW	DOOR SW H
328	INST H	BODY H
329	DOOR SW H	INST H
330	H/LAMP SENSOR	INST H
332	INST H	WASHER SENSOR
333	WASHER SENSOR	332
334	INST H	BODY H
335	S/BELT TIMER	301
336	S/BELT TIMER	INST H
337	DIODE	327
356	AUTO-CHOKE RELAY	INST H
357	DIODE	356
358	DIODE	302
381	CHECK CONNECTOR	301
382	CHECK CONNECTOR	164
383	CHECK CONNECTOR	172
384	CHECK CONNECTOR	174
385	CHECK CONNECTOR	136
386	CHECK CONNECTOR	158
400	SIGNAL SYSTEM	
401	HAZARD F/UNIT	F/BLOCK
402	HAZARD F/UNIT	INST H
404	COM SW (TURN)	INST H
405	FR T/S LAMP RH	COMB SW (TURN)
406	FR T/S LAMP LH	COMB SW (TURN)
409	BODY H	405
410	BODY H	406
415	T/SIGNAL F/UNIT	301
416	T/SIGNAL F/UNIT	INST H
417	INST H	405
418	INST H	406
431	HORN RELAY	401
432	HORN RELAY	HORN
433	HORN	432
434	COMB SW (TURN)	HORN RELAY
441	ENG H NO2	301
442	ENG H NO2	BODY H
445	STOP LAMP SW	F/BLOCK
448	STOP LAMP SW	BODY H
500	ACCESSORY SYSTEM	
501	WIPER MOTOR	541
502	WIPER MOTOR	COMB SW (WOP)
503	WIPER MOTOR	COMB SW (WIP)
505	FR WASHER MOTOR	501
506	COMB SW (WOP)	FR WASHER MOTOR
507	WIPER MOTOR	WIPER AMP
508	RR WASHER	515
509	COMB SW (WIP)	WIPER AMP
510	COMB SW (WIP)	WIPER AMP
511	WIPER AMP	501
512	WIPER AMP	506
513	WIPER AMP	COMB SW (INT)
514	INST H	RR WASHER MOTOR
515	BODY H	FUSE BLOCK
516	INST H	BODY H
517	INST H	BODY H
521	F/BLOCK	INST H
526	INST H	BODY H
527	INST H	BODY H
541	F/BLOCK	INST H
547	F/BLOCK	INST H
551	F/BLOCK	INST H
552	INST H	BODY H
560	FUSE BLOCK	HEATER MOTOR
561	HEATER CONTROL	HEATER MOTOR
563	HEATER MOTOR	HEATER CONTROL
564	HEATER MOTOR	HEATER CONTROL
565	HEATER MOTOR	HEATER CONTROL
567	THERMO SW	132

NO	FROM	TO
568	THERMO SW	COOLING FAN MOTOR
570	CIRCUIT BREAKER	113
587	ROOM LAMP H	CIRCUIT BREAKER
700	SUPPLEMENTAL NUMBER	
740	F/BLOCK	AIR CON RELAY
741	AIR CON RELAY	THERMO CONTROL
742	AIR CON RELAY	560
743	AIR CON RELAY	REV COMPARATOR
744	LOW PRESS SW	THERMO CONTROL
746	LOW PRESS SW	MAG. CLUTCH
748	THERMO CONTROL	THERMO SENSOR
749	THERMO CONTROL	THERMO SENSOR
750	HI PRESS SW	741
751	HI PRESS SW	FAN CONT RELAY
752	FAN CONT RELAY	568
753	FAN CONT RELAY	567
755	CONDENSER FAN	751
757	AIR CON SW	741
758	REV COMPARATOR	COMP RPM SENSOR
759	REV COMPARATOR	COMP RPM SENSOR
760	REV COMPARATOR	AIR CON SW
761	REV COMPARATOR	321
762	REV COMPARATOR	742
782	INST H	INHIBITOR RELAY
783	STOP SW	INHIBITOR RELAY
784	STOP SW	COMB SW
785	COMB SW	ASCD AMP
786	ASCD AMP	784
787	ASCD AMP	SOLENOID VALVE
788	INST H	787
789	ASCD AMP	SERVO VALVE
790	ASCD AMP	SERVO VALVE
791	ASCD AMP	COMB SW
792	ASCD AMP	COMB SW
793	INST H	ASCD RELAY
794	ASCD AMP	INST H
795	ASCD AMP	782
796	ASCD AMP	448
797	ASCD RELAY	781
798	ASCD RELAY	782
900	GROUND	
901	BODY GROUND 1	BODY GROUND 2
903	IGN RELAY	901
904	ACC RELAY	917
905	LIGHTING RELAY	901
906	LIGHTING RELAY	909
908	S/COMB LAMP RH	901
909	S/COMB LAMP LH	901
912	H/LAMP SENSOR	901
913	WIPER AMP	901
914	WIPER MOTOR	917
915	FR T/S LAMP RH	908
916	FR T/S LAMP LH	909
917	BRAKE LEVEL SW	901
919	WASHER SENSOR	901
920	WASHER SENSOR	901
930	AUTO-CHOKE RELAY	901
937	S/BELT TIMER	901
940	THERMO CONTROL	950
942	INST H	901
948	COMB SW (INT)	950
950	COMB SW (WIP)	942
951	ENG REV SW	901
954	ANTENNA GROUND	ENG GROUND
955	BODY GROUND	901
960	BODY H	983
961	HEATER	901
965	ROOM LAMP	912
972	BODY GROUND	965
976	BOOST SW	999
978	CONDENSER FAN	901
979	COOLING FAN	901
980	FAN CONT RELAY	901
983	ROOM LAMP H	990
987	ENG H NO2	901
988	CLUTCH SW	950
995	ASCD AMP	901
997	SOLENOID VALVE	901
998	ASCD RELAY	901

10

194

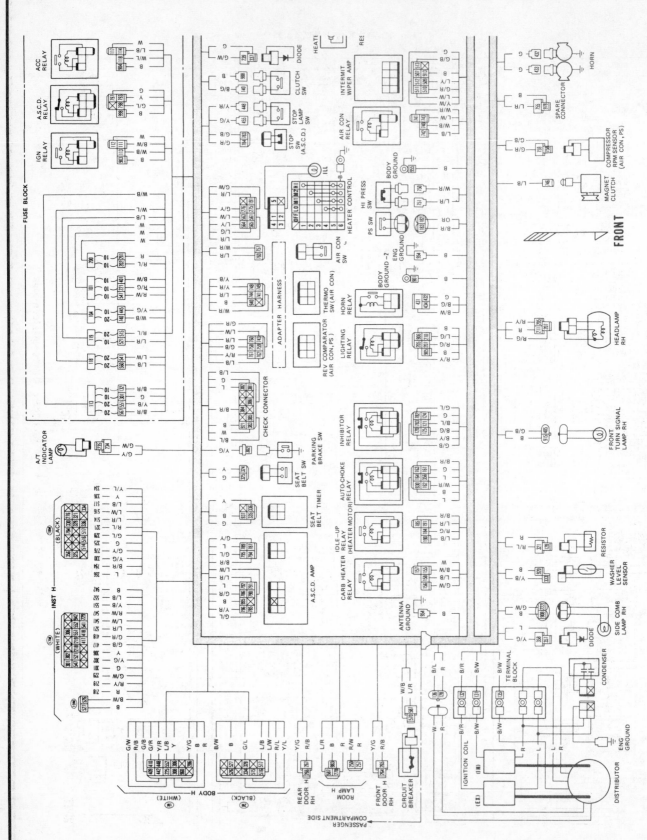

Fig. 10.71 Wiring diagram (N. American SGL models)

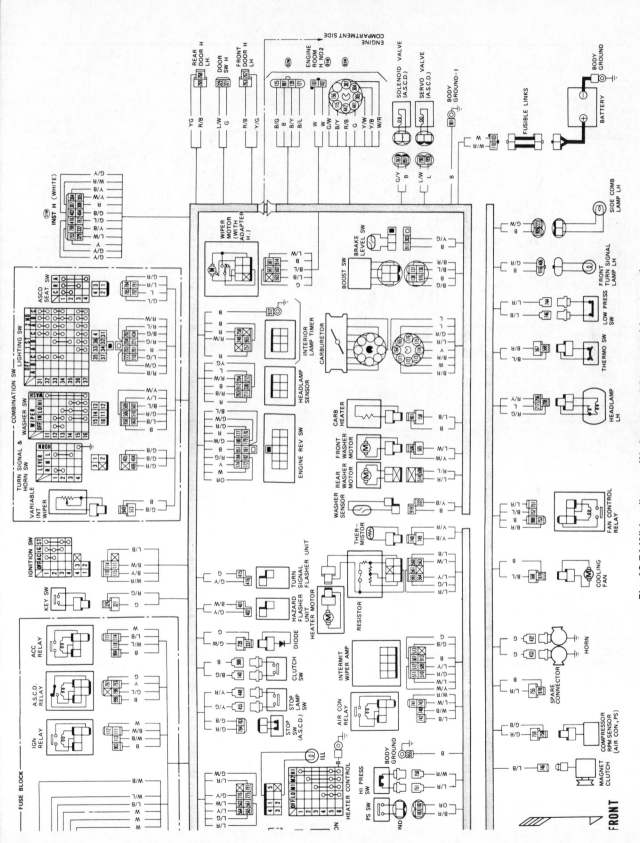

Fig. 10.71 Wiring diagram (N. American SGL models) (continued)

10

Fig. 10.72A Key to Fig. 10.72

NO	FROM	TO
100	ENGINE ELECTRICAL SYSTEM	
101	ENG H NO2	F/BLOCK
102	ENG H NO2	101
103	F/LINK	101
104	F/BLOCK	101
110	F/LINK	IGN SW
111	IGN SW	IGN RELAY
112	IGN RELAY	101
113	IGN RELAY	F/BLOCK
114	IGN SW	AC RELAY
115	IGN SW	ENG H NO2
116	F/BLOCK	111
117	AC RELAY	101
118	AC RELAY	F/BLOCK
119	F/BLOCK	114
120	INHIBITOR RELAY	115
121	INHIBITOR RELAY	ENG H NO2
124	INHIBITOR RELAY	301
125	INHIBITOR RELAY	SPARE CONNECTOR
128	RESISTOR	DISB H
131	F/BLOCK	111
132	F/BLOCK	TERMINAL BLOCK
135	TERMINAL BLOCK	131
136	BOOST SW	TERMINAL BLOCK
137	BOOST SW	132
138	BOOST SW	125
139	ENG H NO2	138
140	CLUTCH SW	138
155	CAB HEATER RELAY	131
156	CAB HEATER RELAY	ENG H NO2
157	CAB HEATER RELAY	102
158	CAB HEATER RELAY	HEATER
161	AUTO-CHOKE RELAY	132
162	AUTO-CHOKE RELAY	307
163	AUTO-CHOKE RELAY	132
164	CARB	AUTO-CHOKE RELAY
165	CARB	164
171	CARB	132
172	CARB	ENG REV SW
173	CARB	171
174	CARB	ENG REV SW
175	CARB	744
176	CARB	ENG REV SW
177	RESISTOR	ENG REV SW
179	222	ENG REV SW
180	ENG REV SW	132
181	ENG REV SW	568
182	P/S SW	ENG REV SW
183	P/S SW	132
184	ENG REV SW	IDLE-UP RELAY
185	IDLE-UP RELAY	132
190	IDLE-UP RELAY	560
191	IDLE-UP RELAY	HEATER CONTROL
200	LIGHTING SYSTEM	
200	F/BLOCK	101
201	F/BLOCK	COMB SW (LAMP)
202	COMB SW (LAMP)	F/BLOCK
203	COMB SW (LAMP)	H/LAMP RH
204	COMB SW (LAMP)	H/LAMP LH
205	LIGHTING RELAY	HEADLAMP RH
206	HEADLAMP LH	205
207	LIGHTING RELAY	HEADLAMP RH
208	HEADLAMP LH	207
210	COMB SW (LAMP)	LIGHTING RELAY
218	INST H	203
219	INST H	205
221	COMB SW (LAMP)	F/BLOCK
222	COMB SW (LAMP)	S/COMB LAMP RH
223	S/COMB LAMP LH	222
225	BODY H	222
229	INST H	222
234	AT INDICATOR LAMP	222
235	AT INDICATOR LAMP	276
239	DIODE	222
250	ROOM LAMP H	547
257	ROOM LAMP H	BODY H
261	BODY H	257
275	HEATER CONTROL	222
276	HEATER CONTROL	INST H
286	BODY H	445
300	METER,GAUGES AND WARNING SYSTEM	
301	F/BLOCK	INST H
302	INST H	HAND BRAKE SW
303	BRAKE LEVEL SW	302
304	ENG H NO2	INST H
305	INST H	ENG H NO2
306	INST H	BODY H
307	INST H	ENG H NO2
308	INST H	257
324	SEAT BELT SW	336
325	SEAT BELT SW	INST H
326	KEY SW	221
327	KEY SW	DOOR SW H
329	DOOR SW H	INST H
335	S/BELT TIMER	301
336	S/BELT TIMER	INST H
337	DIODE	327
356	AUTO-CHOKE RELAY	INST H
357	DIODE	356
358	DIODE	302
381	CHECK CONNECTOR	301
382	CHECK CONNECTOR	164
383	CHECK CONNECTOR	172
384	CHECK CONNECTOR	174
385	CHECK CONNECTOR	136
386	CHECK CONNECTOR	158
400	SIGNAL SYSTEM	
401	HAZARD F/UNIT	F/BLOCK
402	HAZARD F/UNIT	INST H
404	COMB SW (TURN)	INST H
405	COMB SW (TURN)	FR T/S LAMP RH
406	COMB SW (TURN)	FR T/S LAMP LH
409	BODY H	405
410	BODY H	406
415	T/SIGNAL F/UNIT	301
416	T/SIGNAL F/UNIT	INST H
417	INST H	405
418	INST H	406
431	HORN RELAY	401
432	HORN RELAY	HORN
433	HORN	432
434	COMB SW (TURN)	HORN RELAY
441	ENG H NO2	301
442	ENG H NO2	BODY H
445	STOP LAMP SW	F/BLOCK
448	STOP LAMP SW	BODY H
500	ACCESSORY SYSTEM	
501	WIPER MOTOR	541
502	COMB SW (WIP)	WIPER MOTOR
503	COMB SW (WIP)	WIPER MOTOR
504	WIPER MOTOR	COMB SW
505	FR WASHER MO	501
506	CMB SW (WIP)	FR WASHER MO
508	RR WASHER MO	515
514	RR WASHER MO	INST H
515	BODY H	F/BLOCK
516	BODY H	INST H
517	BODY H	INST H
521	F/BLOCK	INST H
526	INST H	BODY H
527	INST H	BODY H
541	F/BLOCK	INST H
547	INST H	FUSE BLOCK
551	F/BLOCK	INST H
552	INST H	BODY H
560	HEATER MOTOR	F/BLOCK
561	HEATER MOTOR	HEATER CONTROL
563	HEATER MOTOR	HEATER CONTROL
564	HEATER MOTOR	HEATER CONTROL
565	HEATER MOTOR	HEATER CONTROL
567	THERMO SW	132
568	THERMO SW	COOLING FAN
700	SUPPLEMENTAL NUMBER	
740	F/BLOCK	AIR CON RELAY
741	AIR CON RELAY	THERMO CONTROL
742	AIR CON RELAY	560
743	AIR CON RELAY	REV COMPARATOR
744	LOW PRESS SW	THERMO CONTROL
746	LOW PRESS SW	MAG CLUTCH
748	THERMO CONTROL	THERMO SENSOR
749	THERMO CONTROL	THERMO SENSOR
750	HI PRESS SW	741
751	HI PRESS SW	FAN CONT RELAY
752	FAN CONT RELAY	568
753	FAN CONT RELAY	567
755	CONDENSER FAN	751
757	AIR CON SW	741
758	REV COMPARATOR	COND RPM SENSOR
759	REV COMPARATOR	COND RPM SENSOR
760	REV COMPARATOR	AIR CON SW
761	REV COMPARATOR	177
762	REV COMPARATOR	742
900	GROUND	
901	BODY GROUND 1	BODY GROUND 2
903	IGN RELAY	901
904	ACC RELAY	903
905	LIGHTING RELAY	902
906	LIGHTING RELAY	905
908	S/COMB LAMP RH	901
909	S/COMB LAMP LH	901
914	WIPER MOTOR	917
915	FR T/S LAMP RH	908
916	FR T/S LAMP LH	909
917	BRAKE LEVEL SW	901
921	CHECK CONNECTOR	901
930	AUTO-CHOKE RELAY	901
937	BUZZER (L/SW)	901
940	THERMO CONTROL	901
942	INST H	901
950	COMB SW (WIP)	942
951	ENG REV SW	901
954	ANTENNA GROUND	ENG GROUND
955	BODY GROUND	901
960	BODY H	901
961	HEATER	901
976	BOOST SW	913
978	CONDENSER FAN	901
979	COOLING FAN	901
980	FAN CONT RELAY	901
987	ENG H NO2	901
988	CLUTCH SW	901

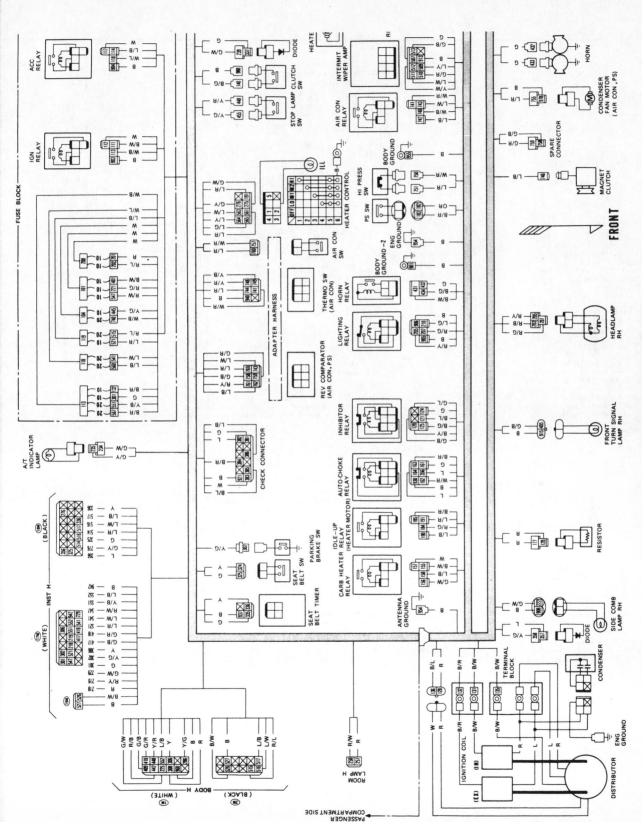

Fig. 10.72 Wiring diagram (N. American G models)

10

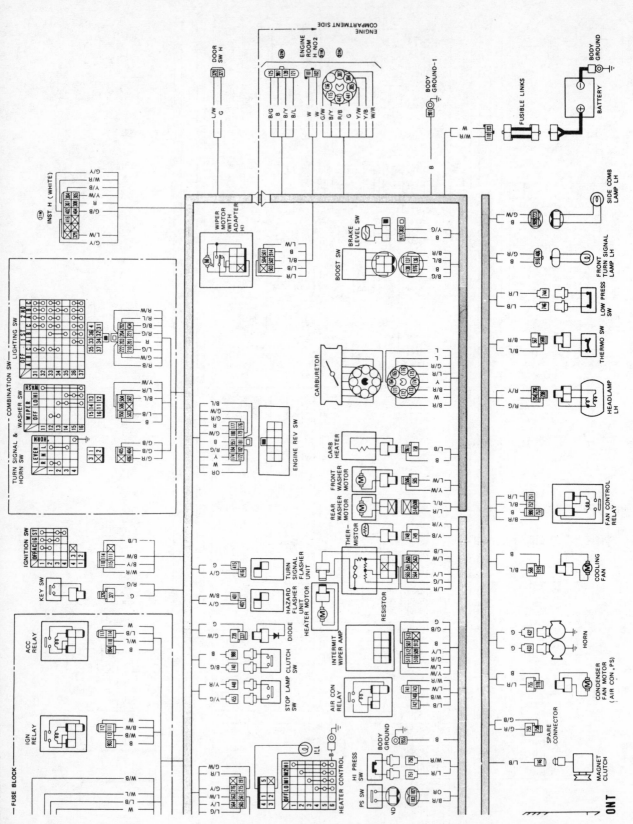

Fig. 10.72 Wiring diagram (N. American G models) (continued)

Fig. 10.73A Key to Fig 10.73

NO	FROM	TO
200	LIGHTING SYSTEM	
218	MAIN H	METER
219	MAIN H	METER
229	MAIN H	METER
231	ASCD MAIN SW	229
232	ASCD MAIN SW	276
236	HAZARD L SW	229
237	HAZARD L SW	271
238	RR DEFOG SW	229
239	RR DEFOG SW	271
271	ILL CONT SW	METER
272	ILL CONT SW	229
277	G/BOX LAMP	229
279	MAIN H	271
283	CIG LIGHTER	229
284	CLOCK	229
285	CLOCK	271
295	AUDIO	229
296	AUDIO	271
300	METER, GAUGES AND WARNING SYSTEM	
301	MAIN H	METER
302	MAIN H	WARNING LAMP
304	MAIN H	METER
305	MAIN H	METER
306	MAIN H	METER
307	MAIN H	WARNING LAMP
308	MAIN H	WARNING LAMP
311	TACHOMETER	301
321	TACHOMETER	MAIN H
322	METER	301
325	MAIN H	CHIME
328	MAIN H	WARNING LMAP
329	MAIN H	CHIME
330	MAIN H	WARNING LAMP
332	MAIN H	WARNING LAMP
334	MAIN H	WARNING LAMP
336	MAIN H	WARNING LAMP
345	WARNING LAMP	301
356	WARNING	MAIN H
400	SIGNAL SYSTEM	
402	HAZARD L SW	MAIN H
404	HAZARD L SW	MAIN H
413	METER	417
414	METER	418
416	HAZARD L SW	MAIN H
417	HAZARD L SW	MAIN H
418	HAZARD L SW	MAIN H
500	ACCESSORY SYSTEM	
514	RR WIP AND WASH SW	MAIN H
516	RR WIP AND WASH SW	MAIN H
517	RR WIP AND WASH SW	MAIN H
520	RADIO	DECK
521	DECK	MAIN H
522	DOOR SP RH	SPEAKER H
523	DOOR SP RH	SPEAKER H
524	DOOR SP LH	RADIO
525	DOOR SP LH	RADIO
526	MAIN H	AUDIO
527	MAIN H	AUDIO
530	INST SP	524
531	INST SP	525
541	CIG LIGHTER	MAIN H
545	CLOCK	541
547	CLOCK	MAIN H
551	RR DEFOG SW	MAIN H
552	RR DEFOG SW	MAIN H
553	WARNING LAMP	552
700	SUPPLEMENTAL NUMBER	
781	ASCD MAIN SW	301
782	ASCD MAIN SW	MAIN H
788	ASCD MAIN SW	MAIN H
793	ASCD MAIN SW	MAIN H
794	MAIN H	METER
900	GROUND	
931	METER	BODY GROUND
932	G/BOX LAMP	942
933	WARNING LAMP	942
934	METER	942
936	CLOCK	942
939	WARNING LAMP	754
942	CIG LIGHTER	MAIN H
943	BODY GROUND	942
944	RR WIP AND WASH SW	942
946	AUDIO	BODY GROUND
949	ILL CONT SW	942
952	TACHOMETER	942
953	METER	942
954	CHIME	942
996	ASCD MAIN SW	949

10

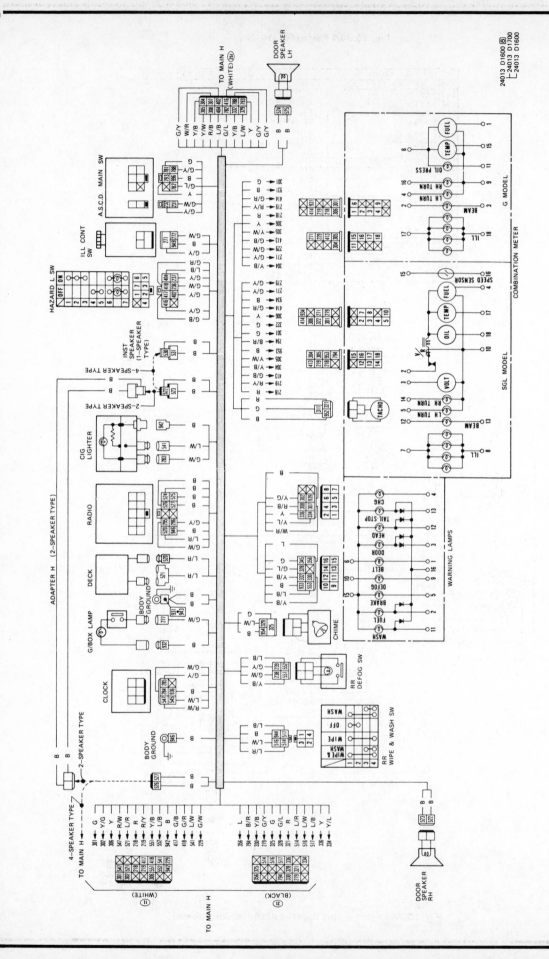

Fig. 10.73 Instrument wiring harness (N. American models)

Fig. 10.74A Key to Fig. 10.74

NO	FROM	TO	REMARKS
100	ENGINE ELECTRICAL SYSTEM		
101	MAIN H	ALTERNATOR	
102	MAIN H	ALTERNATOR	
103	ALTERNATOR	102	
115	MAIN H	ST MOTOR	
125	MAIN H	INHIBITOR SW	AT
139	MAIN H	NEUTRAL SW	MT
156	MAIN H	THERMO SW	
300	METER,GAUGES AND WARNING SYSTEM		
304	MAIN H	OIL PRESS SW	
305	MAIN	THERMAL T/M	
307	MAIN	ALTERNATOR	
400	SIGNAL SYSTEM		
441	MAIN H	BACK-UP LAMP SW	MT
441	MAIN H	INHIBITOR SW	AT
442	MAIN H	BACK-UP LAMP SW	MT
442	MAIN H	INHIBITOR SW	AT
900	GROUND		
987	NEUTRAL SW	MAIN H	MT
989	INHIBITOR SW	MAIN H	AT
999	THERMO SW	987 OR 989	

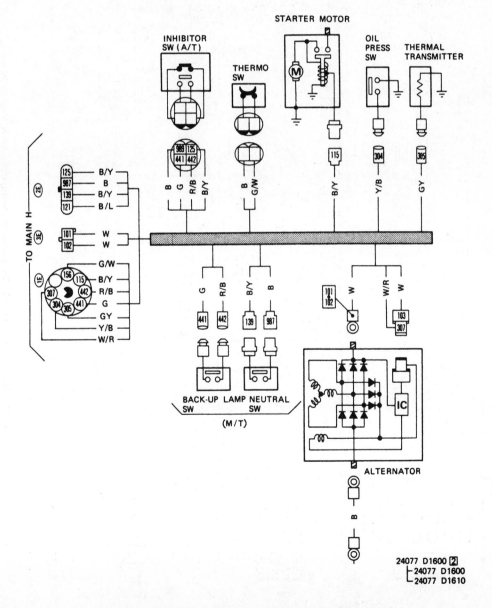

Fig. 10.74 Engine wiring harness (N. American models)

10

Fig. 10.75A Key to Fig. 10.75

NO	FROM	TO	REMARKS
200	LIGHTING SYSTEM		
225	MAIN H	STOP AND TAIL SENS	
226	REAR COMB L RH	MAIN H	
230	LICENSE L RH	226	
231	LICENSE L LH	230	
232	SIDE MARKER RH	226	
233	SIDE MARKER LH	227	
258	DOOR SW RH	MAIN H	
259	DOOR SW LH	258	
286	LUGGAGE LAMP	MAIN H	
300	METER, GAUGES AND WARNING SYSTEM		
306	TANK UNIT	MAIN H	
328	MAIN H	STOP AND TAIL SENS	SGL
334	TANK UNIT	MAIN H	
400	SIGNAL SYSTEM		
409	MAIN H	REAR COMB L RH	
410	MAIN H	REAR COMB L LH	
442	MAIN H	REAR COMB L RH	
443	REAR COMB L LH	442	
446	REAR COMB L RH	STOP AND TAIL SENS	SGL
447	REAR COMB L LH	446	SGL
448	MAIN H	STOP AND TAIL SENS	SGL

NO	FROM	TO	REMARKS
500	ACCESSORY SYSTEM		
515	BACK DOOR H	MAIN H	
516	BACK DOOR H	MAIN H	
517	BACK DOOR H	MAIN H	
526	RR SPEAKER RH	MAIN H	
527	RR SPEAKER RH	MAIN H	
528	RR SPEAKER LH	526	
529	RR SPEAKER LH	529	
552	BACK DOOR H	MAIN H	
900	GROUND		
960	MAIN H	BODY GROUND	
961	TANK UNIT	960	
962	REAR COMB L RH	960	
963	REAR COMB L LH	960	
977	STOP AND TAIL SENS	960	
979	LICENSE L RH	960	
980	LICENSE L LH	960	SGL
988	BACK DOOR H	960	
989	LUGGAGE LAMP	960	
995	SIDE MARKER RH	960	
996	SIDE MARKER LH	960	

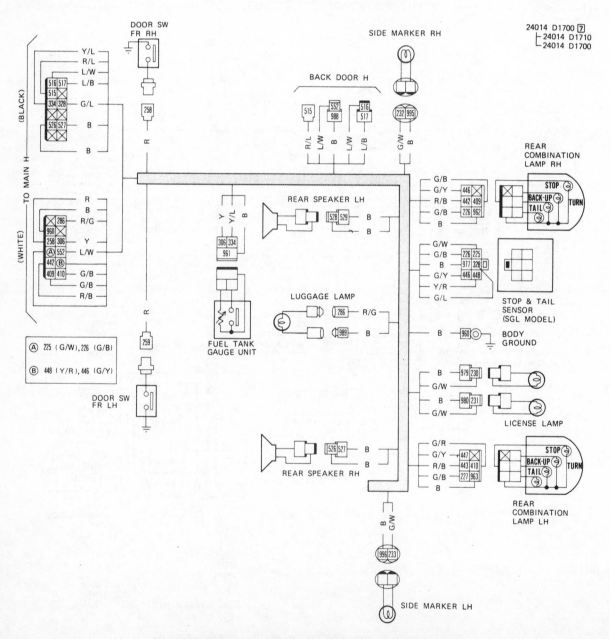

Fig. 10.75 Body wiring diagram (N. American, 3-door models)

Fig. 10.76A Key to Fig. 10.76

NO	FROM	TO	REMARKS
200	LIGHTING SYSTEM		
225	MAIN H	STOP AND TAIL SENS	SGL
226	REAR COMB L RH	STOP AND TAIL SENS	SGL
227	REAR COMB L LH	226	
230	LICENSE L RH	225	
231	LICENSE L LH	230	
232	SIDE MARKER RH	225	
233	SIDE MARKER LH	231	
258	DOOR SW FR RH	MAIN H	
259	DOOR SW FR LH	258	
260	DOOR SW RR LH	259	
261	DOOR SW RR RH	260	
286	LUGGAGE LANP	MAIN H	
300	METER.GAUGES AND WARNING SYSTEM		
306	TANK UNIT	MAIN H	
328	MAIN H	STOP AND TAIL SENS	SGL
334	TANK UNIT	MAIN H	
400	SIGNAL SYSTEM		
409	MAIN H	REAR COMB L RH	
410	MAIN H	REAR COMB L LH	
442	MAIN H	REAR COMB L RH	
443	REAR COMB L LH	442	
446	REAR COMB L RH	STOP AND TAIL SENS	SGL

NO	FROM	TO	REMARKS
447	REAR COMB L LH	446	
448	MAIN H	STOP AND TAIL SENS	SGL
500	ACCESSORY SYSTEM		
515	BACK DOOR H	MAIN H	
516	BACK DOOR H	MAIN H	
517	BACK DOOR H	MAIN H	
526	RR SPEAKER RH	MAIN H	
527	RR SPEAKER RH	MAIN H	
528	RR SPEAKER LH	526	
529	RR SPEAKER LH	529	
552	BACK DOOR H	MAIN H	
900	GROUND		
960	MAIN H	BODY GROUND	
961	TANK UNIT	960	
962	REAR COMB L RH	960	
963	REAR COMB L LH	960	
977	STOP AND TAIL SENS	960	SGL
979	LICENSE L RH	960	
980	LICENSE L LH	960	
988	BACK DOOR H	960	
989	LUGGAGE LAMP	960	
995	SIDE MARKER RH	960	
996	SIDE MARKER LH	960	

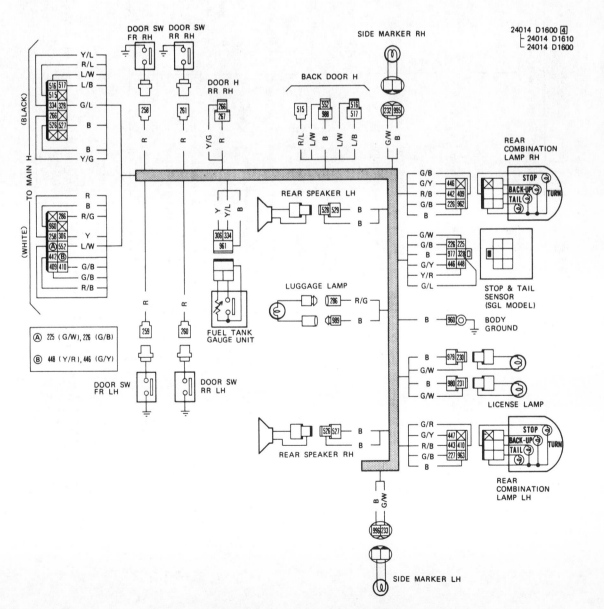

Fig. 10.76 Body wiring diagram (N. American, 5-door models)

10

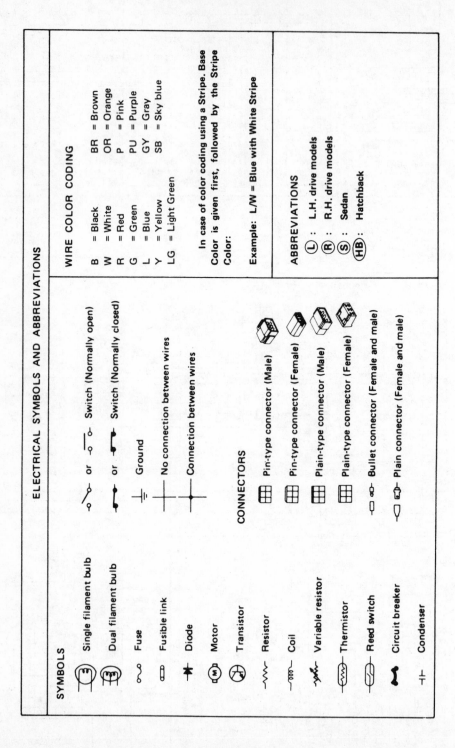

Fig. B. Reading guide and colour code for non-N. American model wiring diagrams

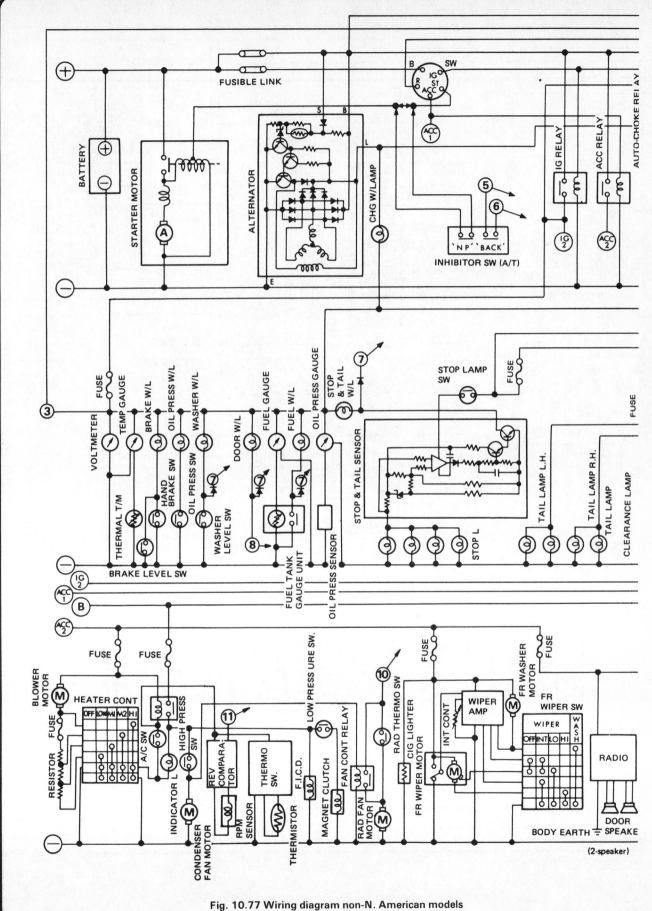

Fig. 10.77 Wiring diagram non-N. American models

10

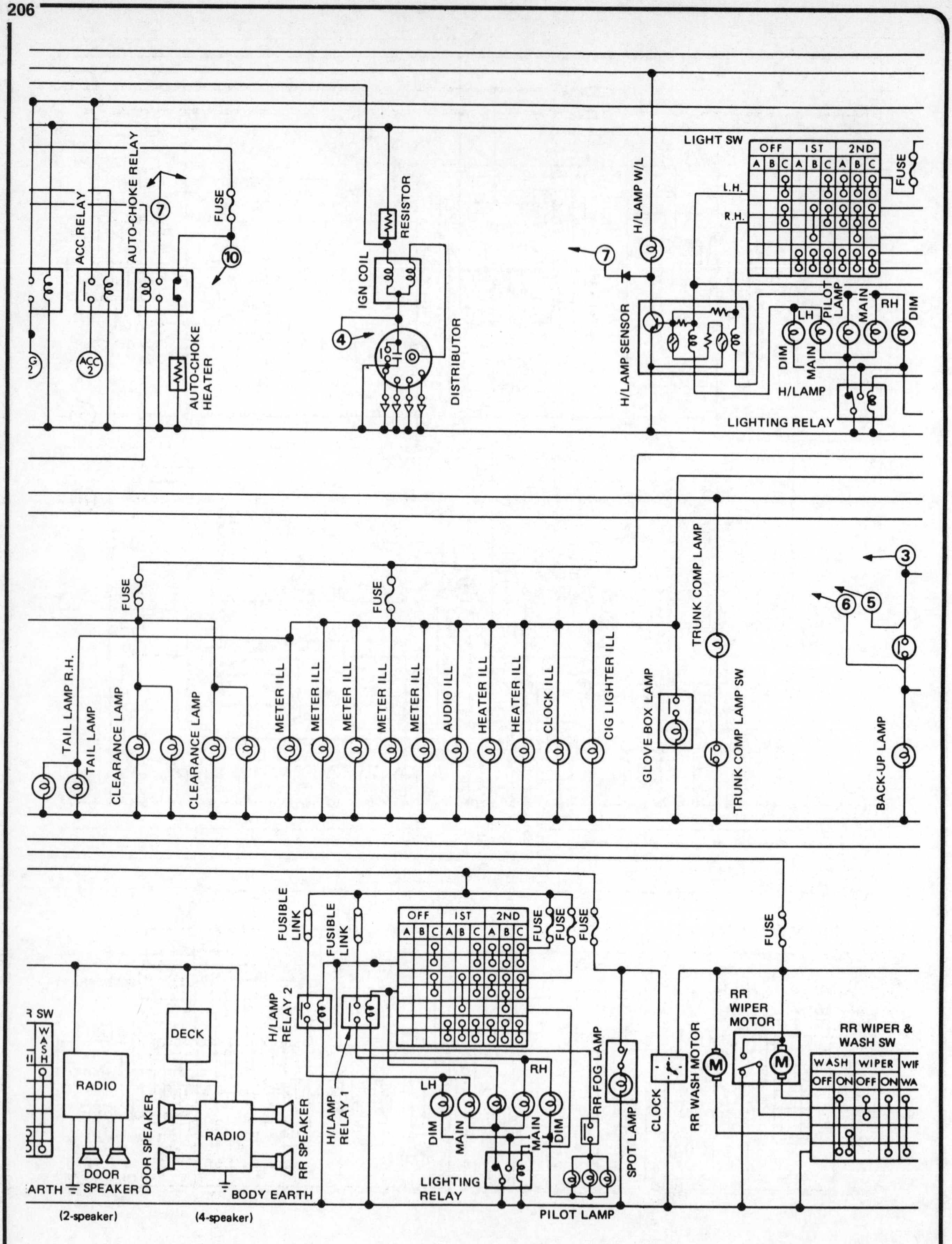

Fig. 10.77 Wiring diagram non-N. American models (continued)

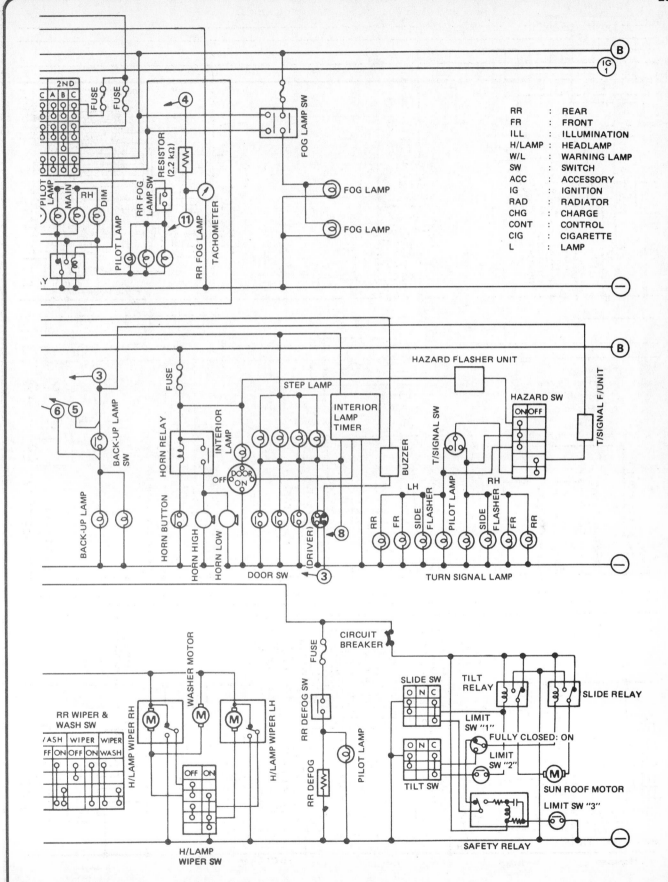

Fig. 10.77 Wiring diagram non-N. American models (continued)

10

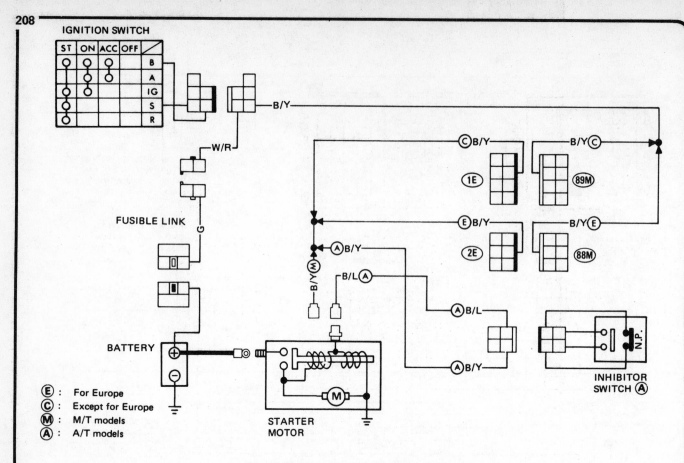

Fig. 10.78 Wiring diagram – starter circuit

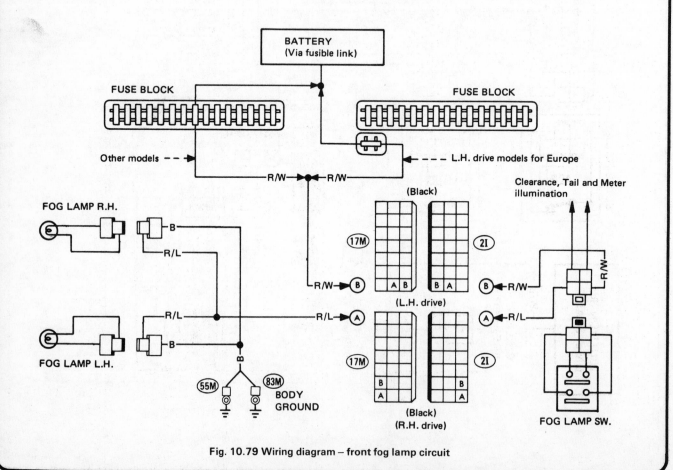

Fig. 10.79 Wiring diagram – front fog lamp circuit

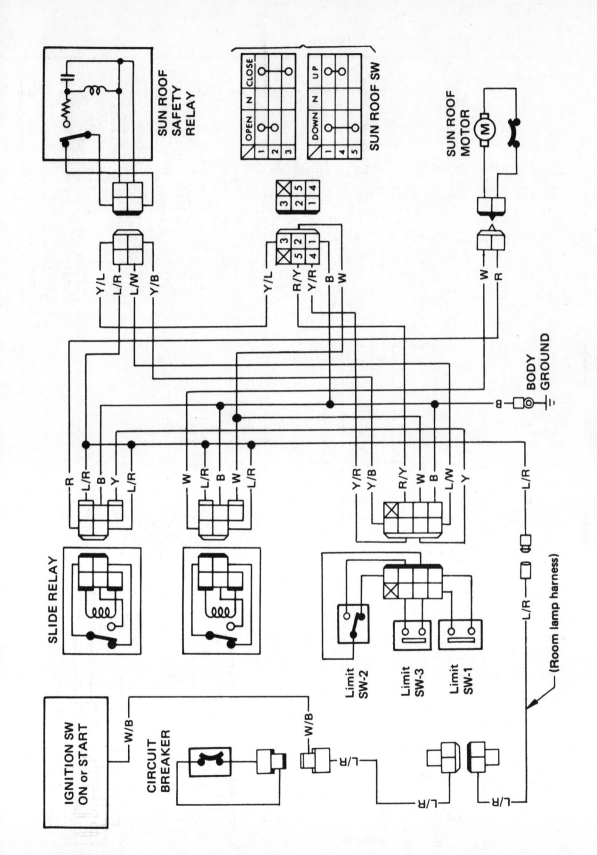

Fig. 10.80 Wiring diagram – electric sunroof circuit

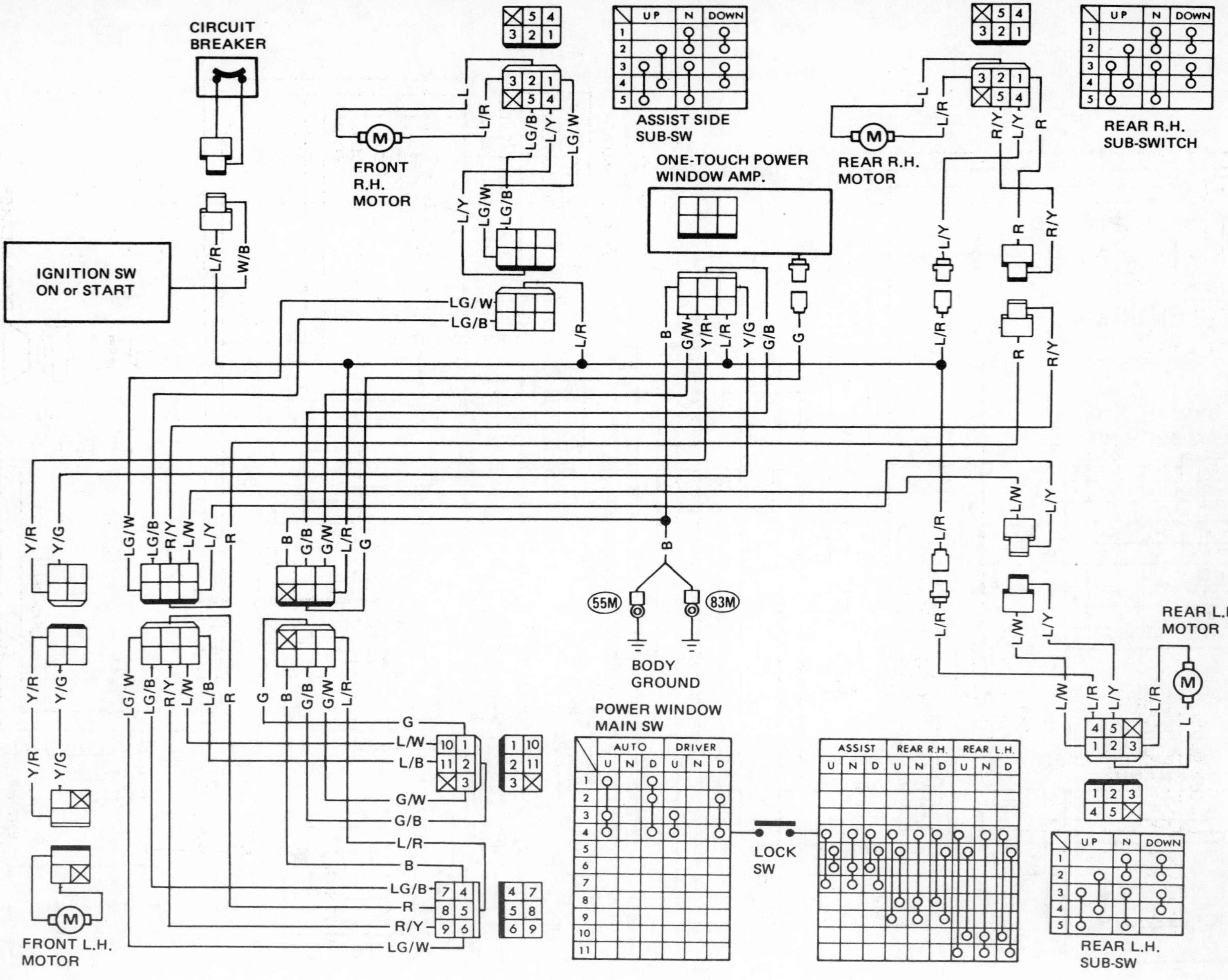
CIRCUIT BREAKER
IGNITION SW ON or START
FRONT R.H. MOTOR
ASSIST SIDE SUB-SW
ONE-TOUCH POWER WINDOW AMP.
REAR R.H. MOTOR
REAR R.H. SUB-SWITCH
BODY GROUND
55M
83M
POWER WINDOW MAIN SW
LOCK SW
REAR L.H. MOTOR
REAR L.H. SUB-SW
FRONT L.H. MOTOR

Fig. 10.81 Wiring diagram – power window circuit

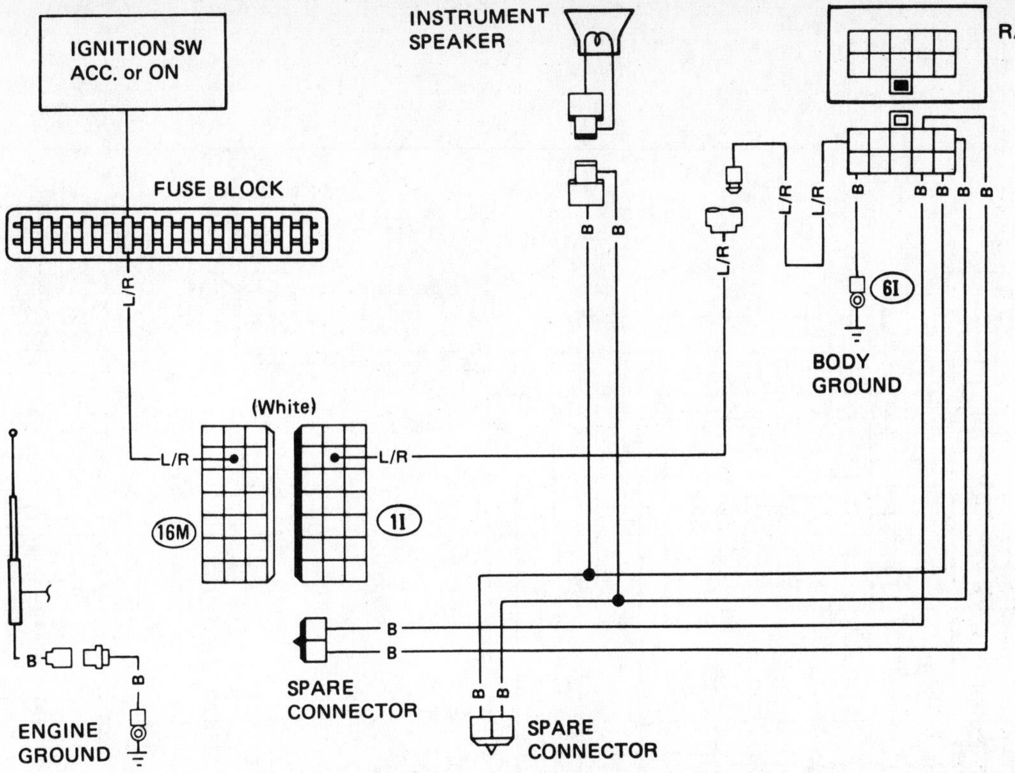

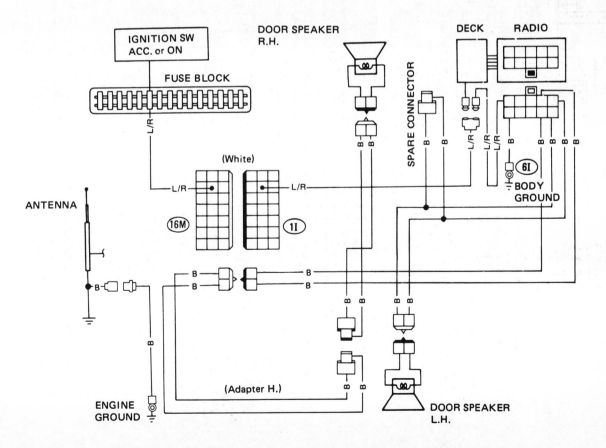

Fig. 10.82 Wiring diagram – 1-speaker radio system

Fig. 10.83 Wiring diagram – 2-speaker radio/cassette system

10

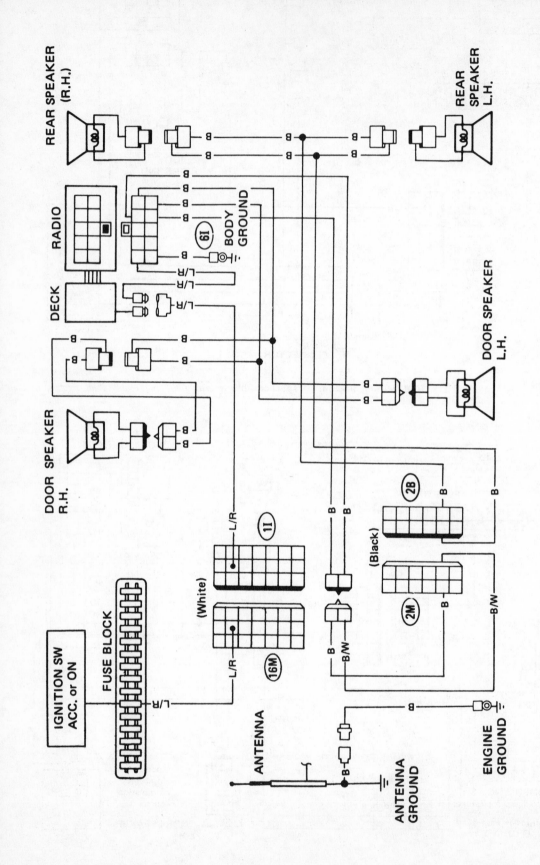

Fig. 10.84 Wiring diagram — 4-speaker radio/cassette system

L.H. drive models for Europe

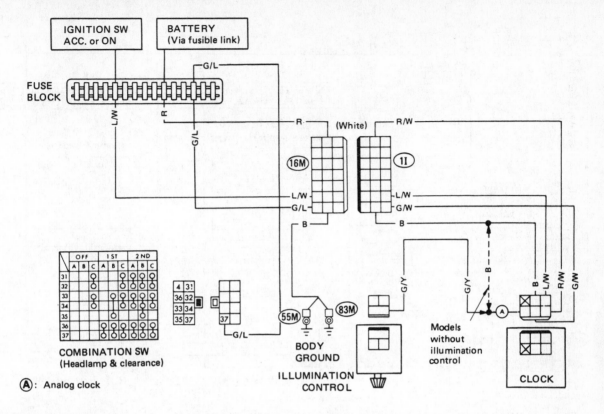

A: Analog clock

Other models

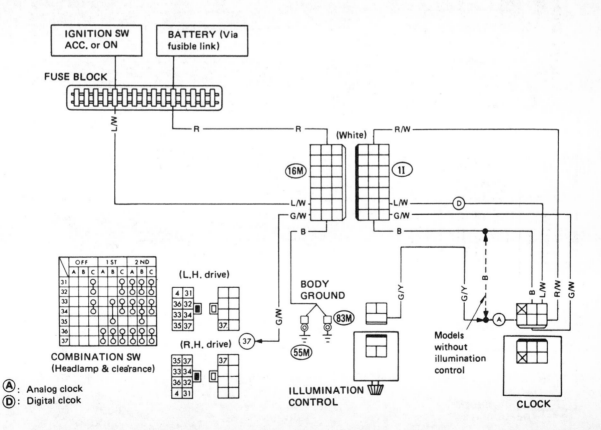

A: Analog clock
D: Digital clcok

Fig. 10.85 Wiring diagram – clock; LH drive European and other models

10

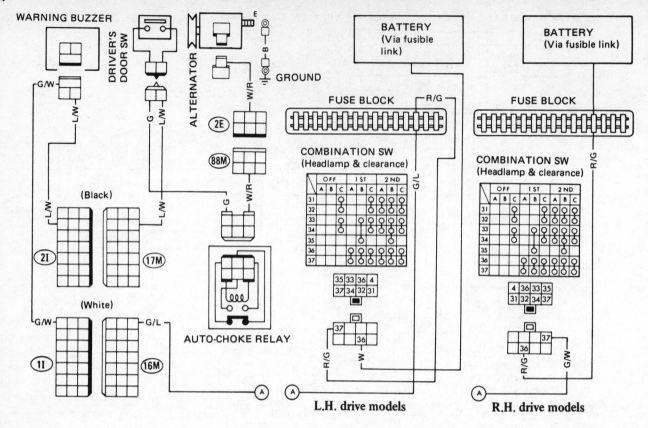

Fig. 10.86 Wiring diagram – warning buzzer circuit

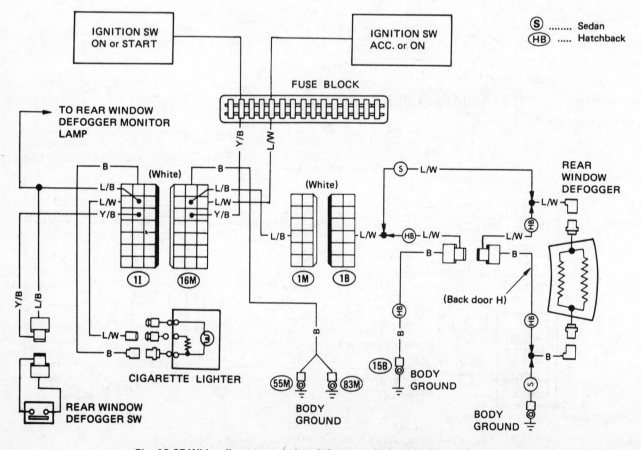

Fig. 10.87 Wiring diagram – window defogger and cigarette lighter circuit

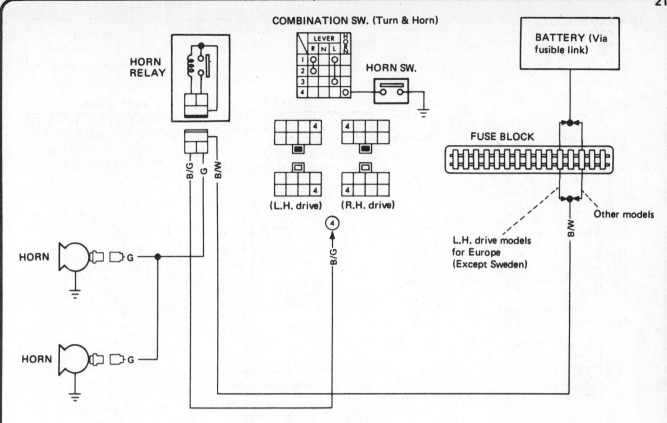

Fig. 10.88 Wiring diagram – horn circuit

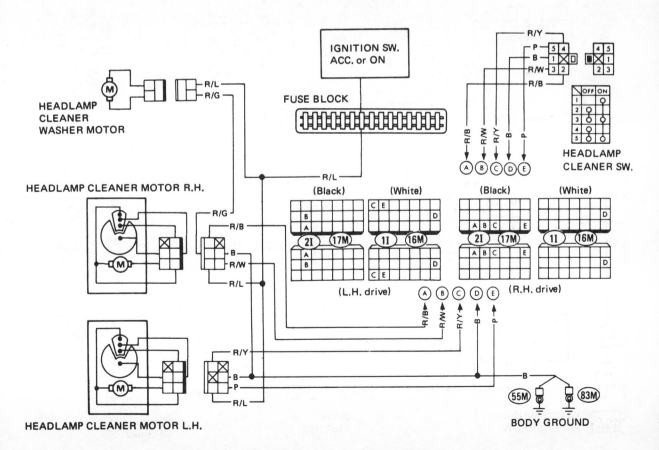

Fig. 10.89 Wiring diagram – headlamp wiper and washer circuit

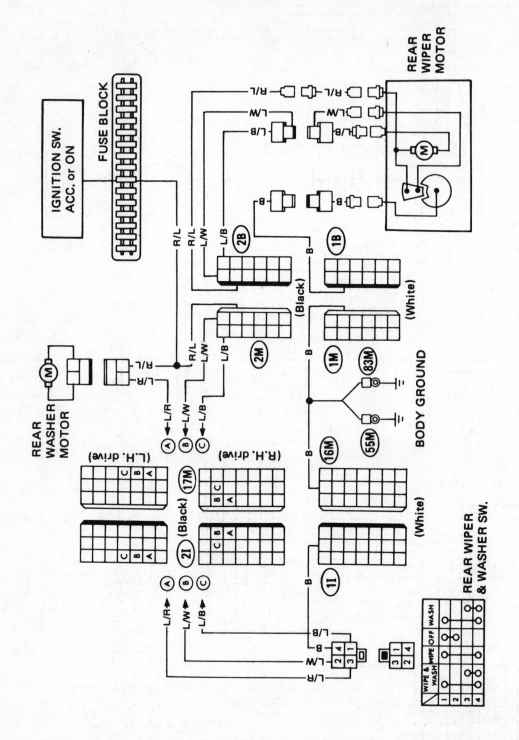

Fig. 10.90 Wiring diagram — rear window wiper and washer circuit

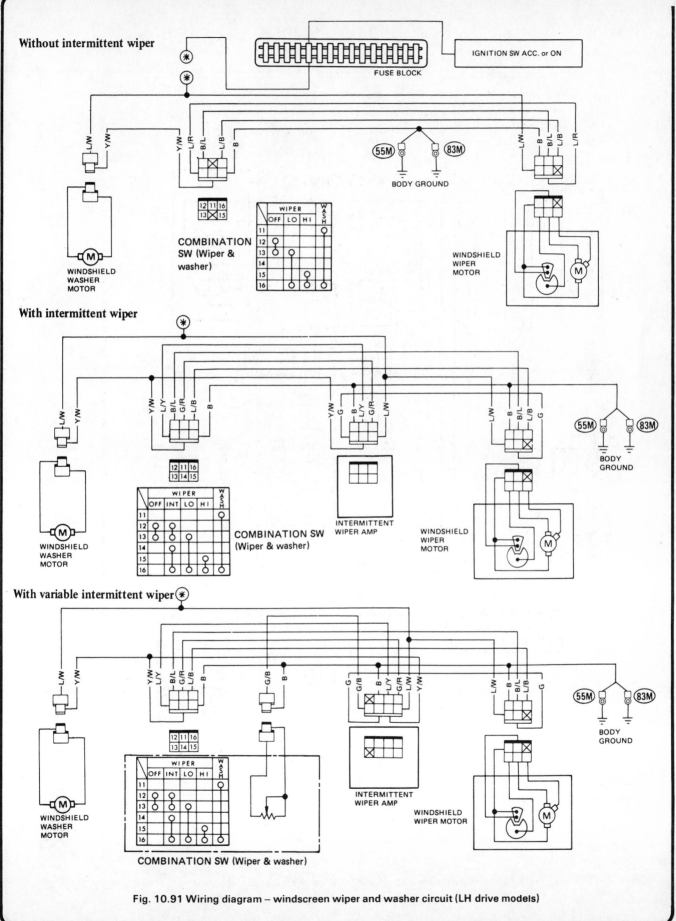

Fig. 10.91 Wiring diagram – windscreen wiper and washer circuit (LH drive models)

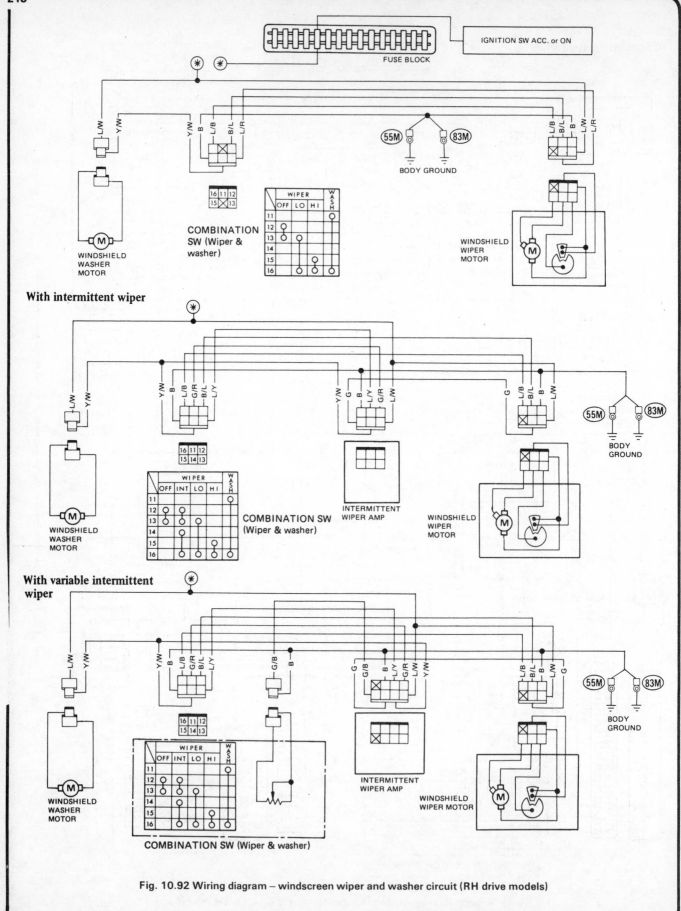

Fig. 10.92 Wiring diagram – windscreen wiper and washer circuit (RH drive models)

219

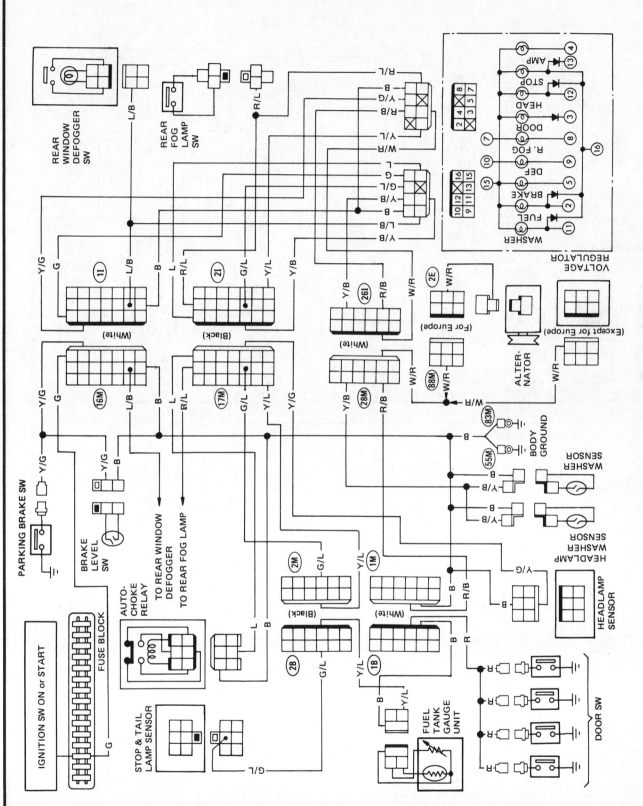

Fig. 10.93 Wiring diagram – warning lamps circuit (LH drive models)

10

220

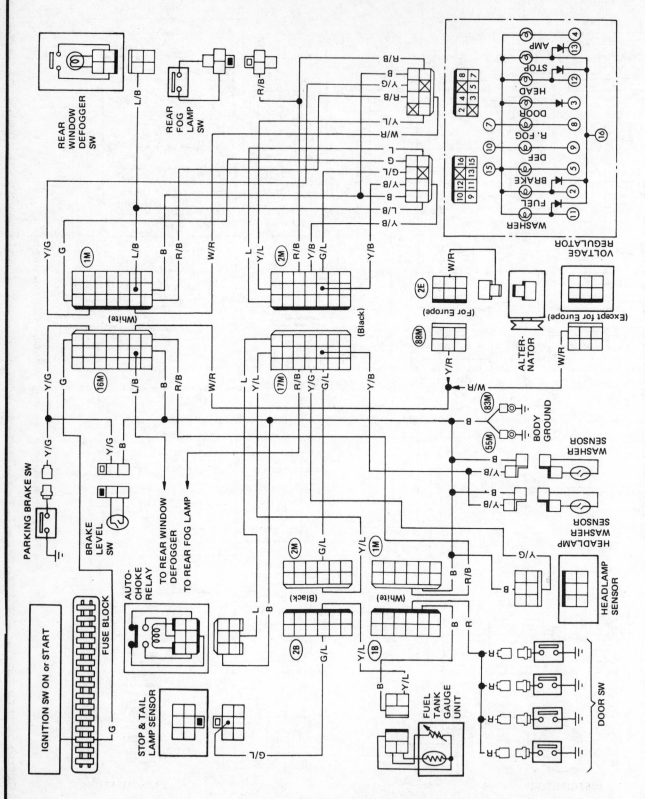

Fig. 10.94 Wiring diagram — warning lamps circuit (RH drive models)

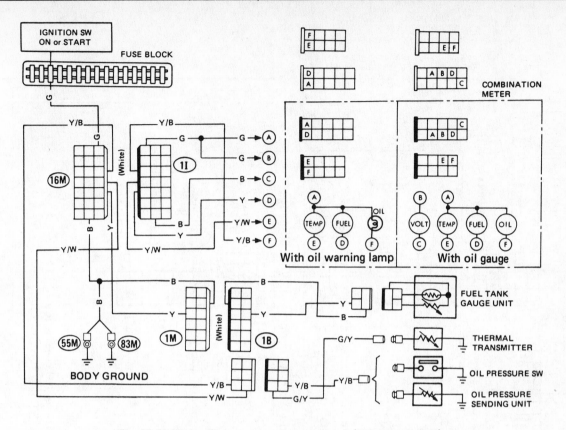

Fig. 10.95 Wiring diagram – instruments circuit (RH drive models)

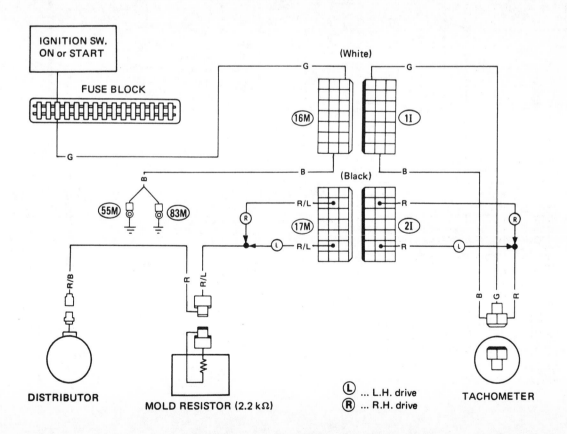

Fig. 10.96 Wiring diagram – tachometer circuit

10

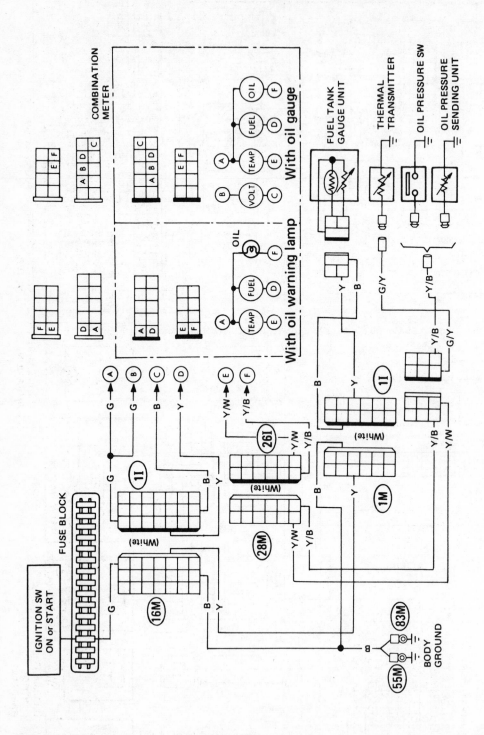

Fig. 10.97 Wiring diagram – instruments circuit (LH drive models)

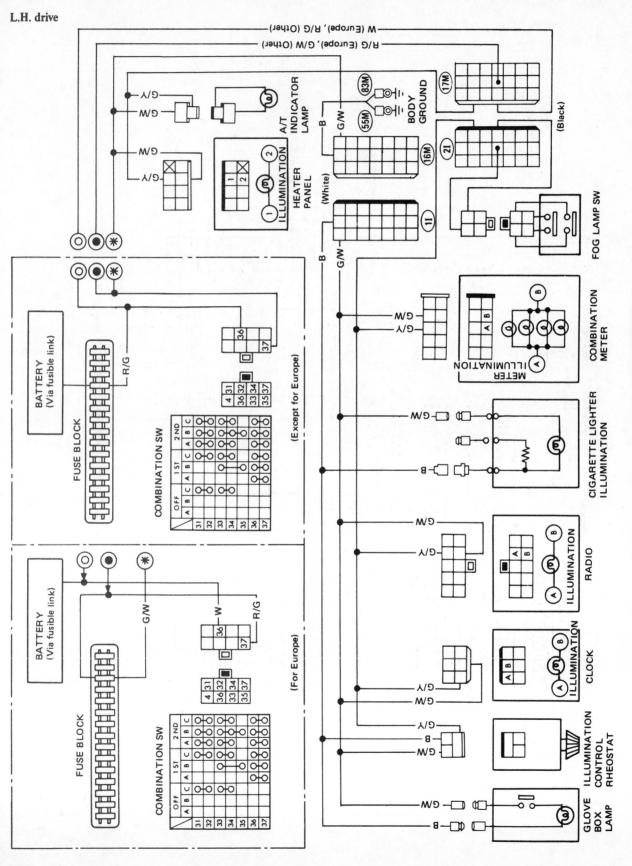

Fig. 10.98 Wiring diagram – instrument panel with illumination rheostat

10

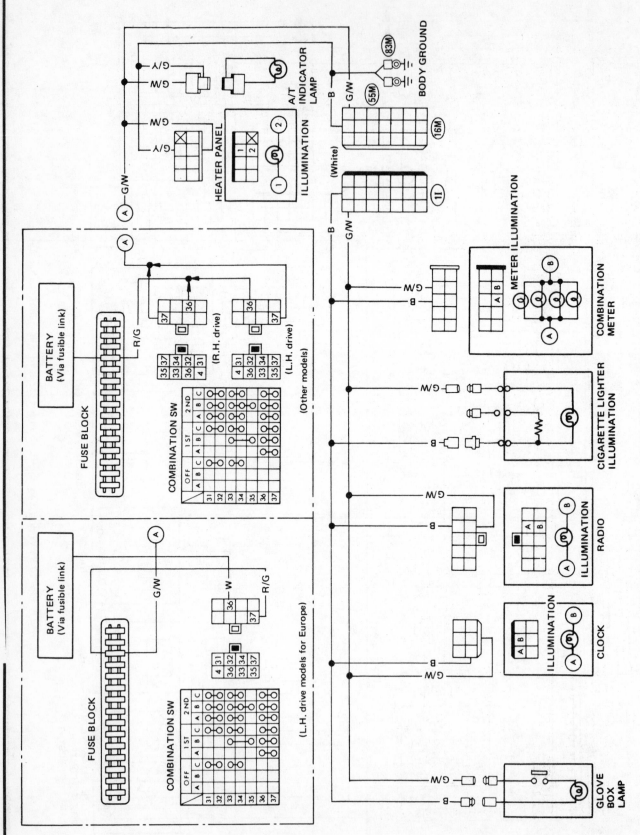

Fig. 10.99 Wiring diagram – instrument panel without illumination rheostat

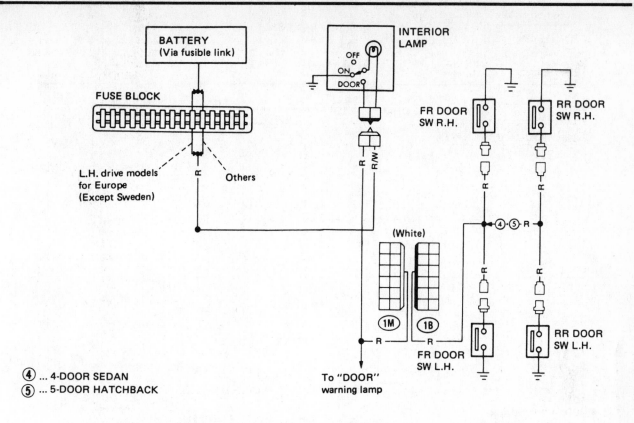

Fig. 10.100 Wiring diagram – interior and stop lamps circuit without interior lamp timer

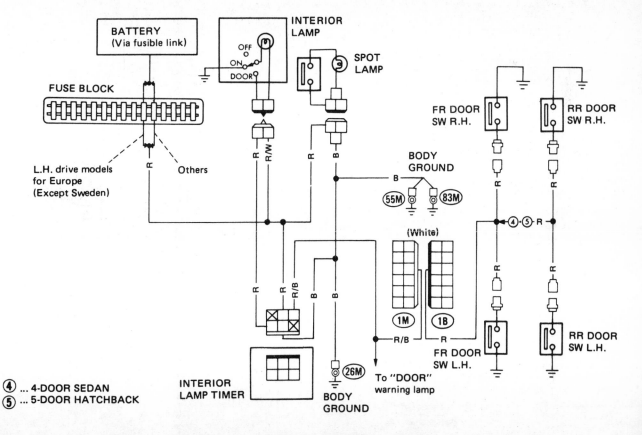

Fig. 10.101 Wiring diagram – interior and stop lamps circuit with interior lamp timer

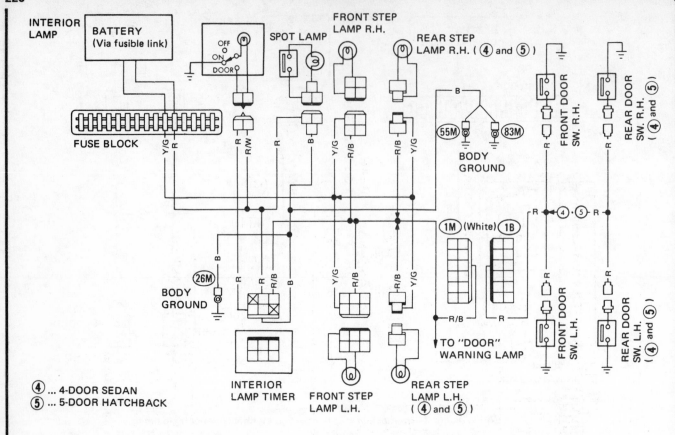

Fig. 10.102 Wiring diagram – interior and stop lamps circuit with interior lamp timer and stop lamps

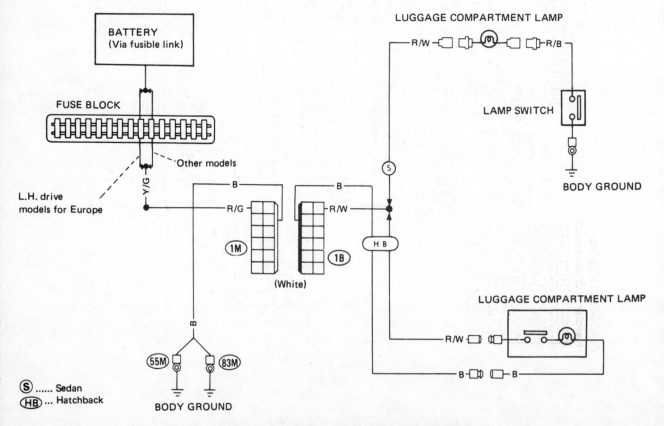

Fig. 10.103 Wiring diagram – luggage compartment lamps

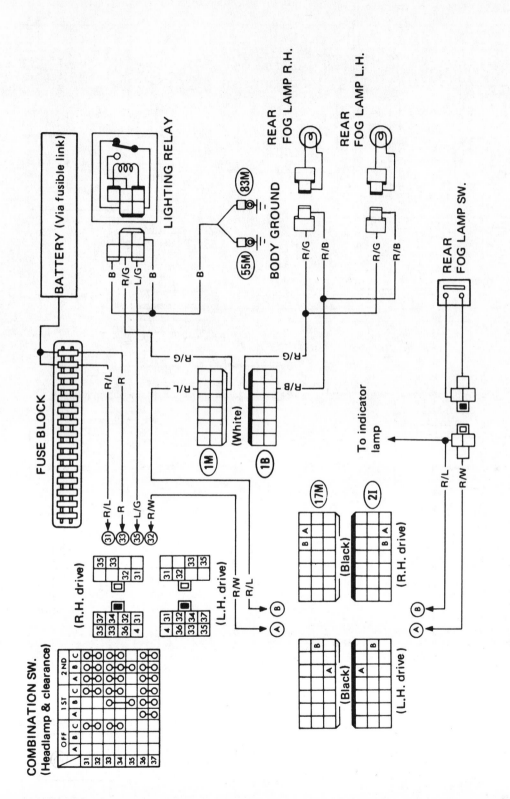

Fig. 10.104 Wiring diagram — rear foglamps

10

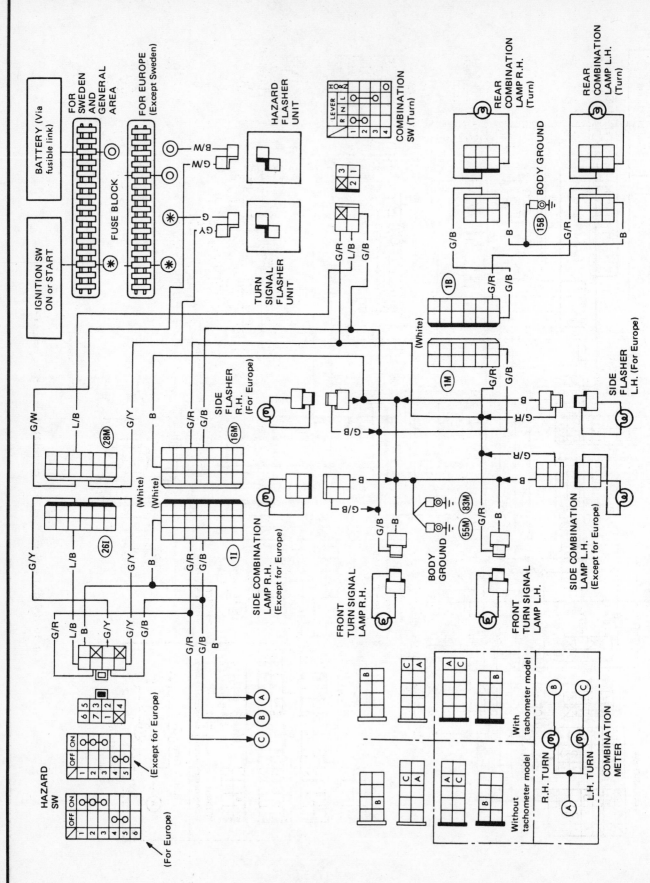

Fig. 10.105 Wiring diagram – turn signal and hazard warning lamps (LH drive models)

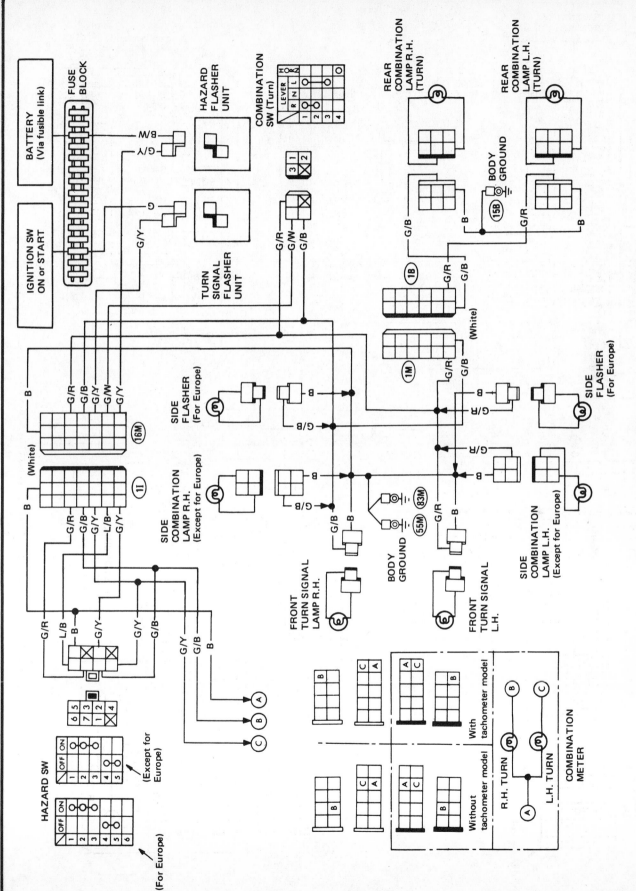

Fig. 10.106 Wiring diagram – turn signal and hazard warning lamps (RH drive models)

10

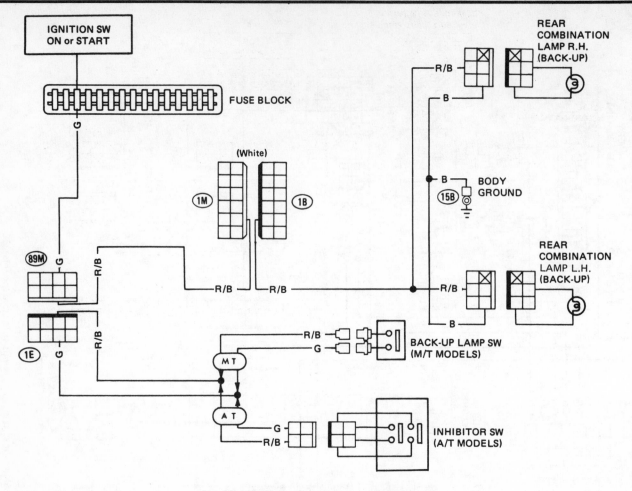

Fig. 10.107 Wiring diagram – reversing lamps

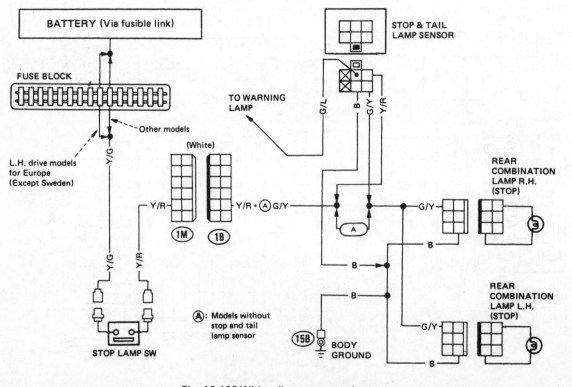

Fig. 10.108 Wiring diagram – stop-lamps

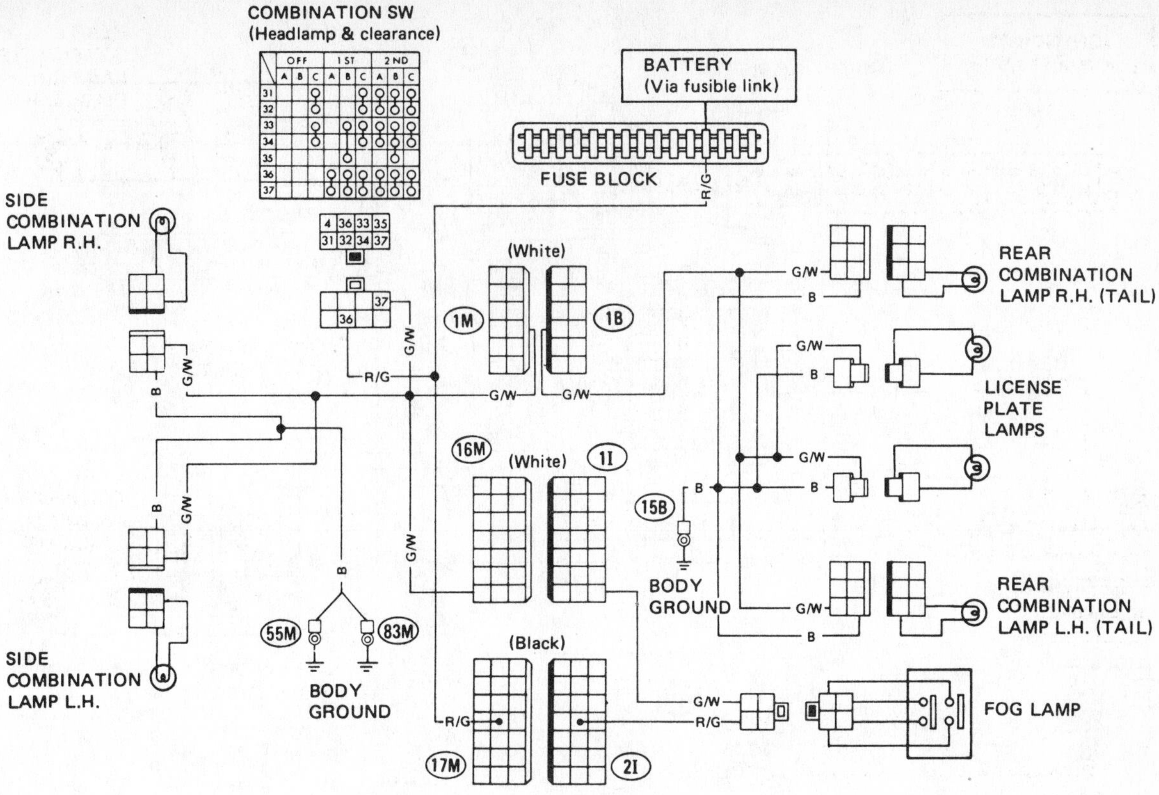

COMBINATION SW (Headlamp & clearance)

BATTERY (Via fusible link)

FUSE BLOCK

SIDE COMBINATION LAMP R.H.

REAR COMBINATION LAMP R.H. (TAIL)

LICENSE PLATE LAMPS

BODY GROUND

REAR COMBINATION LAMP L.H. (TAIL)

SIDE COMBINATION LAMP L.H.

BODY GROUND

FOG LAMP

Fig. 10.109 Wiring diagram – clearance, license plate and tail lamps

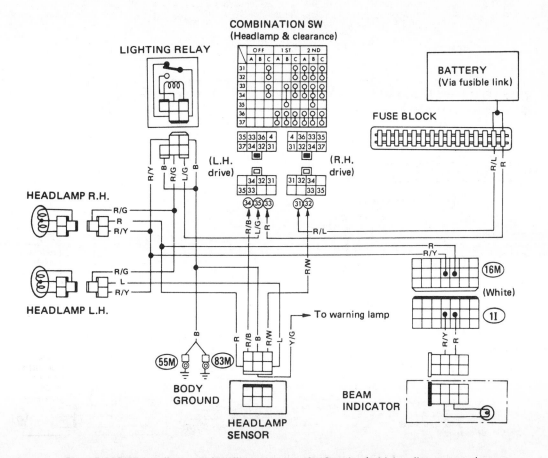

LIGHTING RELAY

COMBINATION SW (Headlamp & clearance)

BATTERY (Via fusible link)

FUSE BLOCK

(L.H. drive)

(R.H. drive)

HEADLAMP R.H.

HEADLAMP L.H.

To warning lamp

BEAM INDICATOR

BODY GROUND

HEADLAMP SENSOR

Fig. 10.110 Wiring diagram – headlamps, except for Sweden (with headlamp sensor)

10

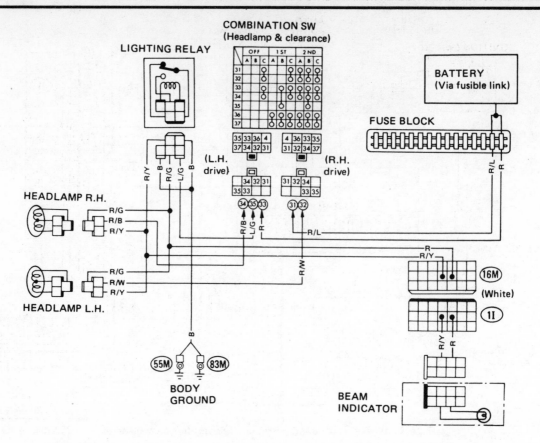

Fig. 10.111 Wiring diagram – headlamps, except for Sweden (without headlamp sensor)

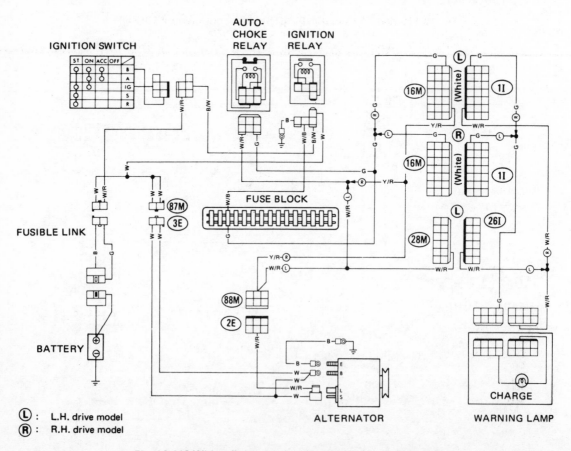

Ⓛ : L.H. drive model

Ⓡ : R.H. drive model

Fig. 10.112 Wiring diagram – charging system circuit (Europe)

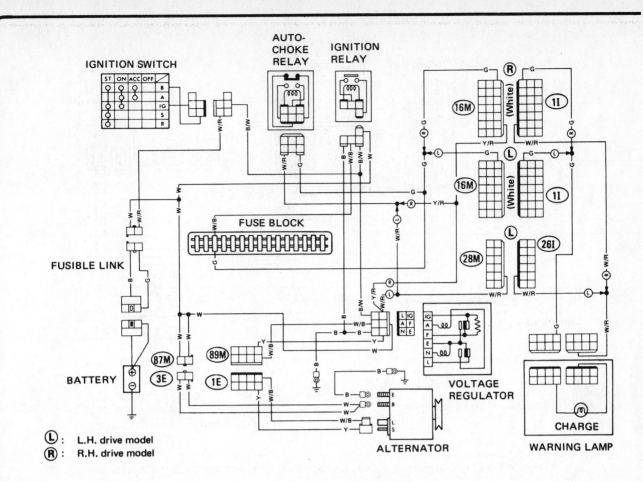

Fig. 10.113 Wiring diagram – charging system circuit (except Europe)

Chapter 11 Suspension and steering

Refer to Chapter 13 for specifications and information applicable to 1984 and later models

Contents

Specifications

Front suspension

Type	Independent with Macpherson struts and coil springs
Camber	0°45' negative to 0°45' positive
Caster	0°40' to 2°10'
Steering axis inclination	13°40' to 15°10'
Toe-in (curb weight)	0 to 2.0 mm (0 to 0.08 in)
Full lock turning angle:	
Inner wheel	36 to 40°
Outer wheel	30 to 34°

Rear suspension

Type	Independent with telescopic struts, coil springs, link rods and radius rod
Camber	0 to 1°30'
Toe-in	5.0 to 8.0 mm (0.20 to 0.30 in)

Steering

Type	Rack and pinion with safety column. Power-assisted steering on certain models
Number of turns lock to lock	3.6
Turning circle	9.75 m (32.0 ft)
Rack grease type/specification	Multi-purpose lithium-based grease, to NLGI No 2 (Duckhams LB 10)
Power-steering fluid type/specification	Dexron type ATF (Duckhams D-Matic)
Power-steering fluid capacity	1.0 litre (1.76 Imp pt, 1.06 US qts)

Torque wrench settings
Front suspension

	Nm	lbf ft
Strut gland nut	100	74
Piston rod self-locking nut	70	52
Strut upper mounting nuts	40	30
Strut lower clamp bolts	100	74
Lower balljoint to track control arm bolts	65	48
Lower balljoint taper pin nut	65	48
Track control arm fixing bolt and nuts	100	74
Track control arm support plate bolts	100	74

Rear suspension

Parallel link bracket bolts	100	74
Strut upper mounting nuts	40	30
Parallel link pivot bolts	100	74
Radius rod pivot bolts	90	66
Radius rod bracket to strut	70	52
Strut piston rod nut	40	30
Strut gland nut	100	47

Steering

Steering wheel nut	45	33
Lower joint pinch-bolts	40	30
Column lower bracket bolts	14	10
Column upper bracket bolts	14	10
Tilt lever nut at stop position	11	8
Tilt lever fixing bolt	12	9
Tilt joint fixing bolt	35	26
Tie-rod balljoint taper pin nut	35	26
Tie-rod end locknut	40	30
Steering gear mounting bolts	75	55
Rack adjuster plug locknut	55	41
Power steering pipe union nut	45	33
Power steering high pressure hose to pump	65	48
Power steering high pressure hose to gear	45	33

1 General description

The front suspension is of independent type incorporating Macpherson struts and coil springs.

The rear suspension is also independent using telescopic struts, coil springs and locating links.

The steering gear is of rack and pinion type with a safety steering column.

Power-assisted steering is available on certain models.

Refer to Chapter 8 for details of hubs and wheels.

2 Maintenance

1 With the elimination of suspension lubrication points, the largest part of regular maintenance consists of visual inspection.

2 With the help of an assistant raise the front end of the vehicle and support it securely. Turn the steering from full lock to full lock and check the rack bellows for splits. Steering bellows which have split completely in two sections can often only be detected in the full lock position.

3 Have your assistant move the steering wheel slightly in both

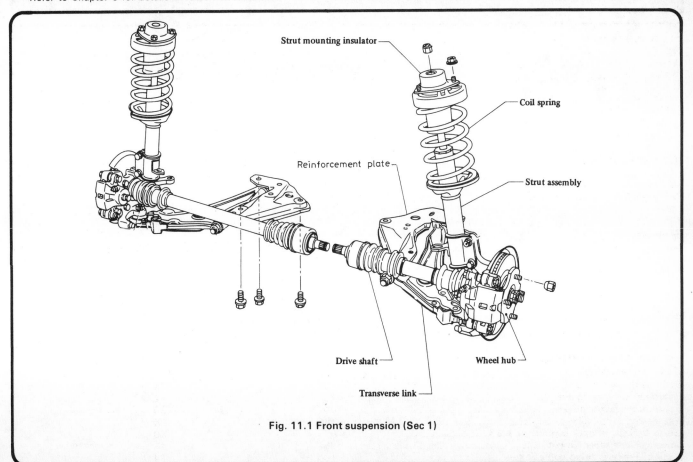

Fig. 11.1 Front suspension (Sec 1)

Strut mounting insulator

Coil spring

Reinforcement plate

Strut assembly

Drive shaft

Wheel hub

Transverse link

11

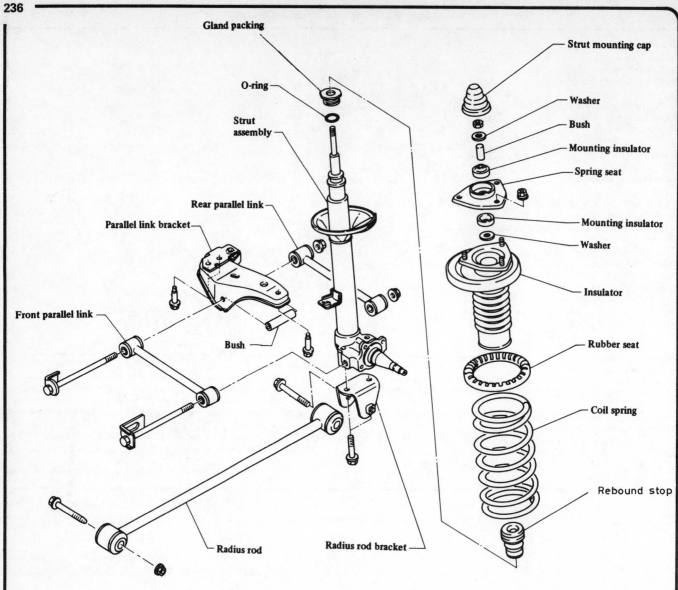

Gland packing

O-ring

Strut assembly

Rear parallel link

Parallel link bracket

Front parallel link

Bush

Radius rod

Radius rod bracket

Strut mounting cap

Washer

Bush

Mounting insulator

Spring seat

Mounting insulator

Washer

Insulator

Rubber seat

Coil spring

Rebound stop

Fig. 11.2 Rear suspension components (left-hand side) (Sec 1)

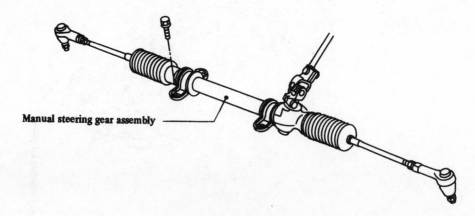

Manual steering gear assembly

Fig. 11.3 Manual steering gear (Sec 1)

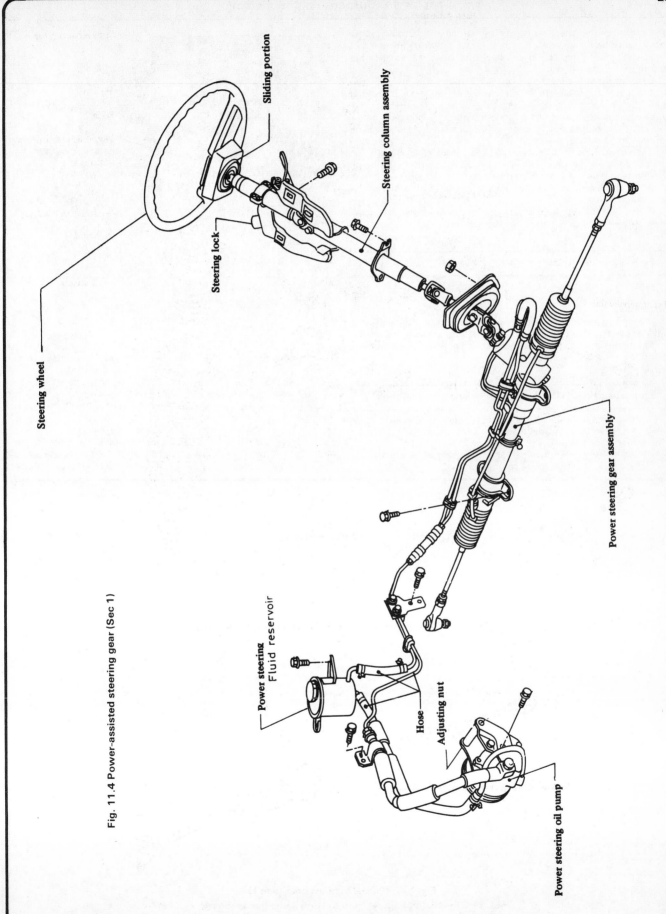

Steering wheel

Sliding portion

Steering column assembly

Steering lock

Power steering gear assembly

Power steering
Fluid reservoir

Hose

Adjusting nut

Power steering oil pump

Fig. 11.4 Power-assisted steering gear (Sec 1)

11

directions while you check for wear in the tie-rod end balljoints at the steering arms on the stub axle carrier. Even the slightest movement of the tie-rod before the steering arm begins to move will indicate the need to renew the balljoint.

4   Lost motion at the steering wheel will confirm wear in the tie-rod end balljoints or if these are in good order then wear in the steering rack or pinion teeth must be the reason.

5   Check all suspension bushes for wear by using a long bar to prise the suspension component. Any non-rotational movement will indicate the need to renew the bushes.

6   Depress each corner of the vehicle in turn by carefully standing on the end of the bumper. Step off, when the vehicle should return to its normal road height. If the vehicle tends to bounce (oscillate) before settling then the strut has lost its damping characteristic and must be renewed.

7   If the vehicle is equipped with power steering, keep a regular check on the fluid hoses and renew if cracked or deteriorated.

3.2 Front suspension lower balljoint

3   Front suspension lower balljoint – renewal

1   Refer to Chapter 8 and remove the driveshaft.
2   Unscrew the nuts and separate the balljoint from the track control arm (photo).
3   Unscrew the nut from the balljoint taper pin and then using a suitable splitter tool, disconnect the balljoint from the stub axle carrier.
4   Refitting is a reversal of removal, but use new nuts to secure the balljoint to the track control arm.

4   Front suspension strut – removal, overhaul and refitting

1   Raise the front end of the vehicle and support it securely on axle stands placed under the bodyframe side-members.
2   Remove the roadwheel.
3   Disconnect the brake hydraulic line from the suspension strut.
4   Place a jack under the track control arm.

5   Remove the bolts which clamp the base of the strut to the stub axle carrier.
6   Loosen but do not remove, the nut on top of the strut piston rod.
7   Unscrew and remove the nuts from the suspension strut top mounting at the suspension strut turret within the engine compartment.
8   Withdraw the strut from under the front wing.
9   A leaking or faulty strut can be overhauled in the following way.
10 First remove the coil spring from the strut. To do this, use purpose made spring compressors (available from most motor accessory

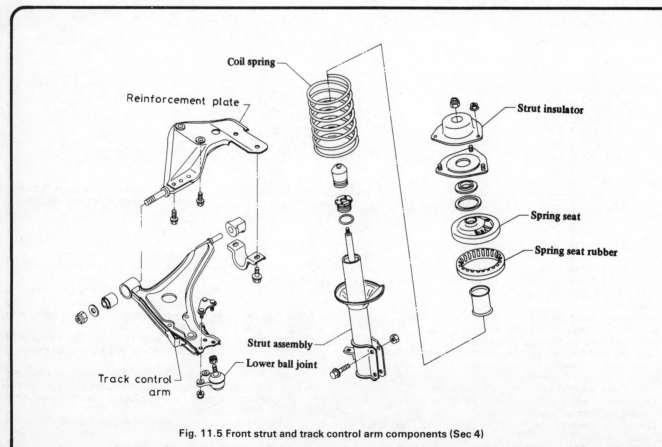

Fig. 11.5 Front strut and track control arm components (Sec 4)

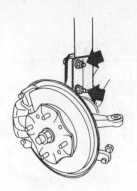

Fig. 11.6 Front strut lower clamp (Sec 4)

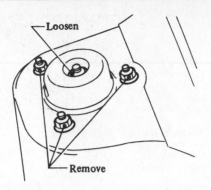

Fig. 11.7 Front strut upper mounting nuts (Sec 4)

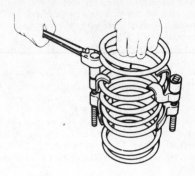

Fig. 11.8 Typical spring compressors (Sec 4)

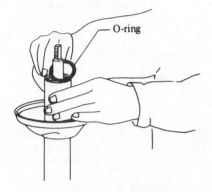

Fig. 11.9 Strut O-ring (Sec 4)

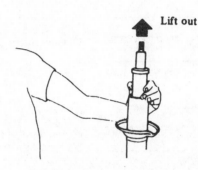

Fig. 11.10 Withdrawing strut internal parts (Sec 4)

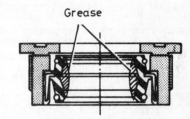

Fig. 11.11 Strut gland nut. Area to grease arrowed (Sec 4)

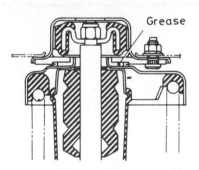

Fig. 11.12 Strut upper mounting. Area to grease arrowed (Sec 4)

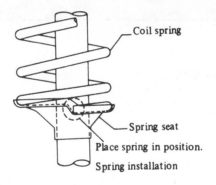

Fig. 11.13 Front coil spring correctly seated (Sec 4)

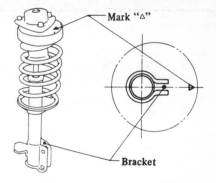

Fig. 11.14 Front strut spring seat and upper mounting alignment (Sec 4)

stores) to compress the spring until the strut top mounting insulator can be turned by hand.

11 Remove the nut from the top of the piston rod.

12 Remove the spring and mounting components. Unless the spring is to be renewed, the clamps can be left in place, otherwise release them very gently.

13 Remove the gland nut from the top of the strut tube.

14 Extract the O-ring and the guide bush.

15 Withdraw the piston/cylinder assembly.

16 Drain the fluid from the cylinder and the outer casing.

17 If the reason for dismantling was caused by a fluid leak from the gland, renew the seal and packing/gland nut assembly.

18 If the shock absorber has faulty damping action then a repair kit must be obtained which will contain the piston rod cylinder, bottom valve and guide bush as a matched set.

19 Commence reassembly by fitting the piston rod/cylinder into the strut tube.

20 Pour in exactly 290 ml (10.2 fluid oz) of strut fluid and fit the guide bush.

21 Fit the gland nut and O-ring having greased them beforehand. Take great care not to damage the lips of the packing. It is recommended that the shoulder on the piston is temporarily taped as a protective measure.

22 Tighten the gland nut to the specified torque wrench setting.

23 Hold the strut in its normal attitude and give it several full strokes to remove trapped air from the fluid. Give several more strokes with the strut inverted.

24 Fit the clamped coil spring to the strut followed by the rebound rubber, upper mounting and piston rod nut. Apply grease as shown to the upper mounting.

25 Release the spring compressor slowly and make sure that the lower end of the coil locates correctly in the spring seat and that the mark on the upper strut mounting is in alignment with the jaws of the clamp at the base of the strut.

26 Offer the strut into position, tighten the upper mounting nuts and clamp bolts.

27 Attach the brake hydraulic line to the strut.

28 Refit the roadwheel and lower the vehicle to the floor.

11

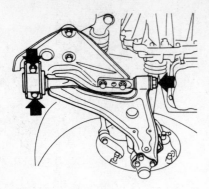

Fig. 11.15 Track control arm pivot nut and clamp bolts (Sec 5)

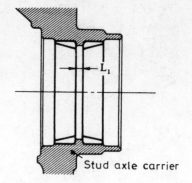

Fig. 11.16 Stub axle carrier bearing outer track spacer thickness (L1) (Sec 6)

5 Front suspension track control arm – removal and refitting

1   Raise the front end of the vehicle and support it securely under the bodyframe side-members.
2   Remove the roadwheel.
3   Disconnect the suspension balljoint from the track control arm by unscrewing the three nuts.
4   Unscrew the pivot nut and clamp bolts and remove the arm from the support plate.
5   The support plate can be removed after removing the fixing bolts.
6   The flexible bushes are renewable. Press or draw the front bush out or into its seat. The rear bush can be gripped in the jaws of a vice while the control arm is twisted out of it. Use brake fluid or soapy water to ease the fitting of the new bushes.
7   Refitting the support plate and control arm is a reversal of removal. Finally tighten all nuts and bolts to the specified torque when the car has been lowered to the floor.

6 Front suspension stub axle carrier – removal and refitting

1   This is described in Chapter 8, Section 7, paragraphs 1 to 12.
2   If the stub axle carrier is to be renewed, dismantle it also as described in Chapter 8, Section 7, but the new stub axle carrier will require a new bearing spacer, the thickness of which must be calculated in the following way.
3   Once the bearing tracks have been pressed into the stub axle carrier, measure the distance (L1) between their inboard edges. From this dimension subtract 0.53 mm (0.0209 in).
4   The resulting figure must then be matched against the eighteen spacers available, their thicknesses being indicated alphabetically.

Spacer mark	Thickness
A	3.910 to 3.940 mm (0.1539 to 0.1551 in)
B	3.970 to 4.000 mm (0.1563 to 0.1575 in)
C	4.030 to 4.060 mm (0.1587 to 0.1598 in)
D	4.090 to 4.120 mm (0.1610 to 0.1622 in)
E	4.150 to 4.180 mm (0.1634 to 0.1646 in)
F	4.210 to 4.240 mm (0.1657 to 0.1669 in)
G	4.270 to 4.300 mm (0.1681 to 0.1693 in)
H	4.330 to 4.360 mm (0.1705 to 0.1717 in)
I	4.390 to 4.420 mm (0.1728 to 0.1740 in)
J	4.450 to 4.480 mm (0.1752 to 0.1764 in)
K	4.510 to 4.540 mm (0.1776 to 0.1787 in)
L	4.570 to 4.600 mm (0.1799 to 0.1811 in)
M	4.630 to 4.660 mm (0.1823 to 0.1835 in)
N	4.690 to 4.720 mm (0.1846 to 0.1858 in)
O	4.750 to 4.780 mm (0.1870 to 0.1882 in)
P	4.810 to 4.840 mm (0.1894 to 0.1906 in)
Q	4.870 to 4.900 mm (0.1917 to 0.1929 in)
R	4.930 to 4.960 mm (0.1941 to 0.1953 in)

5   Select the most suitable spacer and then follow the reassembly operations described in Chapter 8, Section 7, paragraphs 17 to 37.

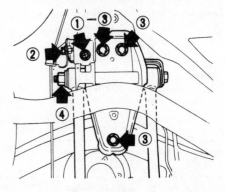

Fig. 11.17 Rear suspension attachment (Sec 7)

1   Exhaust pipe mounting   3   Parallel link bracket bolts
    (LHS only)   4   Link pivot nut
2   Handbrake cable guide bracket

7 Rear suspension parallel link bracket – removal and refitting

1   Raise the rear of the vehicle and support securely under the bodyframe members. Remove the roadwheel.
2   If the link bracket is being removed from the exhaust pipe side, disconnect the mounting bracket.
3   Unbolt the handbrake cable bracket.
4   Unscrew the three bolts from the parallel link bracket. Before disturbing the position of the bracket, mark its setting using quick-drying paint around its edge or within its elongated bolt holes. This will aid alignment at refitting.
5   Unscrew the nut and withdraw the parallel link pivot bolt.
6   Refitting is a reversal of removal, but observe the following points.
7   Use a new nut for the pivot bolt.
8   Check and adjust the rear wheel alignment as described in Section 25 of this Chapter.

8 Rear suspension parallel link and radius rod – removal and refitting

1   Raise the rear of the vehicle and support it securely under the bodyframe side-members.
2   Remove the roadwheel.
3   Mark the two parallel links as they must not be interchanged.
4   The rear link can be unbolted and removed as can the radius rod, simply by unscrewing the connecting nuts or bolts (photos).
5   If the front link is to be removed then the bracket will have to be withdrawn as described in Section 7.

8.4A Rear suspension strut bottom connections

8.4B Radius rod to body bracket

6   The flexible bushes may be renewed by means of a press or by using a bolt, nut, washers and a distance piece.
7   Refitting is a reversal of removal, but use a new nut on the link pivot bolt.

9   Rear suspension strut and spring – removal, overhaul and refitting

1   Raise the rear of the vehicle, support securely under the bodyframe sidemembers and remove the roadwheel.
2   Disconnect the hydraulic brake line and cap the end of the pipe to prevent loss of fluid.
3   Remove the split and clevis pins, disconnect the handbrake cable from the shoe lever.
4   The strut may be removed complete with brake assembly and hub inner bearing. Alternatively the latter components may be removed from the strut, if the strut is to be overhauled or renewed.
5   Disconnect the parallel links and the radius rod from the strut.
6   Support the weight of the strut and remove the upper mounting nuts (photos).
7   Withdraw the strut/spring assembly from under the rear wing.
8   Removal of the coil spring and overhaul of the strut are as described for the front strut in Section 4, but note the mark on the spring seat which must be towards the front of the vehicle.
9   Refitting is a reversal of removal, but adjust the hub bearings as described in Chapter 8 and bleed the brake hydraulic system as described in Chapter 9.

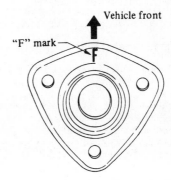

Fig. 11.18 Rear strut spring seat marking (Sec 9)

10   Rear suspension unit – removal and refitting

1   If desired, either side of the rear suspension may be removed complete.
2   Raise the rear of the vehicle and support securely under the body side-members.
3   Remove the roadwheel.
4   Disconnect the brake pipe and cap the end to prevent loss of fluid.
5   If the suspension being removed is on the exhaust pipe side, disconnect the exhaust mounting bracket.

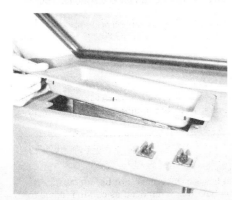

9.6A Removing rear compartment tidy tray for access to strut mounting (Hatchback)

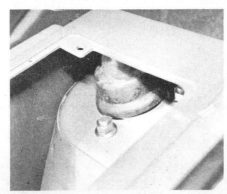

9.6B Rear strut top mounting

9.6C Rear strut top mounting (Hatchback)

11

6   Disconnect the handbrake cable from the lever at the backplate.
7   Disconnect the radius rod from the body.
8   Mark the setting of the parallel link bracket and then remove the fixing bolts.
9   Unscrew the suspension strut upper mounting nuts.
10 Withdraw the complete suspension unit from the vehicle.
11 Refitting is a reversal of removal, but bleed the brake hydraulic system and check and adjust the rear wheel alignment.

11 Steering rack bellows – renewal

1   Unscrew the nut from the tie-rod end balljoint taper pin and then using a suitable splitter tool, disconnect the balljoint from the steering arm of the stub axle carrier (photo).
2   Release the locknut on the balljoint and then counting the number of turns, unscrew the balljoint off the end of the tie-rod.
3   Release the rack bellows inner clamping band and pull the bellows off the tie-rod.
4   If grease is adhering to the inside of the bellows, estimate its quantity and smear an equivalent amount onto the rack teeth with the rack extended.
5   Fit the new bellows and clamp band.
6   Screw on the balljoint the same number of turns as was recorded at removal. Connect it to the steering arm.
7   Do not tighten the locknut until the wheel alignment has been checked and if necessary adjusted, as described in Section 24.

12 Tie-rod end balljoint – renewal

1   Carry out the operations described in paragraphs 1 and 2 of the preceding Section.
2   Screw on the new balljoint the same number of turns as was recorded at removal. Connect it to the steering arm.

3   Do not tighten the locknut until the wheel alignment has been checked and if necessary adjusted, as described in Section 24.
4   It is not unusual to find that when attempting to tighten a balljoint taper pin (ball-stud) nut the taper pin rotates in the tapered eye of its connecting component so preventing tightening of the nut.
5   To overcome this condition, never grease the taper pin and apply pressure with a lever or jack to the balljoint housing so forcing the taper pin further into its seat while the nut is being tightened.

13 Steering wheel – removal and refitting

1   Disconnect the battery negative lead.
2   Prise off the central horn pad or remove the spoke covers with horn pushes by extracting the screws from the rear of the spokes, depending upon vehicle model (photo).
3   Unscrew the steering wheel retaining nut and pull the wheel from the tapered splined shaft. If it is tight, try rocking it but on no account strike the reverse side of the wheel or the end of the shaft as the built-in safety features of the column will be damaged. Use a small puller similar to the one shown . The steering wheel hub has tapped holes provided for this purpose (photo).
4   Before fitting the steering wheel, smear the splines with grease and align the punch marks (photo).
5   Tighten the nut to the specified torque.

14 Steering shaft lower joint – removal and refitting

1   Set the steering wheel and the front road wheels in the straight-ahead position.
2   Unscrew and remove the joint pinch-bolts (photo).
3   If necessary, prise the jaws of the joint open slightly and then pull it upwards to disengage it from the steering gear pinion shaft.
4   Now pull the joint downward off the main steering shaft and remove it.

11.1 Tie-rod end balljoint separating tool

13.2 Steering wheel horn pad

13.3 Unscrewing steering wheel nut

13.4 Steering wheel alignment marks

ST27180001
Fig. 11.19 Typical steering wheel puller
(Sec 13)

14.2 Steering rack mounting clamp

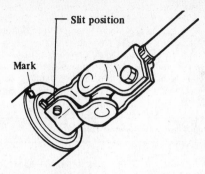

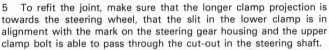

Fig. 11.20 Steering shaft lower joint alignment (Sec 14)

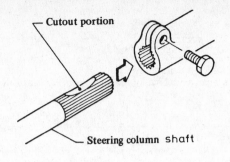

Fig. 11.21 Steering shaft pinch-bolt cut-out (Sec 14)

5   To refit the joint, make sure that the longer clamp projection is towards the steering wheel, that the slit in the lower clamp is in alignment with the mark on the steering gear housing and the upper clamp bolt is able to pass through the cut-out in the steering shaft.
6   Screw in the bolts and tighten to the specified torque wrench setting.

---

15 Steering column (non-tilt type) – removal, overhaul and refitting

---

1   Remove the steering wheel (Section 13).
2   Remove the shaft lower joint (Section 14).
3   Remove the shrouds from the upper column.
4   Remove the steering column switch (Chapter 10).
5   Remove the heater ducts (Chapter 2).

6   Unbolt the lower end of the steering column from the pedal bracket.
7   Unbolt the upper end of the column and lower it onto the front seat.
8   Withdraw the column assembly from the vehicle interior. Retain the sliding plate.
9   If required, the flexible cover on the bulkhead can be removed after unscrewing the three securing bolts.
10 If the bearings are worn they may be renewed in the following way, but before doing this, check the length (A) of the column. If it is not as specified, then the assembly has probably been compressed as a result of front end collision and it must be renewed complete.
11 Before dismantling the column, release the lock by turning the ignition key.
12 To remove the upper bearing, extract the circlip, washer and wave washer and pull out the bearing.
13 Extract the second circlip.

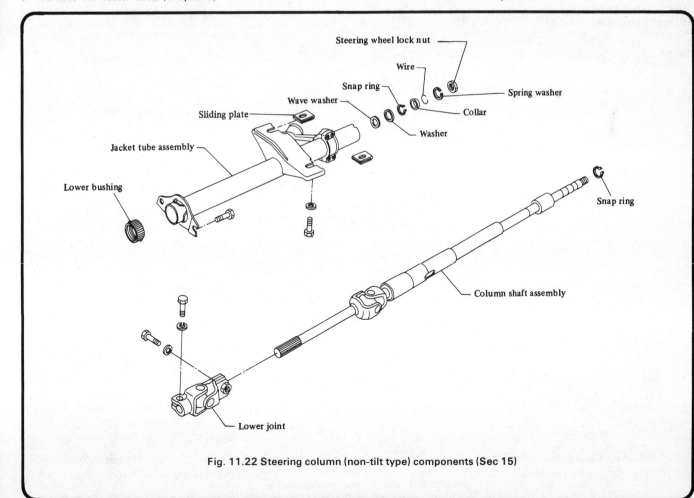

Fig. 11.22 Steering column (non-tilt type) components (Sec 15)

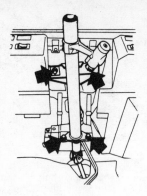

Fig. 11.23 Steering column mounting bolts (Sec 15)

14 Push the shaft downward out of the column tube.
15 Remove the lower bush and then press the new one into position.
16 Grease the bush and insert the shaft.
17 Grease the upper bearing and then fit the first circlip, the bearing, wave washer, washer and second circlip. Note that the radius face of both circlips must be towards the bearing.
18 Offer the column into position making sure that the sliding plates at the upper mounting are in position.
19 Screw in all bolts finger tight then once the column is correctly aligned, tighten them to the specified torque.
20 Refit the steering column switch, the shrouds and the steering wheel.
21 Reconnect the lower joint as previously described.

16 Steering column (tilt type) – removal, overhaul and refitting

1 The removal operations are similar to those described in the preceding Section except that three bolts are used at the upper mounting bracket.
2 With the column removed, first check its length to ensure that it has not suffered deformation. If it is not within specification, it must be renewed as an assembly.
3 To dismantle the tilt mechanism, remove the small bolt which secures the tilt joint.

Fig. 11.24 Steering column flexible cover bolts (Sec 15)

Fig. 11.25 Specified non-tilt type steering column length (Sec 15)

A = 615.0 to 616.0 mm (24.21 to 24.25 in)

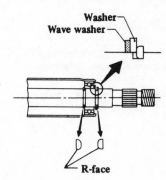

Fig. 11.26 Steering column top bearing circlips (Sec 15)

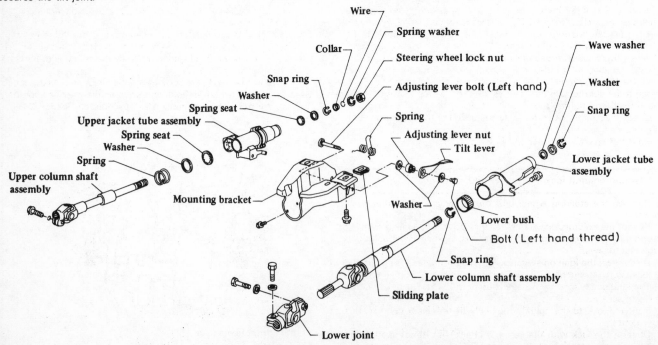

Fig. 11.27 Components of the tilt-type steering column (Sec 16)

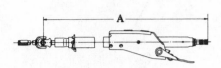

Fig. 11.28 Specified length of tilt-type steering column (Sec 16)

A = 661.0 to 662.0 mm (26.02 to 26.06 in)

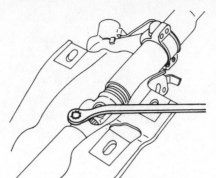

Fig. 11.29 Unscrewing tilt-joint bolt (Sec 16)

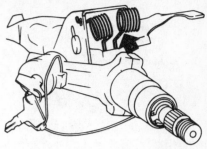

Fig. 11.30 Tilt mechanism springs (Sec 16)

Fig. 11.31 Method of compressing shaft spring (Sec 16)

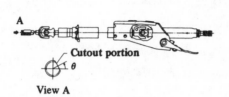

Fig. 11.32 Tilt alignment with shaft joint (Sec 16)

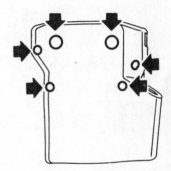

Fig. 11.33 Steering column shroud fixing screws (Sec 17)

4   Release the double spring and separate the components.

5   Unbolt and remove the column upper mounting bracket.

6   Removal and refitting of the shaft and bearings is similar to the procedure described in Section 15, but note that a coil spring is fitted at the upper end of the shaft. When reassembling, compress the spring by binding the coils with wire. The wire must of course be withdrawn later. Grease the bearings and make sure that the radius face of the circlips is towards the upper bearing.

7   When fitting the tilt mechanism, set the tilt joint at the specified angle to the shaft joint cut-out as shown in the diagram, Fig. 11.32.

8   Fit the tilt adjusting lever to its splined nut and tighten the nut just enough to be able to turn the lever to contact its stop. Screw in (left-hand thread) and tighten the retaining bolt.

9   Check that the tilt lever moves from its stop to the release position through an angle of 80°.

10 Refit the column as described in Section 15.

17 Steering column lock – removal and refitting

1   Remove the steering wheel and the upper column shrouds (six screws).

2   Extract the column lock clamp screws. Do this by drilling or using a proprietary screw extractor or if all else fails, by sawing through them at the clamp jaws.

3   Disconnect the ignition switch wiring plug (Chapter 4) and remove the lock/switch assembly.

4   The ignition switch may be detached from the lock after extracting the fixing screws.

5   Refit the lock to the column, but only fit the shear head screws finger tight.

6   Operate the lock with the key and check that its tongue locates smoothly in the steering shaft cut-out. Adjust the lock alignment if necessary.

7   Fully tighten the lock screws until their heads break off.

18 Steering gear (manual) – removal and refitting

1   Raise the front of the vehicle and support it securely on axle stands.

2   Disconnect the tie-rod balljoints from the steering arms on the stub axle carriers.

3   Release but do not remove, the steering gear mounting bolts.

4   Remove the steering shaft lower joint as described in Section 14.

5   Remove the previously loosened mounting bolts and withdraw the steering gear from the vehicle.

6   Refitting is a reversal of removal, align the lower joint as described in Section 14 and tighten all nuts and bolts to the specified torque.

7   Check the front wheel alignment as described in Section 24.

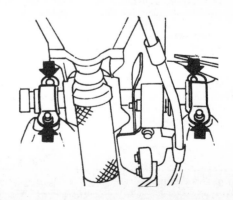

Fig. 11.34 Steering gear mounting clamps (Sec 18)

11

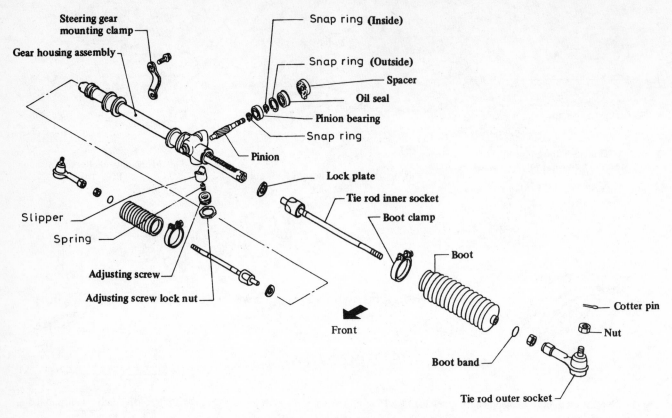

Fig. 11.35 Manual steering components (Sec 18)

19 Steering gear (power-assisted) – maintenance

1   Regularly check the fluid level in the steering pump reservoir. Do this when the system is cold by unscrewing the cap with dipstick attached and reading off the fluid level.
2   Top up if necessary with specified fluid to bring the level within the marked area on the dipstick.
3   Periodically check the condition of the system hoses and renew if they are in anything but first class condition.
4   Keep the pump drivebelt correctly tensioned as described in Chapter 2.

20 Steering gear (power-assisted) – removal and refitting

1   Raise the front end of the vehicle and support securely on stands.
2   Disconnect the flexible hose and rigid pipe from the steering gear and allow the fluid to drain. Cap the pipes to prevent the entry of dirt.
3   Disconnect the tie-rod end balljoints from the steering arms on the stub axle carriers.
4   Refer to Section 14 and remove the steering shaft lower joint.
5   Release the fluid lines from their clips on the steering gear.
6   Unscrew the steering gear mounting bolts and withdraw the gear from under the front wheel arch.
7   Refitting is a reversal of removal, but on completion, check the front wheel alignment and fill and bleed the steering hydraulic system.

21 Steering gear – overhaul

1   Overhaul of either the manual or power steering gear is not recommended. It is far more satisfactory to obtain a new or factory reconditioned unit after the original unit has reached the end of its long service life.

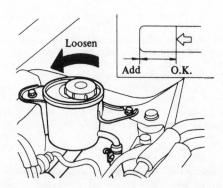

Fig. 11.36 Power steering pump and dipstick (Sec 19)

2   Renewal of the bellows and tie-rod ends may certainly be undertaken as described in earlier Sections of this Chapter.
3   Should a quantity of grease be lost due to a split rack bellows then fresh grease may be introduced at the rack adjuster housing in the following way.
4   Release the locknut and unscrew the threaded adjuster plug.
5   Extract the coil spring and slipper.
6   Pack specified grease into the opening, fit the slipper, spring and tighten the adjuster plug fully.
7   With manual steering unscrew the adjuster plug through 10 to 15° or on power-assisted steering 20 to 25°. Tighten the locknut without disturbing the setting of the plug.
8   The adjustment described in the preceding paragraph may be checked in the event of rack 'knock' becoming evident or the occurrence of stiff steering.

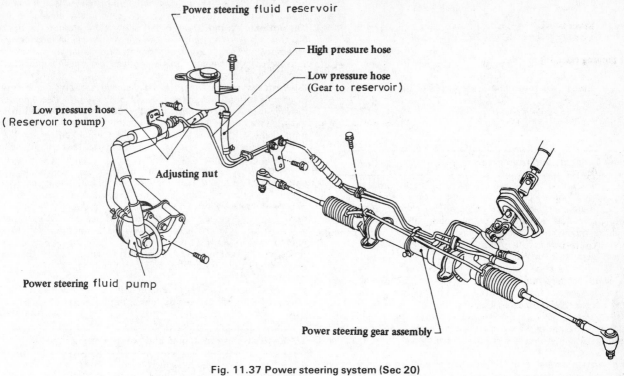

Fig. 11.37 Power steering system (Sec 20)

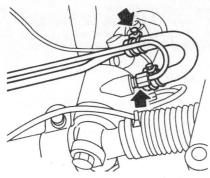

Fig. 11.38 Power steering gear fluid line attachment (Sec 20)

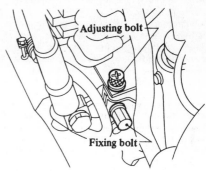

Fig. 11.39 Power steering pump mounting and belt tensioning bolt
(Sec 22)

22 Power-assisted steering pump and reservoir – removal and refitting

1   Slacken the pump mounting bolt, turn the belt tensioning bolt anti-clockwise and then swivel the pump so that the drivebelt can be removed.
2   Disconnect the fluid hoses from the pump, allow the fluid to drain. Then cap the hoses to prevent the entry of dirt.
3   Remove the mounting bolts and withdraw the pump.
4   The fluid reservoir can be removed after disconnecting the fluid hoses from it.
5   Refitting is a reversal of disconnection and removal, but adjust the tension of the drivebelt as described in Chapter 2 and fill and bleed the system as described in the next Section.

23 Power-assisted steering system – filling and bleeding

1   Using only fluid which is clean and of the specified type, fill the system by pouring it into the reservoir until it reaches the 'FULL' mark on the dipstick.

2   Raise the front wheels clear of the floor and support the vehicle securely. Then turn the steering wheel gently from lock to lock ten times.
3   Check the fluid level and top up if necessary.
4   Start and run the engine until the temperature of the fluid in the pump reaches 60 to 80°C (140 to 176°F). Test this with a contact type thermometer on the pump body.
5   Switch off and top up as necessary to the 'FULL' mark.
6   Run the engine for another five seconds, switch off and add more fluid if required.
7   Turn the steering wheel from lock to lock quickly ten times and top up again.
8   Start the engine and while it is idling, repeat the operations described in paragraphs 6 and 7.
9   Should air still be present in the system, indicated by air bubbles in the reservoir fluid or the steering wheel turning stiffly, turn the steering from lock to lock between five and ten times with the engine idling and hold the steering each time at full lock position for five seconds.
10 While holding at full lock, check for a fluid leak in a hose or pipe union.
11 On no account hold the steering in the full lock position for more than fifteen seconds at a time.

11

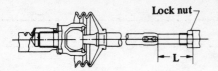

Fig. 11.40 Tie-rod basic setting (Sec 24)

L = 44.6 mm (1.756 in)

24 Steering angles and front wheel alignment

1   Accurate front wheel alignment is essential to provide good steering and roadholding characteristics and to ensure slow and even tyre wear. Before considering the steering angles, check that the tyres are correctly inflated, that the front wheels are not buckled, the hub bearings are not worn or incorrectly adjusted and that the steering linkage is in good order, without slackness or wear at the joints.
2   Wheel alignment consists of four factors:
Camber, is the angle at which the road wheels are set from the vertical when viewed from the front or rear of the vehicle. Positive camber is the angle (in degrees) that the wheels are tilted outwards at the top from the vertical.
Castor, is the angle between the steering axis and a vertical line when viewed from each side of the vehicle. Positive castor is indicated when the steering axis is inclined towards the rear of the vehicle at its upper end.
Steering axis inclination, is the angle when viewed from the front or rear of the vehicle between vertical and an imaginary line drawn between the upper and lower strut mountings.
Toe, is the amount by which the distance between the front inside edges of the roadwheel rims differs from that between the rear inside edges. If the distance between the front edges is less than that at the rear, the wheels are said to toe-in. If the distance between the front inside edges is greater than that at the rear, the wheels toe-out.
3   Camber and castor are set during production. Any deviation from specified tolerances must therefore be due to collision damage or grossly worn suspension components.

4   To check the front wheel alignment, first make sure that the lengths of both tie-rods are equal when the steering is in the straight-ahead position. The tie-rods can be set initially as shown in the diagram after having released the locknuts and rotated the tie-rod.
5   Obtain a tracking gauge. These are available in various forms from accessory stores or one can be fabricated from a length of steel tubing suitably cranked to clear the sump and bellhousing and having a setscrew and locknut at one end.
6   With the gauge, measure the distance between the two wheel inner rims (at hub height) at the rear of the wheel. Push the vehicle forward to rotate the wheel through 180° (half a turn) and measure the distance between the wheel inner rims, again at hub height, at the front of the wheel. This last measurement should differ from the first by the appropriate toe-in according to specifications (see Specifications Section).
7   Where the toe-in is found to be incorrect, release the tie-rod balljoint locknuts and turn the tie-rods equally. Only turn them a quarter of a turn at a time before re-checking the alignment. Do not grip the threaded part of the tie-rod/balljoint during adjustment and make sure that the bellows outboard clip is free otherwise the bellows will twist as the tie-rod is rotated. Always turn both rods in the same direction when viewed from the centre line of the vehicle otherwise the rods will become unequal in lengths. This would cause the steering wheel spoke position to alter and cause problems on turns with tyre scrubbing.
8   On completion, tighten the tie-rod end locknuts without disturbing their setting, check that the balljoint is at the centre of its arc of travel.

25 Rear suspension angles and wheel alignment

1   As with the front suspension, all steering angles for the rear suspension with the exception of toe are set in production.
2   Check the toe-in exactly the same way as described in the preceding Section, but where adjustment is required, then the parallel link brackets will have to be moved in the following way.
3   Release the bolts on one bracket and set it at the mid position of the total movement available by the elongated bolt holes. Tighten the bolts.
4   Release the bolts on the opposite bracket and swivel it as necessary to obtain the specified toe-in. Tighten the bolts on completion.

26 Fault diagnosis – suspension and steering

Symptom	Reason(s)
Suspension	
Vehicle wanders	Worn hub bearings
	Incorrect wheel alignment
	Worn control arm balljoint
Wheel wobble or vibration	Roadwheels out of balance
	Roadwheel buckled
	Incorrect front wheel alignment
	Faulty suspension strut
	Weak coil spring
Pitching or rolling on corners	Faulty suspension strut
	Weak or broken coil spring
Manual steering	
Lost motion at steering wheel	Wear in tie-rod end balljoints
	Worn rack or pinion teeth
	Incorrect wheel alignment
	Seized tie-rod end balljoint
	Dry rack assembly
	Bent shaft or column
Vibration transmitted to steering wheel	Roadwheels require balancing
	Incorrect front wheel alignment
	Roadwheel buckled
No return action of steering wheel	Castor angle out of specification
Power-assisted steering – In addition to the faults listed for manual steering	
Lack of assistance or jerky action	Low fluid level
	Slipping pump drivebelt
Noisy operation especially on turns	Air in system
	Low fluid level
	Worn pump
	Clogged hose or filter

11

Chapter 12 Bodywork

Contents

Specifications

Type ....
All-steel welded
Four-door Saloon
Five-door Hatchback
Three-door Hatchback

Dimensions and weights ....
These are given in the Introductory Section at the beginning of this Manual.

Torque wrench settings	Nm	lbf ft
Bumper bracket to body bolts	40	30
Bumper shock absorber mounting bolts	40	30
Hatchback tailgate hinge bolts	18	13
Front seat mounting bolts	12	9
Seat belt upper anchor bolt	30	22
Seat belt lower anchor bolt	30	22
Seat belt reel housing bolt	30	22

1 General description

The bodywork is of all-steel, welded, unitary construction and is available in 4-door saloon, 3-door hatchback or 5-door hatchback versions.

The front wings are detachable in the interest of economical repair.

2 Maintenance – bodywork and underframe

1   The general condition of a vehicle's bodywork is the one thing that significantly affects its value. Maintenance is easy but needs to be regular. Neglect, particularly after minor damage, can lead quickly to further deterioration and costly repair bills. It is important also to keep watch on those parts of the vehicle not immediately visible, for instance the underside, inside all the wheel arches and the lower part of the engine compartment.

2   The basic maintenance routine for the bodywork is washing – preferably with a lot of water, from a hose. This will remove all the loose solids which may have stuck to the vehicle. It is important to flush these off in such a way as to prevent grit from scratching the finish. The wheel arches and underframe need washing in the same way to remove any accumulated mud which will retain moisture and tend to encourage rust. Paradoxically enough, the best time to clean the underframe and wheel arches is in wet weather when the mud is thoroughly wet and soft. In very wet weather the underframe is usually cleaned of large accumulations automatically and this is a good time for inspection.

3   Periodically, it is a good idea to have the whole of the underframe of the vehicle steam cleaned, engine compartment included, so that a thorough inspection can be carried out to see what minor repairs and renovations are necessary. Steam cleaning is available at many garages and is necessary for removal of the accumulation of oily grime which sometimes is allowed to become thick in certain areas. If steam cleaning facilities are not available, there are one or two excellent grease solvents available which can be brush applied. The dirt can then be simply hosed off.

4   After washing paintwork, wipe off with a chamois leather to give an unspotted clear finish. A coat of clear protective wax polish will give added protection against chemical pollutants in the air. If the paintwork sheen has dulled or oxidised, use a cleaner/polisher combination to restore the brilliance of the shine. This requires a little effort, but such dulling is usually caused because regular washing has been neglected. Always check that the door and ventilator opening drain holes and pipes are completely clear so that water can be drained out. Bright work should be treated in the same way as paintwork. Windscreens and windows can be kept clear of the smeary film which often appears, by adding a little ammonia to the water. If they are scratched, a good rub with a proprietary metal polish will often clear them. Never use any form of wax or other body or chromium polish on glass (photos).

3 Maintenance – upholstery and carpets

1   Mats and carpets should be brushed or vacuum cleaned regularly to keep them free of grit. If they are badly stained remove them from the vehicle for scrubbing or sponging and make quite sure they are dry before refitting. Seats and interior trim panels can be kept clean by wiping with a damp cloth. If they do become stained (which can be more apparent on light coloured upholstery) use a little liquid detergent and a soft nail brush to scour the grime out of the grain of the material. Do not forget to keep the headlining clean in the same way as the upholstery. When using liquid cleaners inside the vehicle do not over-wet the surfaces being cleaned. Excessive damp could get into the seams and padded interior causing stains, offensive odours or even rot. If the inside of the vehicle gets wet accidentally it is worthwhile taking some trouble to dry it out properly, particularly where carpets are involved. *Do not leave oil or electric heaters inside the vehicle for this purpose.*

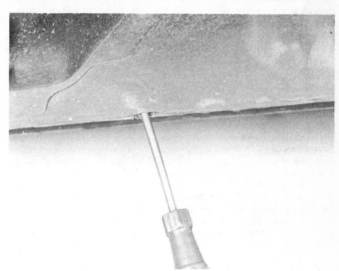

2.4A Sill drain hole

2.4B Sill drain hole

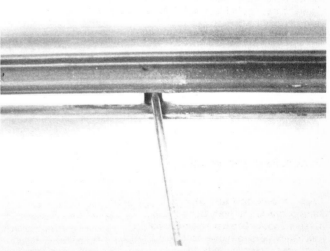

2.4C Door drain hole

12

4 Minor body damage – repair

The photographic sequences on pages 254 and 255 illustrate the operations detailed in the following sub-sections.

Repair of minor scratches in bodywork

If the scratch is very superficial, and does not penetrate to the metal of the bodywork, repair is very simple. Lightly rub the area of the scratch with a paintwork renovator, or a very fine cutting paste, to remove loose paint from the scratch and to clear the surrounding bodywork of wax polish. Rinse the area with clean water.

Apply touch-up paint to the scratch using a fine paint brush; continue to apply fine layers of paint until the surface of the paint in the scratch is level with the surrounding paintwork. Allow the new paint at least two weeks to harden: then blend it into the surrounding paintwork by rubbing the scratch area with a paintwork renovator or a very fine cutting paste. Finally, apply wax polish.

Where the scratch has penetrated right through to the metal of the bodywork, causing the metal to rust, a different repair technique is required. Remove any loose rust from the bottom of the scratch with a penknife, then apply rust inhibiting paint to prevent the formation of rust in the future. Using a rubber or nylon applicator fill the scratch with bodystopper paste. If required, this paste can be mixed with cellulose thinners to provide a very thin paste which is ideal for filling narrow scratches. Before the stopper-paste in the scratch hardens, wrap a piece of smooth cotton rag around the top of a finger. Dip the finger in cellulose thinners and then quickly sweep it across the surface of the stopper-paste in the scratch; this will ensure that the surface of the stopper-paste is slightly hollowed. The scratch can now be painted over as described earlier in this Section.

Repair of dents in bodywork

When deep denting of the vehicle's bodywork has taken place, the first task is to pull the dent out, until the affected bodywork almost attains its original shape. There is little point in trying to restore the original shape completely, as the metal in the damaged area will have stretched on impact and cannot be reshaped fully to its original contour. It is better to bring the level of the dent up to a point which is about $\frac{1}{8}$ in (3 mm) below the level of the surrounding bodywork. In cases where the dent is very shallow anyway, it is not worth trying to pull it out at all. If the underside of the dent is accessible, it can be hammered out gently from behind, using a mallet with a wooden or plastic head. Whilst doing this, hold a suitable block of wood firmly against the outside of the panel to absorb the impact from the hammer blows and thus prevent a large area of the bodywork from being 'belled-out'.

Should the dent be in a section of the bodywork which has a double skin or some other factor making it inaccessible from behind, a different technique is called for. Drill several small holes through the metal inside the area – particularly in the deeper section. Then screw long self-tapping screws into the holes just sufficiently for them to gain a good purchase in the metal. Now the dent can be pulled out by pulling on the protruding heads of the screws with a pair of pliers.

The next stage of the repair is the removal of the paint from the damaged area, and from an inch or so of the surrounding 'sound' bodywork. This is accomplished most easily by using a wire brush or abrasive pad on a power drill, although it can be done just as effectively by hand using sheets of abrasive paper. To complete the preparation for filling, score the surface of the bare metal with a screwdriver or the tang of a file, or alternatively, drill small holes in the affected area. This will provide a really good 'key' for the filler paste.

To complete the repair see the Section on filling and re-spraying.

Repair of rust holes or gashes in bodywork

Remove all paint from the affected area and from an inch or so of the surrounding 'sound' bodywork, using an abrasive pad or a wire brush on a power drill. If these are not available a few sheets of abrasive paper will do the job just as effectively. With the paint removed you will be able to gauge the severity of the corrosion and therefore decide whether to renew the whole panel (if this is possible) or to repair the affected area. New body panels are not as expensive as most people think and it is often quicker and more satisfactory to fit a new panel than to attempt to repair large areas of corrosion.

Remove all fittings from the affected area except those which will act as a guide to the original shape of the damaged bodywork (eg headlamp shells etc). Then, using tin snips or a hacksaw blade, remove all loose metal and any other metal badly affected by corrosion. Hammer the edges of the hole inwards in order to create a slight depression for the filler paste.

Wire brush the affected area to remove the powdery rust from the surface of the remaining metal. Paint the affected area with rust inhibiting paint; if the back of the rusted area is accessible treat this also.

Before filling can take place it will be necessary to block the hole in some way. This can be achieved by the use of zinc gauze or aluminium tape.

Metal gauze is probably the best material to use for a large hole. Cut a piece to the approximate size and shape of the hole to be filled, then position it in the hole so that its edges are below the level of the surrounding bodywork. It can be retained in position by several blobs of filler paste around its periphery.

Aluminium tape should be used for small or very narrow holes. Pull a piece off the roll and trim it to the approximate size and shape required, then pull off the backing paper (if used) and stick the tape over the hole; it can be overlapped if the thickness of one piece is insufficient. Burnish down the edges of the tape with the handle of a screwdriver or similar, to ensure that the tape is securely attached to the metal underneath.

Bodywork repairs – filling and re-spraying

Before using this Section, see the Sections on dent, deep scratch, rust holes and gash repairs.

Many types of bodyfiller are available, but generally speaking those proprietary kits which contain a tin of filler paste and a tube of resin hardener are best for this type of repair. A wide, flexible plastic or nylon applicator will be found invaluable for imparting a smooth and well contoured finish to the surface of the filler.

Mix up a little filler on a clean piece of card or board – measure the hardener carefully (follow the maker's instructions on the pack) otherwise the filler will set too rapidly or too slowly.

Using the applicator apply the filler paste to the prepared area; draw the applicator across the surface of the filler to achieve the correct contour and to level the filler surface. As soon as a contour that approximates to the correct one is achieved, stop working the paste – if you carry on too long the paste will become sticky and begin to 'pick up' on the applicator. Continue to add thin layers of filler paste at twenty-minute intervals until the level of the filler is just proud of the surrounding bodywork.

Once the filler has hardened, excess can be removed using a metal plane or file. From then on, progressively finer grades of abrasive paper should be used, starting with a 40 grade production paper and finishing with 400 grade wet-and-dry paper. Always wrap the abrasive paper around a flat rubber, cork, or wooden block – otherwise the surface of the filler will not be completely flat. During the smoothing of the filler surface the wet-and-dry paper should be periodically rinsed in water. This will ensure that a very smooth finish is imparted to the filler at the final stage.

At this stage the 'dent' should be surrounded by a ring of bare metal, which in turn should be encircled by the finely 'feathered' edge of the good paintwork. Rinse the repair area with clean water, until all of the dust produced by the rubbing-down operation has gone.

Spray the whole repair area with a light coat of primer – this will show up any imperfections in the surface of the filler. Repair these imperfections with fresh filler paste or bodystopper, and once more smooth the surface with abrasive paper. If bodystopper is used, it can be mixed with cellulose thinners to form a really thin paste which is ideal for filling small holes. Repeat this spray and repair procedure until you are satisfied that the surface of the filler, and the feathered edge of the paintwork are perfect. Clean the repair area with clean water and allow to dry fully.

The repair area is now ready for final spraying. Paint spraying must be carried out in a warm, dry, windless and dust free atmosphere. This condition can be created artificially if you have access to a large indoor working area, but if you are forced to work in the open, you will have to pick your day very carefully. If you are working indoors, dousing the floor in the work area with water will help to settle the dust which would otherwise be in the atmosphere. If the repair area is confined to one body panel, mask off the surrounding panels; this will help to minimise the effects of a slight mis-match in paint colours. Bodywork fittings (eg chrome strips, door handles etc) will also need to be masked off. Use genuine masking tape and several thicknesses of newspaper for the masking operations.

Before commencing to spray, agitate the aerosol can thoroughly, then spray a test area (an old tin, or similar) until the technique is mastered. Cover the repair area with a thick coat of primer; the thickness should be built up using several thin layers of paint rather than one thick one. Using 400 grade wet-and-dry paper, rub down the surface of the primer until it is really smooth. While doing this, the work area should be thoroughly doused with water, and the wet-and-dry paper periodically rinsed in water. Allow to dry before spraying on more paint.

Spray on the top coat, again building up the thickness by using several thin layers of paint. Start spraying in the centre of the repair area and then, using a circular motion, work outwards until the whole repair area and about 2 inches of the surrounding original paintwork is covered. Remove all masking material 10 to 15 minutes after spraying on the final coat of paint.

Allow the new paint at least two weeks to harden, then, using a paintwork renovator or a very fine cutting paste, blend the edges of the paint into the existing paintwork. Finally, apply wax polish.

5 Major body damage – repair

1   The repair of collision damage or making good severe corrosion damage to major structures or suspension attachment points should be left to your dealer or body repair specialist as special jigs and gauges will be required to ensure that alignment of the structure is maintained. This is essential to good steering and roadholding.

6 Front bumper (without shock absorbers) – removal and refitting

1   Disconnect the battery negative lead.
2   Remove the front direction indicator lamps (Chapter 10).
3   Remove the headlamp wash/wipe mechanism if so required.
4   Remove the radiator grille (Section 8).
5   Remove the front foglamps, if fitted.
6   Remove the end screws which attach the bumper to the front wing.

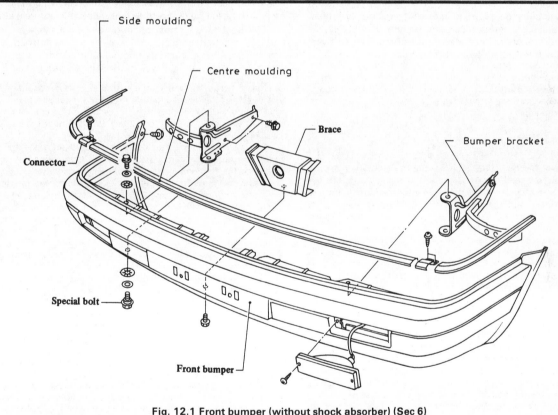

Fig. 12.1 Front bumper (without shock absorber) (Sec 6)

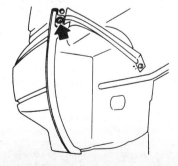

Fig. 12.2 Bumper end screws to wing (Sec 6)

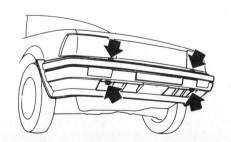

Fig. 12.3 Bumper upper and lower fixing screws (Sec 6)

12

These photos illustrate a method of repairing simple dents. They are intended to supplement *Body repair - minor damage* in this Chapter and should not be used as the sole instructions for body repair on these vehicles.

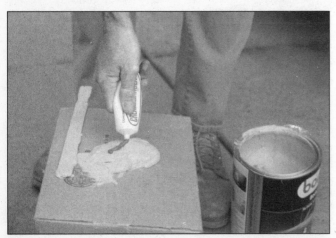

1   If you can't access the backside of the body panel to hammer out the dent, pull it out with a slide-hammer-type dent puller. In the deepest portion of the dent or along the crease line, drill or punch hole(s) at least one inch apart . . .

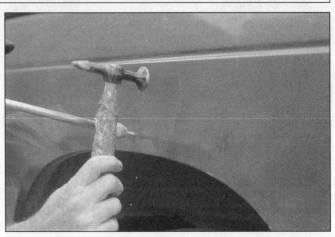

2   . . . then screw the slide-hammer into the hole and operate it. Tap with a hammer near the edge of the dent to help 'pop' the metal back to its original shape. When you're finished, the dent area should be close to its original contour and about 1/8-inch below the surface of the surrounding metal

3   Using coarse-grit sandpaper, remove the paint down to the bare metal. Hand sanding works fine, but the disc sander shown here makes the job faster. Use finer (about 320-grit) sandpaper to feather-edge the paint at least one inch around the dent area

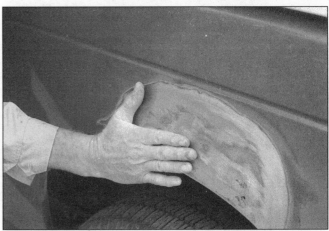

4   When the paint is removed, touch will probably be more helpful than sight for telling if the metal is straight. Hammer down the high spots or raise the low spots as necessary. Clean the repair area with wax/silicone remover

5   Following label instructions, mix up a batch of plastic filler and hardener. The ratio of filler to hardener is critical, and, if you mix it incorrectly, it will either not cure properly or cure too quickly (you won't have time to file and sand it into shape)

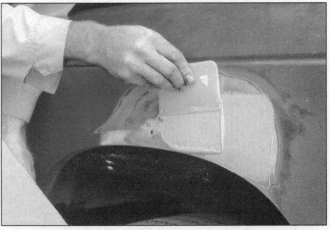

6   Working quickly so the filler doesn't harden, use a plastic applicator to press the body filler firmly into the metal, assuring it bonds completely. Work the filler until it matches the original contour and is slightly above the surrounding metal

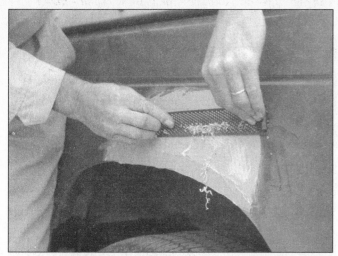

7 Let the filler harden until you can just dent it with your fingernail. Use a body file or Surform tool (shown here) to rough-shape the filler

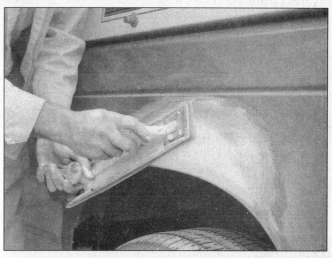

8 Use coarse-grit sandpaper and a sanding board or block to work the filler down until it's smooth and even. Work down to finer grits of sandpaper - always using a board or block - ending up with 360 or 400 grit

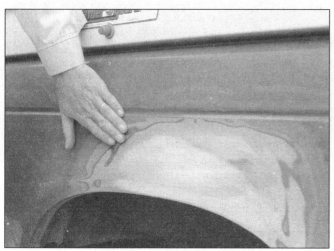

9 You shouldn't be able to feel any ridge at the transition from the filler to the bare metal or from the bare metal to the old paint. As soon as the repair is flat and uniform, remove the dust and mask off the adjacent panels or trim pieces

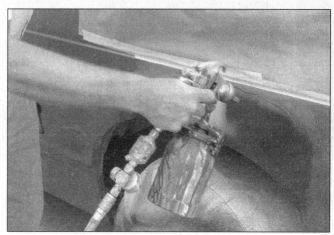

10 Apply several layers of primer to the area. Don't spray the primer on too heavy, so it sags or runs, and make sure each coat is dry before you spray on the next one. A professional-type spray gun is being used here, but aerosol spray primer is available inexpensively from auto parts stores

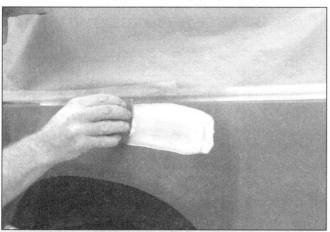

11 The primer will help reveal imperfections or scratches. Fill these with glazing compound. Follow the label instructions and sand it with 360 or 400-grit sandpaper until it's smooth. Repeat the glazing, sanding and respraying until the primer reveals a perfectly smooth surface

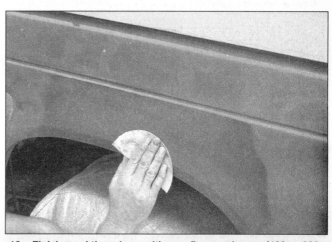

12 Finish sand the primer with very fine sandpaper (400 or 600-grit) to remove the primer overspray. Clean the area with water and allow it to dry. Use a tack rag to remove any dust, then apply the finish coat. Don't attempt to rub out or wax the repair area until the paint has dried completely (at least two weeks)

12

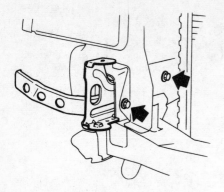

Fig. 12.4 Bumper bracket bolts (Sec 6)

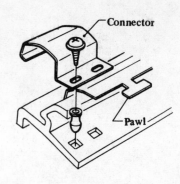

Fig. 12.5 Bumper moulding connector (Sec 6)

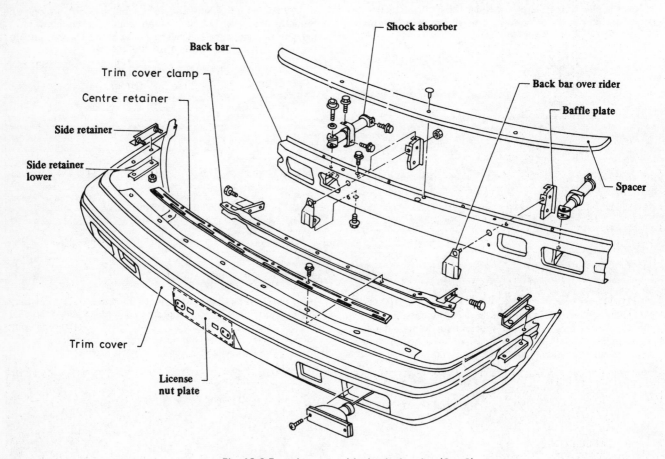

Fig. 12.6 Front bumper with shock absorber (Sec 6)

7   Remove the bumper fixing bolts from the upper and lower edges.
8   Remove the bumper bracket bolts and lift the bumper away.
9   The moulding may be removed from the centre and the ends of the bumper by bending the pawl of the connector straight.
10 Reassembly and refitting are reversals of removal and dismantling; tighten nuts to the specified torque.

7   Front bumper (with shock absorbers) – removal and refitting

1   This type of bumper is mounted on gas-filled shock absorbers and will absorb parking impact without deformation of the bumper material.

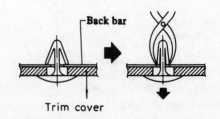

Fig. 12.7 Squeezing bumper trim cover clip legs together (Sec 7)

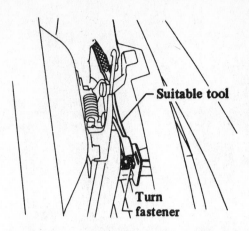

Fig. 12.8 Twisting legs of grille clip (Sec 8)

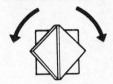

Rotate turn fastener 45°

Fig. 12.9 Grille clip head and opening (Sec 8)

2   Disconnect the battery negative lead.
3   Remove the front direction indicator lamps.
4   Remove the radiator grille (Section 8).
5   Extract the bumper end screws which attach it to the front wing. The forward end of the wing protector will have to be released to do this.
6   Extract the bolts which secure the bumper trim cover clamp.
7   Remove the side retainer nuts and the bumper stay bolts.
8   Unbolt the shock absorber mountings and withdraw the bumper assembly from the vehicle.
9   The bumper can be dismantled by removing the centre retainer and separating the trim cover clamp.
10   Pinch the trim cover clip legs together and prise them out. Separate the trim cover from the bumper bar.
11   Reassembly and refitting are reversals of removal and dismantling, tighten nuts to the specified torque.

8   Radiator grille – removal and refitting

1   Open the bonnet.
2   Grip the legs of the centre turn fastener and twist them through 45°.
3   Release the side turn fasteners by twisting them in a similar way.
4   Remove the radiator grille (photo).
5   When refitting, align the fastener heads so that they pass through the cut-outs and then turn them through 45°.

9   Cowl top grille – removal and refitting

1   Open the bonnet and remove the wiper arms (Chapter 10).
2   Extract the screws from the grille and release the clips which secure the protective cover for the wiper linkage (photo).
3   Refitting is a reversal of removal.

8.4 Removing radiator grille

9.2A Wiper linkage cover

9.2B Wiper motor cover

12

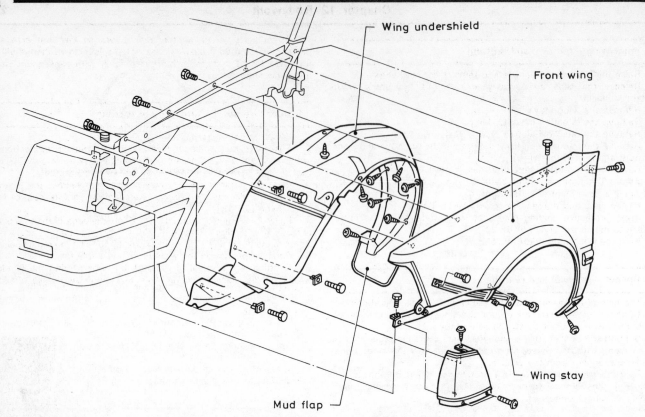

Fig. 12.10 Front wing protective shield and fixing screws (Sec 10)

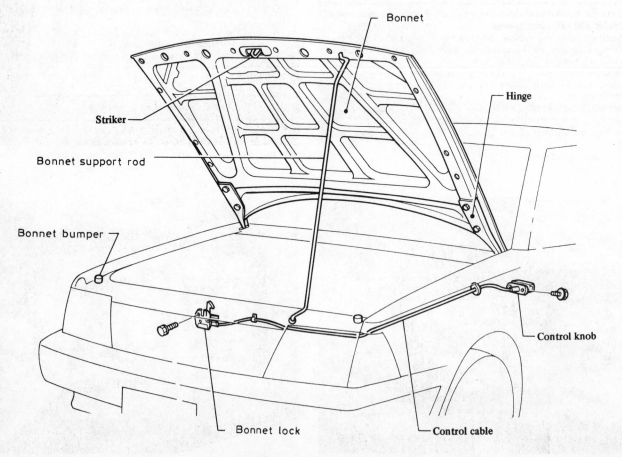

Fig. 12.11 Bonnet and release control (Sec 11)

10 Front wing – removal and refitting

1 Raise the front of the vehicle and remove the roadwheel.
2 Release the clips and screws and remove the under wing protective shield.
3 Remove the wing stay.
4 Remove the direction indicator lamp.
5 Remove the radio aerial if so equipped.
6 Remove the row of wing fixing bolts from the top edge and from the front and rear of the wing.
7 Cut along the mastic joints and then remove the wing.
8 Before fitting the new wing, clean the mating flanges on the body and apply a fresh bead of suitable mastic.
9 Fit the wing and tighten the screws and bolts.
10 Apply protective coating under the wing and refinish the outer surface to match the body colour.
11 Refit the front lamp and radio aerial.

11 Bonnet – removal and refitting

1 The help of an assistant will be required for these operations.
2 Open the bonnet and mark around the hinges on the underside of the bonnet with a pencil or with masking tape (photo).
3 Support the bonnet on the shoulders and lower the stay.
4 Working with one person at each side, unscrew the hinge bolts and lift the bonnet from the vehicle.
5 Refitting is a reversal of removal, but do not fully tighten the hinge bolts until the bonnet has been closed and checked for alignment within the wing channels.

12 Bonnet lock and cable – removal, refitting and adjustment

1 Open the bonnet and disconnect the cable from the lock.
2 Unbolt and remove the lock.
3 Working inside the vehicle, remove the facia panel under-cover.
4 Remove the bonnet release lever fixing bolt and withdraw the cable into the vehicle interior.
5 Refit by reversing the removal operations, but before fully tightening the lock bolts, check that the striker will enter the jaws of the lock centrally.
6 Check the bonnet for smooth positive closure. Adjust by moving the lock up or down after the height setting buffers have been set, to ensure that the surface of the bonnet is flush with the tops of the wings.

7 Do not attempt to set the bonnet lock so low that excessive pressure is required to close the bonnet. If this is down then it will be found very hard to operate the release lever with consequent strain upon the cable.

13 Door trim panel – removal and refitting

1 Wind the door glass up fully.
2 Prise back the escutcheon plate behind the window winder handle and then insert a piece of wire with a small hook at its end. Pull out the clip and then remove the handle and escutcheon plate.
3 Pivot the armrest cover upwards and then extract the armrest screws and take off the armrest. Remove the remote control lock escutcheon (photos).
4 Insert the fingers or a broad blade under the edge of the trim panel and using a jerking movement release the trim panel fixing clips. Remove the panel and as it comes away, disconnect the radio speaker.
5 Carefully peel away the waterproof sheet (photos).
6 Refitting is a reversal of removal, but when fitting the window winder handle, place the spring clip in position in the handle, offer the

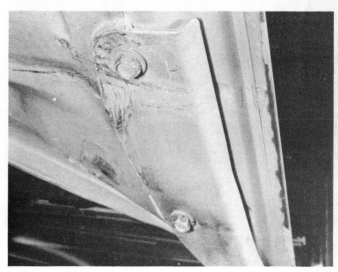

11.2 Bonnet hinge

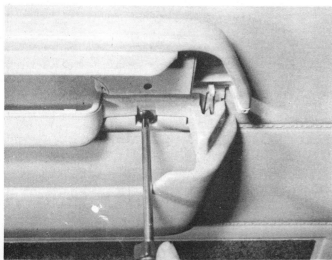

13.3A Removing an armrest screw

13.3B Door remote control escutcheon plate

12

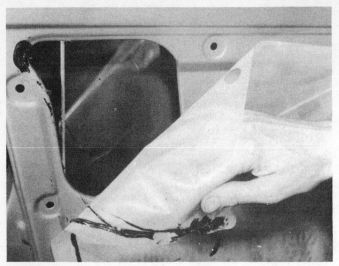

13.5A Door waterproof sheet

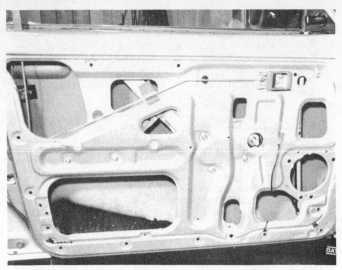

13.5B Door with trim panel removed

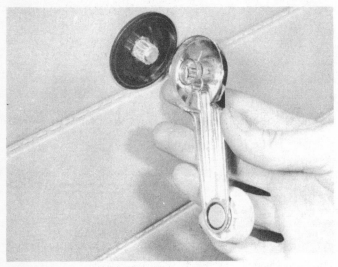

13.6 Window regulator handle showing clip

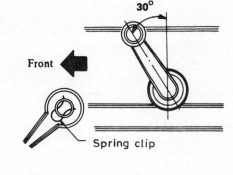

Fig. 12.12 Front door window winder handle and clip (Sec 13)

handle to the splined shaft so that it is at 30° to the vertical when the window is fully closed. Strike the handle a blow with the hand when it will be locked onto the shaft (photo).

14 Front door window glass and regulator – removal and refitting

1   Remove the door trim panel as described in the preceding Section.
2   Temporarily refit the winder handle and lower the glass fully.
3   Extract the screws which clamp the glass to the guide channel. Remove the glass inner and outer weather seal strips.
4   Pull the glass upwards and by tilting it, remove it from the door.
5   If the regulator is to be removed, unscrew the bolts and withdraw it through the large aperture.
6   Refitting is a reversal of removal. The glass may be adjusted by slightly moving the position of the side or lower guide channels to give smooth operation.
7   Apply grease to the lower guide channel.

15 Front door lock – removal and refitting

1   Remove the door trim as described in Section 13.

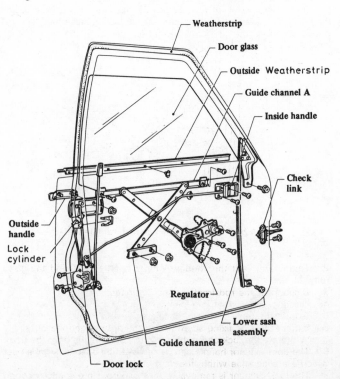

Fig. 12.13 Front door lock and window regulator (Sec 14)

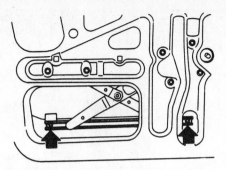

Fig. 12.14 Glass guide channel screws (Sec 14)

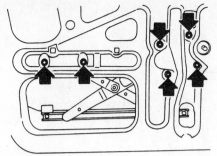

Fig. 12.15 Window regulator securing screws (Sec 14)

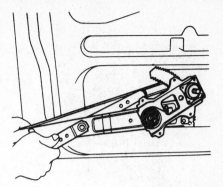

Fig. 12.16 Removing window regulator from front door (Sec 14)

15.5 Door lock remote control handle

15.6 Door lock screws

15.9 Door exterior lock

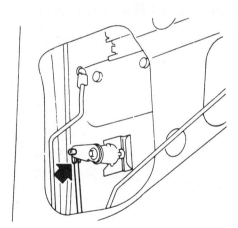

Fig. 12.17 Lock cylinder control rod (Sec 15)

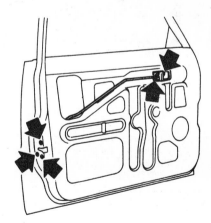

Fig. 12.18 Door lock and remote control screws (Sec 15)

2   Temporarily refit the window winder handle and wind the glass fully up.
3   Disconnect the rod from the lock cylinder.
4   Disconnect the door lock plunger rod.
5   Extract the remote control handle screws (photo).
6   Extract the lock fixing screws from the door edge (photo).
7   Withdraw the lock and remote control assemblies from the door.
8   The door exterior handle can be removed by unscrewing the nuts which are accessible within the door cavity.
9   The lock cylinder is removable by prising out the spring securing clip which again is accessible within the door cavity (photo).

16 Rear door glass and regulator – removal and refitting

1   Remove the door trim panel in a similar way to that described in Section 13, except that the top section of the armrest must be prised off to obtain acess to the armrest fixing screws.
2   Temporarily refit the winder handle and lower the glass fully.
3   Remove the bolts which attach the door glass to the guide channel.
4   Loosen the bolt which secures the lower end of the glass divider.
5   Pull the main glass upwards and remove it.

12

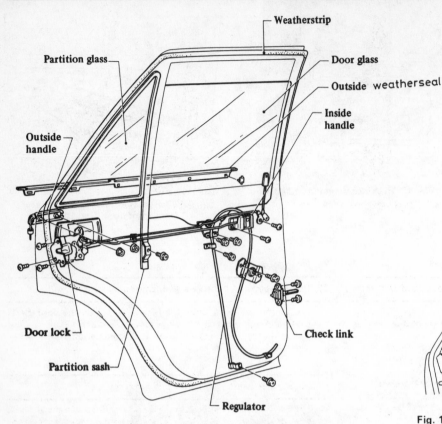

Fig. 12.19 Rear door lock and window regulator components (Sec 16)

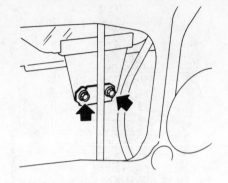

Fig. 12.20 Rear door glass to guide channel connection (Sec 16)

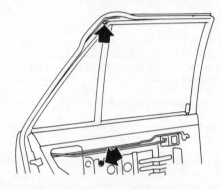

Fig. 12.21 Rear door glass divider lower bolt and upper screw (Sec 16)

6   The fixed quarter glass can be removed if the divider top screw is removed and the upper end moved towards the front of the vehicle.
7   Unscrew the regulator bolts and withdraw the mechanism through the door aperture.
8   Refitting is a reversal of removal.

17 Rear door lock – removal and refitting

1   The operations are very similar to those described in Section 15.

18 Door – removal, refitting and adjustment

1   Remove the side trim panel at the footwell.
2   Disconnect radio speaker and other harness connecting plugs which are located behind the panel.
3   Disconnect the door check link by removing the fixing bolts (photo).
4   On vehicles equipped with power-operated windows or electric door locks, remove the trim panel as described in Section 13 and disconnect the wiring plugs within the door cavity. Pull the wiring out of the door grommet.
5   Open the door fully and support its lower edge on jacks or blocks with pads of rag as protectors.
6   Mark the location of the hinges on the door edge as an aid to refitting and then remove the hinge bolts and lift the door away (photo).
7   Refitting is a reversal of removal, but should the door require adjustment then the door bolts should be slightly released to enable the door to be moved in or out to make it flush with the adjacent body panels.
8   If the door requires alignment within the bodyframe then release the hinge bolts on the body pillar. These are accessible after detaching the rear section of the front wheel protective shield and reaching up from under the wing.
9   If the door has been moved then the lock striker must be adjusted to ensure smooth positive closure (photo).

Fig. 12.22 Rear door regulator bolts (Sec 16)

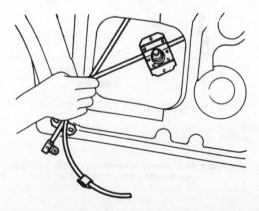

Fig. 12.23 Removing rear door regulator (Sec 16)

18.3 Door check strap

18.6 Door hinge

18.9 Door lock striker

19 Rear quarter trim panel (Hatchback) – removal and refitting

1   Open the front foor fully.
2   Remove the rear seat cushion and back as described in Section 38.
3   Prise the channel trim from the edge of the centre pillar.
4   Prise the top of the armrest using a flat blade and remove the armrest screws.
5   Pull the trim panel away using the fingers or a wide blade inserted between the panel and the body.
6   Ease the panel away until the seat belt anchor plate can be unbolted and passed through the slit in the trim panel.
7   Refitting is a reversal of removal.

20 Power-operated windows and locking system

1   The motor and lock switch are accessible within the door cavity once the door trim panel has been removed (Section 13).
2   The power units are not repairable and must be renewed if faulty.
3   Refer also to Chapter 10.

21 Luggage boot lid – removal and refitting

1   The lid is remotely operated to unlock by means of a cable and a lever beside the driver's seat. The cable must be disconnected from the lock before the lid can be removed from the vehicle.

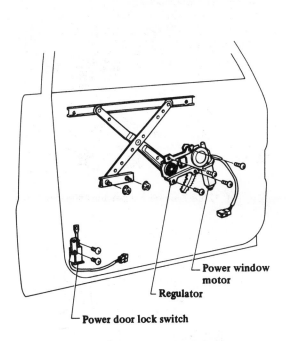

Power window motor
Regulator
Power door lock switch

Fig. 12.24 Front door power-operated window and lock mechanism (Sec 20)

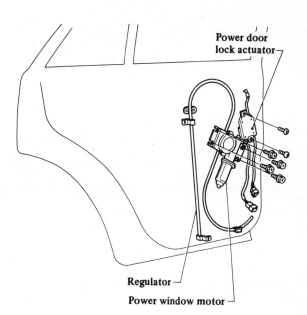

Power door lock actuator
Regulator
Power window motor

Fig. 12.25 Rear door power-operated window and lock mechanism (Sec 20)

12

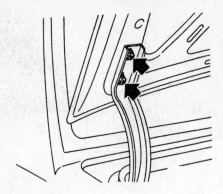

Fig. 12.26 Luggage boot hinge (Sec 21)

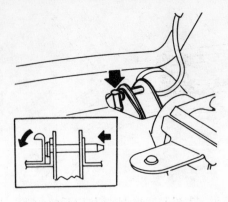

Fig. 12.27 Luggage boot hinge pivot pins (Sec 21)

2   Open the boot lid fully and remove the cable clamp adjacent to the lock.
3   Slip the cable end fitting out of the slot in the operating lever on the lock.
4   Mark around the hinges on the underside of the lid with a pencil or masking tape to facilitate refitting.
5   Have an assistant support the lid and unbolt the hinges from the lid and lift it from the vehicle.
6   The counterbalance torsion bars can be removed if required using a suitable tool to unlock and gently release their tension.
7   The hinges have removable pivot pins which can be knocked out once access is obtained by removal of the seat back and parcel shelf.
8   Refitting is a reversal of removal, but leave the hinge bolts finger tight until the alignment within the body aperture has been checked. Move the lid if necessary within the limits of the elongated hinge bolt holes.
9   Adjust the position of the cable clamp so that the cable release operates easily without excessive tension.
10   Move the striker as necessary to ensure positive closure without any tendency for the lid to rattle.

22 Tailgate – removal and refitting

1   Open the tailgate fully and remove the small finisher panel.
2   Disconnect the wiring harness plugs for the rear wiper motor and the heated rear window.
3   Disconnect the rear washer fluid pipe.
4   Have an assistant support the tailgate and then disconnect the support stay.
5   Mark around the hinges on the tailgate with pencil or masking tape as an aid to refitting and then remove the hinge bolts and lift the tailgate from the vehicle.
6   If required, the hinges can be removed if the roof trim and lining are detached at the rear edge to give access to the bolts.
7   Refitting is a reversal of removal, but before tightening the hinge bolts to the tailgate, close it to check for correct alignment. The tailgate may be moved within the limits of the elongated bolt holes to achieve this, but the striker will then need adjustment to ensure smooth positive closure.

23 Luggage boot, tailgate and fuel filler flap remote controls

1   The cable operated control is located on the floor beside the driver's seat (photo).
2   Remove the driver's seat (Section 37).
3   Remove the kick-plate from the door opening and the finisher from the lower end of the centre pillar.
4   Peel back the carpet and unbolt the remote control lever from its floor bracket.

5-door Hatchback

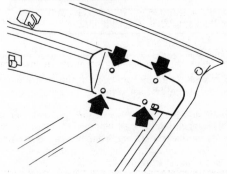

3-door Hatchback

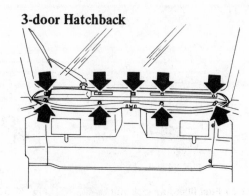

Fig. 12.28 Tailgate finisher panels (Sec 22)

Fig. 12.29 Tailgate stay (Sec 22)

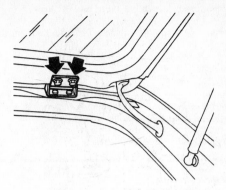

Fig. 12.30 Tailgate hinge bolts (Sec 22)

23.1 Remote control handle

Luggage boot release

5   Open the boot lid and remove the cable clamp which is adjacent to the lock.
6   Slip the cable end fitting out of the lock cut-out.
7   Withdraw the cable and unbolt the lock.

Tailgate release

8   Open the tailgate and remove the trim from the lower rear panel.
9   Slip the cable from the lock. Withdraw the cable and unbolt the lock.

Fuel filler flap opener

10   Remove the luggage boot side trim panel (Saloon) or the luggage compartment side trim panel (Hatchback). These are held by clips and screws.

11   Disconnect the fuel filler lid lock rod from the lock lever.
12   Remove the nuts which hold the lock lever assembly.
13   Disconnect the cable clamp and slip the cable end fitting out of the lock.
14   Refitting is a reversal of removal, but adjust the cable of the boot lock by moving the position of the clamp to give the clearance shown in Fig. 12.33.

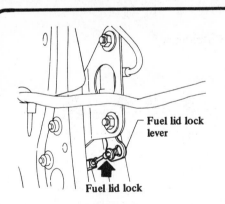

Fig. 12.31 Fuel filler flap lock and lever (Sec 23)

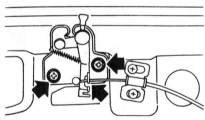

Fig. 12.32 Tailgate lock bolts (Sec 23)

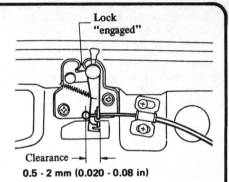

Clearance 0.5 - 2 mm (0.020 - 0.08 in)

Fig. 12.33 Tailgate lock cable adjustment (Sec 23)

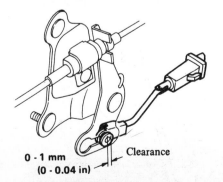

0 - 1 mm (0 - 0.04 in) Clearance

Fig. 12.34 Fuel filler flap lock lever adjustment (Sec 23)

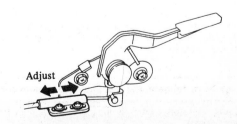

Adjust

Fig. 12.35 Control handle adjustment (Sec 23)

12

15 When refitting the fuel filler lock lever leave the nuts slack and adjust the clearance between the lever and the lid rod end to between 0 and 1.0 mm (0 and 0.04 in).
16 Finally adjust the position of the control handle so that any slackness in the inner cable is eliminated.

24 Rear bumper (without shock absorber) – removal and refitting

1 Extract the screws which secure the ends of the bumper to the rear wings.
2 Unscrew the bumper bracket bolts.

3 Disconnect the rear number plate wiring plugs and withdraw the bumper.
4 Any further dismantling should be carried out as described in Section 6.
5 Refitting is a reversal of removal, tighten all nuts and bolts to the specified torque.

25 Rear bumper (with shock absorber) – removal and refitting

1 Disconnect the ends of the bumper from the rear wing.
2 Remove the side and rear finisher.

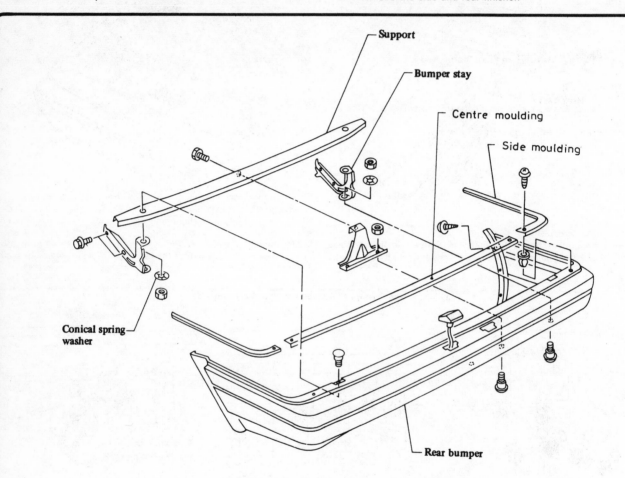

Fig. 12.36 Rear bumper (without shock absorber) (Sec 24)

Fig. 12.37 Rear bumper to wing connection (Sec 24)

Fig. 12.38 Rear bumper bracket bolts (Sec 24)

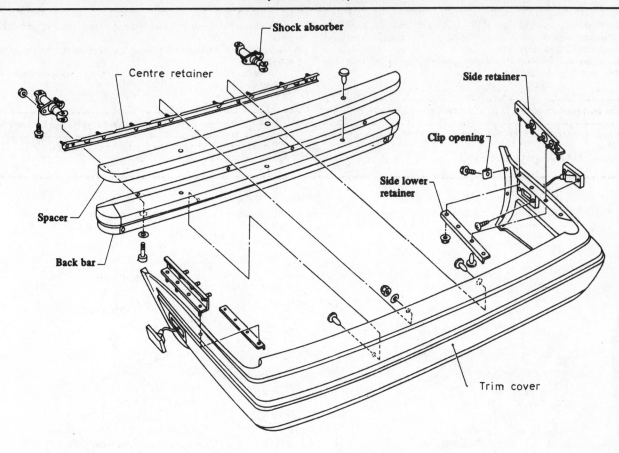

Fig. 12.39 Rear bumper (with shock absorber) (Sec 25)

Fig. 12.40 Side and rear finisher bolts (Sec 25)

Fig. 12.41 Bumper to rear wing and panel nuts (Sec 25)

Fig. 12.42 Rear side window control levers (Sec 26)

3   Unscrew the nuts which hold the bumper to the wing and the rear panel.
4   Unbolt the shock absorbers from the body.
5   The trim can be detached from the bumper bar after cutting off the clips and removing the nuts. Renew the clips at reassembly.
6   Refit by reversing the removal operations, but set the bumper height (top surface to floor) as follows:
3-door Hatchback 498.0 to 548.0 mm (19.61 to 21.57 in)
5-door Hatchback 509.0 to 559.0 mm (20.04 to 22.01 in)
7   Tighten all nuts and bolts to the specified torque.

26 Rear side window opener (Hatchback) – removal and refitting

1   This is of remote cable-operated type.
2   Remove the front and rear seats (Sections 37 and 38).

3   Pull off the knobs from the control levers and then remove the screws and withdraw the lever console.
4   Remove the front door kickplate and seat belt anchor bracket. Peel back the carpet.
5   Extract the screws from the bracket at the window glass also the one from the cable conduit.
6   Prise out the finisher/speaker cover and release the cable conduit bracket now exposed.
7   Remove the mounting and cable clamp screws from the lever console.
8   Withdraw the cable through the aperture left by removal of the finisher/speaker cover.
9   Refitting is a reversal of removal, but set the cable in the following way.
10   With the screw loose at the end of the cable at the control lever, set the control lever in position A with the window just closed to touch the weatherstrip. Tighten the cable screw fully.

12

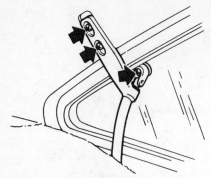

Fig. 12.43 Rear side window bracket (Sec 26)

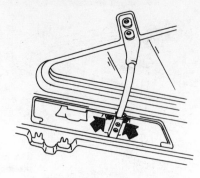

Fig. 12.44 Rear side window cable conduit bracket (Sec 26)

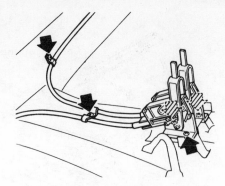

Fig. 12.45 Rear side window control cables (Sec 26)

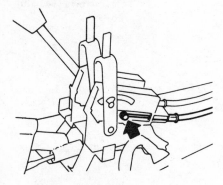

Fig. 12.46 Control cable end fitting screw (Sec 26)

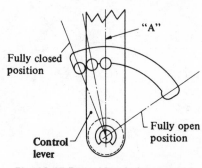

Fig. 12.47 Rear side window control lever setting diagram (Sec 26)

27 Windscreen – removal

1   The windscreen is bonded into the frame and removal or refitting by the home mechanic is not recommended.
2   The glass is positioned on spacers at its lower edge and after installation two hours should elapse before driving the vehicle to allow time for the bonding material to harden.
3   Clips are used to retain the windscreen trim.

28 Rear window (Saloon)– removal and refitting

1   The removal and refitting of this glass is best left to specialists but for those wishing to tackle the job, carry out the following operations.
2   Release the rubber surround from the bodywork by running a blunt, small screwdriver around and under the rubber weatherstrip both inside and outside the car. This operation will break the adhesive of the sealer originally used. Take care not to damage the paintwork or catch the rubber surround with the screwdriver.
3   Have your assistant push the inner lip of the rubber surround off the flange of the window body aperture. Once the rubber surround starts to peel off the flange, the screen may be forced gently outward by careful hand pressure. The second person should support and remove the screen complete with rubber surround.
4   Fit a new weatherseal to the glass and ensure that all old sealant is removed from the body flange. Scrape it away and then clean it off with a fuel-soaked cloth.
5   Apply a bead of sealant to the body flange all round the window aperture.
6   Cut a piece of strong cord greater in length than the periphery of the glass and insert it into the body flange locating the channel of the rubber surround.
7   Offer the glass to the body aperture and pass the ends of the cord, previously fitted and located at bottom centre, into the vehicle interior.
8   Press the glass into place, at the same time have an assistant pull the cords to engage the lip of the rubber channel over the body flange.
9   Remove any excess sealant with a paraffin-soaked rag.

29 Tailgate glass – removal and refitting

Three-door models
1   The glass is set in a rubber weatherseal and may be removed after disconnecting the demister element connecting leads. The operations are as described in Section 26.

Five-door models
2   The glass is bonded to the frame as described for the windscreen in Section 25.

30 Rear quarter window (five-door Hatchback) – removal and refitting

1   The window glass is set in a rubber weatherseal and is removed and refitted as described for the rear window in Section 26.

31 Rear side window (three-door Hatchback) – removal and refitting

1   Remove the catch or remote control bracket and conduit (Section 24) from the glass.
2   Remove the centre pillar inner trim panel.
3   Release the exterior trim clip by turning it through 90°, remove the trim to give access to the window hinges.
4   Remove the hinge bolts and lift the window from the vehicle.
5   Refitting is a reversal of removal.

32 Rear parcels shelf (Saloon) – removal and refitting

1   Remove the rear seat cushion and back as described in Section 38.

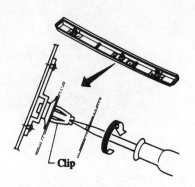

Fig. 12.48 Rear side window trim clip
(Sec 31)

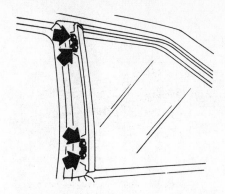

Fig. 12.49 Rear side window hinge bolts
(Sec 31)

Fig. 12.50 Centre console front fixing
screws (Sec 33)

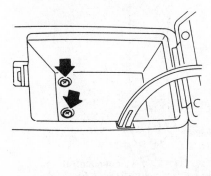

Fig. 12.51 Console fixing screws (three-
door Hatchback) (Sec 33)

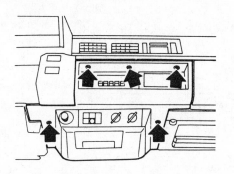

Fig. 12.52 Lower escutcheon panel
screws (Sec 34)

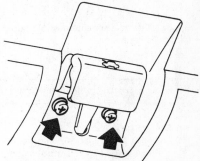

Fig. 12.53 Bonnet release control lever
(LHD) (Sec 34)

Fig. 12.54 Heater control panel screws
(Sec 34)

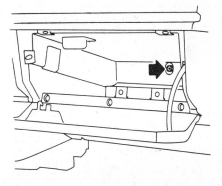

Fig. 12.55 Facia fixing bolt inside glove
box (Sec 34)

2   Prise out the fixing clips using a suitable blade.
3   Refitting is a reversal of removal.

33 Centre console – removal and refitting

1   Flip down the front cover plate and remove the two fixing screws.
2   Prise out the small rectangular blanking plate and extract the fixing
screws.
3   On three-door Hatchback models only, the fixing screws are
located at the bottom of the console box. On these models with a
remote control side window opener, pull off the control lever knobs
and remove the control box retaining screws.
4   Release the gear lever gaiter and remove the centre console.
5   Refitting is a reversal of removal.

34 Facia panel – removal and refitting

1   Disconnect the battery negative lead.
2   Remove the instrument panel as described in Chapter 10.
3   Extract the screw from the lower escutcheon panel, pull the panel
away until the wiring harness plugs can be disconnected. Remove the
panel.
4   Remove the demister grilles by compressing their retaining tabs.
5   Remove the steering wheel (Chapter 11).
6   Release the steering column tilt lever (where fitted) and lower the
upper column.
7   On left-hand drive models, unbolt the bonnet release control lever.
8   Extract the heater control panel screws.
9   Working inside the glove box, remove the fixing bolt, also the

12

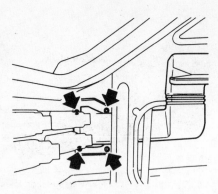

Fig. 12.56 Stale air extractor grille fixing nuts (five-door
Hatchback) (Sec 35)

37.2 Front seat mounting

remaining facia fixing bolts from the ends and within the aperture left
by removal of the instrument panel. Withdraw the facia and disconnect
the wiring harness plugs.
10 Refitting is a reversal of removal.

35 Stale air extractor grille – removal and refitting

Five-door Hatchback
1 Remove the side finisher panel from the luggage area. This is
secured with screws.
2 Unscrew the grille fixing nuts and remove it.
3 Refitting is a reversal of removal.

Saloon models
4 Remove the rear seat, rear parcels shelf and pull away the front of
the rear corner finisher.
5 Unscrew the fixing nut and remove the stale air outlet.

36 Body exterior trim and side guards

1 Most of the exterior trim can be removed by prising. Refit by
clipping it into position using a sharp blow from the hand.
2 The side protective strips are retained by self-curing double sided
tape. Removal can only be carried out using a heat gun (30 to 40°C
– 86 to 104°F).

37 Front seat – removal and refitting

1 Operate the seat adjuster lever and move the seat fully rearwards.
2 Unscrew the Torx type bolts from the seat runners (photo).
3 Move the seat fully forward and remove similar mounting bolts
from the rear ends of the runners.
4 Carefully remove the seat from the vehicle interior.
5 Refitting is a reversal of removal.

38 Rear seat – removal and refitting

Saloon
1 Remove the cushion by gripping its front edge and pulling it
upwards to release the tongues from the slots.
2 On models fitted with a centre armrest, extract the fixing screws
and remove it.
3 Extract the fixing screws from the base of the seat back and push
the back upwards to release the tongues from their slots. If it will not
move, have an assistant depress the tongue locking pawls within the
luggage boot.

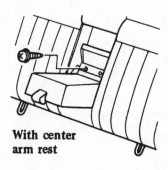

**With center
arm rest**

Fig. 12.57 Centre armrest screw (Sec 38)

Hatchback (single or split type)
4 Release the seat back and fold it forward.
5 Remove the screws which hold the rear anchorages for the
cushion.
6 Lift the seat back upright again and then grip the front edge of the
cushion and lift it upwards to remove the cushion.
7 Remove the seat back pivot screws and remove the seat back.
8 Refitting is a reversal of removal.

39 Seat belts and head restraints – removal and refitting

1 Periodically inspect the safety belts for fraying or other damage. If
evident, renew the belt.
2 Cleaning of the belt fabric should be done with a damp cloth and
a little detergent, nothing else.
3 Never alter the original belt anchorage and if the belts are ever
removed, always take careful note of the sequence of mounting
components. If the washer or collars are incorrectly positioned, the
belt will not swivel as it has been designed to do.
4 On three-door models, the front belt runs behind the rear quarter
panel which will have to be removed to gain access to the lower belt
anchorage. Removal of the panel is described in Section 19.
5 The head restraints are adjustable or removable once the clip at
the base of the mounting tube is depressed.
6 All models have rear seat belt anchorages although the actual
belts are optional extras in territories where their fitting is not
compulsory.

Fig. 12.58 Front seat belt upper anchorage (Sec 39)

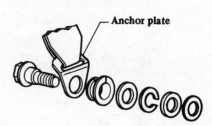

Fig. 12.59 Front seat belt lower anchorage (Sec 39)

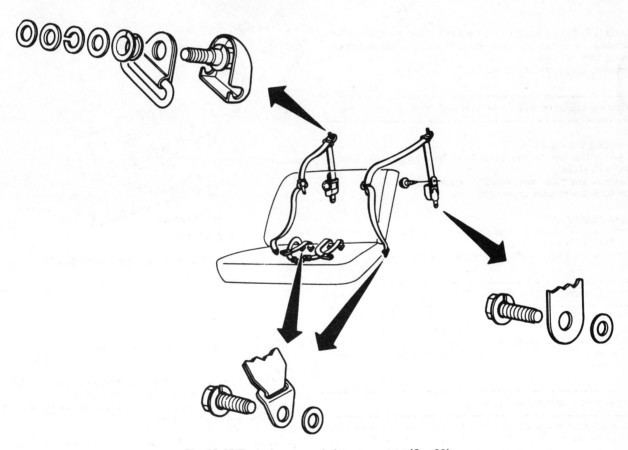

Fig. 12.60 Typical rear seat belt arrangement (Sec 39)

40 Sunroof – removal and refitting

1   Components of the electrically-operated sunroof may be removed in the following way.

Outer lid and finisher plate
2   Open the sunroof until there is a gap of approximately 100.0 mm (3.94 in).
3   Remove the trim clip from the outer lid. The clip is located in front of the finisher plate.
4   If tilt mechanism is fitted, close the outer lid and tilt it. Remove the rear roller from the finisher plate guide. Re-open the outer lid to give the gap indicated in paragraph 2.

5   Push the finisher plate to the rear and then close the outer lid fully.
6   Unscrew and remove the six bolts from each side of the outer lid and lift the lid from the roof. Retain the shims which are located between the lid and the link.
7   Withdraw the finisher plate out through the guide rail cut-out at the same time tilting the plate upwards.
8   Remove the rain rail from the finisher plate.
9   Commence refitting by inserting the finisher plate into the guide rail.
10 Set the link and cable assembly in the fully closed position.
11 Adjust the clearances between the outer lid and the roof aperture so that the side clearances are equal and the front are slightly less than the one at the rear.
12 Temporarily tighten the outer lid to the link and cable assembly.

12

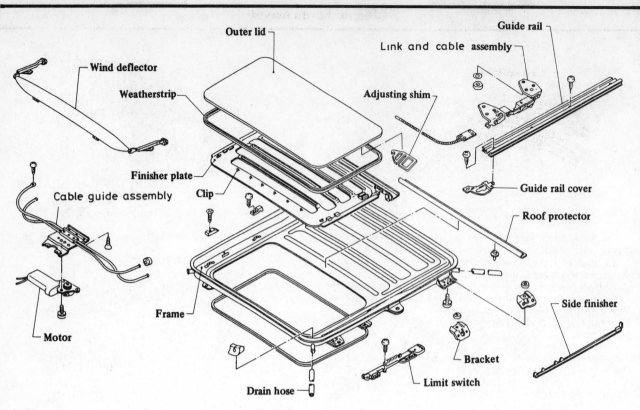

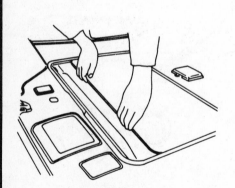

Fig. 12.61 Sunroof components (Sec 40)

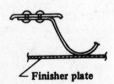

Fig. 12.62 Sunroof finisher plate (Sec 40)

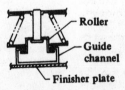

Fig. 12.63 Sunroof retaining bolts (one side) (Sec 40)

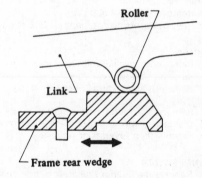

Fig. 12.64 Sunroof frame rear wedge (Sec 40)

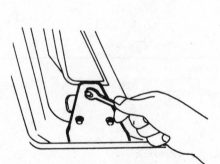

Fig. 12.65 Sunroof finisher plate (without tilt) (Sec 40)

Fig. 12.66 Sunroof finisher plate (with tilt) (Sec 40)

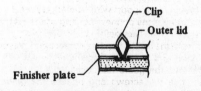

Fig. 12.67 Sunroof finisher plate front edge clip (Sec 40)

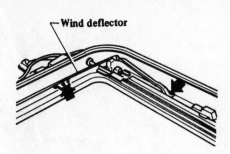

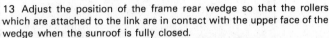

Fig. 12.68 Sunroof wind deflector (Sec 40)

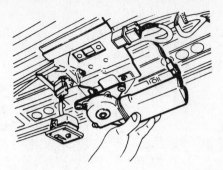

Fig. 12.69 Removing sunroof motor (Sec 40)

13 Adjust the position of the frame rear wedge so that the rollers which are attached to the link are in contact with the upper face of the wedge when the sunroof is fully closed.
14 Using the shims removed at dismantling, adjust the position of the outer lid until it is flush with the surface of the roof.
15 Fit the finisher plate clip to the outer lid.
16 Slide the sunroof to check for smooth operation and tighten the fixing bolts firmly.
17 If a tilt mechanism is fitted, tilt the outer lid and pull the finisher plate forward. Fit the rollers into the guide channel of the finisher plate.
18 Open the outer lid to between 200.0 and 300.0 mm (7.87 and 11.81 mm) from the fully closed position and then fit the clip at the front edge of the finisher plate.

Wind deflector
19 Move the sunroof to the half open position.
20 Extract the screws from the rear of the link.
21 Slide the link from the frame and extract the screws from the front of the link.
22 Remove the wind deflector.
23 Refit by reversing the removal operations.

Motor
24 Remove the interior rear view mirror, sun visors, windscreen pillar trim and the sunroof switch.
25 Remove the welt from the front of the headlining and peel back the headlining.
26 Remove the motor cover and the motor mounting screws.
27 Disconnect the wiring harness and remove the motor.
28 Refitting is a reversal of removal.

Limit switch
29 Remove the interior rear view mirror, sun visors, windscreen pillar trim, centre pillar upper trim with seat belt upper anchorage.
30 Peel back the front part of the headlining.
31 Extract the screws from the limit switch and the cable guide. Remove the limit switch rearwards with the sunroof fully closed.
32 Refit by reversing the removal operations.

Frame, link and cable assembly
33 Remove the outer lid as described earlier.
34 Remove the interior components necessary to be able to peel back the front of the headlining.
35 Release the support wire from its clip at the rear of the headlining.
36 Disconnect the connecting plug at the wiring harness on the right-hand front of the sunroof.
37 Extract the cable bracket screws and disconnect the drain tube.
38 Unbolt and detach the frame.
39 Remove the guide rail cover.
40 Remove the screws and release the guide rail screws from the frame. Slide the finisher plate and rain rail out of the rear of the frame.
41 Remove the motor.
42 Remove the link and cable assembly also the guide rails.
43 Detach the guide rails from the link and cable assembly.
44 Remove the limit switch, wind deflector and cable guide assembly from the frame.
45 Removal and refitting are reversals of removal and dismantling, but observe the following.

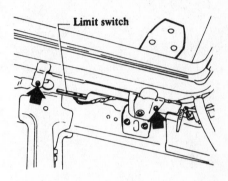

Fig. 12.70 Sunroof limit switch and cable guide (Sec 40)

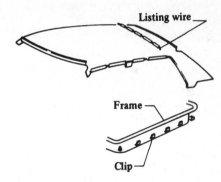

Fig. 12.71 Headlining support wire and clip (Sec 40)

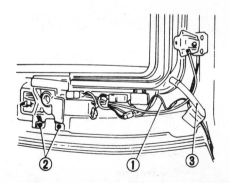

Fig. 12.72 Sunroof frame components (Sec 40)

1 Connecting plug   3 Drain tube
2 Cable guide bracket screws

12

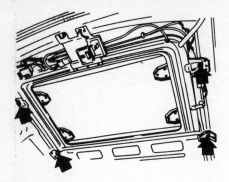

Fig. 12.73 Sunroof frame bolts (Sec 40)

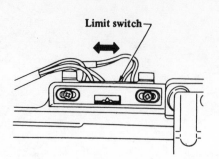

Fig. 12.74 Sunroof limit switch (Sec 40)

41.1 Interior mirror screw

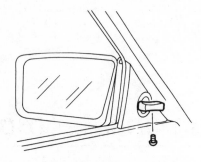

Fig. 12.75 Exterior mirror remote control
(Sec 42)

Fig. 12.76 Exterior mirror finisher plate
seal (Sec 42)

46 Make sure that the top of the cable guide is located between the upper and lower grooves on the limit switch.
47 Apply sealing mastic at the guide rail on the frame side.
48 Set the link and cable assembly in the fully closed position.
49 Adjust the limit switch to obtain the correct first safety stop position (100.0 mm) and then the final fully closed position of the sun roof lid.

41 Interior rear view mirror

1   The mirror is held to its base by a single screw (photo).
2   The mirror base is held to the body by three screws.

42 Exterior rear view mirror

1   Extract the screw from the remote control knob and pull off the knob.
2   Prise off the door finisher triangular shaped plate.

3   Extract the mirror fixing screws and remove the mirror.
4   When refitting the finisher plate, apply a bead of RTV type sealant to prevent any water seepage.

43 Protective shields – removal and refitting

1   Plastic protective shields are fitted in the following positions:

   Under front of engine compartment
   At inner side of wheel arches
   Underside of front wings

2   All the shields are secured by self-tapping screws which are screwed into the body sheet metal or plastic plugs (photos)

44 Grab handles

1   The fixing screws for the grab handles are accessible if the cover plates are prised off using a small screwdriver (photo).

43.2A Removing underwing shield screw from left-hand side

43.2B Removing underwing shield from right-hand side. Note timing marks on crankshaft pulley

44.1 Grab handle screw

Chapter 13 Supplement:
Revisions and information on later models

Contents

1 Introduction

The purpose of this supplement is to provide information on the Nissan Stanza built from 1984 through 1990. There have been a few minor changes and additions, as well as some major changes. The material in the first 12 Chapters of this manual applies unless amendments are given in this Chapter. Therefore, owners of vehicles manufactured between 1984 and 1990 should refer to this Chapter before using the information in the original Chapters of this manual.

An Electronic Fuel Injection (EFI) system has been added to later models. In this Chapter you will find procedures to service this unit. **Warning:** *When working on fuel lines of an EFI system always relieve the residual fuel pressure before loosening any fittings.*

2   Specifications

Engine (C20-series)

Bore diameter	84.50 to 84.55 mm (3.3268 to 3.3287 in)
Valve face angle	44-degrees 45' to 45-degrees 15'

Valve length
intake	106.79 to 107.19 mm (4.2043 to 4.2201 in)
exhaust	107.8 to 108.2 mm (4.244 to 4.260 in)

Connecting rod 1984-86 bearing undersizes
standard	0.2 to 0.3 mm (0.008 to 0.012 in)
limit	0.3 mm (0.012 in)

Piston ring side clearance
top ring
standard	0.04 to 0.08 mm (0.0016 to 0.0031 in)
limit	0.1 mm (0.004 in)

second ring
standard	0.03 to 0.07 mm (0.0012 to 0.0028 in)
limit	0.1 mm (0.004 in)

Ring gap
top
standard	0.25 to 0.35 mm (0.0098 to 0.0137 in)
limit	1.0 mm (0.039 in)

second ring
standard	0.15 to 0.25 mm (0.0059 to 0.0098 in)
limit	1.0 mm (0.039 in)

oil ring
standard	0.2 to 0.6 mm (0.008 to 0.024 in)
limit	1.0 mm (0.039 in)

Torque specifications (C20-series engine)

	Nm	Ft-lbs
Crankshaft pulley bolt (engines without damper)	130	96
Crankshaft damper bolt (engines with damper)	130	96
Crankshaft damper-to-pulley bolts (engines with damper)	9	7
Inlet manifold bolts and nuts	20 to 27	14 to 19
Exhaust manifold nuts	20 to 29	14 to 22
Rocker shaft bolts	18 to 22	13 to 16
Camshaft sprocket bolt	78 to 88	58 to 65
Fuel pump cam bolt	78 to 88	58 to 65
Spark plugs	20 to 29	14 to 22
Rocker arm screw locknuts	18 to 22	13 to 16
Main bearing cap bolts	44 to 54	33 to 40
Connecting rod big-end nuts	32 to 36	24 to 27
Oil pan bolts		
1987 and earlier models	5 to 7	3.6 to 5.1
1988 and later models	7 to 8	5.1 to 5.8
Oil cooler-to-block	16 to 21	12 to 15
Flywheel	98 to 108	72 to 80
Clutch cover	18 to 29	13 to 22
Starter motor bolts	22 to 29	16 to 22
Rear oil seal retainer bolts	4 to 6	2.9 to 4.3
Idler bracket bolt	49 to 59	36 to 43
Cylinder head bolts		
Step 1	29	22
Step 2	78	58
Step 3	Loosen all bolts in reverse sequence	
Step 4	29	22
Step 5	74 to 83	54 to 61

Engine (KA24E engine)

General

Displacement	2389cc (145.78 cu in)
Bore diameter	89 mm (3.30 in)
Stroke	96 mm (3.78 in)
Firing order	1-3-4-2
Compression ratio	8.6

Cylinder block

Piston-to-cylinder clearance	0.020 to 0.040 mm (0.0008 to 0.0016 in)

Camshaft
Cam height .... 44.839 to 45.029 mm (1.7653 to 1.7728 in)
Wear limit of cam height .... 0.2 mm (0.008 in)

Torque specifications (KA24E engine)

	Nm	Ft-lbs
Intake manifold	16 to 21	12 to 15
Exhaust manifold	16 to 21	12 to 15
Cylinder head bolts	see text	
Oil pan bolts	7 to 8	5 to 6
Driveplate bolts	93 to 103	69 to 76
Flywheel bolts	143 to 152	105 to 112
Connecting rod bearing nuts		
Step 1	14 to 16	10 to 12
Step 2 (angle wrench)	60 to 65 degrees clockwise	
Step 2 (torque wrench)	38 to 44	28 to 33

Cooling system
Thermostat opening temperature
    standard .... 82-degrees C (180-degrees F)
    frigid .... 88-degrees C (190-degrees F)

Fuel system
C20/KA24E engines .... Electronic fuel injection (EFI) with electric fuel pump
Idle speed
    manual transmission .... 750 ± 50 rpm
    automatic transmission .... 700 ± 50 rpm (in Drive)
    CO% at idle .... 1.5 ± 1.0 (in Drive)
Fuel pressure
    at idle .... 206 kPa (30 psi)
    moment throttle is fully depressed .... 255 kPa (37 psi)

CA16 engine
Vacuum break clearance
    'RA' .... 3.12 to 3.72 mm (0.1228 to 0.1465 in)
    'R' .... 1.65 to 2.25 mm (0.0650 to 0.0886 in)
      'RA' above 20-degrees C (68-degrees F)
      'R' below 5-degrees C (41-degrees F)

Electrical system
Distributor type
    1986 .... D4N83-16
    1984-85 Canada models
      manual transmission D4N82-01
      automatic transmission D4N82-02
    1987 and later models D4P85-01
Ignition coils
    1985-86 .... CIT-132
      primary resistance (20-degrees C – 68-degrees F) .... 1.03 to 1.27 ohm
      secondary resistance (20-degrees C – 68-degrees F) ...... 8.4 to 12.6 ohm
    1987-89 .... MCC-155A, MCC-155B
      primary resistance (20-degrees C – 68-degrees F) .... 0.8 to 1.0 ohm
      secondary resistance (20-degrees C – 68-degrees F) ...... 7.6 to 11.4 ohm
Starter motor S114-322A
Voltage 12
Normal output .... 1.2 kW
No load
    terminal voltage .... 11 volts
    current .... less than 100
    revolutions .... more than 3900 rpm
Outer diameter of commutator .... more than 29 mm (1.14 in)
Commutator cut depth .... 0.5 to 0.8 mm (0.020 to 0.031 in)
Minimum length of brush .... 11 mm (0.43 in)
Brush spring tension .... 15.7 to 19.6 N (3.5 to 4.4 lb)
Pinion protruding length .... 0.3 to 1.5 mm (0.012 to 0.059 in)

**1990 model
Distributorless ignition
Firing order
1 - 3 - 4 - 2**

981-13-specs Haynes

Cylinder location and distributor rotation

13

Brakes

Disc brakes (1987-on)
  disc (front) minimum thickness* .... 20.0 mm (0.787 in)
  disc (rear) minimum thickness* .... 9.0 mm (0.354 in)
  maximum runout .... 0.07 mm (0.0028 in)
Drum brakes (1987-on)
  drum maximum diameter* .... 230.0 mm (9.06 in)
  out-of-round limit .... 0.03 mm (0.0012 in) max
  radial runout limit .... 0.05 mm (0.002 in) max
Stop light switch to stopper .... 0.3 to 1.0 mm (0.012 to 0.039 in)

Refer to the marks stamped or cast into the disc or drum – they supersede information printed here

Driveaxles

Boot length
  1984-86
    inner CV joint .... 113.4 mm (4.46 in)
    outer CV joint .... 119.4 mm (4.70 in)
  1987-on
    inner CV joint .... 97 to 99 mm (3.82 to 3.90 in)
    outer CV joint .... 96 to 98 mm (3.78 to 3.86 in)

Rear suspension

Wheel bearing
  tightening torque .... 39 to 44 Nm (29 to 33 ft-lb)
  return angle 90-degrees
Rotation starting torque
  with new seal .... 0.78 Nm or less (6.9 in-lb or less)
  with used seal .... 0.39 Nm or less (3.5 in-lb or less)
Rotation starting force at wheel hub bolt
  new seal .... 13.7 Nm or less (10.1 ft-lb or less)
  used seal .... 6.9 Nm or less (5.0 ft-lb or less)

Front suspension

Camber .... -25' to 1-degree 05'
Lower balljoint turning torque
  new parts .... 2.0 to 5.9 Nm (17 to 52 in-lb)
  used parts .... 0.5 Nm or more (4.3 in-lb or more)

Clutch

Mechanical release system
  pedal height ("H") .... 153 to 163 mm (6.02 to 6.42 in)
  pedal free play ("A") .... 12 to 17 mm (0.47 to 0.67 in)
  withdrawal lever play ("B") .... 2.5 to 3.5 mm (0.098 to 0.138 in)
Hydraulic release system
  pedal height ("H") .... 171 to 181 mm (6.73 to 7.13 in)
  pedal free play .... 1 to 3 mm (0.04 to 0.12 in)

---

3   Engine

Cylinder compression check

1   Warm the engine until the water temperature gauge indicator points to the middle of the gauge.
2   Remove the air cleaner.
3   Remove the spark plugs (or on engines with two spark plugs per cylin-der, remove one plug from each cylinder) and disconnect the primary feed wire(s) to the coil(s).
4   Disconnect the anti-dieseling solenoid valve connector.
5   Insert a compression tester into the spark plug hole of the cylinder to be tested.
6   Depress the accelerator pedal to open the throttle valve fully.
7   Crank the engine and read the gauge indicator. Record the reading. Repeat the procedure for all cylinders.

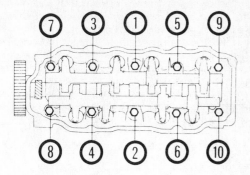

Fig. 13.1   Follow the numbered sequence to tighten the cylinder head bolts (CA20E engine) (Sec 3)

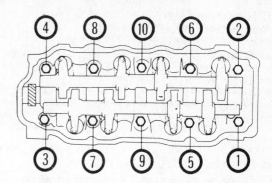

Fig. 13.2   Follow the numbered sequence to loosen the cylinder head bolts (CA20E engine) (Sec 3)

8   Cylinder compression in the lowest cylinder should not be less than 80% of the highest reading. If cylinder compression in one or more cylinders is low, pour a small amount of engine oil into the cylinder through the spark plug hole and retest the compression.

  a) If adding oil helps the compression pressure, chances are the piston rings are worn or damaged.
  b) If pressure stays low, the valve may be sticking or seating improperly.
  c) If cylinder compression is low, and if adding oil does not help the compression, there is leakage past the gasket surface.

Cylinder head bolt tightening sequence (C-series engines)

9   Note the loosening and tightening sequences in the accompanying illustrations.

Hydraulic valve lash adjuster check and replacement

10   Introduced in 1987 in the CA20E engine, the hydraulic valve lash adjusters eliminate the need for periodic valve adjustment. They are located at the valve end of each rocker arm and consist of a small cylinder containing a plunger and check valve. The adjuster becomes pressurized with oil when the engine is started, taking up the clearance between the valve stem and the rocker arm.

11   A faulty lash adjuster is characterized by a fairly loud tapping sound, which will vary with engine RPM. To check the adjuster, begin by removing the rocker arm cover (Chapter 1).

12   Using your finger, push down on the top face of the hydraulic lash adjuster **(see illustration)**. If it depresses 1 mm (0.040-inch) or more, there is a chance that it is partially filled with air. To verify this, reinstall the rocker arm cover and run the engine at 1,000 RPM for approximately ten minutes.

13   Once again, remove the rocker cover and push down on the top of the adjuster. If it still moves 1 mm (0.040-inch) or more, replace it as follows.

14   Remove the rocker shafts following the procedure in Chapter 1.

15   Using a pair of snap-ring pliers, remove the cylinder stopper and slide the hydraulic lash adjuster out of the rocker arm **(see illustration)**. Be careful not to distort the stopper when removing it.

16   Installation is the reverse of the removal procedure. Before inserting the new lash adjuster(s) into the rocker arm(s), it is a good idea to soak them in engine oil for awhile. **Note:** *Anytime the lash adjusters or rocker arms are removed from the engine, keep them in an upright position to prevent air from entering.*

Oil pan removal and installation

17   As of the 1988 model year, RTV sealant is used along the sides of the oil pan and individual gaskets at the front and rear.

18   To detach the pan, remove all of the bolts and insert seal cutter tool no. KV10111100 (or an equivalent tool) between the cylinder block and the oil pan. Using a hammer, knock the tool into the mating joint, then tap it along the length of the oil pan to sever the bond created by the RTV **(see illustration)**. Repeat this procedure on the other side of the pan, then remove the pan from the block. **Caution:** *Do not drive the seal cutter into the oil pump-to-block mating area or the rear oil seal-to-block mating area, as the aluminum mating faces will be gouged.*

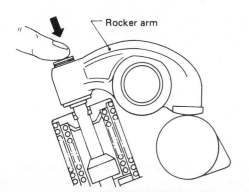

Fig. 13.3   If the hydraulic lash adjusters are in good condition, no play should be felt when you press down on the top face of the adjuster (Sec 3)

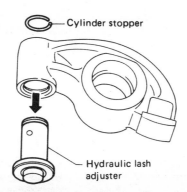

Fig. 13.4   Hydraulic lash adjuster installation details (Sec 3)

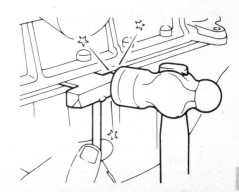

Fig. 13.5   The seal between the oil pan and the engine block must be cut to remove the pan – DO NOT try to pry the pan off (Sec 3)

13

19   Clean all traces of the old RTV material from the block and oil pan. Remove the old gaskets from the front and rear of the pan (they may be stuck to the engine if they aren't on the pan).

20   To install the pan, apply a dab of RTV sealant to the ends of each new gasket **(see illustration)** and place the gaskets in position on the pan.

21   Apply a continuous 3.5 to 4.5 mm (0.138 to 0.177-inch) wide bead of RTV sealant along the groove in the oil pan. Where there is no groove around the bolt holes, apply the sealant to the inside of the bolt holes. The pan must be installed within 5 minutes of sealant application.

22   Position the pan against the block and install the bolts, tightening them to the specified torque. Wait at least 30 minutes before filling the engine with oil.

Oil cooler removal and installation

23   In 1987, an oil cooler was added **(see illustration)**. It is located on the

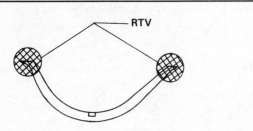

Fig. 13.6   Apply RTV sealant to the shaded areas of the front and rear oil pan gaskets (Sec 3)

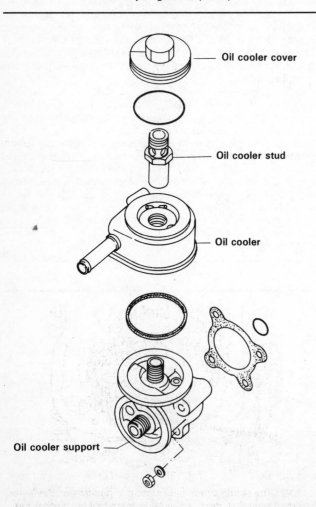

Fig. 13.7   Exploded view of the oil cooler assembly (Sec 3)

right side of the engine and also serves as the oil filter base. As the oil flows through the unit, coolant from the engine is also circulated through it (in a separate passage), and lowers the oil temperature.

24   If the cooler develops a leak between the cooler housing and the support housing, unscrew the cover, remove the stud and separate the cooler from the support. Extract the O-ring and replace it with a new one. Before installing the new O-ring, coat it with clean engine oil.

25   If necessary, the entire cooler can be removed from the engine by unscrewing the four nuts and separating it from the engine block. Always use new gaskets and seals when servicing the oil cooler unit.

Timing chain – removal and installation

Removal

26   The KA24E engine is equipped with a timing chain **(see illustration)** instead of a timing belt. The replacement procedure is somewhat involved, but can be achieved by the do-it-yourselfer as follows.

27   Raise the front of the vehicle and place it securely on jackstands.

28   Remove the under cover and drain the engine oil.

29   Set the number one piston at Top Dead Center (TDC) of its compression stroke. This can be verified by insuring the pointer at the front of the engine is aligned with the TDC marks on the pulley and the distributor rotor is pointing to the no. 1 spark plug wire location on the cap.

30   Remove the drivebelts at the front of the engine, along with the alternator and its brackets.

31   Remove the power steering pump and its brackets.

32   Remove the air conditioning compressor and its mounting brackets.

33   Remove the crankshaft pulley and the oil pump drive boss.

34   Remove the oil pan (see procedure above).

35   Remove the front cover attaching bolts. Note each location and the various sizes used.

36   Remove the rocker cover.

37   Support the engine from above, using an engine hoist.

38   Remove the right-side engine mounting bracket **(see illustration)**, then lower the engine.

39   Remove the front cover.

40   Before removing the timing chain, refer to the accompanying illustration to confirm that the punch marks on the camshaft sprocket and crankshaft sprocket are positioned as shown. Also note the position of the keyways in the sprockets. Remove the chain tensioner, chain guides and the timing chain, along with the sprockets. A special tool will be required to keep the camshaft sprocket from turning. **Caution:** *Do not turn the crankshaft or camshaft with the timing chain removed or serious engine damage will occur.*

Installation

41   Install the timing chain on the camshaft and crankshaft sprockets with the bright silver links of the chain aligned with the punch marks on the sprockets.

42   Install the timing chain and sprockets to the engine and tighten the camshaft sprocket bolt. A holding tool will be required to keep the camshaft sprocket from turning.

43   Install the parts in the reverse order of removal, noting the following:
   a) Use liquid gasket on the front cover to seal it against the engine block.
   b) Be careful not to damage the cylinder head gasket.

Cylinder head removal and installation (KA24E engine)

44   Drain the coolant and release the fuel pressure (see *Releasing fuel pressure* later in this Supplement).

45   Remove the exhaust and intake manifolds and associated hoses and brackets.

46   Remove the rocker cover.

47   Set the number one piston to number one on its compression stroke (see the information above). Once set to TDC, do not rotate the camshaft or crankshaft or serious engine damage could result.

48   Support the timing chain, locking it in position. A special tool is available for this purpose **(see illustration)**. The chain cannot become disengaged from the crankshaft pulley, or the front cover and chain will have to be removed (see above).

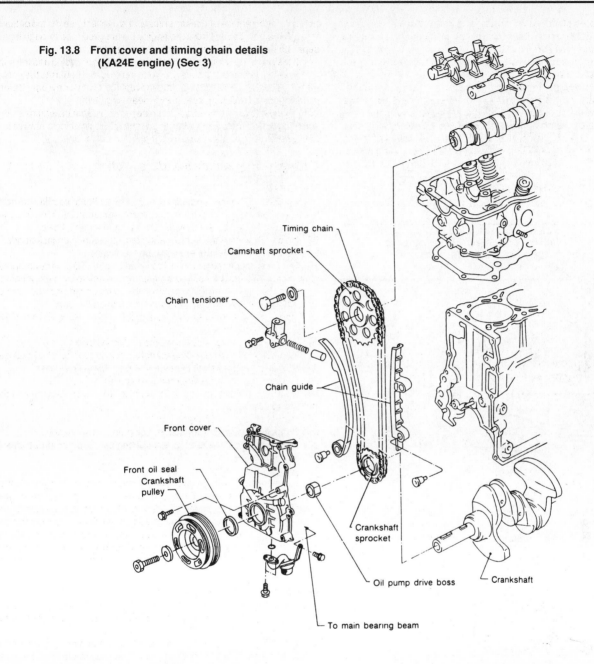

Fig. 13.8 Front cover and timing chain details (KA24E engine) (Sec 3)

Timing chain

Camshaft sprocket

Chain tensioner

Chain guide

Front cover

Front oil seal
Crankshaft
pulley

Crankshaft
sprocket

Oil pump drive boss

Crankshaft

To main bearing beam

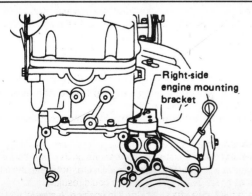

Fig. 13.9 With the engine fully supported from above, remove the right-side engine mounting bracket (Sec 3)

Right-side
engine mounting
bracket

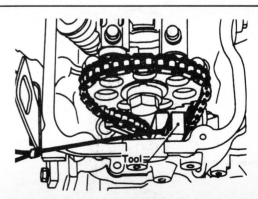

Fig. 13.10 The timing chain must remain in position on the lower crankshaft sprocket. Here, a special holding tool is used for this purpose (Sec 3)

Tool

13

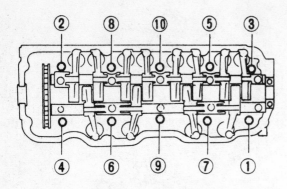

Fig. 13.11   Cylinder head bolt *loosening* sequence (KA24E engine) (Sec 3)

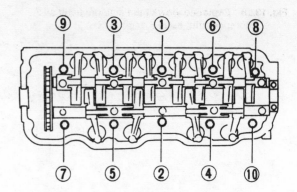

Fig. 13.12   Cylinder head bolt *tightening* sequence (KA24E engine) (Sec 3)

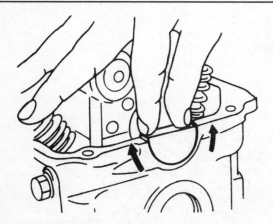

Fig. 13.13   After applying liquid gasket, work the rubber seal into position, spreading the liquid gasket evenly over the surface and ending with the seal flush to the cylinder head (Sec 3)

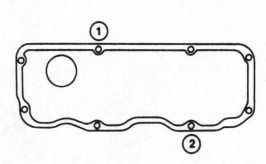

Fig. 13.14   When installing the rocker cover, install these two bolts first . . .

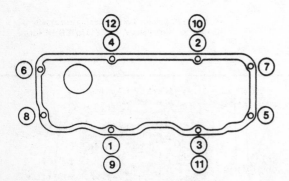

Fig. 13.15   . . . followed by the remaining rocker cover bolts in the order shown (Sec 3)

49   Use wire to secure the timing chain to the camshaft sprocket, remove the sprocket bolt and move the camshaft sprocket (with timing chain attached) out of the way.
50   Remove the bolts which attach the front cover to the cylinder head.

51   Loosen the cylinder head bolts in two or three steps in the order shown in the accompanying illustration.
52   Remove the cylinder head.

53   Install the cylinder head with a new gasket and tighten the bolts in the order shown as follows:
   a) Tighten all bolts to 29 Nm (22 ft-lb).
   b) Tighten all bolts to 78 Nm (58 ft-lb).
   c) Loosen all bolts completely.
   d) Tighten all bolts to 29 Nm (22 ft-lb).
   e) Using an angle wrench, turn each bolt 80 to 85 degrees. If an angle wrench is not available, turn each bolt 74 to 83 Nm (54 to 61 ft-lb).
54   Install the timing chain and the camshaft sprocket. Tighten the sprocket bolt and remove the wire and special holding tool used during removal.
55   Using liquid gasket spread even over the surface, install the rubber plugs (see illustration).
56   Install all parts except the rocker cover in the reverse order of removal.
57   Check the hydraulic valve lifter operation as described previously in this Supplement.
58   Install the rocker cover by tightening the bolts as indicated in the accompanying illustrations.

**Fig. 13.16   Exploded view of the cylinder head and
components (KA24E engine) (Sec 3)**

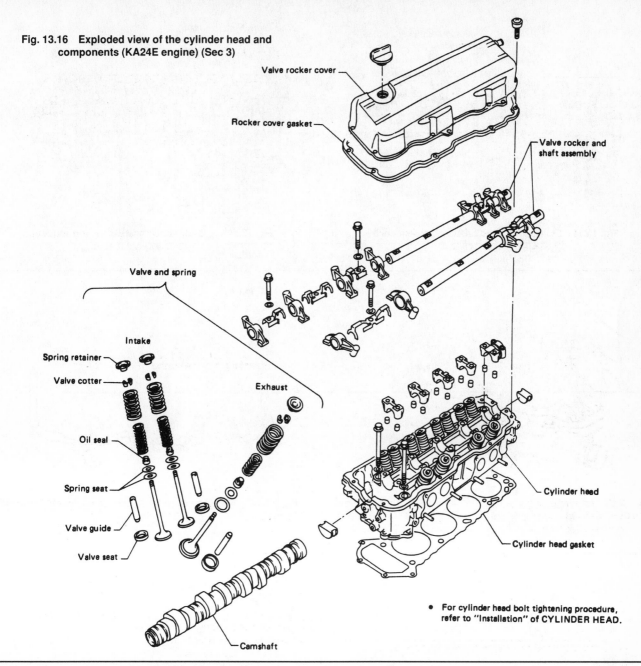

Valve rocker cover

Rocker cover gasket

Valve rocker and
shaft assembly

Valve and spring

Intake

Spring retainer

Valve cotter

Exhaust

Oil seal

Spring seat

Valve guide

Valve seat

Cylinder head

Cylinder head gasket

Camshaft

● For cylinder head bolt tightening procedure,
refer to "Installation" of CYLINDER HEAD.

---

4   Fuel, emission control and exhaust systems

Boost controlled deceleration solenoid

1   The 21E series carburetor installed on the CA16 and CA18 engines
has a boost controlled deceleration solenoid device (BCDD) added **(see
illustration)**. During removal of the carburetor the solenoid electrical lead
will have to be disconnected.

CA18 high speed enricher

2   A high speed enricher has been added to the CA18 carburetor and
does not affect the removal procedure but should be noted during over-

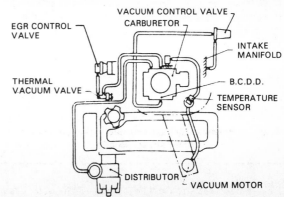

VACUUM CONTROL VALVE
CARBURETOR

EGR CONTROL
VALVE

INTAKE
MANIFOLD

THERMAL
V.ACUUM VALVE

B.C.D.D.

TEMPERATURE
SENSOR

DISTRIBUTOR

VACUUM MOTOR

**Fig. 13.17   The CA16 and CA18 engines have a boost controlled
deceleration solenoid device added (Sec 4)**

13

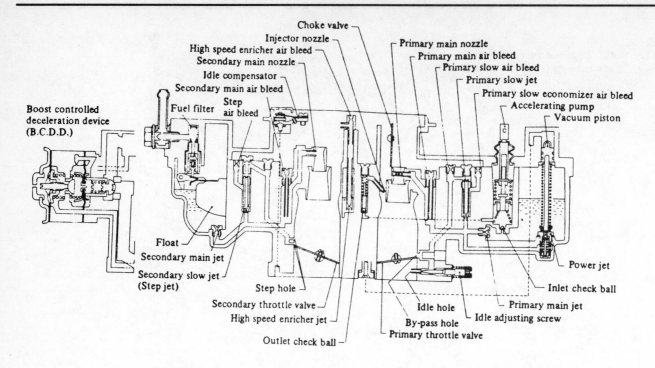

Fig. 13.18   A high speed enricher was added internally to the CA18 carburetor (Sec 4)

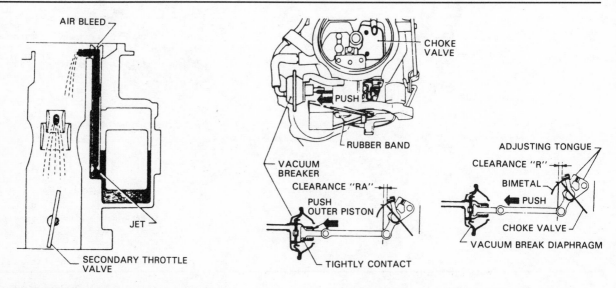

Fig. 13.19   When the velocity of air flowing through the carburetor secondary bore increases, additional fuel is drawn from the enricher nozzle (Sec 4)

Fig. 13.20   With the engine cold, close the choke valve completely by pushing it down (Sec 4)

haul **(see illustration)**. The high speed enricher improves high engine output performance during high speed driving. When the velocity of air flowing through the carburetor secondary bore increases, additional fuel is drawn from the enricher nozzle **(see illustration)**.

Vacuum break inspection and adjustment

3   When the engine is cold, close the choke valve completely by pushing down on the choke valve **(see illustration)**.
4   Push the vacuum break stem straight ahead as far as it will go.

5   Check the clearance "RA", as shown in the accompanying illustration, between the choke valve and the carburetor body.
6   Push the vacuum break stem straight ahead as far as it will go and check clearance "R".
7   If out of adjustment, make the adjustment by bending the vacuum break adjusting tongue.

Electronic Fuel Injection (EFI)

8   Later model engines are now equipped with an electronic fuel injection system (EFI) **(see illustration)**.

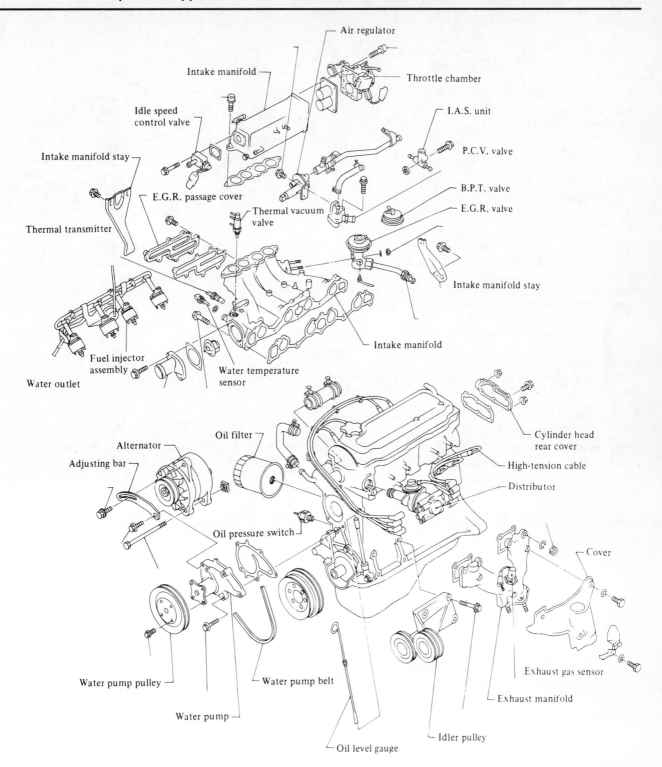

Fig. 13.21   The CA20E engine is equipped with an electronic fuel injection (EFI) system (Sec 4)

9   The amount of fuel injected is determined by the injection pulse duration. For this reason, the pressure differential between the fuel pressure and intake manifold pressure is maintained at a constant level. Since the intake manifold vacuum varies with engine operating conditions, a pressure regulator is placed in the fuel line to regulate the fuel pressure in response to changes in intake manifold pressure.
10   The EFI assembly consists of the following components.

Control unit

The control unit consists of a micro-computer, connectors for signal input, output and power supply, inspection lamps and the diagnostic mode selector. The control unit controls the amount of fuel injected, spark plug switching, automatic transmission lock-up operation, fuel pump operation, idle speed, feedback of the mixture ratio and air regulator switching.

13

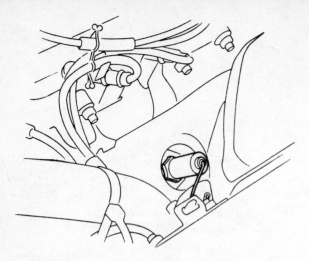

Fig. 13.22   The exhaust gas sensor is screwed into the exhaust manifold and monitors the amount of oxygen in the exhaust gas (Sec 4)

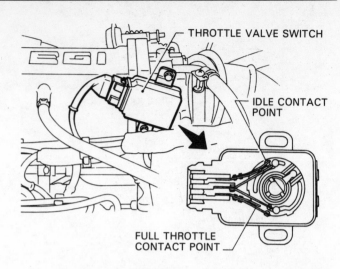

Fig. 13.23   The TVS is attached to the throttle chamber and actuates in response to accelerator pedal movement (Sec 4)

Air flow meter

The air flow meter measures the quantity of intake air and sends a signal to the control unit. Except on California models, a barometric pressure sensor is installed to correct the mixture ratio according to the altitude. During idle, when the amount of intake air is extremely small, the air flows parallel with the flap through the bypass port.

Water temperature sensor

The water temperature sensor is located in the water outlet and monitors changes in coolant temperature.

Exhaust gas sensor

The exhaust gas sensor (see illustration) is screwed into the exhaust manifold and monitors the amount of oxygen in the exhaust gas.

Throttle valve switch (TVS)

The TVS (see illustration) is attached to the throttle chamber and actuates in response to accelerator pedal movement. The switch has an idle contact and a full throttle contact.

Dash pot

To decrease the intake air gradually when the throttle valve is closed, a dash pot is installed on the throttle chamber (see illustration).

Air regulator

The air regulator (see illustration) gives an air bypass when the engine is cold for fast idle during warm-up. A bimetal heater and rotary shutter are built into the air regulator. When the bimetal temperature is low, the air bypass port is open. As the engine starts and electric current flows through a heater, the bimetal begins to rotate the shutter to close the bypass port. The air passage remains closed until the engine is stopped and the bimetal temperature drops.

Fuel injector

The fuel injector is a small, precision solenoid valve. As the EFI control unit outputs an injection signal to each fuel injector, the coil built into the injector pulls the needle valve back and fuel is injected through the nozzle to intake manifold. The amount of fuel injected is controlled by the EFI control unit as an injection pulse duration.

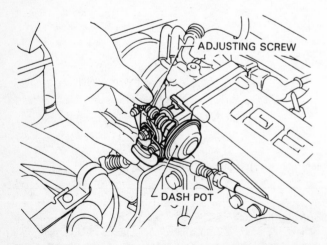

Fig. 13.24   The dashpot is installed on the throttle chamber to decrease intake air gradually when the throttle valve is closed (Sec 4)

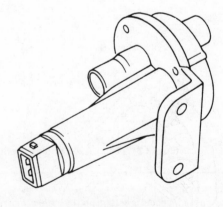

Fig. 13.25   The air regulator provides an air bypass when the engine is cold for fast idle during warm-up (Sec 4)

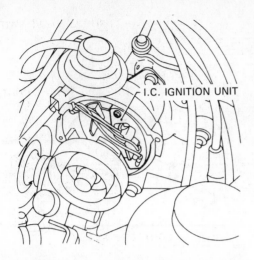

Fig. 13.26   The IC ignition unit sends a signal to the EFI control unit to control the injected fuel (Sec 4)

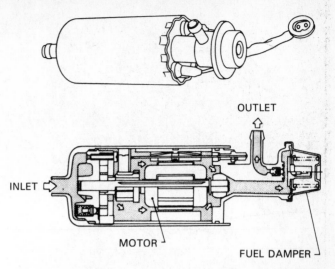

Fig. 13.27   The pressurized fuel system is fed by an electrical pump of the vane roller type (Sec 4)

IC ignition unit

The ignition signal is sent to the EFI control unit to control the injected fuel digitally by monitoring the engine revolution. The signal from the EFI control unit switches the spark plugs from single to dual plug operation and controls the spark timing on automatic transmission models (see illustration).

Fuel pump

The pressurized fuel system is fed by an electrical pump of the vane roller type (see illustration).

Idle-up solenoid valve

The idle-up solenoid valve (see illustration) is attached to the intake manifold. The solenoid valve actuates to stabilize idle speed when the engine load is heavy because of electric load, power steering oil pump, etc.

Releasing fuel pressure

Warning: *Gasoline is extremely flammable, so extra precautions must be taken when working on any part of the fuel system. Do not smoke or allow open flames or bare light bulbs near the work area. Also, do not work in a*
garage if a natural gas-type appliance with a pilot light is present.

11   Before disconnecting any fuel line the system pressure must be released.

Models through 1986

12   Start the engine and let it idle.
13   Disconnect the fuel pressure black electrical connector located under the rear assist seat and carpet (see illustration).
14   After the engine stalls, crank the engine two or three times to ensure the pressure is relieved.
15   Turn the ignition switch Off.
16   Reconnect the fuel pressure black electrical connector.
17   To erase the memory code of the self-diagnosis control unit, disconnect the ground cable at the battery. Move the cable out of the way so it cannot accidentally come into contact with the battery negative post while working on the fuel system.
18   After completing fuel line work, connect the ground cable to the battery.

1987 and later models

19   Remove the fuse for the fuel pump. This is located in the fuse panel in the passenger compartment.

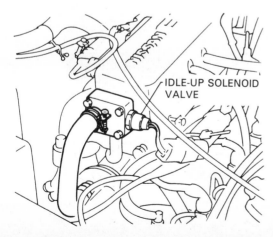

Fig. 13.28   The idle-up solenoid valve is attached to the intake manifold and actuates to stabilize idle speed under engine load (Sec 4)

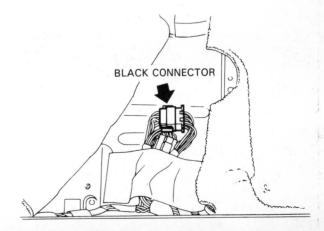

Fig. 13.29   On earlier models with fuel injection, release the fuel pressure by starting the vehicle and disconnecting the fuel pump electrical connector located under the carpet of the rear seat (Sec 4)

13

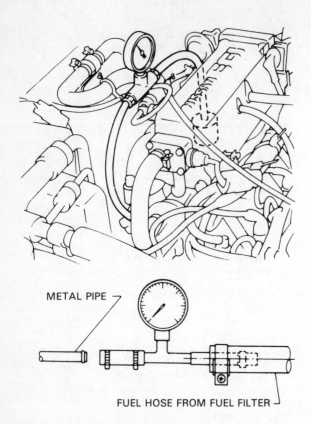

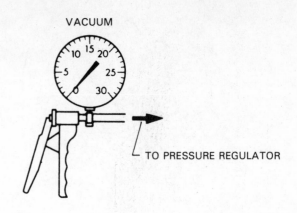

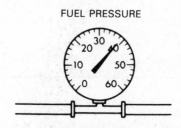

Fig. 13.30   Install a fuel pressure gauge between the
fuel filter and the fuel tube and tighten the hose clamps
securely to prevent fuel leaks (Sec 4)

Fig. 13.31   Connect a vacuum pump to the fuel pressure
regulator (Sec 4)

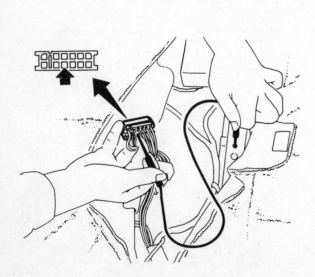

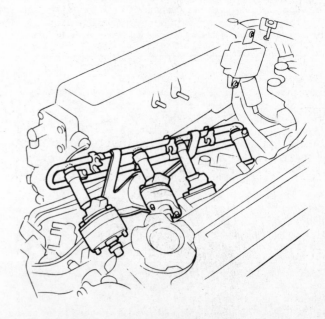

Fig. 13.32   Connect the indicated pin of the body harness under
the assist seat and carpet to ground using a jumper wire (Sec 4)

Fig. 13.33   Remove the injectors with the fuel tube
assembly (Sec 4)

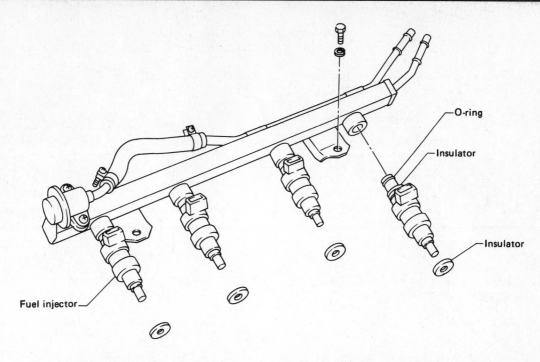

Fig. 13.34   Fuel injectors and fuel tube assembly (1990 model shown) (Sec 4)

20   Start the engine and allow it to run until it stalls.
21   Crank the engine two or three times to make sure all fuel pressure is released.
22   Turn the ignition switch off and replace the fuse.

Fuel pressure check

Warning: *Gasoline is extremely flammable, so extra precautions must be taken when working on any part of the fuel system. Do not smoke or allow open flames or bare light bulbs near the work area. Also, do not work in a garage if a natural gas-type appliance with a pilot light is present.*

23   Release the fuel pressure.
24   Disconnect the fuel hose between the fuel filter and the fuel tube on the engine side.
25   Install a fuel pressure gauge (Nissan part J-2540034 or equivalent) between the fuel filter and the fuel tube as shown **(see illustration)**. Tighten the hose clamps securely to prevent fuel leaks.
26   Have an assistant start the engine and check for fuel leaks.
27   Read the fuel pressure gauge at idle and compare to Specifications. Check the gauge reading the moment the accelerator pedal is fully depressed and compare to Specifications.
28   Stop the engine and disconnect the fuel pressure regulator vacuum hose from the intake collector.
29   Plug the intake collector with a rubber cap.
30   Connect a vacuum pump to the fuel pressure regulator as shown **(see illustration)**.
31   Connect the indicated pin of the body harness under the assist seat and carpet to ground using a jumper wire as shown **(see illustration)**.
32   Turn the ignition switch On.
33   Read the fuel pressure gauge as the vacuum is changed. The fuel pressure should decrease as the vacuum increases. If the results are unsatisfactory, replace the fuel pressure regulator.
34   Turn the ignition to Off.
35   Remove the jumper wire and reposition the assist seat.
36   Disconnect the hand pump from the fuel pressure regulator and connect the vacuum hose to the intake collector.
37   Connect the fuel pressure hose and secure the hose clamps.

Fuel injector removal and installation

Warning: *Gasoline is extremely flammable, so extra precautions must be taken when working on any part of the fuel system. Do not smoke or allow open flames or bare light bulbs near the work area. Also, do not work in a garage if a natural gas-type appliance with a pilot light is present.*

38   Release the fuel pressure.
39   Disconnect the EFI electrical harness connector.
40   Disconnect the inlet and outlet hoses. Place a rag under the end of the hose to catch any leaking fuel.
41   Disconnect the pressure regulator vacuum hose.
42   Remove the fuel pipe securing bolts.
43   Remove the collector with the throttle chamber attached.
44   Remove the injector securing bolts.
45   Remove the injectors with the fuel tube assembly **(see illustrations)**.
46   Remove the injectors from the fuel tube.

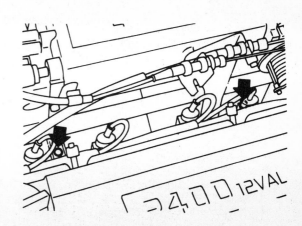

13

Fig. 13.35   The bolts securing the fuel tube (Sec 4)

Fig. 13.36   Carefully cut through the hose to free the injector from the fuel tube assembly (Sec 4)

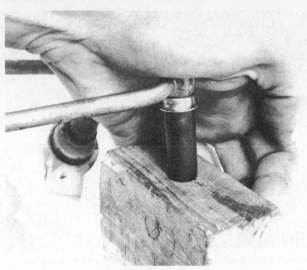

Fig. 13.37   Place the umbrella onto the fuel rail and press the rubber hose onto the fuel rail (Sec 4)

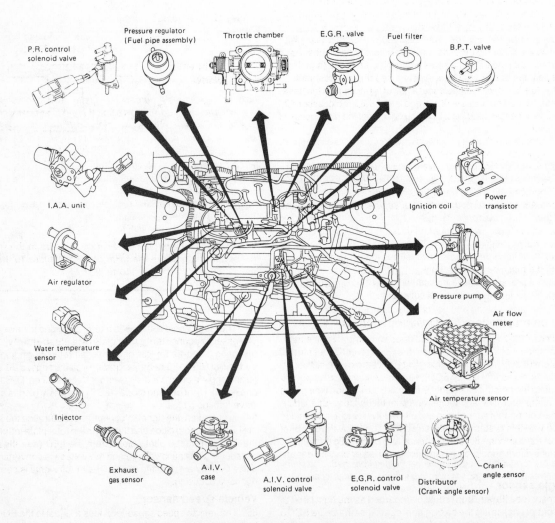

Fig. 13.38   ECCS component locations (Sec 4)

Fig. 13.39   Crank angle sensor location (arrow) and rotor plate (Sec 4)

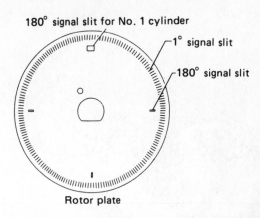

Fig. 13.40   The rotor plate has 360 slits to indicate engine speed and 4 slits for crank angle signal (Sec 4)

47   If any of the individual injectors are to be replaced, determine the injector to be replaced and carefully cut through the hose to free the injector from the fuel tube assembly (see illustration).

48   To install the new injector, wet the new hose (inside diameter) with gasoline, place the umbrella onto the fuel rail and press the rubber hose onto the fuel rail. Be sure the hose seats against the umbrella (see illustration). Repeat the procedure for all injectors needing replacement.

49   Install the fuel line hose clamps about a half of an inch up on the hose.

50   Lubricate the fuel line hoses with fuel and install the injector assembly into the fuel line hoses by pressing it firmly by hand until the hose bottoms onto the injector.

51   Once the hoses are attached insert each injector into its proper port.

52   Install and tighten the hold-down bolt for each injector.

53   Install the metal spring clips onto the injector electrical connector and slip the connector onto each of the injectors.

54   Install a new gasket and set the intake collector in place.

55   Install the Allen head retaining bolts that secure the collector to the intake manifold.

56   Connect all electrical connectors and vacuum/fuel hoses that were disconnected during removal.

57   Connect all wiring harness hold-down straps to the collector.

58   Connect the fuel pipe securing bolts.

59   Connect the pressure regulator vacuum hose.

60   Connect the EFI harness electrical connector.

Emission control system (fuel injected models)

61   Beginning in 1987, all models are equipped with a new engine management/emission control system called the Electronic Concentrated Control System (ECCS). As in the earlier system, it employs a microcomputer (the electronic control unit or ECU), several sensors and output devices to regulate the amount of fuel that is injected, the ignition timing, idle speed, fuel pump operation and the feedback of the mixture ratio, etc. A few additional components have been added, mainly due to a new ignition system used with this system (see illustration). The following is a brief description of the components, but all service and diagnostic procedures related to this system should be carried out by a dealer service department.

Crank angle sensor

62   This sensor (see illustration) could be regarded as the right hand to the ECCS control unit, as it is the basic signal sensor for the entire ECCS system. It monitors engine speed and piston position and it sends a signal to the ECCS control unit (ECU) for control of the fuel injection, ignition timing, idle speed, fuel pump operation and EGR function.

Fig. 13.41   Light passes through the slits in the rotor plate, sending signals in the form of on-off pulses to the control unit (Sec 4)

63   The crank angle sensor has a rotor plate and a wave forming circuit. The assembly consists of a rotor plate (see illustration) with 360 slits representing 1-degree signals of crankshaft rotation (engine speed signal) and four slits for 180-degree signals (two sets spaced 90-degrees apart) (crank angle signal). One slit is larger, representing TDC for the number one piston. Light emitting diodes (LED) and photo diodes are built into the wave forming circuit.

64   In operation, the signal rotor plate passes through the space between the LED and photo diode and the slits in the rotor plate intermittently cut off the light sent to the photo diode from the LED (see illustration). This causes an alternating voltage and the voltage is converted into an on/off pulse by the wave forming circuit. The on/off signal is sent to the control unit for processing.

Vehicle speed sensor

65   The vehicle speed sensor provides a signal to the ECCS control unit for fuel cut and recovery. A reed switch, which is installed in the speedometer unit, transforms vehicle speed into a pulse signal which is sent to the control unit.

13

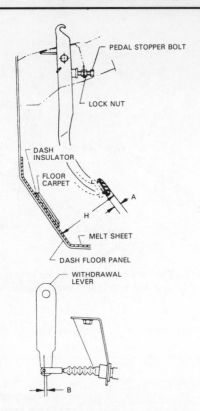

**Fig. 13.42   It is important to have the clutch pedal
height and free play correctly adjusted (Sec 5)**

Idle air adjusting (IAA) unit
66   The idle air adjusting unit, mounted on the end of the air intake chamber (plenum) of the intake manifold, receives a signal from the ECU and maintains the idle speed at the preset value.

Auxiliary air control (AAC) valve
67   Actuated by the ECU, the AAC is cycled on and off to allow an additional amount of air into the intake manifold to regulate idle speed (the longer it is left on, the greater amount of air that can pass through). It is mounted on the IAA unit.

Vacuum control valve
68   Also mounted on the IAA unit is the vacuum control valve. It helps cut down on engine oil consumption by opening up when the engine reaches a certain amount of vacuum upon deceleration, creating a vacuum leak and lowering manifold vacuum.

Exhaust gas temperature sensor (California models only)
69   This sensor, built into the EGR valve, measures the temperature inside the EGR passage and sends a signal to the ECU.

Fuel pressure regulator control solenoid valve
70   This valve, controlled by the ECU, adjusts the amount of vacuum to the fuel pressure regulator, based on the fuel mixture requirements of the engine.

5   Clutch

Pedal height and free play adjustment
1   It is important to have the clutch pedal height and free play correctly adjusted as shown **(see illustration)**. The height of the pedal is the distance it sits away from the floor (distance H in the illustration) and the free play is the pedal slack or the distance the pedal can be depressed before it begins to have any effect on the clutch (measurement A in the illustration).

Both of these measurements can be found in the Specifications for this Chapter. If these measurements are not as specified, the clutch pedal should be adjusted by using the following procedures.
2   First, ensure that the pedal height is correct. If this distance is not correct, loosen the locknut on the pedal stopper or clutch switch. Turn the pedal stopper or clutch switch in toward the pedal until the distance between the top center of the pedal pad and the floor panel is within specifications. Then retighten the pedal stopper/clutch switch locknut. **Note:** *When making this adjustment, be sure that the pedal is not depressed and that the pushrod is not pushed beyond its free play.*
3   Check that the pedal free play is within specifications. To correct the free play, loosen the pushrod lock nut and turn the pushrod until the free play of the pedal is within specifications. Tighten the pushrod locknut.
4   Following all adjustments, fully depress and release the pedal several times to ensure that the clutch linkage is operating smoothly.

Clutch hydraulic release system general information
5   In 1987, the Stanza received a hydraulic clutch release system to replace the clutch cable. The clutch pedal depresses a plunger in the clutch master cylinder, which transmits hydraulic force through a pipe and into a release cylinder, actuating the release cylinder pushrod. The release cylinder pushrod extends and pushes on the release lever, which forces the release bearing into the pressure plate fingers, disengaging the clutch.

Clutch master cylinder removal, overhaul and installation
Note: *Before beginning this procedure, contact local parts stores and dealer service departments concerning the purchase of a rebuild kit or a new master cylinder. Availability and cost of the necessary parts may dictate whether the cylinder is rebuilt or replaced with a new one. If it's decided to rebuild the cylinder, inspect the bore as described in Step 18 before purchasing parts.*

Removal
6   Disconnect the negative cable from the battery.
7   Under the dashboard, disconnect the pushrod from the top of the clutch pedal. It's held in place with a clevis pin.
8   Disconnect the hydraulic line at the clutch master cylinder. If available, use a flare nut wrench on the fitting, which will prevent the fitting from being rounded off. Have rags handy as some fluid will be lost as the line is removed. **Caution:** *Don't allow brake fluid to come into contact with paint as it will damage the finish.*
9   Remove the two nuts which secure the master cylinder to the engine firewall. Remove the master cylinder, again being careful not to spill any of the fluid.

Overhaul
10   Remove the reservoir cap and drain all fluid from the master cylinder. Loosen the clamp and pull the reservoir from the master cylinder body.
11   Push in on the pushrod and remove the valve stopper screw from the underside of the cylinder.
12   Pull back the dust cover on the pushrod **(see illustration)** and remove the stopper ring.
13   Remove the stopper and the pushrod from the cylinder.
14   Tap the master cylinder on a block of wood to eject the piston assembly from inside the bore. **Note:** *If the rebuild kit contains a complete piston assembly, ignore Steps which do not apply.*
15   Separate the spring from the piston.
16   Remove the dust cover, stopper ring and stopper from the pushrod.
17   Carefully remove the seal from the piston.
18   Inspect the bore of the master cylinder for deep scratches, score marks and ridges. The surface must be smooth to the touch. If the bore isn't perfectly smooth, the master cylinder must be replaced with a new or factory rebuilt unit.
19   If the cylinder will be rebuilt, use the new parts contained in the rebuild kit and follow any specific instructions which may have accompanied the rebuild kit. Wash all parts to be re-used with brake cleaner, denatured alcohol or clean brake fluid. DO NOT use petroleum-based solvents.

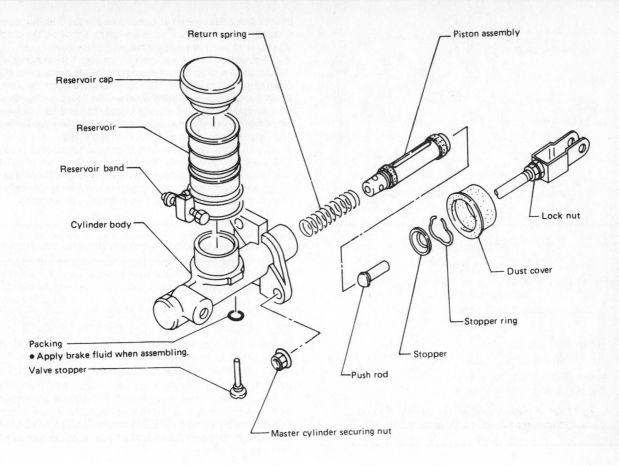

Fig. 13.43   Exploded view of the clutch master cylinder components (Sec 5)

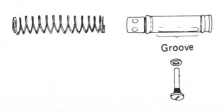

Groove

Fig. 13.44   The groove in the bottom of the clutch master cylinder piston must line up with the valve stopper hole in the cylinder (Sec 5)

20   Attach the piston seal to the piston. The seal lips must face away from the pushrod end of the piston.
21   Assemble the spring on the other end of the piston.
22   Lubricate the bore of the cylinder and the seals with plenty of fresh brake fluid (DOT 3).
23   Carefully guide the piston assembly into the bore, being careful not to damage the seals. Make sure the spring end is installed first, with the groove in the piston aligned with the valve stopper hole in the bottom of the cylinder **(see illustration)**.
24   Position the pushrod and stopper in the bore, compress the spring and install the valve stopper (with a new gasket) and a new stopper ring.

25   Apply a liberal amount of rubber grease or equivalent to the inside of the dust cover and attach it to the master cylinder.
26   Push the reservoir onto the cylinder and tighten the clamp securely.

Installation
27   Attach the master cylinder to the firewall and install the mounting nuts finger tight.
28   Connect the hydraulic line to the master cylinder, moving the cylinder slightly as necessary to thread the fitting properly into the bore. Don't cross-thread the fitting as it's installed.
29   Tighten the mounting nuts securely, then tighten the hydraulic line fitting.
30   Working inside the vehicle, connect the pushrod to the clutch pedal.
31   Fill the clutch master cylinder reservoir with brake fluid conforming to DOT 3 specifications and bleed the clutch system as outlined later in this Section.

Clutch release cylinder removal, overhaul and installation

Note: *Before beginning this procedure, contact local parts stores and dealer service departments concerning the purchase of a rebuild kit or a new release cylinder. Availability and cost of the necessary parts may dictate whether the cylinder is rebuilt or replaced with a new one. If it's decided to rebuild the cylinder, inspect the bore as described in Step 39 before purchasing parts.*

Removal
32   Disconnect the negative cable from the battery.
33   Raise the vehicle and support it securely on jackstands.

13

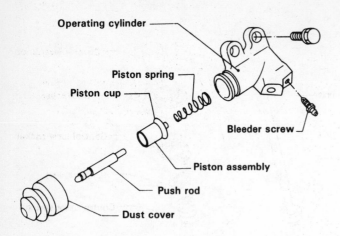

Fig. 13.45 Exploded view of the clutch release cylinder components (Sec 5)

34   Disconnect the hydraulic line at the release cylinder. If available, use a flare nut wrench on the fitting, which will prevent the fitting from being rounded off. Have a small can and rags handy, as some fluid will be spilled as the line is removed.
35   Remove the two release cylinder mounting bolts.
36   Remove the release cylinder.

Overhaul
37   Remove the pushrod and the boot **(see illustration)**.
38   Tap the cylinder on a block of wood to eject the piston and seal. Also remove the spring from inside the cylinder.
39   Carefully inspect the bore of the cylinder. Check for deep scratches, score marks and ridges. The bore must be smooth to the touch. If any imperfections are found, the release cylinder must be replaced with a new one.
40   Using the new parts in the rebuild kit, assemble the components using plenty of fresh brake fluid for lubrication. Note the installed direction of the spring and the seal.

Installation
41   Install the release cylinder on the clutch housing. Make sure the pushrod is seated in the release fork pocket.
42   Connect the hydraulic line to the release cylinder. Tighten the fitting.
43   Fill the clutch master cylinder with brake fluid conforming to DOT 3 specifications.
44   Bleed the system as described in the next Section.
45   Lower the vehicle and connect the negative battery cable.

Clutch hydraulic system bleeding
46   The hydraulic system should be bled to remove all air whenever any part of the system has been removed or if the fluid level has fallen so low that air has been drawn into the master cylinder. The procedure is very similar to bleeding a brake system.
47   Fill the master cylinder with new brake fluid conforming to DOT 3 specifications. **Caution:** *Don't re-use any of the fluid coming from the system during the bleeding operation. Also, don't use fluid which has been inside an open container for an extended period of time.*
48   Raise the vehicle and place it securely on jackstands to gain access to the slave cylinder, which is located on the front of the transaxle.
49   Remove the dust cap which fits over the bleeder valve and push a length of plastic hose over the valve. Place the other end of the hose in a

clear container with about two inches of brake fluid. The hose end must be in the fluid at the bottom of the container.
50   Have an assistant depress the clutch pedal and hold it. Open the bleeder valve on the release cylinder, allowing fluid to flow through the hose. Close the bleeder valve when the flow of bubbles and fluid ceases. Once closed, have your assistant release the pedal.
51   Continue this process until all air is evacuated from the system, indicated by a solid stream of fluid being ejected from the bleeder valve each time with no air bubbles in the hose or container. Keep a close watch on the fluid level inside the master cylinder – if the level drops too low, air will be sucked back into the system and the process will have to be started all over again.
52   Install the release cylinder and lower the vehicle. Check carefully for proper operation before placing the vehicle in normal service.

---

6   Manual transmission

General information
In 1987, a new five speed transaxle was installed in the Stanza. This transaxle, designated the RS5F50A, is similar to, but slightly different from the transaxle that was previously used. If the transmission is being overhauled, use the procedure described in Chapter 6 as a guideline, but refer to the illustrations that accompany this Section, as well as the Specifications that are listed at the beginning of this Chapter. It would also be very helpful to take instant photographs and make sketches of the components as they are disassembled. When disassembling the gearshafts, it is a good idea to string the components onto a wire (a straightened-out coat hanger works well) as they are removed, so they stay in the correct order and don't get mixed up.

---

7   Automatic transmission

Lock-up release system
1   When the accelerator pedal is released completely while the vehicle is in the lock-up mode the lock-up piston in the torque converter will disengage. The same thing will happen when the water temperature is low **(see illustration)**.

Kickdown cable adjustment (1987 and later models)
2   Follow the procedure outlined in Chapter 8, but note that the travel of the cable between full throttle and idle is different (see the Specifications Section at the beginning of this Chapter).

Torque converter installation
3   When installing the torque converter on 1987 and later models, the distance from the transaxle engine mating flange to the face of the welded nuts on the torque converter must be 19 mm (3/4-inch) or greater.

---

8   Driveaxles

Removal, overhaul and installation (1987 and later models)

Left driveaxle removal and installation
1   Follow the procedure in Chapter 8, Section 3.

Right driveaxle removal and installation
2   Follow the procedure in Steps 1 through 6 in Section 3 of Chapter 8.

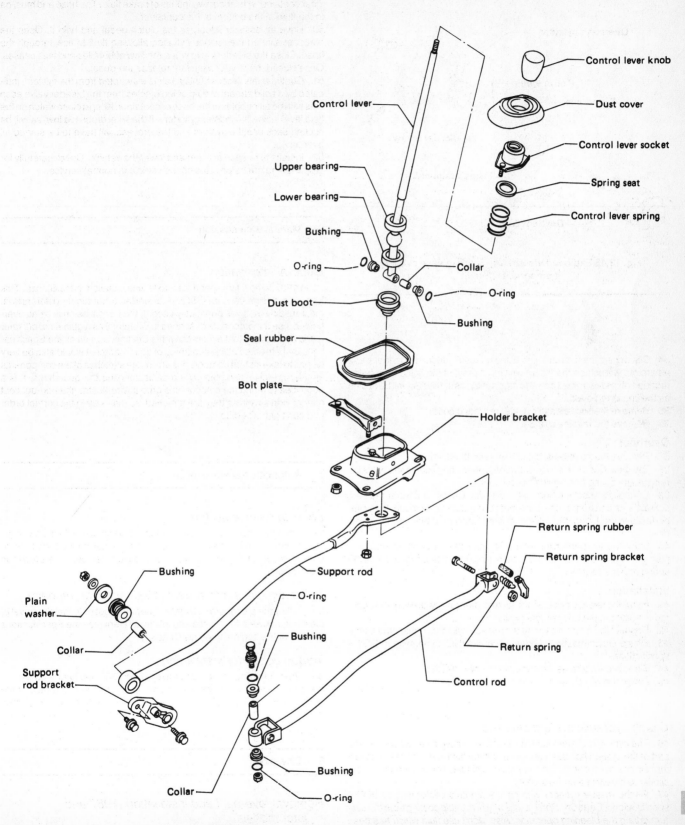

Fig. 13.46   Exploded view of the transaxle gearshift linkage – 1987 and later models (Sec 6)

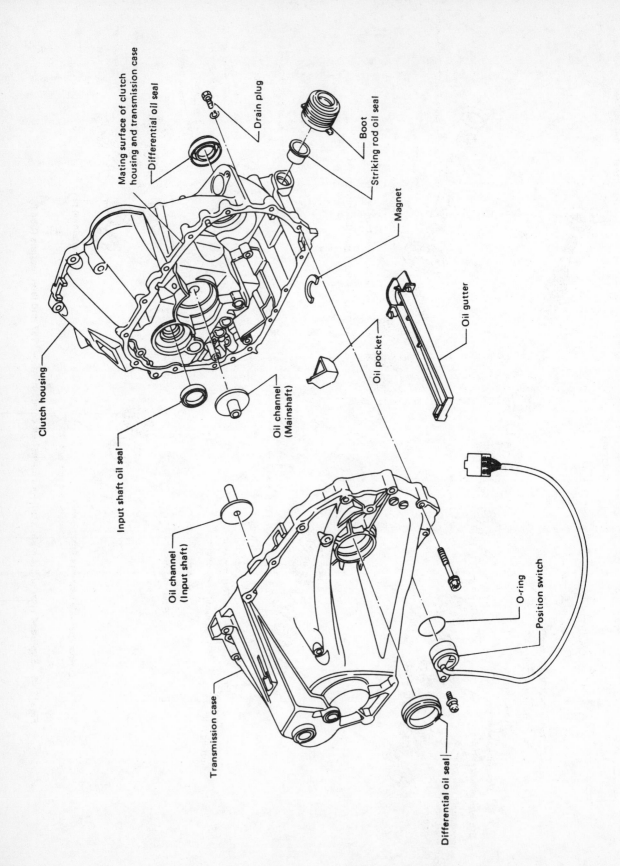

Fig. 13.47   Transmission case components – 1987 and later models (Sec 6)

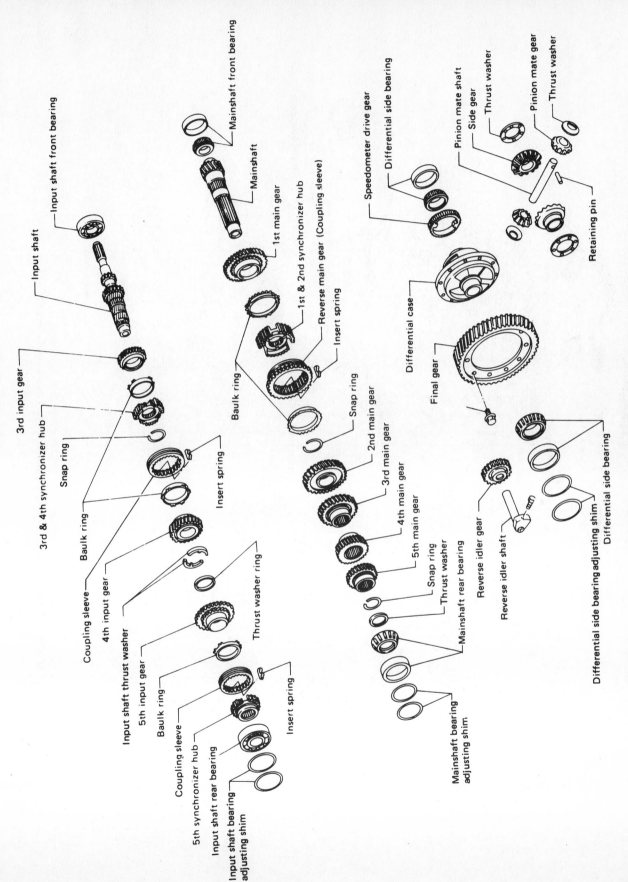

Fig. 13.48   Exploded view of the input shaft and mainshaft components – 1987 and later models (Sec 6)

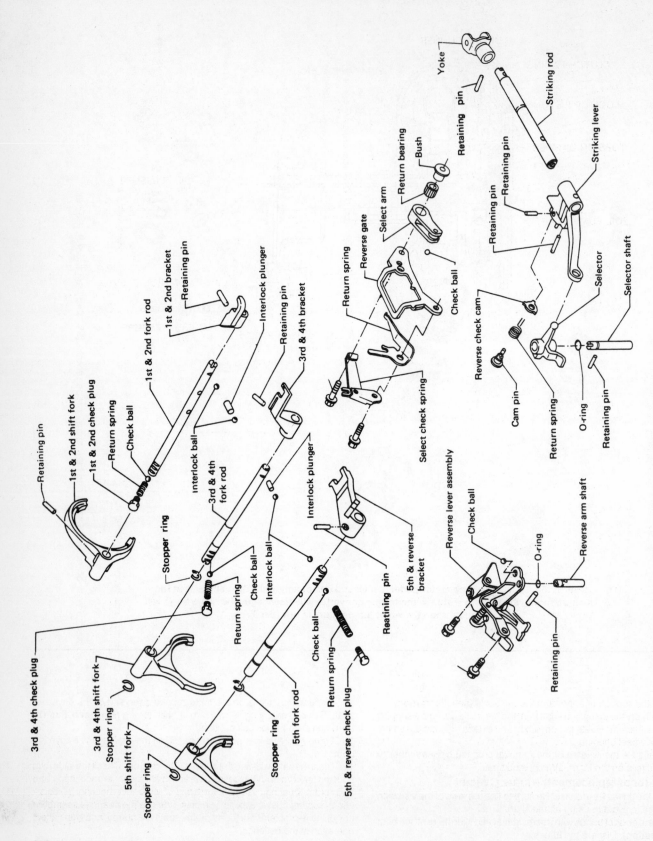

Fig. 13.49   Gear selector components – 1987 and later models (Sec 6)

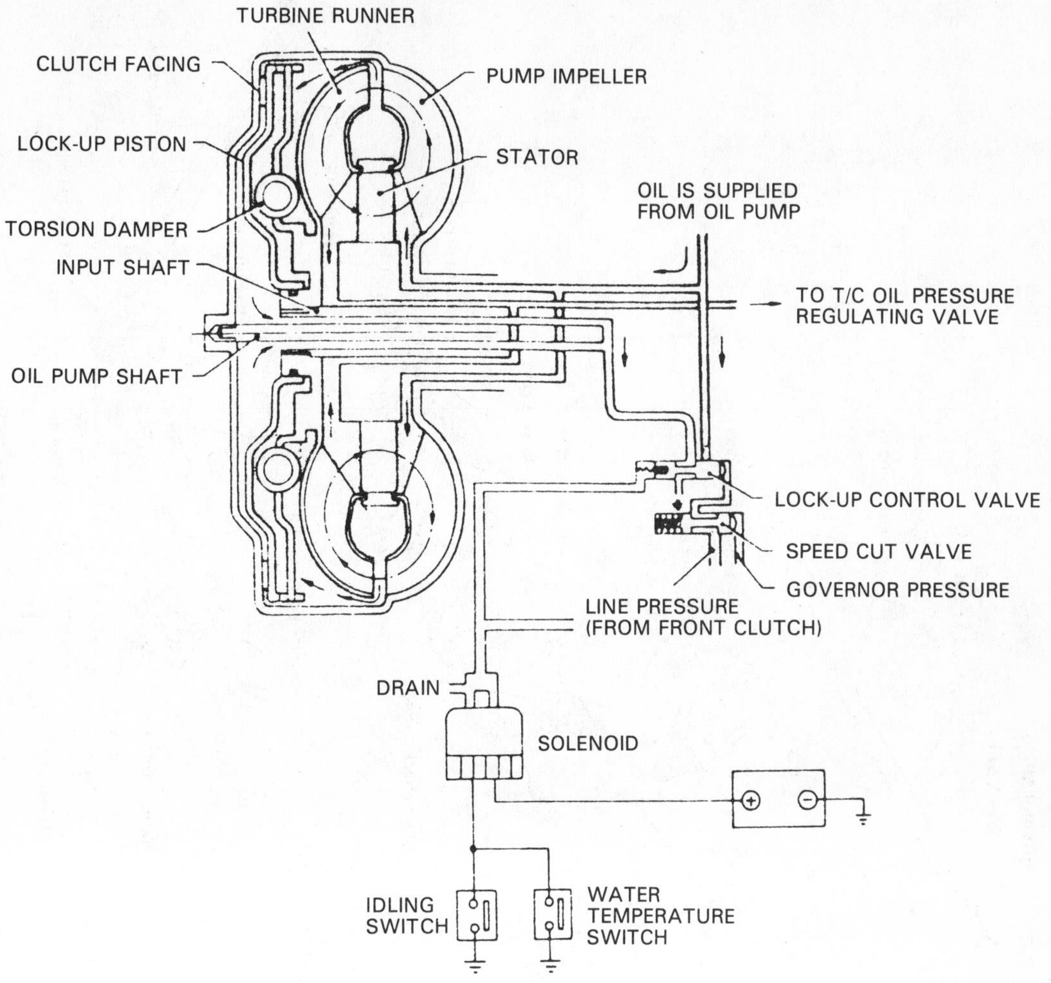

Fig. 13.50   When the accelerator pedal is released completely while the vehicle is in the lock-up mode, the lock-up piston in the torque converter will disengage. The same thing will happen when the water temperature is low (Sec 7)

3   Unbolt the support bearing from the transaxle **(see illustration)**.
4   Carefully pry the extension shaft from the transaxle, using the support bearing as a fulcrum. Guide the driveaxle and extension shaft assembly out the right wheel opening.
5   Installation is the reverse of the removal procedure. Remember to use a new circlip on the inner CV joint stub shaft.

Overhaul (boot replacement) – inner CV joint
6   Mount the driveaxle in a vise. Be sure to line the jaws of the vise with wood or rags to avoid marking up the shaft.
7   Pry open the boot bands with a screwdriver and slide them off the boot **(see illustration)**. Discard the bands.
8   Using white paint or a scribe, make match marks on the slide joint housing and the inner race **(see illustration)**.
9   Pry off snap-ring "A" **(see illustration)**, then remove the slide joint housing from the bearing assembly.

10   Place match marks on the inner race and the end of the driveaxle shaft. Remove snap-ring "C" with a pair of snap-ring pliers **(see illustration)** and slide the joint off the shaft.
11   Using a screwdriver, pry snap-ring "B" off the shaft, then remove the boot.
12   Clean all parts with solvent and allow them to dry. Check the slide joint housing for cracks and excessive wear. Check the inner race, cage and balls of the bearing assembly for signs of wear, overheating (discoloration), scoring, rust and excessive play. Replace the bearing assembly if any of these problems are found. Shiny spots are normal and won't affect operation of the bearing.
13   Before installing the boot, wrap the splines of the axleshaft with tape to avoid damage to the boot when installing it.
14   Slide the inner boot band and boot onto the shaft. Remove the tape and install snap-ring "B", making sure it seats in the groove in the shaft.

13

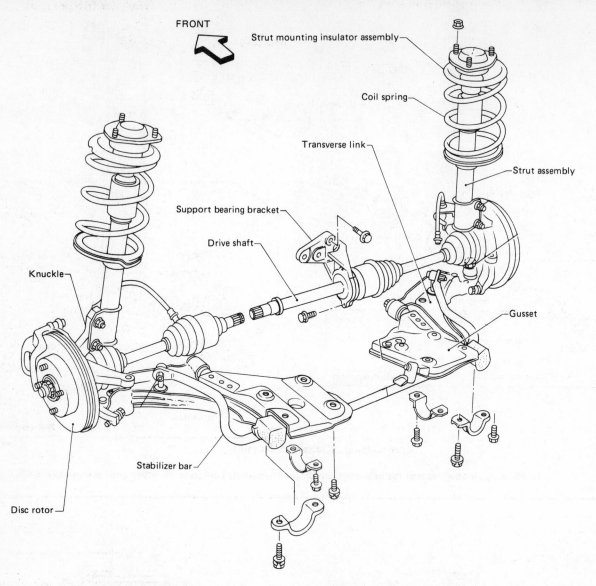

Fig. 13.51   Driveaxle and front suspension layout – 1987 and later models (Sec 8)

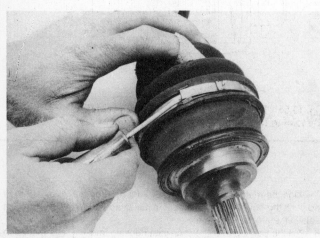

Fig. 13.52   The boot bands can be pried open with a small screwdriver (Sec 8)

Fig. 13.53   Pry the large snap-ring out of the slide joint housing with a small screwdriver (Sec8)

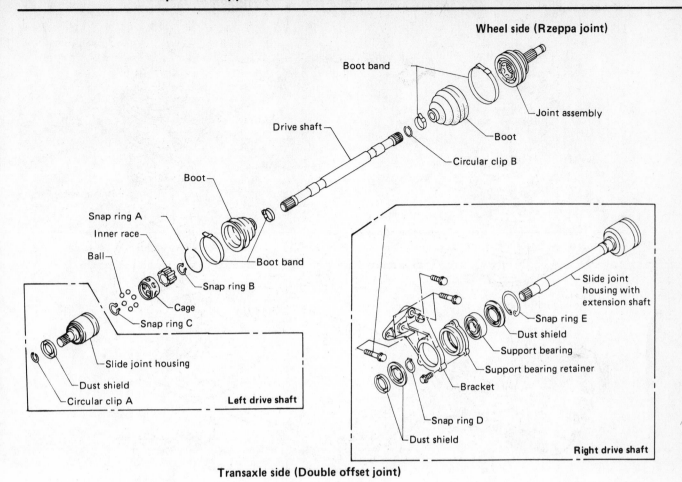

Fig. 13.54   Exploded view of the driveaxle and CV joint assembly components – 1987 and later models (Sec 8)

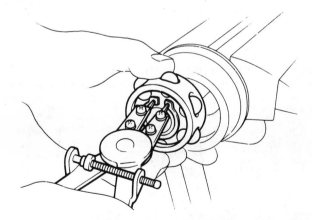

Fig. 13.55   Remove the snap-ring at the end of the shaft with a pair of snap-ring pliers (Sec 8)

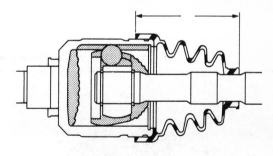

Fig. 13.56   Before tightening the boot bands, adjust the length of the joint to the boot length dimension listed in the Specifications

15   Thoroughly pack the bearing assembly with the CV joint grease supplied in the boot kit. Place the remainder of the grease in the slide joint housing.

16   Mount the CV joint bearing assembly on the driveaxle shaft, aligning the previously applied match marks. Install snap-ring "C".

17   Align the match marks on the slide joint housing and the inner race and push the housing over the race. Install snap-ring "A", making sure it seats in the groove completely.

18   Pull the boot up over the slide joint housing, making sure that each end of the boot seats in the groove.

19   Move the joint in or out, as necessary, to achieve the specified boot length **(see illustration)**. Carefully slip a dull screwdriver under the large

13

Fig. 13.57   To install a new boot band, bend the tang down . . .

Fig. 13.58   . . . and tap the tabs over to hold it in place (Sec 8)

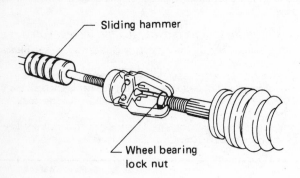

Fig. 13.59   Use a sliding hammer to remove the outer joint from
the driveaxle shaft (Sec 8)

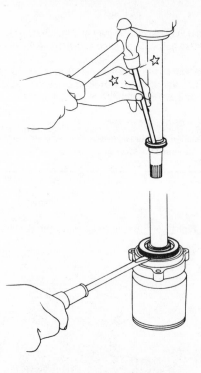

Fig. 13.61   Remove the small dust shield by tapping it off the
shaft with a hammer and punch – the other dust shield can be
pried out of the support bearing bracket with a
screwdriver (Sec 8)

Fig. 13.60   Pack grease into the splined hole, then insert a
wooden dowel into the hole and push down – the dowel will force
the grease into the joint (Sec 8)

end of the boot to equalize the pressure inside the boot, then install and
tighten the boot bands (see illustrations).

Overhaul (boot replacement) – outer CV joint

20   With the driveaxle mounted in a vise, thread the hub nut back onto the
outer CV joint stub shaft. Make match marks on the joint and the axleshaft.
Attach a sliding hammer with a three-jaw gear puller to the wheel bearing
locknut and pull the outer joint off the shaft (see illustration).

21   Pry off the circlip and slide the old boot off the shaft.
22   The outer joint can't be disassembled, but whenever the outer boot is
being replaced, the joint should be thoroughly washed out with solvent to
remove any grit and moisture that may have entered through the torn boot.
23   After the joint has been washed, inspect it carefully for signs of excessive wear, scoring or overheating. If any undesirable conditions are found,
replace the joint.
24   Pack the outer CV joint assembly with CV joint grease (supplied in the
boot kit) through the splined hole in the inner race. Force the grease into
the bearing by inserting a wooden dowel through the splined hole and
pushing it to the bottom of the joint (see illustration). Repeat this procedure until the bearing is completely packed.
25   Wrap the splines of the driveaxle with tape, then slide the new small
boot band and the boot onto the shaft.
26   Install a new circlip on the end of the shaft.

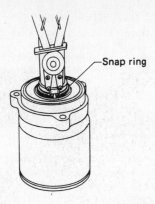

Fig. 13.62 The support bearing and bracket is retained by a snap-ring, but it's also press fit on the shaft (Sec 8)

27 Align the match marks on the joint and the shaft, then tap the outer joint into place. Use only enough force to overcome the resistance of the snap-ring.
28 Position the boot on the joint and seat the small end of the boot in the groove on the shaft. Adjust the joint to the proper length, equalize the pressure inside the boot and install the boot bands (Step 19).

Support bearing replacement
29 Pry the dust shields off the bearing, then tap them off the shaft with a hammer and punch **(see illustration)**.

30 Using a pair of snap-ring pliers, remove the snap-ring from the inner side of the bearing **(see illustration)**.
31 The support bearing is a press fit on the shaft – a hydraulic press will be required to separate the two. The bearing is also a press fit in the retainer. If you don't have access to a press, take the assembly to a dealer service department or an automotive machine shop to have the old bearing removed and a new one installed.
32 Before installing the bearing in the support bracket, check the bracket for cracks. Replace it if any are found.
33 Reassembly is the reverse of the disassembly procedure.

9 Braking system

Warning: *Dust created by the brake system may contain asbestos, which is hazardous to your health. Never blow it out with compressed air and don't inhale any of it. An approved filtering mask should be worn when working on the brakes. Do not, under any circumstances, use petroleum-based solvents to clean brake parts. Use brake cleaner or denatured alcohol only!*

Master cylinder removal, overhaul and installation
1 In 1984 the Nabco master cylinder was redesigned **(see illustration)**.
2 Disconnect the electrical connector from the master cylinder.
3 Disconnect the hydraulic lines using a flare nut wrench. Catch the fluid in a suitable container, being careful not to let any fluid get on painted surfaces.
4 Unscrew the nuts which hold the master cylinder to the front face of the servo unit and pull the master cylinder forward to remove it.

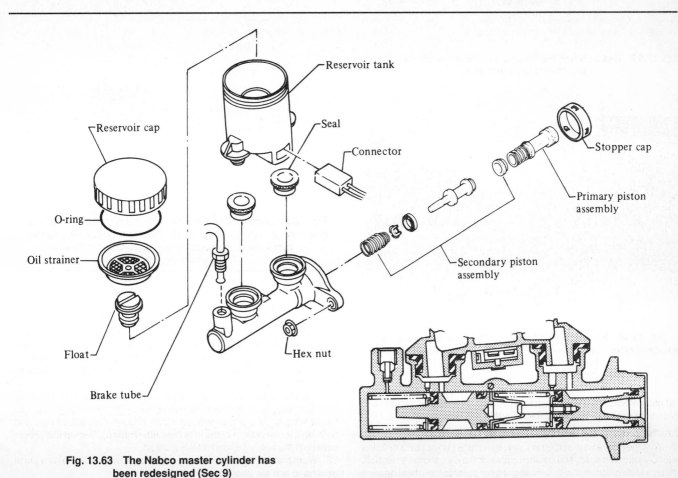

Fig. 13.63 The Nabco master cylinder has been redesigned (Sec 9)

13

5   Clean away external dirt and, using small screwdriver, pry the stopper cap from the master cylinder end.
6   Remove the piston assembly from the master cylinder. Clean all parts in brake fluid and inspect each part for abnormal wear or damage. Examine each of the pistons and the cylinder bore. If they are scored or show signs of corrosion the master cylinder must be replaced. Do not disassemble the primary piston.
7   Remove the seals, noting the direction in which the lips face, and discard them. On 1987 and later models, complete piston assemblies are included in the rebuild kit.
8   Obtain a repair kit which will contain all the necessary new seals and other renewable items.
9   Install the spring into the cylinder and then dip the secondary piston in clean brake fluid and insert it into the cylinder bore.
10   Dip the primary piston in clean brake fluid and insert it into the cylinder.
11   Hold the piston assembly slightly depressed while the stopper cap is installed.
12   If the reservoir is to be removed, pull on it while wiggling it until the stubs on the reservoir release from the rubber collar seals.
13   Replace the seals with new ones and press the reservoir onto the master cylinder.
14   Bench bleed the master cylinder (see the following procedure).
15   Refit the master cylinder and secure the attaching nuts.
16   Connect the hydraulic fluid lines and connect the electrical reservoir to the master cylinder.
17   Fill the reservoir with clean brake fluid and then bleed the complete system as described in Chapter 9 and later in this Supplement for models with ABS brakes.

Bench bleeding the master cylinder

18   Because it will be necessary to apply pressure to the master cylinder piston and, at the same time, control flow from the brake line outlets, it is recommended that the master cylinder be mounted in a vise. Use caution not to clamp the vise too tightly, or the master cylinder body might be cracked.
19   Insert threaded plugs into the brake line outlet holes and snug them down so that there will be no air leakage past them, but not so tight that they cannot be easily loosened.
20   Fill the reservoirs with brake fluid of the recommended type (see *Recommended fluids and lubricants*).
21   Remove one plug and push the piston assembly into the master cylinder bore to expel the air from the master cylinder. A large Phillips screwdriver can be used to push on the piston assembly.
22   To prevent air from being drawn back into the master cylinder, the plug must be replaced and snugged down before releasing the pressure on the piston assembly.
23   Repeat the procedure until only brake fluid is expelled from the brake line outlet. When only brake fluid is expelled, repeat the procedure with the other outlet hole and plug. Be sure to keep the master cylinder reservoir filled with brake fluid to prevent the introduction of air into the system.
24   Since high pressure is not involved in the bench bleeding procedure, an alternative to the removal and replacement of the plugs with each stroke of the piston assembly is available. Before pushing in on the piston assembly, remove the plug. Before releasing the piston, however, instead of replacing the plug, simply put your finger tightly over the hole to keep air from being drawn back into the master cylinder. Wait several seconds for

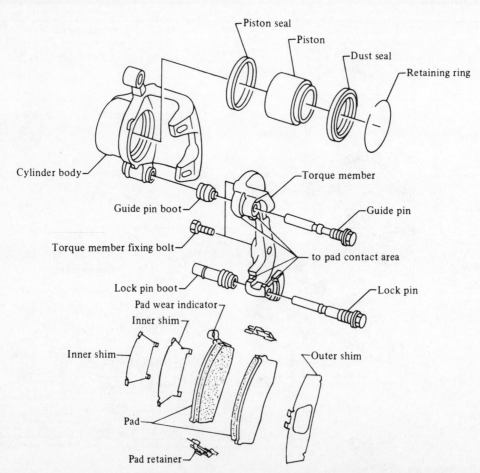

Fig. 13.64   In 1985 an inner shim was added to the front disc brake (Sec 9)

brake fluid to be drawn from the reservoir into the piston bore, then depress the piston again, removing your finger as brake fluid is expelled. Be sure to put your finger back over the hole each time before releasing the piston, and when the bleeding procedure is complete for that outlet, replace the plug and snug it before going on to the other port.

Front disc pad replacement (type AD20V)

25   In 1985 an inner shim was added to the front disc brake **(see illustration)**. Pad replacement remains the same with the exception of the new shim.

Disc brake caliper (type CL28VA)

26   In 1987 the caliper mounting arrangement was redesigned. Two short bolts retain the caliper to two sliding pins in the torque member. Disc pad replacement is performed in the same manner as on earlier models. The caliper overhaul procedure is similar, but the piston dust boot must be installed before the piston and the sliding pins must be lubricated with silicone-based grease when installing them.

Brake disc removal and installation

27   The brake disc on 1987 and later models is much easier to remove than on previous models. Simply raise the vehicle, remove the wheel, caliper and torque plate (Chapter 9) and slip the disc off the front hub.

Rear brake shoe replacement

28   Read the Warning at the beginning of this Section.
29   Remove the brake drum (Chapter 8).

30   Before removing any of the drum brake components, clean the assembly with brake cleaner and allow it to dry. Be sure to position a drain pan under the brake assembly to catch the fluid.
31   Use pliers or a brake spring tool to depress the anti-rattle springs and retainers and turn them 90-degrees to remove them from the pins **(see illustration)**.
32   Unhook the lower return springs from the lower ends of the shoes.
33   Spread the lower ends of the shoes apart and lift them over the anchor plate. Now spread the upper ends of the shoes apart and lift the assembly off the backing plate.
34   Disconnect the parking brake cable from the toggle lever and set the brake shoe assembly on a workbench.
35   Remove the adjuster from between the shoes and clean it thoroughly. Apply a small amount of multi-purpose grease to the threads and pivoting parts.
36   Unhook the upper return spring from each shoe.
37   Pry apart the clip that secures the adjusting/toggle lever pin to the trailing shoe. Remove the pin and transfer the levers and spring to the new trailing brake shoe. Install the pin and secure it with a new clip.
38   Connect the upper return spring between the two shoes. Install the adjuster – make sure it's facing the proper direction. It should also be screwed in to its shortest length.
39   Lubricate the brake shoe contact areas on the backing plate with high-temperature grease – don't overdo it though, as excess grease could contaminate the linings.
40   Connect the parking brake cable to the toggle lever and position the brake shoes on the backing plate. Install the anti-rattle springs and retainers.
41   Install the lower return springs.

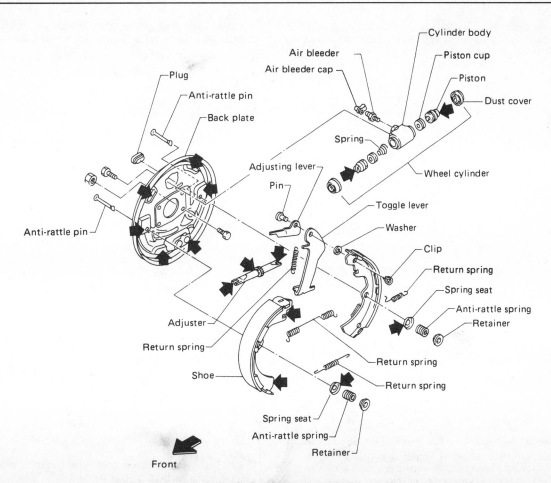

Fig. 13.65   Exploded view of the rear drum brake assembly – 1987 and later models (Sec 9)

13

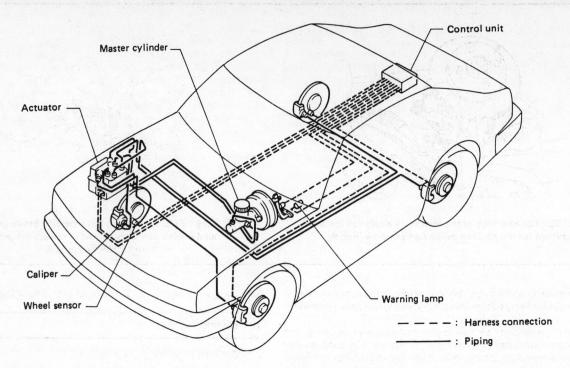

Fig. 13.66   ABS braking system components (Sec 9)

42   Make sure the upper ends of the shoes are inserted into the slots in the wheel cylinder pistons. The lower ends of the shoes must be seated behind the anchor plate.
43   Install the brake drum (Chapter 8) and the wheel. Lower the vehicle to the ground and adjust the brakes by operating the parking brake a few times.

Brake light switch removal, installation and adjustment
44   The brake light switch is the top switch mounted on the brake pedal.

Removal and installation
45   Disconnect the wires leading to the switch.
46   Loosen the locknut located on the pedal side of the switch.
47   Unscrew the switch from the retaining bracket.
48   Installation is the reverse of the removal procedure.
49   Once installed, adjust the switch-to-pedal clearance.

Adjustment
50   Use a feeler gauge inserted between the pedal stopper and the threaded end of the stop lamp switch. Turn the stop lamp switch adjusting nut until the distance between the switch and stopper meets specifications.
51   Tighten the adjusting nut.
52   Confirm that the stop lamps go out when the brake pedal is released.
53   If equipped, adjust the Automatic Speed Control Device (ASCD) switch in the same manner as the stop lamp switch.
54   Press the brake pedal and check the brake lights come on when depressed and go off when released.

ABS braking system

General information
55   An anti-lock braking system has been added to later models. This system uses a series of sensors mounted at each wheel and an electronic control unit (see illustration) to vary the hydraulic pressure in the brake system to prevent the wheels from locking-up during hard deceleration.
56   All repair procedures located around the outer suspension and steering components may be effected by the wheel sensors. If so, the electrical wiring to the sensors can be easily disconnected for servicing.

57   Other than the information given here, the ABS system should be repaired by a qualified mechanic or dealer service department.

Bleeding
58   Note that the four electrical connectors to the ABS actuator (see illustration) must be disconnected prior to bleeding the brakes.

Rear disc brake pad replacement
59   The rear disc brakes, incorporated on some later models, are similar in design to the disc brakes used on the front, with the following differences which should be noted during pad replacement.

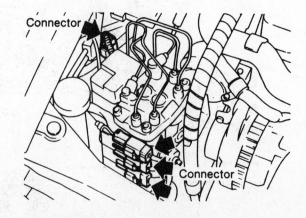

Fig. 13.67   The electrical connectors to be disconnected prior to bleeding the brakes (ABS models only) (Sec 9)

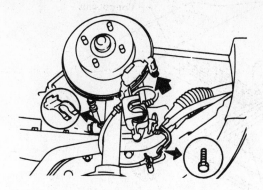

Fig. 13.68   The rear disc brake system is similar to the front, except for the parking brake components (Sec 9)

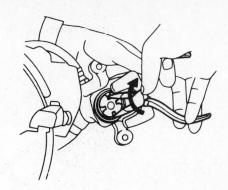

Fig. 13.69   Before installing the new disc brake pads, use needle-nose pliers as shown to retract the piston (turn clockwise) (Sec 9)

60   Prior to swinging the caliper body upwards for disc removal, remove the parking brake fixing bolt, pin bolt and the sliding lock spring **(see illustration)**.

61   Before the new disc pads can be put into the caliper body, the piston must be retracted to allow additional room. This is done by using needle-nose pliers in the recessed areas of the piston to turn the piston clockwise **(see illustration)**. By so doing, the piston will thread itself into the caliper, allowing additional space for the thicker pads.

62   Due to the design of the rear caliper, incorporating the parking brake mechanism, overhaul of the caliper is best left to a professional. Alterna-

tively, new or rebuilt calipers can be purchased and installed.

10   Electrical system

Starter motor general information

1   Starter motor type S114-322A **(see illustration)** was introduced in 1984 for Canadian models and in 1986 was adopted on all N. American models. Removal of the unit is the same as before but a new procedure for overhaul of the internal components is noted below.

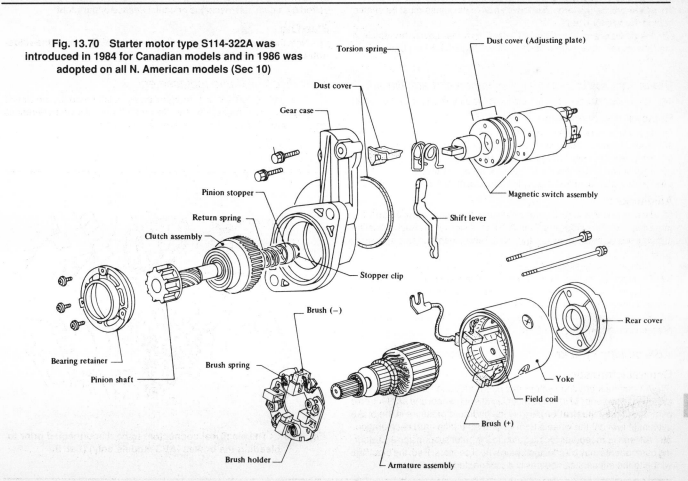

Fig. 13.70   Starter motor type S114-322A was introduced in 1984 for Canadian models and in 1986 was adopted on all N. American models (Sec 10)

Torsion spring

Dust cover (Adjusting plate)

Dust cover

Gear case

Magnetic switch assembly

Pinion stopper

Shift lever

Return spring

Clutch assembly

Stopper clip

Bearing retainer

Pinion shaft

Brush (–)

Brush spring

Rear cover

Yoke

Field coil

Brush (+)

Brush holder

Armature assembly

13

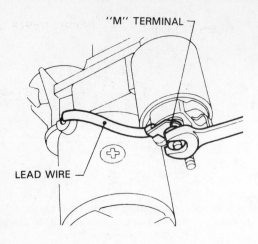

Fig. 13.71   Loosen the nut on the "M' terminal and remove the lead wire (Sec 10)

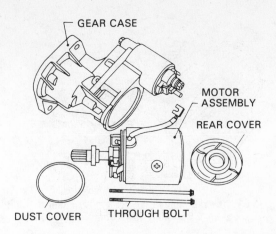

Fig. 13.72   Remove the through bolts and pull the rear cover and motor assembly from the gear case (Sec 10)

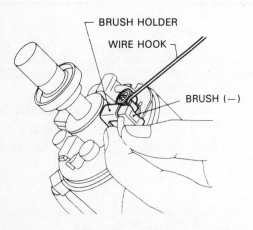

Fig. 13.73   Remove the brush holder by lifting the brush spring and holding it against the side surface of the negative brush (Sec 10)

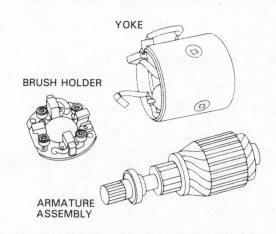

Fig. 13.74   Separate the armature assembly from the yoke (Sec 10)

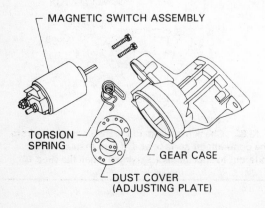

Fig. 13.75   Remove the magnetic switch assembly from the gear case (Sec 10)

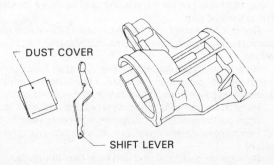

Fig. 13.76   Remove the dust cover and shift lever from the gear case (Sec 10)

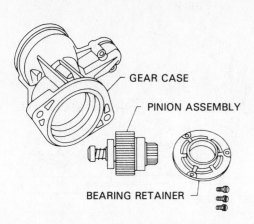

Fig. 13.77   Remove the bearing retainer and lift out the pinion assembly (Sec 10)

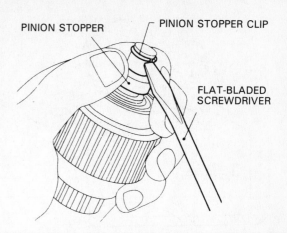

Fig. 13.78   Move the pinion stopper toward the pinion and remove the pinion stopper clip using a flat blade screwdriver (Sec 10)

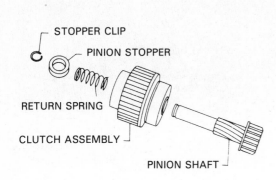

Fig. 13.79   Remove the pinion shaft from the clutch assembly (Sec 10)

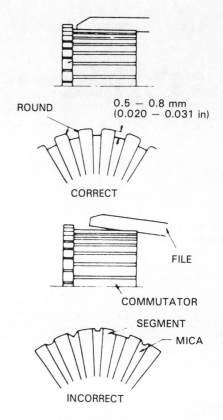

Fig. 13.80   Check the depth of the insulating mica from the commutator surface and, if less than specified, undercut to specifications using a small file (Sec 10)

Starter motor overhaul

2   Loosen the nut on the "M" terminal as shown **(see illustration)** and remove the lead wire.

3   Remove the through bolts from the rear of the starter housing and draw out the rear cover and motor assembly from the gear case **(see illustration)**.

4   Remove the brush holder by lifting the brush spring and holding it against the side surface of the negative brush **(see illustration)**. This causes the negative brush to separate from the commutator.

5   Remove the positive brush from the holder by lifting the brush spring.

6   Draw out the armature assembly from the yoke **(see illustration)**.

7   Remove the magnetic switch assembly from the gear case **(see illustration)**.

8   Remove the dust cover and shift lever **(see illustration)**.

9   Remove the bearing retainer and lift out the pinion assembly **(see illustration)**.

10   Move the pinion stopper toward the pinion and remove the pinion stopper clip with a flat blade screwdriver **(see illustration)**.

11   Remove the pinion shaft from the clutch assembly **(see illustration)**.

12   Inspect the commutator surface for corrosion or cracks. If corrosion is not too severe, lightly sand the commutator with No. 500 grit sandpaper.

13   Check the diameter of the commutator using a vernier caliper and compare results with the Specifications.

14   Check the depth of the insulating mica from the commutator surface and compare to the Specifications **(see illustration)**. If less than specified, undercut to specifications using a small file.

13

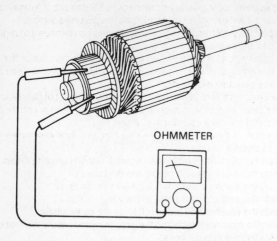

Fig. 13.81   Use an ohmmeter to check continuity between two segments of the armature assembly (Sec 10)

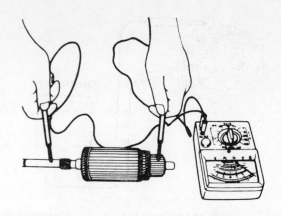

Fig. 13.82   Use the ohmmeter to run an insulation test between each commutator bar and the shaft (Sec 10)

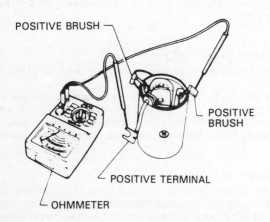

Fig. 13.83   Check continuity between the field coil positive terminal and the positive brushes (Sec 10)

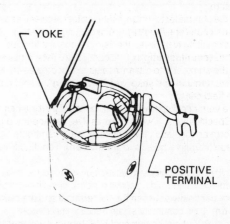

Fig. 13.84   Use the ohmmeter to run an insulation test between the field coil and the positive terminal and yoke (Sec 10)

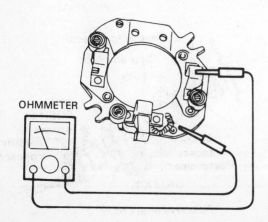

Fig. 13.85   Perform an insulation test between the brush holder (positive side) and its base (negative side) (Sec 10)

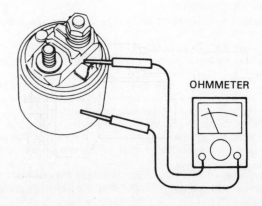

Fig. 13.86   Check continuity between the "S" terminal and the switch body (Sec 10)

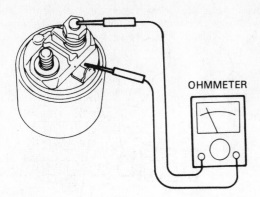

Fig. 13.87   Check for continuity between the "S' terminal and the "M' terminal (Sec 10)

15   Use an ohmmeter to check the continuity between two segments of the armature assembly **(see illustration)**. If there is no continuity, replace the armature.
16   Use the ohmmeter to run an insulation test between each commutator bar and the shaft **(see illustration)**. If continuity exists, replace the unit.
17   Check continuity between the field coil positive terminal and the positive brushes **(see illustration)**. If no continuity exists, replace the field coil.
18   Use the ohmmeter to run an insulation test between the field coil and the positive terminal and yoke **(see illustration)**. If continuity exists, replace the field coil.
19   Use a vernier caliper to check the length of the brushes and compare them to Specifications. If wear is excessive, replace the brushes.
20   Perform an insulation test between the brush holder (positive side) and its base (negative side) **(see illustration)**. If continuity exists, replace the holder.
21   Check the brush holder to see if it moves smoothly. If the brush holder is bent, replace it. If the sliding surface is dirty, clean it with light sandpaper.
22   Check continuity between the "S" terminal and the switch body **(see illustration)**. If no continuity exists, replace the switch.
23   Check for continuity between the "S" terminal and the "M" terminal as shown **(see illustration)** and replace if no continuity is shown.
24   Check the pinion assembly clutch to see that it locks properly when turned in the "drive" direction and rotates smoothly when direction is reversed. If the pinion does not lock in either direction or if unusual resis-

tance is evident apply grease and recheck its movement. If resistance is still present it will be necessary to replace the pinion assembly.
25   Inspect the pinion and ring gear teeth for wear or damage and replace the pinion if damaged.
26   Inspect the ball bearing movement by spinning the race of the ball bearing assembly to ensure smooth movement and replace the assembly if abnormal resistance is present.
27   During assembly of the starter apply a small amount of grease to the reduction gear, the friction surface of the pinion, the shift lever and the sliding surface of the magnetic switch plunger.
28   Assemble the pinion shaft to the clutch assembly and secure it with the pinion stopper clip.
29   Insert the pinion assembly and secure it with the bearing retainer.
30   Install the shift lever and secure the dust cover.
31   Install the magnetic switch assembly to the gear case.
32   Install the armature assembly in the yoke.
33   Install the brushes and brush holder to the commutator.
34   Insert the motor assembly into the gear case and secure the rear cover by installing the through bolts.
35   Connect the lead wire to the "M" terminal and secure it with the nut.
36   Check the pinion protruding length and compare it to the Specifications. Use jumper wires attached to the battery to push out the pinion using the magnetic switch to check the pinion length **(see illustration)**. Also pull the pinion out by hand until it touches the stopper to check. If the protruding length does not meet specification, adjust by removing the dust cover adjusting plate.

Distributor general information
37   In 1986 all N. American models adopted the use of the D4N83-16 type distributor.
38   In 1987, the D4P85-01 type distributor, explained in Section 4 under "crank angle sensor" was installed. Removal and installation is the same as a standard distributor. If a problem develops with the distributor, it must be replaced as a complete unit, as individual parts are not available.

Headlight replacement
39   Later model vehicles are equipped with a slightly different halogen headlight assembly. The halogen bulbs are replaced as follows. **Caution:** *When replacing halogen bulbs, do not touch the glass portion of the bulb – handle only by grasping the plastic base.*
40   Disconnect the negative cable at the battery.
41   Turn the bulb retaining ring counterclockwise until it is free from the reflector, then remove it **(see illustration)**.

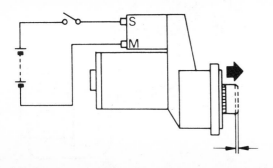

Fig. 13.88   Use jumper wires attached to the battery to push out the pinion using the magnetic switch to check the pinion length (Sec 10)

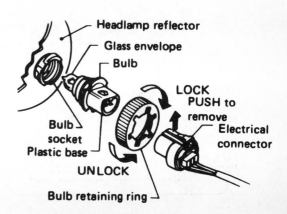

Fig. 13.89   Halogen headlight bulb details (Sec 10)

13

42   Disconnect the electrical harness connector from the back of the bulb.
43   Remove the headlight bulb carefully by grasping the plastic base.
44   Install the new bulb and complete the installation by performing the above steps in reverse order.

Wiring diagrams

Note that wiring diagrams for later model years have been included at the end of this Chapter. Due to space limitations we are not able to provide every diagram for all years; however, the diagrams included are typical of later models.

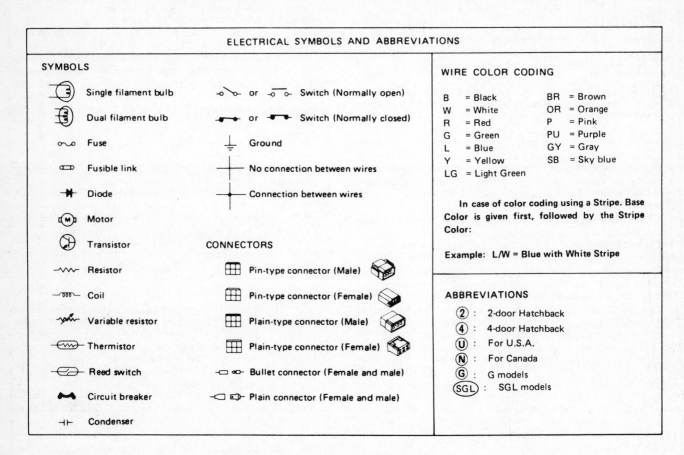

Wiring diagram symbols and abbreviations

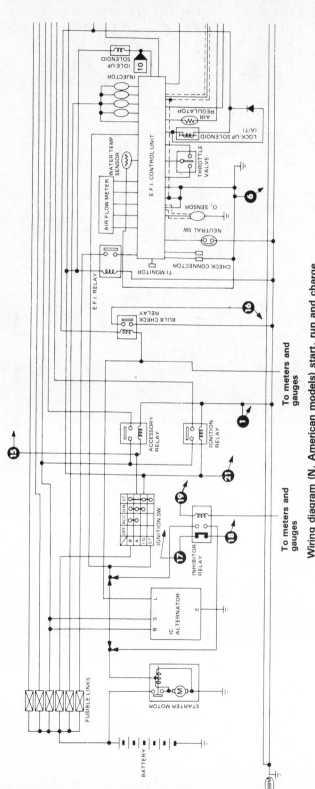

Wiring diagram (N. American models) start, run and charge

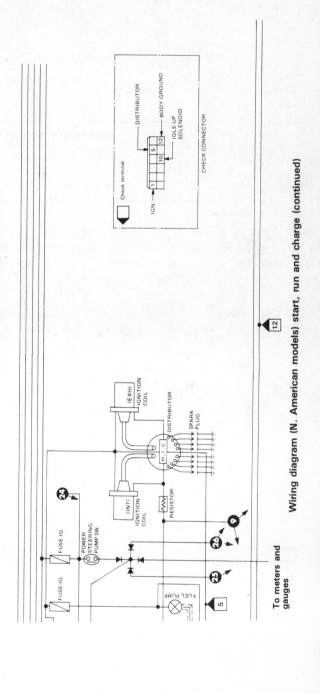

Wiring diagram (N. American models) start, run and charge (continued)

314

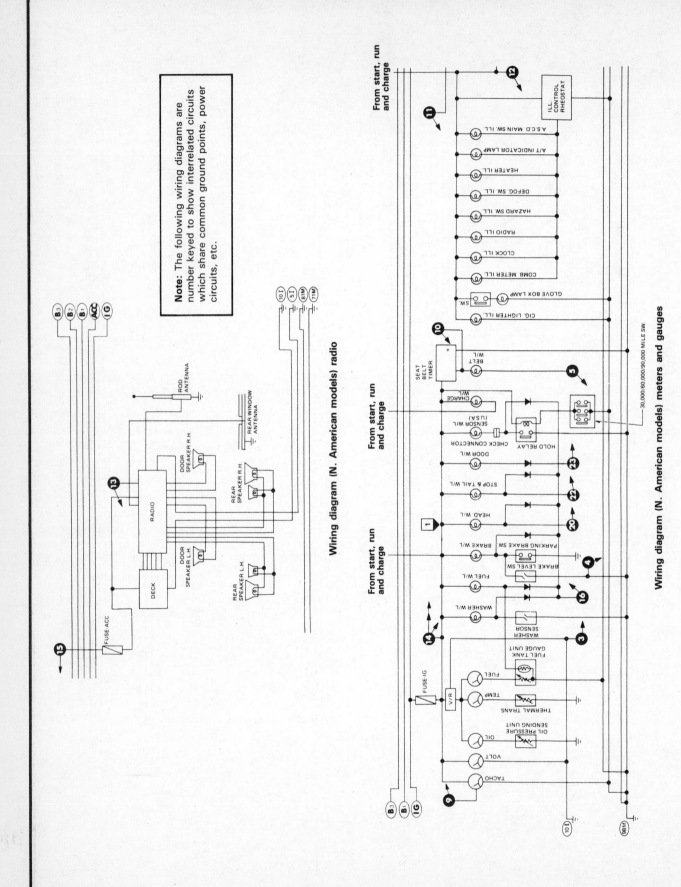

Note: The following wiring diagrams are number keyed to show interrelated circuits which share common ground points, power circuits, etc.

Wiring diagram (N. American models) radio

Wiring diagram (N. American models) meters and gauges

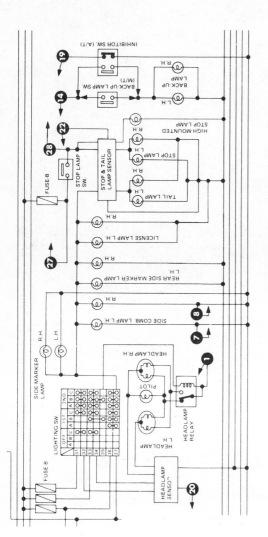

Wiring diagram (N. American models) warning and stop lights

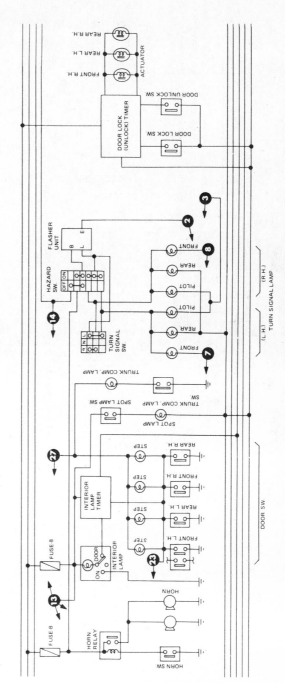

Wiring diagram (N. American models) warning, horn and interior lamps and turn signals

316

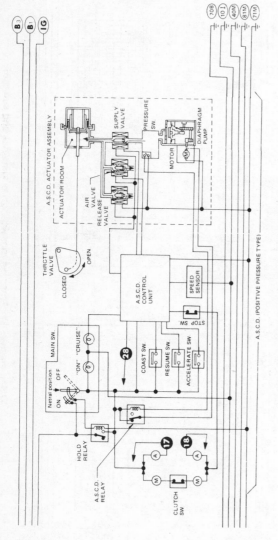

Wiring diagram (N. American models) ASCD speed control

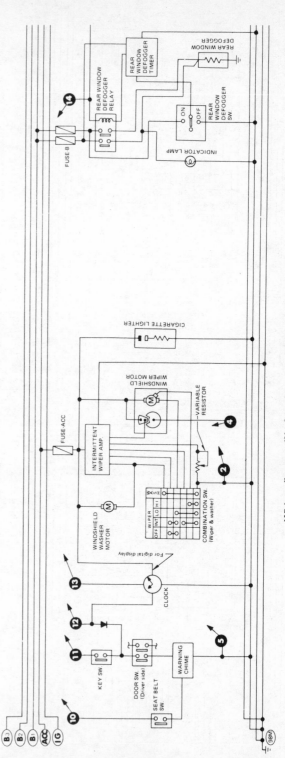

Wiring diagram (N. American models) windshield wiper

Note: The following wiring diagrams are number keyed to show interrelated circuits which share common ground points, power circuits, etc.

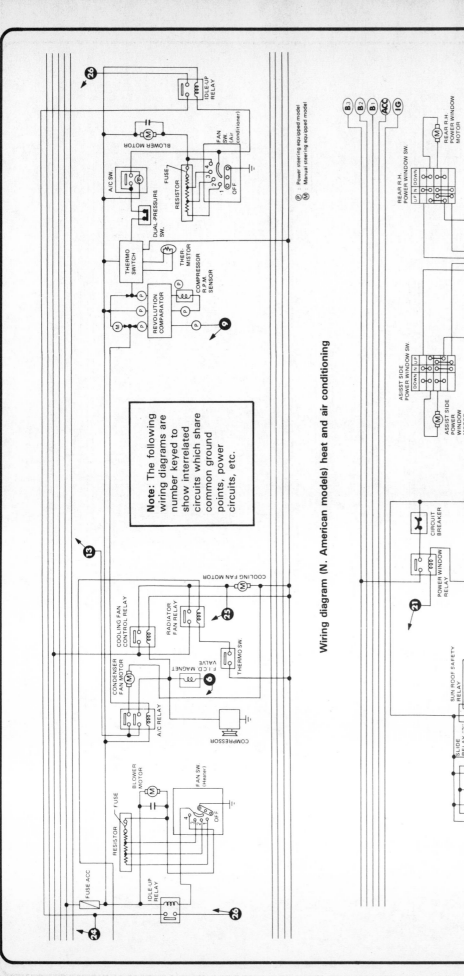

Wiring diagram (N. American models) heat and air conditioning

Wiring diagram (N. American models) power windows and sun roof

Note: The following wiring diagrams are number keyed to show interrelated circuits which share common ground points, power circuits, etc.

(P) : Power steering equipped model
(M) : Manual steering equipped model

13

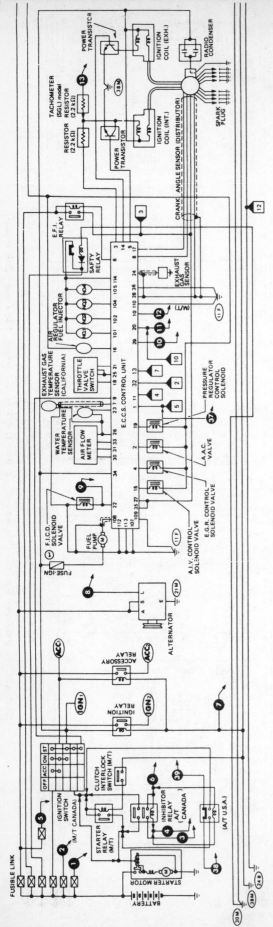

Starting, charging, fuel and emission control circuits (1989 model shown, 1987 and 1988 similar)

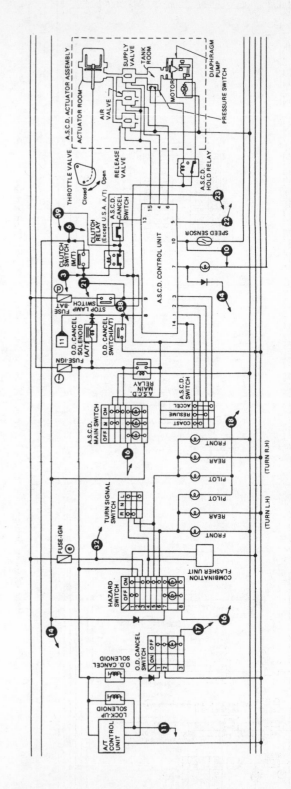

Hazard flasher/turn signal/cruise control circuits (1989 model shown, 1987 and 1988 similar)

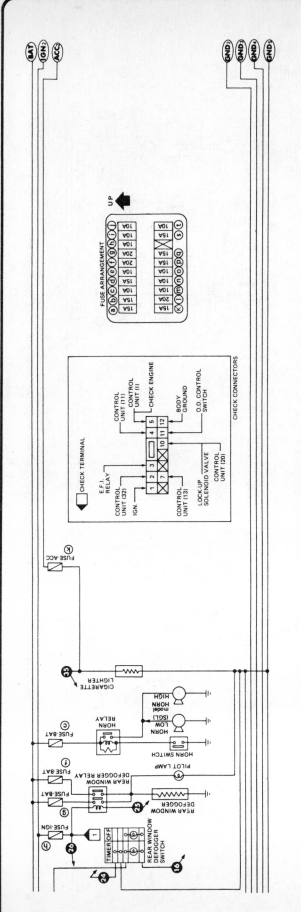

Rear window defogger switch/horn circuit (1989 model shown, 1987 and 1988 similar)

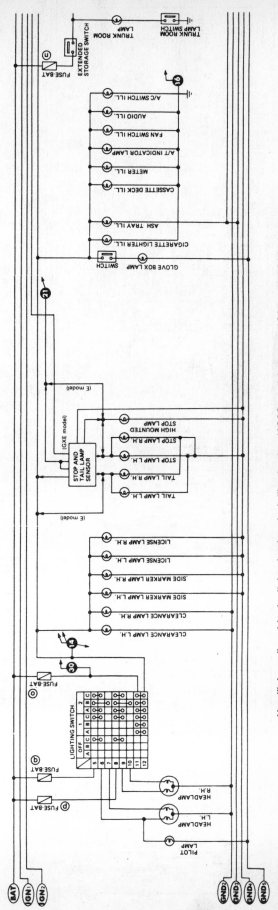

Headlight, tail and brake light circuits, dash illumination (1989 model shown, 1987 and 1988 similar)

13

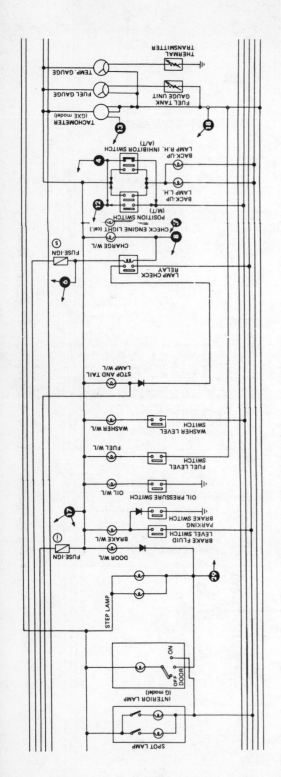

Interior light switch, warning lights, gauges (1989 model shown, 1987 and 1988 similar)

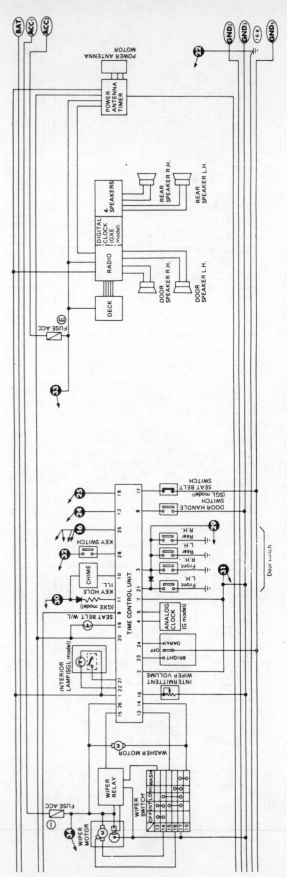

Windshield wiper and radio circuits (1989 model shown, 1987 and 1988 similar)

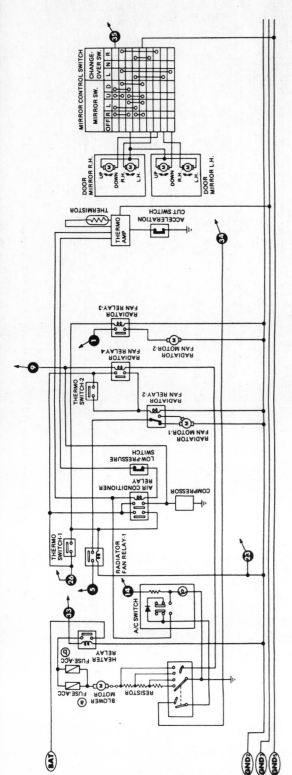

Air conditioning, blower motor, cooling fan and remote mirror control circuits
(1989 model shown, 1987 and 1988 similar)

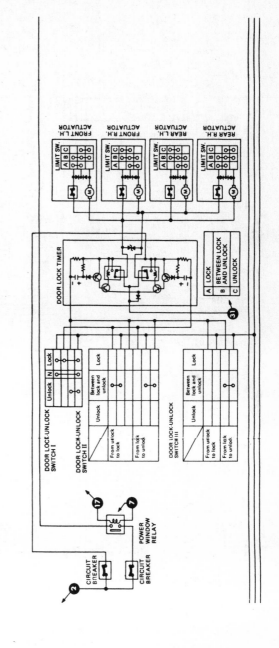

Power door lock circuit (1989 model shown, 1987 and 1988 similar)

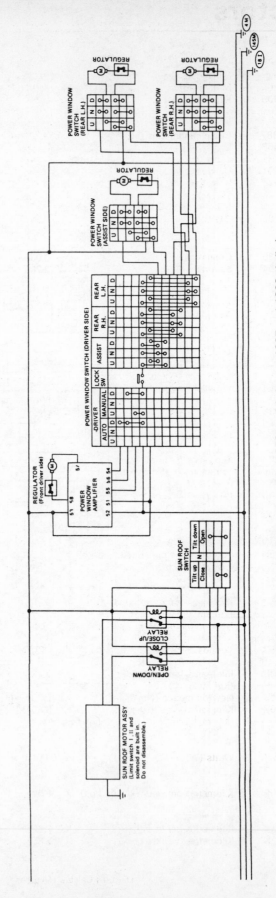

Sunroof and power window circuits (1989 model shown, 1987 and 1988 similar)

Conversion factors

Length (distance)

	X		=		X		=	
Inches (in)	X	25.4	=	Millimetres (mm)	X	0.0394	=	Inches (in)
Feet (ft)	X	0.305	=	Metres (m)	X	3.281	=	Feet (ft)
Miles	X	1.609	=	Kilometres (km)	X	0.621	=	Miles

Volume (capacity)

	X		=		X		=	
Cubic inches (cu in; in³)	X	16.387	=	Cubic centimetres (cc; cm³)	X	0.061	=	Cubic inches (cu in; in³)
Imperial pints (Imp pt)	X	0.568	=	Litres (l)	X	1.76	=	Imperial pints (Imp pt)
Imperial quarts (Imp qt)	X	1.137	=	Litres (l)	X	0.88	=	Imperial quarts (Imp qt)
Imperial quarts (Imp qt)	X	1.201	=	US quarts (US qt)	X	0.833	=	Imperial quarts (Imp qt)
US quarts (US qt)	X	0.946	=	Litres (l)	X	1.057	=	US quarts (US qt)
Imperial gallons (Imp gal)	X	4.546	=	Litres (l)	X	0.22	=	Imperial gallons (Imp gal)
Imperial gallons (Imp gal)	X	1.201	=	US gallons (US gal)	X	0.833	=	Imperial gallons (Imp gal)
US gallons (US gal)	X	3.785	=	Litres (l)	X	0.264	=	US gallons (US gal)

Mass (weight)

	X		=		X		=	
Ounces (oz)	X	28.35	=	Grams (g)	X	0.035	=	Ounces (oz)
Pounds (lb)	X	0.454	=	Kilograms (kg)	X	2.205	=	Pounds (lb)

Force

	X		=		X		=	
Ounces-force (ozf; oz)	X	0.278	=	Newtons (N)	X	3.6	=	Ounces-force (ozf; oz)
Pounds-force (lbf; lb)	X	4.448	=	Newtons (N)	X	0.225	=	Pounds-force (lbf; lb)
Newtons (N)	X	0.1	=	Kilograms-force (kgf; kg)	X	9.81	=	Newtons (N)

Pressure

	X		=		X		=	
Pounds-force per square inch (psi; lbf/in²; lb/in²)	X	0.070	=	Kilograms-force per square centimetre (kgf/cm²; kg/cm²)	X	14.223	=	Pounds-force per square inch (psi; lbf/in²; lb/in²)
Pounds-force per square inch (psi; lbf/in²; lb/in²)	X	0.068	=	Atmospheres (atm)	X	14.696	=	Pounds-force per square inch (psi; lbf/in²; lb/in²)
Pounds-force per square inch (psi; lbf/in²; lb/in²)	X	0.069	=	Bars	X	14.5	=	Pounds-force per square inch (psi; lbf/in²; lb/in²)
Pounds-force per square inch (psi; lbf/in²; lb/in²)	X	6.895	=	Kilopascals (kPa)	X	0.145	=	Pounds-force per square inch (psi; lbf/in²; lb/in²)
Kilopascals (kPa)	X	0.01	=	Kilograms-force per square centimetre (kgf/cm²; kg/cm²)	X	98.1	=	Kilopascals (kPa)
Millibar (mbar)	X	100	=	Pascals (Pa)	X	0.01	=	Millibar (mbar)
Millibar (mbar)	X	0.0145	=	Pounds-force per square inch (psi; lbf/in²; lb/in²)	X	68.947	=	Millibar (mbar)
Millibar (mbar)	X	0.75	=	Millimetres of mercury (mmHg)	X	1.333	=	Millibar (mbar)
Millibar (mbar)	X	0.401	=	Inches of water (inH₂O)	X	2.491	=	Millibar (mbar)
Millimetres of mercury (mmHg)	X	0.535	=	Inches of water (inH₂O)	X	1.868	=	Millimetres of mercury (mmHg)
Inches of water (inH₂O)	X	0.036	=	Pounds-force per square inch (psi; lbf/in²; lb/in²)	X	27.68	=	Inches of water (inH₂O)

Torque (moment of force)

	X		=		X		=	
Pounds-force inches (lbf in; lb in)	X	1.152	=	Kilograms-force centimetre (kgf cm; kg cm)	X	0.868	=	Pounds-force inches (lbf in; lb in)
Pounds-force inches (lbf in; lb in)	X	0.113	=	Newton metres (Nm)	X	8.85	=	Pounds-force inches (lbf in; lb in)
Pounds-force inches (lbf in; lb in)	X	0.083	=	Pounds-force feet (lbf ft; lb ft)	X	12	=	Pounds-force inches (lbf in; lb in)
Pounds-force feet (lbf ft; lb ft)	X	0.138	=	Kilograms-force metres (kgf m; kg m)	X	7.233	=	Pounds-force feet (lbf ft; lb ft)
Pounds-force feet (lbf ft; lb ft)	X	1.356	=	Newton metres (Nm)	X	0.738	=	Pounds-force feet (lbf ft; lb ft)
Newton metres (Nm)	X	0.102	=	Kilograms-force metres (kgf m; kg m)	X	9.804	=	Newton metres (Nm)

Power

	X		=		X		=	
Horsepower (hp)	X	745.7	=	Watts (W)	X	0.0013	=	Horsepower (hp)

Velocity (speed)

	X		=		X		=	
Miles per hour (miles/hr; mph)	X	1.609	=	Kilometres per hour (km/hr; kph)	X	0.621	=	Miles per hour (miles/hr; mph)

Fuel consumption*

	X		=		X		=	
Miles per gallon, Imperial (mpg)	X	0.354	=	Kilometres per litre (km/l)	X	2.825	=	Miles per gallon, Imperial (mpg)
Miles per gallon, US (mpg)	X	0.425	=	Kilometres per litre (km/l)	X	2.352	=	Miles per gallon, US (mpg)

Temperature

Degrees Fahrenheit = ($^\circ$C x 1.8) + 32

Degrees Celsius (Degrees Centigrade; $^\circ$C) = ($^\circ$F - 32) x 0.56

It is common practice to convert from miles per gallon (mpg) to litres/100 kilometres (l/100km), where mpg (Imperial) x l/100 km = 282 and mpg (US) x l/100 km = 235

Index

overhaul (mechanical breaker) — 101
removal and refitting — 99
fault diagnosis — 104
mechanical contact breaker points servicing — 98
spark plugs — 103, 105
specifications — 95
switch
removal and refitting — 104
timing — 98
torque wrench settings — 96, 276
Instrument panel
removal and refitting — 182

J

Jacking — 11

L

Lamp bulbs renewal
exterior — 178
headlamp — 178
interior — 181
Luggage boot lid
removal and refitting — 263
Lubricants and fluids — 12
Lubrication chart — 12

M

Maintenance, routine — 14
Manifolds — 92
Manual transmission — 111 et seq
Manual transmission
components inspection — 122
description — 112, 294
dismantling — 116
fault diagnosis — 130
final drive
adjustment — 129
gearchange linkage
removal and refitting — 115
gear lever
removal, refitting and adjustment — 112
mainshaft bearing
preload adjustment — 130
maintenance — 112
reassembly — 122
removal and refitting — 115
specifications — 111
torque wrench settings — 112
Master cylinder — 154, 299, 303
Mirrors, rear view
exterior — 274
interior — 274

O

Oil cooler — 280
Oil, engine — 24
Oil filter — 24
Oil pump
removal and refitting — 30

P

Piston rings
renewal — 30

R

Radiator
removal, repair and refitting — 54
Radiator grille
removal and repair — 257
Radio and cassette player
removal and refitting — 188
Relays, circuit breakers, limit switches and sensors — 176
Repair procedures, general — 10
Roadwheels
changing — 11
general — 146
size — 138
Routine maintenance — 14

S

Safety first! — 13
Seat belts and head restraints
removal and refitting — 270
front — 270
rear — 270
Spare parts
buying — 7
to carry in car — 19
Spark plug conditions (colour chart) — 105
Spark plugs and HT leads — 103
Speedometer drive cable
renewal — 189
Starter motor
description and testing — 172, 307
overhaul — 173, 309
removal and refitting — 173
Steering (see also Suspension and steering)
angles and front wheel alignment — 248
column (non-tilt type)
removal, overhaul and refitting — 243
column (tilt type)
removal, overhaul and refitting — 244
column lock
removal and refitting — 245
filling and bleeding (power assisted) — 247
gear
overhaul — 246
removal and refitting (manual) — 245
removal and refitting (power assisted) — 246
maintenance (power assisted) — 246
pump and reservoir (power assisted)
removal and refitting — 247
rack bellows
renewal — 242
shaft lower joint
removal and refitting — 242
tie-rod and balljoint
renewal — 242
wheel
removal and refitting — 242
Sump pan
removal and refitting — 29
Sunroof, power-operated
general — 188
removal and refitting — 271
Suspension and steering — 234 et seq
Suspension and steering
description — 235
fault diagnosis — 249
maintenance — 235
specifications — 234, 278
torque wrench settings — 234, 235
Suspension, front (see also Suspension and steering)
lower balljoint
renewal — 238
strut
removal, overhaul and refitting — 238